ॐ Empathy and History ॐ

MAKING SENSE OF HISTORY
Studies in Historical Cultures
General Editor: Stefan Berger
Founding Editor: Jörn Rüsen

Bridging the gap between historical theory and the study of historical memory, this series crosses the boundaries between both academic disciplines and cultural, social, political and historical contexts. In an age of rapid globalization, which tends to manifest itself on an economic and political level, locating the cultural practices involved in generating its underlying historical sense is an increasingly urgent task.

For a full volume listing please see back matter.

EMPATHY AND HISTORY

Historical Understanding in Re-enactment, Hermeneutics and Education

Tyson Retz

berghahn
NEW YORK · OXFORD
www.berghahnbooks.com

First published in 2018 by
Berghahn Books
www.berghahnbooks.com

© 2018, 2022 Tyson Retz
First paperback edition published in 2022

All rights reserved. Except for the quotation of short passages
for the purposes of criticism and review, no part of this book
may be reproduced in any form or by any means, electronic or
mechanical, including photocopying, recording, or any information
storage and retrieval system now known or to be invented,
without written permission of the publisher.

Library of Congress Cataloging-in-Publication Data

A C.I.P. cataloging record is available from the Library of Congress

British Library Cataloguing in Publication Data

A catalogue record for this book is available from the British Library

ISBN 978-1-78533-919-6 hardback
ISBN 978-1-80073-438-8 paperback
ISBN 978-1-78533-920-2 ebook

https://doi.org/10.3167/9781785339196

True happiness, we are told, consists in getting out of one's self;
but the point is not only to get out – you must stay out;
and to stay out you must have some absorbing errand.
—Henry James, *Roderick Hudson*

Contents

Foreword to the Paperback Edition ... ix
Acknowledgements ... xii
List of Abbreviations ... xiv

Introduction ... 1

Part I. Education

Chapter 1. Reforming the Past ... 21
Chapter 2. The Influence of the Philosophy of History ... 35
Chapter 3. A Conceptual Portmanteau ... 57

Part II. Origins

Chapter 4. Empathy and Historicism ... 73
Chapter 5. Historicism, Neo-Kantianism and Hermeneutics ... 91
Chapter 6. Collingwood and the Continent ... 106
Chapter 7. Questions, Answers and Presuppositions ... 121
Chapter 8. Horizons of Context ... 145

Part III. Consequences

Chapter 9. Competing Conceptions ... 173
Chapter 10. Historical Thinking and Historical Consciousness ... 192

Conclusion	213
Bibliography	219
Index	234

Foreword to the Paperback Edition

The book that you are holding, or are viewing on an electronic screen, is richer in its implications and offers more food for thought than its terse title lets on. That is because it has the wit to embrace, rather than smooth over or turn aside from, the fact that empathy has entered historical discourse under the guidance of two rather different academic communities, one consisting of scholars located in schools of education, and the other of philosophers, broadly defined to include theorists working in departments of literature, history, or politics.

As a result of this dual focus, *Empathy and History* is really two studies in one. The first study (present mainly in Part I) is devoted to the work of what Retz calls the 'history educationalists': scholars in schools of education involved in teaching prospective schoolteachers how to go about teaching history to school students. Since empathy first entered the history curriculum in the UK, that is where Retz places most of his attention, although he also touches on counterparts in Canada and Australia. For reasons that Retz explains early in the book, history educationalists in the UK were keen to introduce disciplinary forms of knowledge to school students. However, their ideas about how to do this were formed much less by developments in the discipline than by philosophers of history, above all by R.G. Collingwood. They were especially attracted by Collingwood's notion of 're-enactment', which in the 1970s they relabelled as 'empathy'.

In Part I Retz recounts the 'empathy debate' among the educationalists. In doing so he subtly sets the stage for his own active engagement, in Part II, not only with Collingwood but also with Hans-Georg Gadamer, Quentin Skinner, and other writers concerned with hermeneutics and with philosophy of history. He addresses questions central to Cambridge school contextualism, challenging, in particular, Skinner's understanding of Collingwood's philosophy of history. He invites us to consider the fundamentally critical nature of Collingwood's philosophy and to treat empathy as a kind of question-and-answer logic. Here, the name of the game is to ask questions that will open up the past and will yield meaningful answers. Retz adamantly defends (with help from others) historical inquiry that is grounded in disciplinary procedures. In synthesizing Collingwood and Gadamer on the importance of the logic of question and answer, he offers much that will be of interest to specialists in hermeneutics and the philosophy of history.

In Part III Retz discusses, in Chapter 9, efforts in the 1980s and 1990s to establish a national history curriculum for England and Wales. He then turns, in Chapter 10, to discussion in the 1990s and early 2000s of 'historical consciousness' and related notions, and to attempts in Canada and in Australia to reform history teaching and curricula.

Retz's short but densely packed Conclusion will repay attentive reading. Retz points out the irony surrounding the entry of 'empathy' into the discourse on school history-teaching. History educationalists in the UK in the 1970s and 1980s picked up on empathy because they saw it as 'giving individual content to the general categories through which the past is viewed', and thus as enlivening 'a traditionally dull school subject'. Empathy first entered into thinking about history in Germany, under the name *Einfühlung* (literally 'in-feeling'), rising to prominence in the late nineteenth century, when it became part of an attempt to assert the distinctiveness, and hence the standing, of a humanistic historical discipline faced by the rising prestige of the natural sciences. However, as Retz points out, by the 1950s and 1960s the context had dramatically changed. Academic historians were increasingly drawn to theories from the wider social sciences. A further irony, noted by Retz in Chapter 10, is that from the 1980s onward, history educationalists de-emphasized 'feeling' and instead insisted that pupils should aim 'at understanding the reasons for which people who lived in the past did what they did'.

Yet the word empathy persists. One of the most interesting 'moves' in *Empathy and History* is Retz's shifting of its meaning. He does this unobtrusively, under the cover of his exposure in Part I of the collective murkiness of educationalists' uses of the word. What I would call 'Retzian empathy' is an orientation toward the recovery of meaning. It could be an attempt to enter the heads of people who lived in the past, or it could be the meaning that we attribute to their actions based on our present-day frames of reference, or a fusion of horizons between the past and present. Retz explores all three possibilities, but takes a particular interest in the *verbum interius*, the *vouloir dire* (the 'meaning' or 'wish to say') of the texts (understood broadly). Empathy in history, however, requires attention to specific historical contexts: Retz distances himself from the notion, already criticized by Collingwood and by W. Dilthey, of empathy as a capacity for entering directly into past reality.

To all this I would say 'Yes', but with one reservation, namely, that we ought to nurture more explicitly the 'feeling' of empathy – without, however, the delusion of immediacy. Perhaps we ought to maintain two notions of empathy, Retzian empathy and affective empathy, with the aim of taking account of history's dual status as both cognitive and affective, concerned both with the past as past and with the overhangs of the past in the present (which latter are both structural/material and affective). Recent time in many countries has been marked by two movements, most often sharply opposed to each other, that are both strongly affective in character: populism, and calls for long-deferred justice. Accordingly, at the present moment both an affective empathy (that resists, however, the delusion of immediacy) and empathy as Retz redefines it seem needed.

Allan Megill, Professor of History, University of Virginia
Charlottesville, December 2021

Acknowledgements

The themes in this book trace back to my efforts as an undergraduate at the University of Adelaide to find a project that combined my interests in history, philosophy and politics. Gerry Groot, Clem Macintyre, Peter Mayer, Felix Patrikeeff and John West-Sooby were teachers whose inspiration and encouragement set me on that path.

Education became a fourth interest when I fell somewhat by accident into school teaching. I am grateful to John Whitehouse for introducing me to concepts in historical teaching and learning as well as to the many teachers and students, too numerous to name, who made those days mostly a pleasure.

Stuart Macintyre planted the idea that I retake my place among my natural allies in history and philosophy. He supervised my doctoral studies at the University of Melbourne with a remarkable care, conscientiousness and alacrity, and he remained no less engaged in my research after completion. His influence has been enormous and I am extremely grateful. I am also grateful to Marnie Hughes-Warrington and Andrew Inkpin for reading this work in its earlier form, and to my examiners Allan Megill and Arthur Chapman for their valuable feedback and continued support.

I spent a very productive year with Peter Seixas in his Centre for the Study of Historical Consciousness at the University of British Columbia. Our rousing tennis matches, lunchtime walks and discussions in the courses to which he so kindly allowed me to contribute are memories that I will hold dearly long into the future.

The Faculty of Arts and School of Historical and Philosophical Studies at the University of Melbourne did me a terrific service. A Gilbert Early Career Development Fellowship spurred this work to its completion, and a number of travel grants enabled me to present my research nationally and internationally. Trevor Burnard, Kate Darian-Smith, Antonia Finnane, David Goodman and Volker Prott entrusted me with teaching duties that added to and stimulated my research on historical method, teaching and learning. The many students I taught confirmed my suspicion that the topic was an important one.

I am grateful to Stefan Berger for welcoming this work into the Making Sense of History series. I also owe thanks to him and several others for hosting me in January 2017, when I gave a series of guest lectures and seminars at universities in Europe and the United Kingdom that proved fruitful in putting the finishing touches on the manuscript. Berber Bevernage, Nicola Brauch, Arthur Chapman, James Connelly, Mark Donnelly, Maria Grever, Lucian Hölscher, Daniel Lindmark, Claire Norton and Jörn Rüsen made these genial occasions.

I shared the experience of writing this book with many outstanding people. André Brett was a thoughtful friend and willing interlocutor. Shane Smits, Kate Allan and Gretel Evans brought wit, charm and intelligence to many a conversation. Further back, I owe to my brother Aaron my earliest intellectual debts, none larger than his acquainting me with Dostoevsky's genius.

There throughout were my parents, to whom this book belongs.

Abbreviations

ACARA	Australian Curriculum, Assessment and Reporting Authority
CPS	Centre for Policy Studies
CSE	Certificate of Secondary Education
CSHC	Centre for the Study of Historical Consciousness, University of British Columbia
DES	Department of Education and Science
GCSE	General Certificate of Secondary Education
HCA	History Curriculum Association
HiEP	History in Education Project, Institute of Historical Research, University of London
HMI	Her Majesty's Inspectorate
HMSO	Her Majesty's Stationery Office
HWG	National Curriculum History Working Group
IOE	Institute of Education, University of London
LEA	Local Education Authority
SCHP	Schools Council History Project
SREB	Southern Regional Examinations Board

Introduction

The question behind this book concerns the link between empathy, the history discipline, the philosophy of history and history education. It surfaced a decade ago while I was being instructed in the method of teaching school history. A seminar on the concept of 'historical empathy' left me flummoxed. I knew that if history was to concern itself with the forms of meaning produced by human societies in the past, it must penetrate to the place where these meanings were held and expressed. I knew that history was a perspectival form of inquiry. But alongside concepts such as 'cause and consequence' and 'continuity and change', it was unclear to me how a concept typically described metaphorically as 'putting oneself in another's shoes' was meant to work. What combination of empathy's poetic, aesthetic, cognitive, imaginative and affective qualities were we teachers-in-training expected to go forth and instil?

The concept's variety of meanings methodologically had furnished it with a full range of political implications. Empathy as emotional engagement could appeal to those who endowed the past with an activist potential to change the present. Empathy as imaginative exploration suggested the possibility of freeing history from evidentiary limitations and entering more fully into the experiences of everyday and marginalized people. A more poetic and aesthetic conception seemed to promise a history as wonder divested of worldly entanglements. Construed cognitively as an investigation of historical context, empathy enticed social and liberal democrats hoping to raise appreciation of the plurality of human forms of life in time and space. But some could regard even this seemingly noble ideal as imposing Western categories of historical thinking on societies possessing their own historical cultures and modes of historical representation. At the opposite end of the political spectrum, conservatives could complain that empathy cheated history of its

---

Notes for this section begin on page 15.

time-honoured role in buttressing national attachments and commitment to universal precepts serving as a guide to the future. Empathy struck at the heart of what it meant to do history as a political enterprise.

Since it was launched in England in the early 1970s, history educationalists have tended to answer that empathy is a cognitive act that in some way defines or constitutes historical method.[1] 'Empathy is central to history – one might say structural', wrote one of these educationalists, Peter Lee, in 1983, 'in that without it . . . history cannot begin.'[2] Lee argued that unless historians understand the points of view of the people whose lives they study, there can be no prospect of using historical evidence in a way that explains why they acted the way they did. In the history classroom, teachers and students were to explain the past by reference to the beliefs, values and goals of the people who lived, thought and acted in it. Empathy became the most common term employed by teachers and examiners to characterize a form of historical thinking that yielded an enriched understanding of historical context.

Yet there was no agreement on what empathy meant. Some suggested that empathy was an 'achievement' of having reconstructed the connections between a historical agent's intentions, circumstances and actions. Others saw it as a history-specific instructional 'process' used to illuminate the 'indeterminate area of action' between the context in which the action was taken and its consequence.[3] Selecting empathy from a list that included alternatives such as 'rational understanding', 'understanding' and 'perspective taking', history educationalists linked it with the idea that an understanding of the context in which an action was taken is the basis for explaining why it was taken. They recognized that empathy carried a wider range of meanings in its everyday sense, but were confident that it could be given this meaning in its historical sense.

But for a concept supposedly so central to historical method, empathy was noticeably absent from historians' writings on the historical craft. E.H. Carr believed that historical facts were more than simply given to historians, but this did not imply that to know the facts required historians to establish a kind of contact with the persons attached to them. G.R. Elton maintained that there were only two principles of historical research – to continually ask 'exactly what evidence is there, and exactly what does it mean?' Rather than merely 'hear' what people in the past were saying, historians had to penetrate the past with questions that kept them alert to the variety of possible meanings contained in historical sources. George Kitson Clark acknowledged the difficulty of explaining the past through general categories and suggested that nominalism – the medieval doctrine that no universal or abstract categories exist, only individuals – was a 'healthy dissolvent' that encouraged historians to identify their distinct parts.[4]

Empathy was not the active ingredient in any of these prescriptions. Across the Atlantic, Peter Gay issued a more pronounced call. His investigation of style in historical writing led him to conclude that the 'emotional empathy that is irrelevant to other scientists is a quality he must patiently cultivate'. Like the modern psychoanalyst, Gay's historian worked in the 'tense yet productive coexistence of engagement and detachment'; he must 'penetrate the most secret recesses of his patient's life', yet remain, as Freud put it, 'a stranger to his patient forever'.[5]

Philosophers of history offered a more crystalline picture of empathy's place in historical method. Carl G. Hempel, the German philosopher of science whose 1942 essay 'The Function of General Laws in History' provided a set of problems and thus a research programme for a scholarly field long the stronghold of speculative philosophers in the German, Italian and British idealist traditions, wrote that the 'method of empathy' functioned as a 'heuristic device' for suggesting 'certain psychological hypotheses' that might serve the historian as 'explanatory principles in the case under consideration', but in the end did not constitute a historical explanation. 'In history as anywhere else in empirical science', he argued famously, 'the explanation of a phenomenon consists in subsuming it under general empirical laws . . . the criterion of its soundness is not whether it appeals to our imagination.'[6]

William Dray, the Canadian philosopher of history, described Hempel as propounding the 'covering-law model' of historical explanation and countered it by proposing a theory of empathetic understanding as 'rational explanation' in his 1957 book *Laws and Explanation in History*. The idealist notion of empathy or imaginative understanding 'allowed some merit', in his view, when it was used as a method for displaying the rationale of what was done in the past.[7] Historians achieved understanding when they saw the 'reasonableness' of what a man did, given the situation as he perceived it, and they provided a rational explanation when the connection between his beliefs, motives and actions was established. Dray denied explicitly that this entailed anything more than empirical, evidence-based inquiry: 'To get inside Disraeli's shoes the historian does not simply ask himself: "What would I have done?"; he reads Disraeli's dispatches, his letters, his speeches, &c. – and not with the purpose of discovering antecedent conditions falling under some empirically validated law, but rather in the hope of appreciating the problem as Disraeli saw it.'[8]

The covering law-versus-empathy debate provided a lens through which the history of historical thought could be read by the 1960s, when a body of publications in historiography and the philosophy of history became available for undergraduate and graduate study, among them Fritz Stern's *Varieties of History* (1956), Hans Meyerhoff's *Philosophy of History in Our Time* (1959) and Patrick Gardiner's *Theories of History* (1959).

Gathering pace at the same time were educational theories that treated the subjects studied at school as an induction into distinct forms of knowledge. Spurred by these, history educationalists in England turned to the philosophy of history to establish the subject's conceptual structure. There they found a philosophy of history that had come into existence precisely to defend history's autonomy against Hempel's methodological incursion. From the early 1950s, analytical philosophers of history denied the applicability of the covering-law model to history while using it as a platform for advancing their claims about the *sui generis* character of historical explanation. A peculiar dynamic emerged: these philosophers mostly rejected the model of scientific explanation, deeming it a form of methodological determinism, while meeting the challenge it posed by attempting to shore up with analytical rigour older varieties of humanism and metaphysics, which as predominantly liberal thinkers they had viewed as a hotbed of imprecise thinking and communist politics.[9] Dray's chief complaint against the covering-law doctrine in history was not the difficulty of putting it into practice; rather, it was that it established 'a kind of *conceptual barrier* to a humanistically oriented historiography'.[10]

Specifically, the analytical philosophers of history refurbished R.G. Collingwood's view that 'all history is the history of thought' along largely epistemological lines to provide an account of historical knowledge that avoided his claim – difficult to accept in the new paradigm – that there was no real boundary between epistemology and metaphysics. Collingwood was regarded as having announced a 'rationalist' or 'intentionalist' approach to explaining human actions from the inside, from the standpoint of what agents held in mind while going about the actions that furnish history with its subject matter. In this way, he became associated with empathy's longer history as a method for capturing the individuality of historical phenomena.

Within this intellectual framework, Collingwood was looked upon by history educationalists as proposing a more accessible way of teaching history now that the English school had to appeal to students of varied academic ability. By holding in mind the thought behind past actions, students could attribute the meaning of a past action to a specific historical context and at the same time consider that meaning in relation to their present-day lives. In their quest for the subject's conceptual basis, these educationalists saw historians doing what history students traditionally had not done. They penetrated behind appearances and achieved insight into historical situations; they revived, re-enacted, re-thought and re-experienced the hopes, fears, plans, desires, views and intentions of those they sought to understand.[11] Empathy was laid as the cornerstone of a structure of historical inquiry designed to have students achieve this task.

This disciplinary conception of empathy has sat uncomfortably with some who see it as limiting empathy's potential to contribute to a fuller historical experience in history classrooms. A brief glance at the literature justifies their concerns. Bridget Cooper has suggested that in education generally, empathy 'is not a neat, concrete concept which necessarily permits high objective evaluation, but its complexity must be understood in as many diverse ways as possible because of its centrality to human interaction and to teaching and learning'. The authors of a 1985 study in developmental psychology began by quoting sixteen definitions of the concept before announcing their intention to account for its 'affective-cognitive-communicative features'. An edited volume noted shortly thereafter that even among the different specialisms in psychology – clinical, development and social – there were conflicting views on how the concept should be defined. A recent collection assembling scholars from philosophical and psychological backgrounds further demonstrates empathy's elasticity, with sections devoted to 'empathy and mind', 'empathy and aesthetics' and 'empathy and morality'. Contributors take insights from phenomenology, hermeneutics, clinical psychology, developmental and social psychology, care ethics, neuroscience and ethology to defend and extend the concept, while others caution that empathy can be detrimental to human affairs.[12] Added to this scholarly interest are the host of books available on the popular market, *Zero Degrees of Empathy*, *The Age of Empathy*, *The Art of Empathy*, *The Empathy Factor*, *Roots of Empathy* and many more. Indeed, when Barack Obama declared that America's federal deficit was less of a problem than its 'empathy deficit', we could be sure that empathy was being vigorously discussed.[13]

The disciplinary conception has been regarded as unsatisfactory by educationalists writing from the American social studies tradition of history teaching. Keith Barton and Linda Levstik argue that restricting the concept to a cognitive endeavour limits the contribution it might make to pluralist democracy. 'To engage in meaningful deliberation with those whose ideas differ from our own', they write, 'we must do more than understand them – we must care about them and about their perspectives.' Christopher Blake contends that the disciplinary conception is 'essentially a reductionist one' that presumes 'a false distinctiveness of historical inquiry'. According to him, empathy's integrative and holistic nature 'unites it more widely and diversely than any one discipline can circumscribe'. Jason Endacott has conducted empirical research beginning with the proposition that 'we must first experience affective empathetic arousal' of the historical agents under investigation. The most important task for history educators is therefore to find out how to cultivate 'empathetic engagement' rather than ask what constitutes empathetic understanding.[14] In a similar vein, Deborah Cunningham finds little in the literature that could help teachers understand how the variety of factors specific to their classroom environments work with or against their efforts to cultivate empathy in their students.[15]

It is fair to characterize North American history teaching as more politically and socially oriented than its British counterpart. I say North American history teaching – and not simply US history teaching – because the internationally influential Canadian model of historical thinking also stresses the benefits of historical learning for social democracy. Peter Seixas has acknowledged his debt to the British educationalists whose work on disciplinary concepts informed his framework while observing that he introduced an 'ethical dimension' and emphasized the value of historical thinking for democratic education. The British educationalists behind empathy's formulation as a central structural concept held to a more open-ended ideal of history as a truly liberal education. They believed that a conceptual structure for teaching history emerged from properties internal to history itself, from its distinct logic as a form of knowledge – a belief enabled, as we shall see, by history's roots in idealist philosophy.

The philosophy of history played a less important role in shaping US history education practice, though a joint effort by historians since 2011 to agree upon the skills, knowledge and habits of mind students develop in university history degrees suggests an increasing tendency to define empathy in the language of historical method.[16] The first document of the American Historical Association's 'Tuning Project' to articulate history's disciplinary core bore witness to the full variety of meanings admitted by the concept's application to historical study. The 'practice of historical empathy' assumed the second of six core competencies of a university history education, which required the achievement of six learning outcomes. Students valued history's contribution to lifelong learning and the critical habits of mind essential for effective and engaged citizenship; they developed historical knowledge with range and depth; they appreciated the provisional status of historical knowledge; they contextualized the past in its own terms; they explored different historical and theoretical viewpoints providing perspective on the past; and they recognized their location in history.

A revised version released three years later winnowed out those aspects not concerned with the investigation of historical context and brought the view of US historians more firmly into line with the longer tradition of approaching the concept explored in this book. Empathy was no longer a core competency to be realized through a collection of learning outcomes; the collaborative 'tuning' of a common disciplinary language reeled it back to a learning outcome of a core competency in 'developing historical methods'. It went from being its own competency, with six outcomes acting in its service, to being one of four outcomes required for the achievement of a competency. Students receiving a training in historical method were now to 'develop empathy toward people in the context of their distinctive historical moments', even if earlier in the document they were told that history 'requires empathy for historical actors'. On the one hand, history's disciplinary profile gave an impression that students were to have empathy for past actors in their persons; on the other hand, dressed in the language of historical method, empathy directed inquiry to the conditions that led them to think, believe and act in the ways they did. The latter complemented three other outcomes in appreciating the evidentiary nature of historical accounts, being able to work with complex materials and practising ethical standards in the use and acknowledgement of historical and scholarly sources.

It may be perfectly reasonable to take the view prevalent in psychology and everyday usage that empathy is feeling what another person feels, but such a communion with dead people is a hard task. History students do not have the benefit of being able to confer with their subjects and so cannot 'catch' their feelings. They are obliged to take a second view that empathy involves the cognitive act of attributing a context to another person's behaviour in order to make sense of it. History involves reading historical texts. Empathy in history cannot operate on a basis of emotional contagion, nor do questions regarding empathetic relationships between teachers and students — though they are indeed important educational questions in social development — help with the methodological issue of understanding the dearly departed through the texts they left for us to interpret.

Aspects of the so-called dark side of empathy are relevant here. Fritz Breithaupt warns that 'empathy is not a sugarcoated method of happy community building' — it can arouse negative feelings towards others and put the feelings it captures in others to negative ends. A separate issue concerns lacking a source of moral motivation when empathy replaces our first-personal stance with the perspective of the other person.[17] We may do better for other people by remaining in our own footwear and, perhaps by anger or a sense of injustice, acting on their behalf when precepts to which we are committed are infringed. Another problem again is that empathy's reliance on capturing feelings makes it a poor motivator for moral action when we are separated by distance from those in need. The philosopher Jesse Prinz has discussed a study demonstrating that while people are often willing to help people suffering directly in front of them, a far smaller proportion cross the street to give the same assistance. The psychologist Paul Bloom believes that empathy is a sacred cow whose time has come for the slaughterhouse, making way for a 'rational compassion' capable of extending human goodwill beyond the narrow preferences determined by immediate impulses.[18]

These criticisms hold true for historical understanding. If empathy cannot motivate us to cross a street, how can it inspire us to journey into a past full of characters who take work to understand? The need in history to attribute a context to past actions renders inadequate its formulation as feeling for people who lived in the past, for such a conception is silent on what constitutes a historical context and what is required for identifying it. History requires a commitment to distant peoples and places that feeling alone cannot sustain. The historian must be animated by a sense of importance and relevance reaching beyond the merely immediate. A history of empathy's place in historical thinking shows that it offered a means for treating the past by its own standards and 'in its own terms', when 'in' refers to the attempt by historians to describe a past phenomenon in terms of its own internal elements and categories rather than from the standpoint of any existing scheme – what social scientists and in particular anthropologists call emic and etic perspectives. Empathy penetrated a context said to yield a variety of historical understanding proper to the newly formed history discipline. The purpose of this book is to specify and evaluate the precise nature of that context.

Historically speaking, I argue that the rise of psychology, as well as the shift from metaphysics to epistemology in philosophical reflection upon history, created a space for empathy to offer itself to historical method. From the 1960s in history education, the epistemology or 'forms of knowledge' of the discipline were translated into a pedagogy for the school subject. Empathy was launched as the cornerstone of a particularly historical way of knowing that could help insulate the subject from cross-curricular and integrated approaches. Similarly, in nineteenth-century German historicism and neo-Kantianism, the need to secure for history an epistemological foundation was the context in which empathy became a core element in an effort to shore up the legitimacy of historical thinking and knowledge.

The two main thinkers investigated in this book – R.G. Collingwood and H.-G. Gadamer – were deeply dissatisfied with the individualizing psychologism of this nineteenth-century, epistemologically preoccupied tradition. I share with them this dissatisfaction.

Methodologically speaking, I argue that the individual-to-individual view of empathy found in the educational literature, as well as in interpretations of Collingwood's doctrine of re-enactment, neglects the fact that language is shared and that, consequently, the historical context empathy must uncover is that which gave rise to common forms of life in the past. By drawing attention away from epistemology and towards metaphysics, I attempt to illuminate the object or subject matter that the empathetic inquirer identifies and describes. To focus on the processes of knowing is the work of the epistemologist; to concentrate on what is being known is the work of the metaphysician. With Collingwood, I agree that we should not separate 'the study of knowing from the study of what is known'.[19]

★ ★ ★

This book is a historical investigation into the nature of the historical context that empathetic understanding should attempt to recover. History educationalists have stressed that empathy cultivates an enriched understanding of historical context. But what context? Does understanding the historical context involve grasping the beliefs, values and goals that people held in the past to help us explain why they acted in the ways they did? Or is the context to be understood that in which it was *possible* for people in the past to hold their beliefs as true and to act upon them accordingly? Is it the beliefs themselves, or the conditions under which they were held, that constitutes the 'context' of empathetic understanding?

The conjunction of Collingwood and Gadamer on the importance of the logic of question and answer illuminates, I believe, the historical context that empathetic understanding should attempt to identify and describe. I treat the actions that furnish history with its subject matter as *answers to questions* that arise from *problem contexts* specific to their time and place.

Intellectual historians have recognized that their answer to this question on the nature of the historical context determines in large part the kind of history they write. Over the past two decades, Mark Bevir has defended the historicist and hermeneutic notion that human societies generate meanings that exist at a certain time and place, and that explanations of human meaning must therefore be historical. According to him, 'all historical meanings must derive from hermeneutic meanings since hermeneutic meanings alone have a temporal existence . . . The hermeneutic meaning of a work derives from the intentions of the person for whom the text has that meaning'.[20] Bevir's 'postfoundational intentionalism' holds that although historians do not have a pure or unmediated access to the past (because all experience and reasoning is theory-laden), they are nevertheless able to postulate the existence of a historical object beyond the texts they study in which this meaning is inscribed – past agents' intentional states. 'All meanings arise from the intentional states, notably the beliefs, which individuals attach to texts.'[21] These beliefs are not present in the texts themselves; they are objects historians postulate as those that best make sense of the text. Historians who study *Leviathan* assume, for instance, Hobbes had beliefs he tried to convey in it, and they ascribe to him the beliefs that best make sense of the facts on which they agree.

Pace Bevir, Quentin Skinner has voiced concern that this project of recovering beliefs has given the intellectual historian a misleading and impoverished hermeneutic, by which he means that it falsely identifies the object of historical interpretation and constricts from the outset the grounds on which a historical explanation may be offered. The authors of the political and philosophical treatises that intellectual historians generally study were not simply affirming beliefs; they were intervening in and making a contribution to a pre-existing debate or conversation specific to the time and culture in which they were writing. 'The essential question which we therefore confront, in studying any given text, is what its author, in writing at the time he did write for the audience he intended to address, could in practice have been intending to communicate by the utterance of this given utterance.'[22] Machiavelli did more than merely affirm that force and fraud are indispensable to political success. He launched his contention into a moral and political context that still held to Cicero's humanist account of the *virtus* that brings princely glory. He reminded his readers of Cicero's claim, questioned its authority, satirized it, and thereby opposed and redefined a standard tenet of humanist political theory.[23]

When historians do describe beliefs, a separate problem is that they often begin by asserting whether a belief is true or false before offering an explanation as to why it was held that way. When it is found that a people in the past held a false belief – as, for example, Emmanuel Le Roy Ladurie's peasants of Languedoc believed it was possible to bring harm to others by casting spells on them – the task historians set themselves becomes an inquiry into the causes of a failure of reasoning. They foreclose from the beginning the possibility that the belief may have stemmed from or been held according to a perfectly rational chain of reasoning.[24] Like Bevir's form of intentionalism, Skinner's concept of 'contextualism' posits an object beyond the text to be understood, but rather than the beliefs themselves, it is the preceding or anterior context that gave rise to them, in which they were held and acted upon, that offers historians a richer pasture for explaining human actions in the past.

Empathy enters this discussion when the intentionalist position appears to entail the recovery of past mental states. Skinner has been at pains to distance himself from the theory of mind of the German *Verstehen* school, Collingwood's concept of re-enacting past thought and what he summarizes as 'the discredited hermeneutic ambition of stepping empathetically into other people's shoes'.[25] Bevir accepts a 'weak' account of empathy, reminding historians that they should not emulate natural scientists in searching for causal laws of events, but rejects a 'strong' account that historians should re-enact the mental processes of those they try to understand, on the grounds that it offers them no access to their subjects' pre-conscious and unconscious beliefs, and leaves them unable to transcend the limits their subjects gave to their own work.[26] He cites the followers of Gadamer's ontological hermeneutics and Paul Ricœur's critical hermeneutics as examples of a 'phenomenological scepticism' that highlights the corrupting role subjective prejudices and biases play in any attempt to recover past intentions.[27] Despite our susceptibility to such a theoretical or 'folk-psychological' knowledge, Karsten Stueber has defended 'reenactive empathy' as the default method for gaining knowledge of other persons in the social sciences. By re-enacting and imitating in our own mind the thought processes of other people's behaviour, we can conceive of it as the behaviour of rational agents who act for reasons.[28]

My argument that Collingwood and Gadamer offer a better alternative to empathy makes this study in part an intellectual history of two philosophers' thought. Collingwood scholars debate the extent to which re-enactment, the logic of question and answer, and the theory of absolute and relative presuppositions combine to constitute a coherent philosophical outlook. As Dray and W.J. van der Dussen remark, 'partly because he worked quickly and partly because he did not mind "thinking on paper", his ideas sometimes appear to change significantly over time, and in some cases over a very short time'.[29] Collingwood's best-known work among historians, *The Idea of History*, was not his definitive view on the philosophy of history, but rather a collection of manuscripts and lecture notes written mostly in the mid-1930s and compiled posthumously by his student, T.M. Knox. Gadamer read the book and found in its account of re-enactment the legacy of a naïve historicist epistemology of re-cognition and reconstruction that forgot all new understanding is an integration into something already understood. In *An Autobiography,* on the other hand, Collingwood's account of treating propositions as answers to questions was enough for Gadamer to declare question-and-answer logic the hermeneutical *Urphänomen* or highest principle. That a historical text is made the object of interpretation, both men agreed, means that it puts a question to the interpreter in relation to which the text must be understood.

Gadamer's negative reception of re-enactment followed from his view that the meaning of a text is never reducible to the intentions its author had in producing it. He repudiated the empathy-dependent hermeneutics from which the intentionalist approach to historical interpretation emerged and attempted to supplant it with an ontological hermeneutics recognizing the embedded nature of all understanding. He welcomed the logic of question and answer, on the other hand, because with Collingwood he agreed that to understand a text is to be conducted by its subject matter, which despite being constantly reinterpreted in the dialectical movement of understanding was viewed as residing in a past horizon of meaning separate from the present horizon in which we seek its integration. While Gadamer is often invoked by antifoundationalists to support the claim that there can be no understanding of the past unmediated by present-day concerns and interests, I argue that an underappreciated aspect of his hermeneutics retains historicism's concern with being directed by the distinct questions and meanings the past puts to us. The 'horizon of the question' by which interpreters are conducted when they read a historical text posits an object beyond the text to which it owes its meaning and is thus the source for its understanding. I defend the historicist principle that the meaning of an object resides in its past while allowing for the fact that the interpretation of this meaning always occurs against the backdrop of tradition and prior understanding. By bringing to bear a wider selection of Collingwood's works and theories on Gadamer's interpretation of him, I suggest that the context of the question to which actions were answers yields the subject matter that historians reconstruct.

In an educational culture obsessed with critical thinking, where to be critical and to detect bias sets the investigator from the start, I take Collingwood and Gadamer to be providing the opportunity for an investigation into what it means to be ready to learn from the past, to be directed by its questions and meanings. I do not have in mind a generic 'openness' to the views and experiences of all and sundry. This can all too easily be taken to license an unreflective relativism that equates taking a position on something with pointing out its truth relativity in time, place and culture. Such an openness is in fact indifferent to the past because it believes itself to have landed upon its kernel of truth, which confined to its past context induces no need to reflect upon its possible shared relevance to today.

I have in mind a historical comportment, a structure of readiness to consider the past as a place that might provide us with considerable insight, if only we grant it the capacity to do so. I am suspicious of approaches that study history for a predetermined end – history for environmentalism, history for national solidarity, history for multiculturalism, and others of varied political colourations – because I see in them the potential for history to be used as a vehicle for buttressing present-day orthodoxies and ways of thinking. The so-called lessons we take from history should emerge from history itself, from a preparedness to treat the historical subject matter as a potential beacon into some important element of our lives. There is an element of risk in letting the past assert itself against the present that we may not like what it says, but nothing I propose suggests blind acceptance. My purpose is to clarify how past questions and meanings interplay with our questions and meanings in historical investigation. While I speak of letting the past assert itself against the present, I do not pretend that there is any such thing as a pure or unmediated access to it.

★ ★ ★

'To an analytically minded philosopher', wrote Kant's most recent biographer, 'the biography of a thinker is simply irrelevant, since it says nothing about the truth of his position and adds nothing to the soundness of his arguments.'[30] In providing an educational history of the concept of empathy as well as an intellectual history of its place in the history discipline and in the conjunction of Collingwood and Gadamer's thought, I have had to strike a balance between diachronic description and synchronic analysis. That is, I have had to represent ideas as they were in their specific historical contexts and as they are for the person who continues to think about them. The discussion has to track back and forth between the historical and the analytical.

With my ambition being primarily to historicize the concept of empathy and the currents of thought surrounding it, I adopt the past tense in cases where the continued relevance of the idea might seem to call for the present tense. It is to be held in mind in such instances that I am interested in what the ideas signified rather than whether they are true or false. Of course, the history of ideas is very much the story of individuals and groups responding to ideas they found to be true or false; thus, to state my purpose in terms of signification over truth and falsity does not release me from the duty of inquiring into the validity of the ideas put forward in specific historical contexts. I shift to the present tense in cases where they have been adequately contextualized that they can be treated in this manner.

Added to these considerations about satisfying the expectations of historians and philosophers is the fact that this book investigates a concept used in historical teaching and learning. The history educationalists to whom I refer work in a field geared principally towards the delivery of a professional degree to students training to be school teachers. A good part of this training consists in becoming experienced with the range of models, taxonomies and matrices of historical thinking and historical consciousness that fill the present-day teacher's repertory. I have not sought to add to this toolkit, but rather to sharpen an implement already in it. I hope by this twin account of empathy's educational and intellectual history to clarify for teachers and history education researchers the nature and function of a concept said to be so central to historical inquiry in its varied configurations of pedagogical execution. They should find resources for overcoming longstanding debates on such topics as skills versus content, as well as a matrix for further research on teaching and learning the historical context that should constitute the object of empathetic understanding in history.

Finally, let me be clear that by taking examples from intellectual historians, hermeneutists and philosophers of history, I am not proposing that school students should be studying the texts by Plato or Machiavelli that these thinkers invoke to argue their point. It need only be recalled when these examples arise that empathy in the history classroom is about offering an enriched context of historical understanding, and it is specifying the nature of this context that is our concern. I take the examples to illustrate the historical context that ought to constitute the object of empathetic understanding. This is the preceding or anterior context in which it was possible for historical agents to hold their beliefs as true and to act upon them accordingly.

★ ★ ★

This dual exploration of empathy's educational and intellectual history is composed of three parts and ten chapters. Part I (Chapters 1–3) concentrates on the period in which empathy entered UK history education from the 1950s to the 1970s. Chapter 1 sets this entry against the backdrop of a newfound methodological and theoretical ecumenicism in academic historical practice. History educationalists became interested in distilling the disciplinary essence of the school subject precisely at a time when a proliferation of approaches was blurring the notion of such a clear-cut identity. Chapter 2 explains how the search to establish history's conceptual structure led educationalists to works by philosophers of history attentive to the *sui generis* character of historical knowledge, charting the emergence of a Collingwood-inspired concept of empathy in the Schools Council History Project (SCHP) at the University of Leeds and a rival conception of rational understanding derived from analytical texts at the University of London. Chapter 3 describes how the need for an agreed vocabulary saw empathy win out over its rivals. By drawing on literature emphasizing empathy's hermeneutical character, the preparation is made for a transition to empathy's intellectual history in the middle part of the book.

Part II (Chapters 4–8) is strictly an intellectual history of empathy in German historicism, Collingwood's philosophy of history and Gadamer's hermeneutics. Chapter 4 examines empathy's deployment together with the need in nineteenth-century Germany to offer a historical account of the nation's distinct cultural past. An eighteenth-century revolt against the universalizing pretensions of the French Enlightenment created the conditions for a German historical practice concerned with establishing individual identities. Chapter 5 explores the contributions of nineteenth-century thinkers who sought to secure for history a role in human knowledge by furnishing this empathy-dependent method with a theoretical foundation. Chapter 6 shifts attention fully to Collingwood to contrast the individualizing psychologism of the German historicists with an Italian outlook that proved far more influential in his attempt to reconcile history and philosophy, epistemology and metaphysics. Chapter 7 attends to the claim that re-enactment belongs to a primitive empathetic hermeneutics by examining the doctrine alongside Collingwood's twin theories of question-and-answer and absolute presuppositions. I put forward the case that these two theories illuminate the historical context with which empathetic understanding ought to concern itself. Chapter 8 extends Collingwood's contribution to specifying this context by linking it with what Gadamer termed the dialectic of question and answer. Both men responded to the psychologism of the nineteenth-century empathy tradition in a way that Gadamer did not fully appreciate in receiving Collingwood's thought.

Part III (Chapters 9–10) returns to the educational milieu where Part I left off in the early 1980s. It brings the discussion of empathy's place in history education into the current century while drawing on the themes and patterns presented in Part II. Chapter 9 describes how the philosophical programme behind empathy's launch in the 1970s played out in the development of a national curriculum for England and Wales in the 1980s. Empathy was ultimately omitted, but this did not spell its end. The concept was one of several disciplinary, structural or second-order concepts that were taken up outside England by history curriculum theorists and designers, most prominently in an influential Canadian model of historical thinking. Chapter 10 explains how this model has combined two traditions of historical thought: first, the analytical tradition that gave rise to disciplinary concepts; and, second, the historicist-hermeneutical tradition through which empathy was theorized alongside the concept of historical consciousness that has come to occupy an important place in contemporary history education research. These two traditions of historical thought now vie for the attention of a global network of history educators.

Notes

1. Unlike the more generic terms 'history educator' and 'history education researcher', I use the term 'history educationalist' to refer specifically to an academic working from a university department of education, with an interest primarily in historical teaching and learning in a school curricular context.

2. Peter Lee, 'History Teaching and Philosophy of History', *History and Theory* 22, 4 (1983), 40.

3. Compare Peter Lee and Rosalyn Ashby, 'Empathy, Perspective Taking, and Rational Understanding', and Elizabeth Anne Yeager and Stuart J. Foster, 'The Role of Empathy in the Development of Historical Understanding', in O.L. Davis Jr., Elizabeth Anne Yeager and Stuart J. Foster (eds), *Historical Empathy and Perspective Taking in the Social Studies* (Lanham: Rowman & Littlefield, 2001), 3, 23; Stuart Foster, 'Using Historical Empathy to Excite Students about the Study of History: Can You Empathize with Neville Chamberlain?' *Social Studies* 90, 1 (1999), 18–24.

4. Edward Hallett Carr, *What is History?* (London: Macmillan, 1961), 19–21; G.R. Elton, *The Practice of History* (Sydney: Sydney University Press, 1967), 17, 65, 85; G. Kitson Clark, *The Critical Historian* (London: Heinemann, 1967), 135.

5. Peter Gay, *Style in History* (New York: Basic Books, 1974), 215.

6. C.G. Hempel, 'The Function of General Laws in History', *Journal of Philosophy* 39, 2 (1942), 44–45; reprinted to wider circulation in Patrick Gardiner (ed.), *Theories of History: Readings from Classical and Contemporary Sources* (Glencoe: Free Press, 1959), 344–56.

7. William Dray, *Laws and Explanation in History* (Oxford: Oxford University Press, 1957), 120.

8. Ibid., 129.

9. Kerwin Lee Klein, *From History to Theory* (Berkeley: University of California Press, 2011), 49–51.

10. William Dray, 'The Historical Explanation of Actions Reconsidered', in Sidney Hook (ed.), *Philosophy and History: A Symposium* (New York: New York University Press, 1963), 133.

11. Except where they appear differently in direct quotations and in other writers' usage, I hyphenate 're-think' and 're-enact', as Collingwood did, to retain their sense as technical terms in his philosophy of history.

12. Bridget Cooper, *Empathy in Education: Engagement, Values and Achievement* (London: Continuum, 2011), 7–8; Arnold P. Goldstein and Gerald Y. Michaels, *Empathy: Development, Training, and Consequences* (Hillsdale: Lawrence Erlbaum Associates, 1985), 1–5; Nancy Eisenberg and Janet Strayer (eds), *Empathy and its Development* (Cambridge: Cambridge University Press, 1987), ix; Amy Coplan and Peter Goldie (eds), *Empathy: Philosophical and Psychological Perspectives* (Oxford: Oxford University Press, 2011).

13. 'Obama to Graduates: Cultivate Empathy: "The World Doesn't Just Revolve around You"', Northwestern University Commencement Speech, 19 June 2006. As President, Obama continued to spread his empathy message in commencement speeches across the country.

14. I have changed 'empathic' to 'empathetic' in the few instances where authors use the former. While the shorter form is indeed the original, *empathetic* has prevailed as the preferred adjective in all but certain styles of scientific, modern self-help and spiritual writing.

15. Keith C. Barton and Linda S. Levstik, *Teaching History for the Common Good* (Mahwah: Lawrence Erlbaum, 2004), 207; Christopher Blake, 'Historical Empathy: A Response to Foster and Yeager', *International Journal of Social Education* 13, 1 (1998), 26; Jason L. Endacott, 'Reconsidering Affective Engagement in Historical Empathy', *Theory and Research in Social Education* 38, 1 (2010), 8; Deborah L. Cunningham, 'Understanding Pedagogical Reasoning in History Teaching through the Case of Cultivating Historical Empathy', *Theory and Research in Social Education* 35, 4 (2007), 592–630. See also Sarah Brooks, 'Historical Empathy in the Social Studies Classroom: A Review of the Literature', *Journal of Social Studies Research* 33, 2 (2009), 213–34.

16. 'Tuning the History Discipline in the United States', *American Historical Association*. Retrieved 23 November 2017 from https://www.historians.org/teaching-and-learning/tuning-the-history-discipline.

17. Fritz Breithaupt, 'Empathy for Empathy's Sake: Aesthetics and Everyday Empathic Sadism', in Aleida Assmann and Ines Detmers (eds), *Empathy and its Limits* (New York: Palgrave Macmillan, 2015), 162; Jesse J. Prinz, 'Is Empathy Necessary for Morality?' and Peter Goldie, 'Anti-empathy', in Coplan and Goldie (eds), *Empathy*, 211–29 and 302–17 respectively.

18. Prinz, 'Is Empathy Necessary for Morality?' 220; see also by the same author, 'Against Empathy', *Southern Journal of Philosophy* 49, 1 (2011), 214–33; Paul Bloom, *Against Empathy: The Case for Rational Compassion* (New York: HarperCollins, 2016).

19. R.G. Collingwood, *The Idea of History*, rev. edn [1946] Jan van der Dussen (Oxford: Oxford University Press, 1994), 3.

20. Mark Bevir, *The Logic of the History of Ideas* (Cambridge: Cambridge University Press, 1999), 76; see also Mark Bevir, 'In Defence of Historicism', *Journal of the Philosophy of History* 6, 1 (2012), 111–14.

21. Mark Bevir, 'How to Be an Intentionalist', *History and Theory* 41, 2 (2002), 213.

22. Quentin Skinner, 'Meaning and Understanding in the History of Ideas', *History and Theory* 8, 1 (1969), 48–49.

23. Quentin Skinner, 'Belief, Truth and Interpretation', Keynote Address, Intellectual History: Traditions and Perspectives, Ruhr Universität Bochum, 18 November 2014.

24. Quentin Skinner, *Visions of Politics, Volume 1: Regarding Method* (Cambridge: Cambridge University Press, 2002), 35–36.

25. Ibid., 120.

26. Bevir, *Logic*, 157–58.

27. Ibid., 76–77, 121, 123–24.

28. Karsten Stueber, *Rediscovering Empathy: Agency, Folk Psychology, and the Human Sciences* (Cambridge, MA: MIT Press, 2006).

29. W.H. Dray and W.J. van der Dussen, editors' introduction to *The Principles of History: And Other Writings in Philosophy of History* (New York: Oxford University Press, 1999), xv. Although unfinished, Collingwood gave Knox permission to publish his manuscript 'The

Principles of History' as a separate book, which he had hoped would be his final word on the philosophy of history. How Knox edited the manuscript and included it in *The Idea of History* has been a topic of vigorous discussion among Collingwood scholars. The original manuscript was lost until 1995, when it was discovered in the Oxford University Press archive. In 1978, Collingwood's widow deposited several thousand pages of unpublished manuscripts in the New Bodleian Library at Oxford. A new version of *The Idea of History* appeared in 1994, edited by Jan van der Dussen, containing important lectures from 1926 and 1928. I rely particularly on the 1928 'Die manuscript' Collingwood cited in his *Autobiography* as being such a breakthrough in his thought.

30. Manfred Kuehn, *Kant: A Biography* (Cambridge: Cambridge University Press, 2001), 19.

Part I

EDUCATION

Amid the growing claims of natural science it is difficult
to find a place for the teaching of history.
—James Bryce, 1907

CHAPTER 1

Reforming the Past

'Foreigners tell us that in education, as in all else, we have no care for method', wrote a founding member of the Historical Association, C.H.K. Marten, in an early symposium on the teaching of history.[1] The foreigners he had in mind were Germans, where the rise of historicism and the nationalist proclivities of the Romantic movement had imbued history education with an anthropological purpose to discover the origins of humankind and human institutions.

In the spirit of British gradualism, by contrast, the so-called great tradition of history teaching in England worked under the assumption that a shared story, filled with moral and patriotic examples and drawn from a relatively agreed set of historical facts, could equip students with the knowledge needed for civic life and participatory democracy. As a record of good and evil done on the world, history supplied the content for a kind of moral training, where students found examples to emulate or abjure from the great men and women who lived in the past. The role of history teachers consisted in placing before the student instances of exemplary conduct and exploits. Delivered mostly in the style of an edifying homily, they had small reason to extend their practice beyond a drilling in dates, names and events. It was a tradition in which teachers didactically transmitted the facts of historical knowledge to passive students who demonstrated their mastery through repeated short tests. Indeed, for the first two-thirds of the twentieth century, W.C. Sellar and R.J. Yeatman's caricature of English history, *1066 and All That,* spoke a certain truth: 'History is not what you thought. *It is what you can remember.*'[2] The content to remember was mainly political history, with some social and economic aspects; it was mainly English, with some European, from Julius Caesar to the First World War.[3]

Notes for this section begin on page 33.

A sense that the subject was not meeting the demands of contemporary education began to seize history teachers in the 1960s. Martin Booth, the head of history at a Harlow comprehensive school, conducted a pioneering study inside four schools that suggested students had the ability to structure historical knowledge in ways that could make the subject 'vital and relevant'. Booth worried that as the teachers of other school subjects appealed for more teaching time, the danger would grow that a 'utilitarian society' would treat the 'impractical discipline of history with mild contempt'. He drove home the message that teaching methods required as much consideration as teaching content. For history to contribute to 'creative, divergent thought', learning in the subject had to be based on 'independent activity' rather than 'unthinking receptivity'.[4]

Booth's appeal for methodological innovation in school history came at a time when the practice of history in universities was becoming increasingly interdisciplinary. Historians since the interwar period had expressed their dissatisfaction with the nominalist individualism of mainstream English history. The rise of social history in the 1960s was fuelled by a recognition that history was richer and more explanatory when social theories were brought to bear on its subject matter.

Much of the initial impetus came from economic historians. R.H. Tawney argued in his inaugural lecture at the London School of Economics (LSE) in 1932 that individual historical phenomena contained elements in common with other phenomena and that generalization in the manner of the social sciences was therefore possible. 'The generalisations of the historian, like those of the anthropologist and sociologist, take the form . . . not of propositions claiming universal validity, but of statements of the relations between phenomena within the framework of a specific epoch or civilisation.'[5]

Tawney's LSE colleague, Eileen Power, in her own inaugural lecture the following year, pleaded further for historians to dispose of the view that historical facts could be known by purely inductive, intuitive reasoning, and to look forward instead to 'a social science *par excellence*' built upon a cooperation between anthropology, sociology, economics and history, open to deductive analysis and able to find 'dependable uniformity and regularity' in society.[6] Her future husband and Cambridge economic historian, M.M. Postan, had reservations about the intellectual calibre of historians of 'cautious and painstaking disposition', whose 'critical attitude to minutiae' and the 'unique and unrepeatable' came at the expense of theoretical synthesis and scientific generalization. His target were the neo-Kantian philosophers of history, those who had 'succeeded in spreading the view of history as an impregnable stronghold of non-scientific knowledge' by defining it as a 'vehicle of specific forms of cognition'.[7] Though Postan did not name his neo-Kantian philosophers, he almost certainly had in mind Benedetto Croce,

R.G. Collingwood and, particularly, Michael Oakeshott, whose *Experience and its Modes* spoke of historical experience as an abstract and defective 'arrest' of the totality of experience, which entailed a descriptive and nontheoretical historical practice. 'History', held Oakeshott, 'is the narration of a course of events which, in so far as it is without serious interruption, explains itself . . . the method of the historian is never to explain by means of generalization but always by means of greater and more complete detail.'[8]

Marxist historians held similar concerns. Christopher Hill took aim at the Whig-liberal tradition of locating the source of historical explanation in the free will of the individual, admitting of 'flights of fancy', he believed, by divesting history of 'ponderable, analysable, material factors'. It was a tradition worth exposing for Hill not because it any longer held respect in the academic world, but because it still informed most of the history taught in English schools: 'the history, that is to say, of all but the specialist historians'.[9] He articulated a moderate version of Marxism that could 'help contemporary historians to preserve a sense of proportion between social forces and the men through whom they work, between statistics and poetry, necessity and freedom'.[10] History could be reduced neither to the will of individuals, 'great' or otherwise, nor to the economic forces that produce political results. Maurice Dobb made the same point when he argued that Marxist materialism was an aid to research, a guide to problem-solving, a general hypothesis, not a substitute for history itself. 'That the shaping of individuals by their social *milieu* and of social groups by their relations to the mode of production is a simple formula which can yield a direct answer to every historical problem', he wrote, 'no serious Marxist has ever maintained.'[11]

The vastly altered intellectual landscape of the 1960s was one in which a new generation of Marxist historians sensed a new optimism about history's relevance for the present. This is part of the story told by Geoff Eley in his reflection on the state of historiography over the past four or five decades: 'We saw it not only as an aid to effective political thinking but also as a tool for honing a critical social consciousness and for making our way toward a workable political ethos.'[12] Critics of the empiricist tradition such as Gareth Stedman Jones wrote of a profession in 'arrested intellectual development', conceptually bankrupt and impervious to the syncretic advances in theory and practice transforming historiography elsewhere, particularly in France under the *Annalistes* and social thought of Althusser and Lévi-Strauss. Stedman Jones excoriated 'the legacy of a tenacious and antique liberal individualism' in English historical culture, the 'scientific sermon' that was history when accumulated facts provided the basis for moral lessons, the belief that theory or interpretations came to light after all facts had been collected, and in cases where sociological structures had been acknowledged as exercising an influence on individuals' behaviour, that no concomitant attempt had been made to formulate the concepts for an expanded methodological repertory. He credited Carr with having finally made clear that the composition of facts appears differently depending upon the angle from which they are approached, but found his conception of history accounted inadequately for the 'differential temporality of linked historical structures', by which he concluded that it failed to illustrate how a heterogeneous theoretical practice, up to the task of dislodging the liberal orthodoxy, might look.[13]

However slow it was to take hold, methodological heterogeneity had entered the mainstream by 1971. It was 'a good moment to be a social historian', Eric Hobsbawm famously proclaimed.[14] A 'general historization' of the social sciences had taken place in response to the immensely changed global circumstances that marked this period of human history. The struggles for political and economic emancipation in colonial and semicolonial countries drew the attention of governments, international and research organizations, and along with them social scientists, to what were problems of historic transformation. Hobsbawm celebrated the fact that these problems, previously at the margins of academic orthodoxy in the social sciences, were being taken up by a new generation of politically engaged social historians.[15]

In a separate essay appearing alongside a reprint of Stedman Jones' assault on British empiricism, Hobsbawm attempted to correct the conventional errors of a pervasive 'vulgar Marxism'.[16] A crude economic determinism, a simple base-superstructure model of society, a view of history simply as the story of class struggle, a penchant for historical laws and a presumption of historical inevitability had to yield to a more sophisticated Marxism that brought history and the social sciences together to account for both stability and disruption, one that accommodated the individual by showing how human agency was at work in individuated societies, which sometimes controlled or refashioned economic determinants while at other times were controlled and refashioned by them. 'It is equally important that internal tensions may sometimes be reabsorbed into a self-stabilizing model by feeding them back as functional stabilizers, and that sometimes they cannot.'[17]

Yet the view that each society had its own dynamic was not incompatible with the view that social history had a generalizing or totalizing potential, captured in the title of Hobsbawm's *Dædalus* article, 'From Social History to the History of Society'. Theory was needed to pull together its various modes and sites of social explanation. For the British Marxist historians assembled around Hobsbawm and the journal *Past and Present,* launched in 1952, this had been pursued by strengthening the international networks initiated at the 1950 International Historical Congress in Paris, where a Social History Section had been created, and made possible by the recent translation of classic and modern European theory, which was being integrated into undergraduate and graduate curricula. Eley understood while a student at Oxford in the late 1960s that history was insufficient by itself; it needed 'theory' enlisted from other disciplines. A core feature of the intellectual conjuncture that brought history into dialogue with the social sciences was its ecumenicism, an open-endedness of intellectual discovery also characteristic of the radical political movements of the time.[18]

The ferment of new ideas and approaches in economic, urban, social and family history spurred a considerable increase in the number of university-employed practitioners and PhD-inspired scholarship. Looking back on this period from an educational perspective, Alaric Dickinson has called it the 'golden age' of British history and British historians.[19] Important works by professional historians included Christopher Hill's *The Century of Revolution 1603–1714* (1961), Asa Briggs's *Victorian People* (1954), E.P. Thompson's *The Making of the English Working Class* (1963), and Lawrence Stone's *The Crisis of the Aristocracy 1558–1614* (1965). These books appealed to a wide audience and, by Dickinson's analysis, inspired many teachers and senior secondary school students. Significantly for school history, they challenged the traditional supremacy of political history that had long provided structural coherence to school history courses, and the shift in subject matter in general led to an upsurge of interest in the scholarly techniques of history.

These developments in historical practice and theorization affected the way teachers entering the profession imagined their task in the 1960s and 1970s.[20] The installation of an enlarged methodological armoury made possible by the new openness to influences from sociology and anthropology, as well as an interest in the everyday experiences of the oppressed and dispossessed, transformed the concerns of academic historians and thus the content base of history degrees. Those graduates who went on to become history teachers entered the profession with a substantially different knowledge and conceptual set from those who had formed an understanding of history's purpose and procedures in previous decades.

Particularly influential was the historian E.P. Thompson. His celebrated ambition to rescue the everyday person 'from the enormous condescension of posterity' enunciated a methodological ethics that underlay later attempts in education to mobilize empathy as a concept for understanding the distinct context in which people thought and acted in the past. Thompson's *Making* set the standard for a history in which people became the movers of historical change, 'a study in an active process, which owes as much to agency as to conditioning'. Historians' criterion of judgement was not whether a person's actions were justified in the light of subsequent evolution; rather, they had to assume that the aspirations of everyday people 'were valid in terms of their own experience', and the task became showing how real people in real contexts were agents in their own making.[21] According to Eley, Thompson's 'historical ethnography' was underpinned by a 'politics of empathy', 'an intense and vehement valuing of the lives and histories of ordinary people', which presupposed a readiness for entering into their mental worlds, reconstructing their hidden rationalities and suspending one's own context-bound assumptions.[22]

In France the *Annales* school of historiography, founded interbellum by Marc Bloch and Lucien Febvre, had forged the concept of *histoire des mentalités* as a way of capturing the unconscious level of social behaviours in past peoples. A need in French historiography to account for elements such as the crowd in the French Revolution had created a space for social explanation and brought the discipline into contact with sociology much earlier than in Britain. In the context of a postwar questioning of European cultural pre-eminence, this making of room for history's forgotten received further impulse. History's crisis was not a malady affecting history alone; it was, in Febvre's words, 'a great crisis of human understanding'.[23] The natural ally of the *Past and Present* group, *Annales* historiography turned the historian's gaze beyond the political arena to horizons of physical nature, the countryside, population, demographics, exchanges and manners, which provided a point of contact for all the social sciences. For Bloch, the vast terrain of history demanded that the historian be in possession of the full range of techniques of the social sciences: 'Few sciences, I believe, are forced to use so many dissimilar tools at the same time . . . man's actions are the most complex in the animal kingdom, because man stands upon nature's summit.'[24]

Fernand Braudel engineered this union in three distinct timeframes, delineated magisterially in his *La Méditerranée et le Monde Méditerranéen à l'Époque de Philippe II* (1949). First, the plurality of time manifested in man's connection with his geographical milieu, the *longue durée* of nearly immobile history. Second, the slow history of conjunctions – the history of economics and society often marked by war, famine or other such calamity – interpolated in this course of time and rejigged its structures and interdependencies. Finally, the history of events impressed themselves on an individual scale as brief and dramatic oscillations of the traditional historical flow. In this symbiosis of history and the social sciences, whose purpose was a synthesis of the totality of human phenomena (*histoire totale*), the concept of *mentalité* solidified as the master category of social structure, and consequently the category through which past societies were researched and presented. The focus shifted to the human and therefore required varying degrees of humane understanding.

Amid these shifts in the way history was being written were shifts in thinking about the nature and purpose of education. It was an atmosphere in which educationalists began to feel ill at ease with traditional methods and content, prompting them to reflect on the presuppositions of their educational orthodoxies. They asked themselves what shape the English national narrative took now that its global supremacy had vanished, as well as how history merited a place in the curriculum in an age that measured itself in terms of scientific, technological and entrepreneurial advances.

Then there were shifts in the way teachers were being trained in university departments of education. From as early as the 1920s, there had been debate over whether teachers should be experts in their subject or experts in teaching. Teachers from training colleges, mostly women who taught in primary schools, had received hardly any education in history, while the male teachers who filled posts in secondary schools had traditionally been qualified to teach by their possession of university degree and thus entered the classroom with little or no training in teaching.[25]

The 1960s was a period of momentous change in education. Reforms in primary schooling were prompted by the Plowden Report of 1967, the Circular 10/65 reorganized secondary schools along comprehensive lines, and in 1972 the school leaving age was raised to sixteen. The Robbins Committee Report, published in 1963, led to the establishment of sixteen new universities, doubling the numbers in higher education over the next decade. The redesignation of teacher training colleges as colleges of education, closely linked to the universities, and the introduction of the Bachelor of Education degree led to a threefold expansion of the higher education sector.[26] As summarized in an account of the search to find the 'right kind of history' in England, in 'colleges of education and in universities, educational theory was being energetically advanced, while the advent of comprehensive schools generated new demands and ideas about what to teach and how to teach it. The results of this "pedagogic ferment" would profoundly affect how history was taught in schools'.[27]

Educational psychology was well placed to play a leading role in the expanded departments of education. Since the 1920s, it had established itself to such a degree that in the following decades the majority of professors of education were psychologists. J.B. Thomas has quoted evidence of a proliferation of courses and a related expansion of monographs, new book series and journals in which educational psychologists published at a higher rate than in any other area of psychology.[28]

The significance of the growth of educational psychology is that it provided a framework for developing a host of new educational research programmes. From the late 1950s until well into the 1970s, the theories of conceptual development of the Swiss psychologist Jean Piaget provided British educationalists with the framework for understanding the school curriculum, students' performance, as well as the means for classifying and systematizing the types of thinking required for different school subjects.[29] Piaget's principal contribution to psychology, or genetic epistemology as he preferred to say, was a delineation of the basic structures of thought that characterize children at different ages or stages of development. Relying on logical formalism and an epistemology founded on biological principles, his famously painstaking observations of children provided portraits of their developmental course and suggested the mechanisms that enable them to transition to higher stages of development, from the sensorimotor stages of infancy to the intuitive stage of early childhood, or from the concrete operational stage of middle childhood to the formal operational stage of adolescence.[30]

The view of history through the Piagetian lens was not edifying. A particularly influential study was that of Roy Hallam, who after conducting research with one hundred subjects aged eleven to sixteen, reported that only two were able to think at the highest, 'formal', operational level.[31] He concluded that thinking skills develop later in history than in science or mathematics and accordingly recommended that exercises demanding inferential thought be avoided in place of concrete topics of simple cause-effect relationships. Faced with hypothetical inferences and moral dilemmas, history, for Hallam, 'can perplex the most intelligent of adults'.[32]

The Piagetian research agenda predominated. Booth reported that at least twenty-four theses and dissertations on historical learning from a Piagetian perspective were conducted in the United Kingdom from 1955 to 1983, all concluding that 'children find it harder to think hypothetically and deductively [in history] than in other disciplines'.[33] This conclusion was hardly encouraging and the push for curricular reform had to come from an educational psychology that cast history's prospects in a more propitious light.

Such a model was provided by the educational writings of the American psychologist Jerome Bruner. His tenet was that 'any subject can be taught effectively in some intellectually honest form to any child at any stage of development'.[34] In contrast to Piaget's 'ages and stages' framework for the development of conceptual thought, which tended to emphasize limitations over possibilities, Bruner's idea that 'the curriculum of a subject should be determined by the most fundamental understanding that can be achieved of the underlying principles that give structure to that subject' appealed to those who wished to champion history's disciplinary principles at a time when the subject was coming under increasing pressure from social and integrated studies. Whereas previously school history stood relatively detached from its academic parent, Bruner's insistence that the 'ablest scholars and scientists' had a part to play in identifying the 'basic structure' of the school subjects drew history educationalists into questions concerning the nature, purposes and procedures of historical thinking and knowing, traditionally the subject matter of the philosophy of history. Guided by this educational thought, they launched a search for history's *sui generis* character just as the widening of history's methodological purview was blurring such disciplinary distinctions among academic historians.

Paul H. Hirst, an educational philosopher in the Institute of Education at the University of London, articulated a complementary argument for disciplinary distillation.[35] Responding to the need to give positive content to the term 'liberal education', Hirst contended that a liberal education is one that treats knowledge as the understanding of experience in a unique way. The task thus became specifying the objective differences in the 'forms of knowledge' that distinguish the disciplines and school subjects from each other and from the unitary approaches to developing mental abilities in a combined curriculum.

Hirst criticized the view, rooted in the Greek notion that knowledge achieves its own satisfaction in the mind by corresponding to what is external to it in reality, that attaining knowledge alone develops the mind in ways that promote the living of a good and virtuous life. The problem with this view when used as the basis for liberal educational programmes was that it provided no conceptual vocabulary by which the achievement of knowledge or fruits of learning could be publicly registered or tested. Whatever forms of private awareness of the mental processes there may be in the individual whose knowledge comes to correspond to an external reality, it is by means of publicly accepted symbols that conceptual articulation becomes objectified for the individual in learning, 'for the symbols give public embodiment to the concepts . . . The result of this is that men are able to come to understand both the external world and their own private states of mind in common ways, sharing the same conceptual schema by learning to use symbols in the same manner'.[36] In this way, Hirst conceived the forms of knowledge as the basic articulations whereby the whole of human experience has become intelligible to man, and through which, by means of a liberal education, experience is filtered in the everyday world. Although unmentioned by Hirst, historical knowledge would seem to have a special place here. 'To acquire knowledge', according to him, 'is to become aware of experience as structures, organised and made meaningful in some quite specific way, and the varieties of human knowledge constitute the highly developed forms in which man has found this possible. To acquire knowledge is to learn to see, to experience the world in a way otherwise unknown, and thereby come to have mind in a fuller sense.'[37]

It is because the forms of knowledge involve us in coming to look at experience in particular ways that Hirst referred to them as disciplines. Unlike the fields of knowledge bound simply by their subject matter and that employ whatever concepts, skills and techniques are necessary for investigating that subject matter, disciplines were seen to exhibit logically distinct forms of expression that depend on some particular kind of test against experience, which apply to the full spectrum of the discipline's subject matter. The sciences, for instance, depend on empirical experimental and observational tests, and mathematics on deduction from certain sets of axioms. As for history, Hirst believed a strong case could be made for it as a discipline owing to its particular 'logical features', though it was beyond his scope to specify what these features might be. Once identified by specialists in the discipline, the conduct of liberal education would be composed of immersion in paradigmatic examples of the forms of knowledge, first to understand the way in which the concepts and criteria 'work' in particular cases, then through a sufficient generalization of these over the range of the discipline's subject matter, to begin to experience the world in this distinctively structured manner.[38]

Against this background, an article by Mary Price, 'History in Danger', proved pivotal in creating the groundswell for history education reform. Price recognized that since the Second World War, teachers had been engaged in a 'prolonged and searching questioning of the traditional school subjects . . . and of the methods of teaching and examining them', which pressed them 'more often to say why their subject should form an essential part in the education of the young'.[39] The roll-out of comprehensive schools was bringing students of mixed abilities under the one roof, generating a need to provide less academic and more relevant subjects, either by integrating history, geography and religious education into the humanities or by focusing on contemporary issues in social studies. Price thought it was 'deplorable' to suppose that only academically gifted children could study history profitably. Moreover, the cross-curricular approach embodied in humanities diluted history, while the current affairs content of the social studies disregarded history altogether. Accordingly, Price implored history teachers to help themselves by establishing a 'forum for the exchange of experiment and thought in the teaching of history', such as the periodical *English in Education* had achieved for that subject.[40]

Price's proposal came to fruition soon afterwards. She 'proved a prophetess', wrote one commentator two decades later.[41] In May 1969, the Historical Association released its first number of the periodical *Teaching History*; published quarterly, it became the primary forum for debate in the following decades. More significantly, as Dickinson has suggested, Price may have influenced the Schools Council's decision to fund a major project in history curriculum development.[42] She noted in her article that the body was only 'marginally interested' in history compared with other subjects.[43] Yet in March 1972, it awarded a grant of £126,000 for such an investigation. The Schools Council History 13–16 Project (SCHP) began its work at the University of Leeds in September 1972 to help teachers find ways of encouraging more student interaction in their study of history and to reconsider the subject's role in the various forms of cross-disciplinary studies being developed in schools.

The Newsom Report and the Schools Council paper *Humanities for the Young School Leaver* had by this time disseminated the idea that the use of the imagination in history could respond to students' 'needs' by giving them an insight into the lives of those who lived in the past. 'Even more important, perhaps, than this scientific approach to factual evidence', said the first, 'is an ability to enter imaginatively into other men's minds. What is to be cultivated here is psychological sensitivity and intuitive awareness rather than rational fact finding . . . People count . . . People make history.'[44] The Schools Council distinguished a 'hard-won detachment' from a 'lack of engagement that has marked some traditional courses in humanities subjects'. This detachment involved 'an imaginative effort to take up the other man's point of view, or to investigate its limitations . . . To balance the discipline of the facts there has to be a discipline of the imagination'.[45]

But while the 1960s saw imagination accorded a new importance in historical teaching and learning, empathy was not yet its bedfellow. A 1971 pamphlet produced for the Historical Association by Jeanette Coltham and John Fines, *Educational Objectives for the Study of History*, provided the first instance of their being considered alongside one another.[46] The pamphlet has been commended for having 'inspired a revolution' in the teaching and learning of history by pioneering an approach based on Bruner's idea of introducing students to the skills of the historian.[47] This meant classifying for the first time the specific components that distinguish learning in history from learning in other subjects.

Coltham and Fines applied to history the taxonomy of educational objectives of the American educational psychologist Benjamin Bloom to classify progress in learning as a series of developmental steps identifiable by particular affective and cognitive behaviours. Bloom's team had undertaken the ambitious task of defining and classifying a full range of such opaque educational terms as thinking, problem-solving and understanding. The taxonomy aimed to establish a set of differentiated educational symbols that would permit teachers, examiners, curriculum writers and educational researchers to determine and communicate the effectiveness of their educational programmes through a common language and hence with greater precision.[48] For example, a teacher who wished to have students 'understand' a particular phenomenon might categorize their understanding as 'translation' if they described the phenomenon in terms similar to those originally used to describe it. If, on the other hand, students were able to summarize and explain the phenomenon by reordering the material in their own words, the next-highest category, 'interpretation', might apply to the understanding.

Coltham and Fines applied empathy and sympathy to Bloom's affective domain, which in the taxonomy included objectives that describe changes in interest, attitudes, values, the development of appreciation and adequate adjustment.[49] Empathy and sympathy appeared under the 'conative behaviour' or 'attitude toward the past' *imagining* – one of three such behaviours with 'attending' and 'responding' – used to describe an effort on the part of the student to enter into 'the shoes' or 'the skins' of persons they encountered in the past, identifying with them so as to be able to affirm their viewpoints on problems that were contemporary to them. The concepts thus served to increase students' willingness to receive and respond to historical content before introducing the cognitive or disciplinary procedures of investigation, which comprised the bulk of the document.[50]

In Bloom's taxonomy, receiving and responding were classified as separate educational objectives, characterized at the highest levels by students' ability to maintain their attention on a selected stimulus in spite of competing and distracting stimuli (receiving), and by their exhibiting an attachment to this stimulus accompanied by a feeling of satisfaction, pleasure, zest or other such emotion (responding).[51] Imagining thus served to sensitize students to the content of history in ways that made them more willing to apply their intellects thereafter. But while imagining described only the formation of an image in the mind, they suggested that sympathy and empathy were needed to bring the historical imagination to life. Creating much confusion later, they defined sympathy as the 'power of entering into another's feelings or mind', and empathy as the 'power of entering into another personality' and 'imaginatively experiencing his experience'. For the history student to achieve 'something more than external acquaintance', according to them, 'sympathetic and empathetic behaviours are necessary'. Coltham and Fines considered such behaviours to be 'very specific to the study of history', in which 'a person's action can be understood only by seeing some problem, predicament or decision from his point of view, or a biography is achieved only by breathing life into an assembly of many small pieces of evidence'.[52]

Educational Objectives had a profound effect, if not for the intricate framework it established, then for the debate it generated by trying to systematize the various components of historical thinking. Peter Lee reflected four decades after its publication that although Coltham and Fines made advances in identifying the distinguishing features of historical learning, they failed in the subsequent task of categorizing them into a set of observable objectives by imposing upon the subject a conceptually muddled and ultimately unworkable framework.[53] In spite of its flaws, which stemmed from the fact that it was the first study of its kind and that its model, Bloom's taxonomy, was itself a complex document, the point to note is that empathy was envisaged as a concept able to motivate and engage students in their study of historical material. It had not yet reached the status of a central structural concept. In its earliest formulation, it sprang from a need to revitalize an endangered school subject and, in an increasingly heterogeneous historical practice in the universities, alongside a strand emphasizing the human and social aspects of the historian's task.

We turn in the next chapter to the ways in which texts in the philosophy of history offered themselves to history educationalists as resources for specifying history's conceptual structure, as well as empathy's place within that structure.

Notes

1. C.H.K. Marten, 'The Teaching of History in Schools: Practice', in F.W. Maitland et al., *Essays on the Teaching of History* (Cambridge: Cambridge University Press, 1901), 84.
2. W.C. Sellar and R.J. Yeatman, *1066 and All That: A Memorable History of England, Comprising All the Parts You Can Remember, Including 103 Good Things, 5 Bad Kings and 2 Genuine Dates* (London: Methuen, 1930).
3. David Sylvester, 'Change and Continuity in History Teaching 1900–93', in Hilary Bourdillon (ed.), *Teaching History* (London: Routledge, 1994), 9–11.
4. Martin B. Booth, *History Betrayed?* (London: Longmans, 1969), xi, 120–22.
5. R.H. Tawney, 'The Study of Economic History' (1932), in N.B. Harte (ed.), *The Study of Economic History: Collected Inaugural Lectures 1893–1970* (London: Frank Cass, 1971), 98–99.
6. Eileen Power, 'On Medieval History as a Social Study' (1933), in Harte (ed.), *Study of Economic History,* 112–18.
7. M.M. Postan, 'History and the Social Sciences' (1935), in his *Fact and Relevance: Essays on Historical Method* (Cambridge: Cambridge University Press, 1971), 15–17.
8. Michael Oakeshott, *Experience and its Modes* (Cambridge: Cambridge University Press, 1933), 143.
9. Christopher Hill, 'A Whig Historian', *Modern Quarterly* 3, 1 (1938), 284.
10. Christopher Hill, 'Marxism and History', *Modern Quarterly* 3, 2 (1948), 62.
11. Maurice Dobb, 'Historical Materialism and the Role of the Economic Factor', *History* 36, 126–27 (1951), 7.
12. Geoff Eley, *A Crooked Line: From Cultural History to the History of Society* (Ann Arbor: University of Michigan Press, 2005), 2.
13. Gareth Stedman Jones, 'The Pathology of English History', *New Left Review* 46 (Nov–Dec 1967), 29, 42–43.
14. Eric J. Hobsbawm, 'From Social History to the History of Society', *Daedalus* 100, 1 (1971), 43.
15. Ibid., 23.
16. Eric J. Hobsbawm, 'Karl Marx's Contribution to Historiography', in Robin Blackburn (ed.), *Ideology in Social Science: Readings in Critical Social Theory* (New York: Pantheon Books, 1972), 270–71. Stedman Jones' *New Left Review* article was reprinted in this volume as 'History: The Poverty of Empiricism', 96–115.
17. Hobsbawm, 'Marx's Contribution', 280.
18. Eley, *Crooked Line*, 17–40.
19. Alaric Dickinson, 'What Should History Be?', in Ashley Kent (ed.), *School Subject Teaching: The History and Future of the Curriculum* (London: Kogan Page, 2000), 94–95.
20. Chris Husbands, Alison Kitson and Anna Pendry, *Understanding History Teaching* (Maidenhead: Open University Press, 2003), 10.
21. E.P. Thompson, preface to the 1963 edition of *The Making of the English Working Class*, rev. edn (Harmondsworth: Penguin, 1980), 8, 12.
22. Eley, *Crooked Line,* 56.
23. Lucien Febvre, *Combats pour l'Histoire* (Paris: Armand Colin, 1953), 26: '[La] crise de l'histoire n'a pas été une maladie spécifique frappant l'histoire seule. Elle a été, elle est un des grands aspects – l'aspect proprement historique d'une grande crise de l'esprit humain.'
24. Marc Bloch, *The Historian's Craft,* trans. Peter Putnam (New York: Alfred A. Knopf, 1953), 68.

25. Richard Aldrich, 'The Training of Teachers and Educational Studies: The London Day Training College, 1902–1932', *Paedagogica Historica* 45, 5–6 (2004), 627; David Cannadine, Jenny Keating and Nicola Sheldon, *The Right Kind of History: Teaching the Past in Twentieth-Century England* (Basingstoke: Palgrave Macmillan, 2011), 78, 141–42.

26. Richard Aldrich, *The Institute of Education 1902–2002: A Centenary History* (London: Institute of Education University of London, 2002), 164.

27. Cannadine, Keating and Sheldon, *Right Kind of History*, 157.

28. J.B. Thomas, 'Psychology of Education in the UK: Development in the 1960s', *Educational Studies* 33, 1 (2007), 54.

29. Samuel S. Wineburg, 'The Psychology of Learning and Teaching History', in David C. Berliner and Robert C. Calfee (eds), *Handbook of Educational Psychology* (New York: Simon & Schuster/Macmillan, 1996), 427.

30. Howard Gardner, *The Mind's New Science: A History of the Cognitive Revolution* (New York: Basic Books, 1985), 116–18.

31. R.N. Hallam, 'Piaget and Thinking in History', in Martin Ballard (ed.), *New Movements in the Study and Teaching of History* (London: Temple Smith, 1970), 166.

32. Ibid.

33. M.B. Booth, 'Skills, Concepts, and Attitudes: The Development of Adolescent Children's Historical Thinking', *History and Theory* 22, 4 (1983), 103–4.

34. Jerome S. Bruner, *The Process of Education* (Cambridge, MA: Harvard University Press, 1960), 31–33.

35. Paul H. Hirst, 'Liberal Education and the Nature of Knowledge', in Reginald D. Archambault (ed.), *Philosophical Analysis and Education* (London: Routledge & Kegan Paul, 1965).

36. Ibid., 123–24.

37. Ibid., 124–25.

38. Ibid., 130–33.

39. Mary Price, 'History in Danger', *History* 53, 179 (1968), 342.

40. Ibid., 344, 346

41. Vivienne Little, 'A National Curriculum in History: A Very Contentious Issue', *British Journal of Educational Studies* 38, 4 (1990), 320.

42. Dickinson, 'What Should History Be?', 95.

43. Price, 'History in Danger', 346.

44. Ministry of Education, *Half Our Future: A Report of the Central Advisory Council for Education (England)* (The Newsom Report) (London: HMSO, 1963), 166.

45. Schools Council, *Humanities for the Young School Leaver: An Approach through English* (London: HMSO, 1968), 10.

46. Jeannette Coltham and John Fines, *Educational Objectives for the Study of History: A Suggested Framework,* pamphlet no. 35 (London: Historical Association, 1971).

47. Nicola Sheldon, 'Jeanette Coltham's, John Fines' and Peter Rogers' Historical Association Pamphlets: Their Relevance to the Development of Ideas about History Teaching Today', *International Journal of Historical Learning, Teaching and Research* 9, 1 (2010), 9–10.

48. Benjamin S. Bloom (ed.), *Taxonomy of Educational Objectives: The Classification of Educational Goals,* vols 1–2 (London: Longmans, 1956–64).

49. Ibid., vol. 1, 7

50. Coltham and Fines, *Educational Objectives*, 5–7.

51. Bloom, *Taxonomy of Educational Objectives,* vol. 2, 176–80.

52. Coltham and Fines, *Educational Objectives*, 7–8.

53. Peter Lee, 'Reflections on Coltham's and Fines': Educational Objectives for the Study of History – A Suggested Framework and Peter Rogers': The New History, Theory into Practice', *International Journal of Historical Learning, Teaching and Research* 9, 1 (2010), 14.

CHAPTER 2

The Influence of the Philosophy of History

> I got a lot of my ideas from reading Collingwood the philosopher, where he said history is rethinking the thoughts of the past. Actively you rethink them and it evokes empathy – a word I brought into history teaching, which caused me a lot of trouble.
> —David Sylvester, first director of the Schools Council History Project[1]

Concerned with questions over the nature of historical understanding, the composition of historical knowledge and the procedure of historical explanation, the philosophy of history provided history educationalists with a source for defining the subject's distinct characteristics. Two figures working in separate university departments of education in the late 1960s played particularly important roles in bringing it to bear on the method of teaching school history.

First, David Sylvester, a graduate of Balliol College, Oxford, received a Diploma in Education in 1956 and went on to teach history at Chesterfield Grammar School and St Paul's College, Cheltenham, where he was head of history from 1962 to 1967. He then entered the Department of Education at the University of Leeds as a lecturer of historical method, a position he had to relinquish, though remaining at Leeds, to direct the Schools Council History Project (SCHP) from its inception in 1972 to 1975.

The second figure was William Hedley Burston, a graduate of the University of Bristol and head of the history department at the Institute of Edu-

---

Notes for this section begin on page 54.

cation (IOE) at the University of London from the 1950s until his death in 1981. Given the title of Professor of Education in 1972, he was known inside the IOE for his cantankerous temperament and insistence that history teaching must be informed, if it were to be genuine history teaching, by the kind of analysis offered by philosophers of history. His student and later colleague Peter Lee recounts that Burston's unpopularity stemmed from his inability to find ways of relating his ideas to the teachers in training, who did not always see the purpose of his philosophical ruminations. Burston's importance was not in the particular recommendations he made for history teaching, but in his stance that any serious attempt to think about the nature and purpose of history teaching had to draw on the contributions of philosophers of history and developmental psychologists. For the former, he was most influenced by the work of W.H. Walsh and his friend Michael Oakeshott, followed by R.G. Collingwood and William Dray. For the latter, his work drew heavily on his close acquaintance at the University of Birmingham, Edwin Peel, an educational psychologist of the Piagetian mould.

As the first director of the widely successful SCHP that cemented empathy's place in school history teaching, Sylvester's approach must take pride of place in this account of empathy's conceptual development. This approach owed much to the educational writings of M.W. Keatinge, F.G. Happold and M.V.C. Jeffreys. Keatinge in the 1910s had advocated the use of historical sources as a way of initiating students to the modern scientific historical method by setting them problems to study through careful analysis of historical sources. A decade later, Happold linked the apprehension of historical content to the imagination rather than the intellect and provided extracts from primary sources to demonstrate how reconstruction can help students realize 'an event might have appeared very different to those who were living at the time from what it does to us'.[2] But perhaps most pivotal for Sylvester was Jeffreys' articulation of the 'historical sense', 'an habitual disposition', he believed, 'to see the whole historical process, or some selected part or aspect of it, in its developmental perspective, and to make inferences as to the nature of the process and the laws that govern it'.[3] An antidote to the kind of thinking that was about to plunge the world into another war, the historical sense entailed having a philosophical attitude to history rather than a practical or romantic one. Jeffreys' method for developing a philosophical attitude was the 'line of development' – 'a central theme from which subsidiary investigations can radiate as far as time and the pupils' intelligence allow'.[4] He explained how this connected to a philosophical attitude in the following passage:

> A boy of nine or ten, studying London buses from an excellent book issued by London Transport, could appreciate the principles of trial and error, the drag of tradition, acceleration of the rate of change, and so on. That is to say, the ele-

ments of a philosophy of history are not beyond the young pupil, provided that the material in which he works is sufficiently simple. But give the same boy a course of lessons on the Puritan Revolution, and he will acquire the knowledge that Oliver Cromwell cut off the head of King Charles I after fighting some battles, and will understand precisely nothing.[5]

Sylvester applied the line of development in his first book, *The Story of Medicine*.[6] It provided teachers with a resource for studying the development of medicine from the prehistoric age to the formation of the World Health Organization in 1948. The book also helped teachers who wished to concentrate on a particular 'patch' or period of history in detail. This patch approach, which complemented the line of development, began with the motive of discovering as much as possible about the character of life in some other age for its own sake, and so was seen to greatly extend the imaginative experience of those who pursued it. A 1952 Her Majesty's Stationery Office (HMSO) pamphlet had put it the following way: 'The teacher who is pursuing a "patch" approach will endeavour rather [than fasten attention on the historical events themselves] to bring out the behaviour, beliefs and everyday life peculiar to the time, those things which seemed important to men and women . . . not those things which are important to us now.'[7]

Sylvester's next publication was the more substantial *History for the Average Child*. Produced at a time when the government was considering raising the school leaving age, it pressed the case that the purpose of school history, or any school subject for that matter, consisted in initiating young people 'to what that subject is'. This meant teaching history as it is known to historians; not as the recitation of memorized facts, a reliance on textbook accounts or the supplying of missing words to an emasculated content, but 'as a way of finding out, of selecting and of writing about events in the past'.[8] By Sylvester's analysis, what the historian did that the history student traditionally had not done was imaginatively reconstruct the thoughts, points of view, motives and feelings of the people encountered in studying the past. The 'major problem' in teaching the subject was 'essentially a problem of *resurrection, of how to make the dead live, the intangible tangible, the past present*'.[9] In this respect, an aim of history teaching was 'to reflect in the teaching the dictum of R.G. Collingwood that: "To the boy or girl the activities whose history he or she is studying are not spectacles to be watched but experiences to be lived through".'[10]

On the back of these two publications, Sylvester was sought by Roy Wake, Her Majesty's staff inspector for history, and Joe Hunt, head of history at the City of London School and chairman of the School Council's History Committee, to direct the SCHP. Wake himself had published an article claiming that history is concerned with method and that the received or information subject it had traditionally been needed to make way to it becoming an involvement subject. 'This matter of method is not something to be introduced, if one is lucky, at some advanced level; it *must* be built into history teaching from the time it begins.'[11] He advocated a syllabus based on a series of probes into the past, a form of questioning of original sources valid at every level of intellectual development and leading to satisfying answers at every level. 'The real aim', he wrote, 'is to make people live in their time and their place. There are many forms of scholarship, many gifts of teaching to admire, but the one I admire the most is that which can use all the relevant techniques, that assemble great stacks of evidence, and then, quite hiding them, makes a person or persons, their day, their lives, their hopes and fears, live.'[12]

Wake saw in Sylvester somebody who could produce through the SCHP the materials required to execute on a wide scale the objectives they had set down independently in their writings. The Project was neither the product of an extremist fringe nor of teacher-controlled curriculum initiatives; rather, it looked to formalize what were widely considered to be examples of current best practice. Sylvester criticized Coltham and Fines' pamphlet for introducing an excessive number of objectives (forty to fifty); he wanted a workable model based on four or five objectives.

The SCHP's manifesto *A New Look at History* set out this new approach. Whereas 'imaginative reconstruction' had in previous documents typically described the act of understanding another's point of view, capturing their feelings and recognizing their thoughts in order to interpret their motives, empathy entered the stage with the SCHP as the concept that served this function. Classified alongside 'analysis' and 'judgement' as 'abilities' – itself one of four educational outcomes for history together with 'ideas', 'experience' and 'interest' – 'empathy' appeared as follows:

> *Empathy.* Analysis and judgement must be illuminated by imagination to provide the understanding of people of the past that characterizes the historian's perspective. He has to be able to enter into the minds and feelings of all the persons involved in an event and appreciate their differing attitudes without necessarily approving of their motives if he is to understand why, given their situation, they acted as they did.[13]

What is critical to note is that empathy's function in providing a human context for understanding past actions, and in this manner for understanding the complexities of agency and causation in human affairs, was intended specifically to counter 'rational fact finding' teaching methods and 'the heresy of arguing from covering law or claiming that history repeats itself'.[14] Moreover, empathy's rationale was linked directly to Collingwood's philosophy of history. In expressing their conception of the nature of history, the SCHP authors stated that 'history involves some attempt to rethink the past, to re-enact it and to empathise with the people concerned in any past situation', and then followed this statement by quoting from Collingwood's *Autobiography*: 'You are thinking historically . . . when you say about anything, "I see what the person who made this (wrote this, used this, designed this, &c.) was thinking".'[15]

Elsewhere, Collingwood was invoked in connection with the 'perpetual act of resurrection' in which students, teachers and historians reconstruct the past the better to make it real and present to them. His dictum 'all history is the history of thought' meant that to reconstruct the past involves responding imaginatively and intellectually to the evidence that constitutes the raw material of history.[16] This more vivid focus on the people being studied in history, with their own characters, hopes, failings and fears, cohered with the wider educational objective of making school content more relevant to students' needs.

Even so, this account does not explain why empathy, a term Collingwood never employed and one more readily associated with psychology than history, was chosen to label this emic procedure of studying bygone peoples in terms of their own perceptions and categories of experience. Sylvester selected empathy because he wanted a single word (*projection* was the only single-word alternative) and wished to avoid phrases like 'rational understanding' or 'imaginative reconstruction' that, he worried, would too easily be paraphrased as 'sensible ideas' or 'making it up'. Peter Lee and Rosalyn Ashby have explained that empathy held an advantage over such alternatives in that it was short and, as an imported term to history, it could be given a meaning. Once empathy was adopted by the SCHP, it stuck.[17] But although it may have entered history teaching phraseology *faute de mieux*, its purpose was clear: to cultivate an understanding that the actions of people who lived in the past, which often strike the present-day observer as unintelligent or even foolish, were reasonable in light of the circumstances they faced.

Sylvester recruited Denis Shemilt in 1974 to evaluate the SCHP. The latter was in the final stages of a sociological statistical piece of research in the Institute of Education at the University of Leeds. Having no training in history, Sylvester gave him tutorials in SCHP philosophy, which meant reading Collingwood in particular. Sylvester opposed the prevailing illuminative or ethnographic method of evaluation adopted by other Schools Council projects. He wanted hard data able to show, contra the Piagetians, that formal operational or abstract thinking was being reached before the age of sixteen in the trial schools.

While the results did not confirm that this was the case, they did suggest that the SCHP students had a superior understanding of the complexities of evaluating sources and of discussing historical questions.[18] Indeed, the most striking aspect of the *Evaluation* – by Lee's assessment 'the most important landmark in both research and curriculum development in history education in the UK in the second half of the twentieth century'[19] – was the extent to which an education in historical method and history's inner logic was pitched to counteract the determinism or necessity of scientific explanations of cause and effect. In order for history to be relevant to the present, it had to be able to illuminate connections between past and present, and this appreciation of continuity and change 'is precluded if the inevitability of progress is assumed and historic causation thought akin to that of the chemistry laboratory'.[20]

In the first course segment, 'What is History?', the model for an inquiry-based, problem-solving pedagogy concerned with people, their actions and perceptions of events was approached by introducing students to the idea of reconstructing from evidence, discussing the problems of reconstruction and addressing the question of historical explanation in the form of the delineation of agents' motives. Sylvester's imprint was obvious. A decade earlier in *History for the Average Child,* he had argued against throwing students into the haystack of history, assuming along the way that they would pick up conceptions of what history is, calling instead for courses to begin with carefully structured lessons on the nature of history as a mode of inquiry.

In the third segment, 'Inquiry in Depth' (one topic drawn from Britain 1815–51, the American West and Elizabethan England), students were to gain self-knowledge and awareness of what it means to be human by concentrating on the ideas, beliefs, values and attitudes of people who lived in a different time and place. They were 'to empathize with the ideas and motives of his predecessors, and to reconstruct frames of reference within which those ideas and motives can seem both rational and justifiable. Insofar as "empathetic reconstruction" complements "experimental re-enactment" in Natural Science', went this new approach, 'it is integral to the philosophy of each and every course segment'.[21]

Empathy was thus conceived as the means by which historical explanations of motivated action were achieved. Shemilt reported that 73 per cent of the SCHP subjects construed motivated action as the mainspring of history, while only 22 per cent of control subjects held the same assumption.[22] As for how they were to understand past motives, 9 per cent of control students took empathetic reconstruction to be important, compared with 32 per cent of SCHP subjects. In spite of the number of students willing to recognize the importance of being able to see, for example, European encroachment from the perspective of a Native American, Shemilt acknowledged that this did not necessarily translate into them being able to empathize accurately or productively with that perspective.[23]

Although Sylvester repeatedly invoked Collingwood, he made no effort to use Collingwood's theories as a basis for establishing empathy's disciplinary, philosophical and methodological credentials. Shemilt's attention after the *Evaluation* turned to doing so. 'Like any beautiful woman', he began in 1984, 'the theory of "empathetic reconstruction" excites the devotion of some and the censure of others.' Its devotees saw in it 'the essence of the historian's craft, the divine wind that breathes life into the dry bones of the past, turns dust to flesh, and inspires pupils to commune with their predecessors'. Its critics saw in it the hallmark of an 'unhistorical at best and fraudulent at worst' kind of new history, one that 'savours of profundity without demanding much thought, and imitates a methodology that looks historical but is susceptible to no rational analysis'.[24]

Shemilt conceded that such mockery was not entirely unmerited, for even those who agreed that empathy held a place in school history found it difficult to settle on a definition distinguishing the concept from tolerance, sympathy for others, imagination, creativity or some variety of interpersonal skill. This meant that there could be no agreement as to why empathy should be taught. Some saw it as a socially useful skill or attitude of mind that history helps cultivate, which, first, justified the subject's retention in the school curriculum and, second, could foster altruistic behaviour in students' everyday lives. If this were the case, Shemilt mused, 'the lady's beauty may appear more marketable than the philosopher's scruples', but he found no evidence substantiating this connection. He favoured a second rationale beginning from the premise that the study of history is worthy in itself and that empathetic reconstruction is an integral part of that study.[25] In other words, empathy earned a rightful place in the history classroom owing to the unquestioned role it was seen to play in historical studies in general.

This claim that empathy occupies a legitimate place in the history discipline led Shemilt to consider three interpretations of 'Collingwood's empathizing historian'.[26] Each dealt in a different manner with what he termed the 'empathetic crux' of the 'black-box problem'. The inputs into the black box consisted of those aspects of a historical situation of which the agent in question was aware – the 'knowns' of the situation, as well as the outputs, the agent's actions. The empathizing historian's chief task, as Shemilt conceived it, consisted in disclosing the contents of the black box unknown to the agent, that is, in identifying the unstated assumptions on which the outputs were based, which involved being able to distinguish between a situation as the agent articulated it and the situation that the historian, with historical hindsight, attributes to the agent.

The three portraits are significant less for the light they shine on Collingwood's philosophy and more for signposting the range of interpretations educationalists could ascribe to him. First, the 'psyche-snatcher' was a 'stealer of souls' able to overcome temporal and epistemological constraints to relive the thoughts and feelings of historical agents by direct intuition. Shemilt considered this view of empathetic reconstruction preposterous, for it assumed that the perceptual experiences of others are phenomenally apprehensible to another. Nor did this kind of 'mystic communion' with the past bear any relation to Collingwood's notion of re-enactment. The prefix *re* signified a critical distance obliterated by the idea of direct transposition.

Second, Collingwood's 'time-traveller' could project his own psyche into the past and mentally relive events from the situation, though not from the standpoint, of the historical agent. By remaining a creature of the present and making no claim to correspondence of thought or feeling, the products of the hypothetical transferal of positions acquired the status of a rational explanation, not intuitive fact. Shemilt knew that a problem with this view was its reliance on a transhistorical conception of human nature. The historian who applies universal precepts of how people act to understand, for instance, how a strong, ambitious and self-confident man like Caesar perceived his situation (S_1) before crossing the Rubicon could, by the same reasoning, determine how these perceptions resulted in Caesar having certain feelings, thoughts and intentions. The historian's view of what S_1 must have been shapes all subsequent explanations. Then there was the problem Shemilt discovered among the SCHP trial students: merely knowing how Caesar perceived his situation did not explain why he took his particular course of action and not another.

Finally, the 'necromancer' depicted Collingwood's historian as a conjurer of images of the past that a contemporary audience would find recognizable, intelligible and plausible. Unlike the earlier portraits that kept the black box's content hidden and thus as something to unearth, it appeared to this historian as a glass box to be fathomed from the exterior, thus removing the need for *re*-enactment or *re*construction. The historian always *constructs* the past and brings it back to life not by recreating it, but by using the conceptual apparatus of the present to create models of mind different from those of the present into which evidence about past agents can be integrated and made intelligible. The conceptual distance separating an alien past from a familiar present is the space in which this empathetic construction takes place. Unfamiliar mentalities are recast in ways that make them recognizable while retaining their distinctive and diacritical features.

In presenting the three portraits, Shemilt quoted passages from Collingwood's *The Idea of History* to raise points of approval and disapproval. By his reading of the philosopher-historian, the psyche-snatcher eliminated the need for a historical method; the time-traveller's conception of a universal human nature read the present onto the past; the necromancer, though accepting of epistemological, ontological and temporal constraints, restricted history to the conceptual schemes of the present and so left unilluminated the nature of the past that, if it is to be history, must still form the basis of this construction. Given Shemilt's admission that there was little in the models that Collingwood could have supported, it is perplexing he nevertheless applied Collingwood's name to them. Although the portraits may be said to exhibit features that emerge from a reading of Collingwood, that no one of them took Collingwood's account of re-enactment as a starting point for elucidating the concept of empathy suggests that Shemilt was mistaken to refer to a Collingwoodian empathizing historian.

In Shemilt's defence, it may be noted that his purpose was less to contribute to the philosophy of history than to shore up the legitimacy of a new educational concept by applying to empathy the symbols and language used by philosophers of history. He addressed himself to history educationalists working with a new concept, not to philosophers of history engaged in the subtleties of Collingwood's thought. Shemilt's achievement consisted in showing that empathy raised questions germane to the full spectrum of historical approaches. The portraits did little to advance understanding of Collingwood's theories, but they made a strong case for the notion that with empathy came questions fundamental to the way in which historians conceive their task. In particular, the idea articulated through the black-box metaphor that historical study involves grasping the *unstated assumptions* upon which thought and action were based is one given a special importance when we turn in Part II to Collingwood's twin theories of question-and-answer and absolute presuppositions.

★ ★ ★

This Leeds perspective of Sylvester, Shemilt and the SCHP stood in contrast to the London perspective of Burston and Lee.

Burston, who Sylvester refers to as the great guru of history teaching at the IOE, disapproved of the SCHP's practice of using primary sources and its precept that history teaching must induct students into the world of the academic historian. His sense of what school history teaching could achieve corresponded to G.R. Elton's counsel on the subject. Three years after the Cambridge historian responded to Carr's *What is History?* in *The Practice of History,* Elton weighed in on the debate about why and how school history should be taught.[27] He mocked the notion that the scholarly methods of academic history could be inculcated in students under the age of fifteen. Any conscientious attempt to demonstrate what 'history is really about' was more likely to reduce students' interest in the subject and dissuade them from pursuing it at university. For those who did proceed to study university history, according to Elton, the standard school approach had already impaired their capacity to develop advanced techniques by having produced in them 'prematurely aged minds', minds that had been encouraged to believe that they were already competent in the academic study of history, but in truth were closed to new knowledge and unwilling to think *de novo*. The universities had then to extirpate this belief by diversifying the range of courses of study, by introducing superficially practised themes and by throwing in before the student titbits of philosophical and historiographical material.

School history had rather to focus on cultivating a fascination for the past, not on cultivating scholarly techniques. By actively stimulating the imagination, history could help form balanced, receptive minds, open to new ideas but capable of assessing them against traditional ideas, aware of humankind in all its differences across time and space and responsible to itself and others in the knowledge that actions have consequences of sometimes intended and sometimes unintended significance. Instilling an awareness of the range of human experiences through time could counteract intellectual weaknesses such as an excessive concentration on one line of thought, an absence of understanding for other points of view, an absence of imaginative understanding – which Elton labelled empathy – intolerance and an overriding concern with the present. By opening students to all the past contains, history could prepare students for adult life, first, by unsettling false assurances of rightness produced by a limited range of experiences and, second, by unsettling false assurances that one's own preoccupations and needs are universal. With customary aplomb, Elton ruled: 'Let the schools feed the imagination, enlarge mental capacity, and lay the foundations of universal sympathy; we shall soon enough, at the university, attend to the search for truth and the promotion of precise analytical thought'.[28]

With Elton, Burston rejected the trend of bringing school history into line with academic history, but this did not mean he rejected the idea that teaching school history should be based upon the features distinct to the discipline. Burston and the IOE researchers who worked under him treated history as *sui generis*; that is, while educational psychology and practical teaching experience were seen to reveal certain problems of method, only by discovering what was analytically true of the nature of history by philosophical examination could the logic of historical explanation be found, upon which teaching had to be structured.[29]

The qualifier 'analytical' must be stressed here. Influenced greatly by W.H. Walsh, Professor of Logic and Metaphysics at the University of Edinburgh, who guest lectured for Burston at the IOE and whose *Introduction to Philosophy of History* structured a course for the teachers-in-training, Burston saw no place for 'speculative philosophy of history', such as that found in Spengler and Toynbee's historical metaphysics, as an instructive kind of inquiry for history teaching.[30] Rather, what Walsh had termed 'critical philosophy of history' provided the means for identifying the forms of knowledge that could channel the delivery of historical content through methods true to history's logic of explanation.

The logic of explanation of critical philosophy of history represented one of three options available. First, as raised earlier by Postan's objections to neo-Kantian philosophy of history, idealists such as Collingwood and Oakeshott, concerned as they were seen to be with illustrating the uniqueness of events and hostile to any overarching explanatory framework, looked no further for the causes of events than the events themselves. As Oakeshott put it: 'History accounts *for* change by means of a full account *of* change.'[31] To narrate an individual event calls for no explanation outside the event itself, for providing the full account brings into view its connections and makes them its own. Burston believed that this idealist view offered an accurate picture of how the historian in fact proceeds.

Second, the historian could appeal to general laws or what Dray termed 'covering laws'. The argument that historical explanation operates on the basis of such laws had been put most vigorously by Hempel. In his famous essay, he claimed that no difference separates history from the natural sciences: 'both can give an account of their subject-matter only in terms of general concepts, and history can "grasp the unique individuality" of its objects of study no more and no less than can physics or chemistry'.[32] Hempel's view belonged to a larger effort in logical positivism to show that there is a close connection between explanation, prediction and confirmation in the natural sciences, as set out in 1945 by Karl Popper in *The Open Society and its Enemies*.

In spite of the influence in philosophy of this attempt to subsume historical explanation under the covering-law natural scientific model, it held little credibility among historians. One contributor to Burston's 1967 collection, *Studies in the Nature and Teaching of History,* in a separate article, put it piercingly: 'As the historian penetrates deeper into the individual features of his study, laws seem to become more and more limited, till they become laws with only one or two cases, and finally only the one under review – a very embarrassing situation for a general law!'[33]

But while it could be denied that the historian sets out to formulate patterns of regularity in the human world after the manner of the scientist in the physical world, the idea that the study of human behaviour presupposes general propositions about human nature and how people are likely to act in certain situations meant that, for Burston, as Walsh maintained, covering laws could not be wholly rejected. For example, those we might take into the study of the formation of an 'alliance' between two counties would supply the working assumptions that both sides had something to gain from the agreement, that they engaged in a bargain in which each side contributed something, that one side's involvement in military conflict was a *casus belli* for the other and so on. The difference between history and natural science is that the latter, in setting out to establish the bases upon which future behaviour may be predicted, makes such propositions the object of its researches, whereas for history their function ends when historical thinking ends.[34] In Walsh's words: 'History differs from the natural sciences in that it is not the aim of the historian to formulate a system of general laws; but this does not mean that no such laws are presupposed in historical thinking.'[35]

Burston ultimately found a logic for history teaching in a third variety of historical explanation provided by Walsh's work on colligation. A concept implicit in the idealist view of history and given analytical content by Walsh, colligation involved taking an individual event as the starting point, working outwards to discover its relation to other events with which it shared a common purpose or inner relationship, forming a conception of an intelligible whole on these bases and then returning to the individual aspects to illuminate them in the light of it.[36] Walsh stressed the importance that the idealists had attached to human actions for such a method of explanation. 'It is the fact that every action has a thought-side', he wrote, 'which makes this whole thing possible. Because actions are, broadly speaking, the realization of purposes, and because a single purpose or policy can find expression in a whole series of actions, whether carried out by one person or by several, we can say in an intelligible sense that some historical events are intrinsically related.'[37]

To the extent that Burston grounded teaching procedures in the logic of historical explanation, his reflections on the merits and defects of these three theories were significant. It is unlikely that Sylvester would have placed equal stock in them, for he approached the philosophy of history from the perspective of an educationalist searching to revitalize his subject, and not so much from the standpoint that its teaching methods were direct objects of its logic. Burston took from Walsh's concept of colligation the procedure of historical explanation, but inverted it in his instruction for teachers. 'The teacher can and should proceed in the reverse order to the historian', he advised, 'whereas the latter starts with an event, proceeds to its explanation, and then to associate it with other events, the teacher should start by explaining the general movement and proceed from this to the event and its individual characteristics.'[38] Thus the reign of a king would commence with an explanation of his purposes and policies and the obstacles confronting him; the Congress of Vienna with an explanation of the policies of the Great Powers; and Parliamentary Reform with an explanation of the electoral situation and need for reform.

This inversion of history's logic of explanation, proceeding from the general to the particular, served the purpose of counteracting the movement to make 'mini-historians' out of students and all that implied about the place of primary sources in the school history classroom. Rather than use primary sources to explain from the individual to the general, he suggested that teachers set an overall context before considering individual historical cases. Colligating events according to their common purposes offered itself as a pedagogical device for establishing the general context from which individual explanations could be offered. In this way, it also provided an initiation into Burston's conception of historical thinking, one formulated in direct opposition to the line-of-development approach proposed by Jeffreys, which was gaining favour in the early 1950s and applied later by Sylvester in the SCHP.

Burston objected to the line of development because it 'assumes in advance that the principal explanation of an event lies within the topic'; that is, it restricted the content of historical explanation to the content found solely within the topic of investigation.[39] For example, the source for explaining developments in transport, a topic Sylvester championed, could come from no other source than the topic of transport itself. As in Butterfield's formulation of 'Whig history', it imposed a forward-looking view on the past that reduced history to the study of how human beings arrived at the present, producing a distorted image of the development of present-day institutions by divorcing them from their full context in different past periods.

Burston's alternative, the 'theme method', which he credited fully to Walsh, sought not to form an explanatory chain by including only those events known with hindsight to have contributed to the development of an existing institution, but rather to start with the events themselves and to form the chain out of those aspects of an event illuminated by the explanation of another.[40] This meant that to colligate events in the theme method rested largely upon the teacher's ability to make the kinds of generalizations able to guide students through the initial stage of study, generalizations in the sense that a statement such as 'England went to war in 1914' could provide an entry point for considering the many factors that contributed to that collective action. Although covering laws did not survive Burston's examination, the idea that the historian always begins with a hypothesis meant that teachers must commence by referring to general categories of events and concepts. In dealing with the French Revolution, they may need to adduce examples from economics and social theory on the causes and consequences of inflation, just as the terms 'inflation', 'democracy' and 'despotism' may need to be explained by reference to present-day examples.[41]

Yet like any system of generalizing, this practice of colligating concepts and events consisted in an act abstraction not to be confused with the explanation of an individual event. As Isaiah Berlin explained in the maiden article of *History and Theory* in 1960, the most rigorous and universal of scientific models – mathematics and physics – draw their strength from their ability to operate at the highest possible level of abstraction from natural characteristics; they are reliable as scientific models because they deliberately reject 'all but certain selected ubiquitous and recurrent similarities'.[42] Moving down the scale, as sciences become richer in content, they become less susceptible to classification and less reliable as general theories or scientific models. 'Exclusion – neglect of what is beyond the defined frontiers – is entailed in model-building as such.'[43] Hence a specialist branch such as economic history can claim a greater degree of scientificity than general history because it excludes from consideration those aspects of human activity not related to production, consumption, exchange and distribution. The more economic history were to consider such aspects as the springs of human action and the states of mind and moralities attached to them, the less it would be able to serve as an instrument of analysis and prediction.

Since history in the idealist tradition distinguished itself from sociology and the natural sciences by the fact that it eschewed general theories and tried to illuminate individual historical phenomena themselves – what Postan disparaged as the overly narrow focus on the unique and unrepeatable – for Burston, the true mainspring of historical explanation remained where Collingwood had located it in the intentions, purposes and designs expressed in human action – the 'inside' or the 'thought' side of an action being the basis for explaining the 'outside' or external activity.[44] So while colligation in Walsh's words was 'a peculiarity of historical thinking . . . consequently of great importance when we are studying the nature of historical explanation', it was insufficient by itself, and what teachers needed were supplementary activities that drew attention back to individuals and the agency expressed in their actions.[45] 'To teach significantly, to collate events coherently, to make a narrative intelligible', Burston concluded:

> the history teacher must always teach at a constant level of generality, and, until the Sixth form at least [final two years of secondary school], this must be a high level of generality. Yet this involves a correspondingly high degree of abstraction, and we get further and further away from the actions and purposes of individuals which are the ultimate basis of all history. As history becomes coherent and intelligible to the boy, so it loses reality and vividness as the story of real men and women in the past.[46]

This attention to the actions and purposes of individuals served as the most basic principle for ensuring that the study of history remained a 'historical' rather than 'practical' exercise. These were Oakeshott's terms to distinguish a past whose significance consisted in the fact that it had been influential in determining the present, which was the essence of Whig history, and a past whose *differentia specifica* constituted forms of experience that could be 'arrested' in the world to which they belonged.[47] The practically minded filtered the past through present-day values, concepts and norms; the historically minded valued the contrast that the past provides with the present. History involves a reconstruction of a past life we can experience in imagination, as it stood alone, irrespective of its position as a stage in the development of the present.

Oakeshott's distinction oriented teachers and students in two different directions. Whereas the practical teacher might say of the House of Lords 'Let me tell you its history, how it developed into the present situation', the historical teacher might say 'let me tell you what it *was*, and how people used it *in the past*'.[48] Rather than telling the history of an existing institution from the vantage point of its place and function in the present, and in so doing obviating the need to imagine it as it once was, the institution could be regarded as a link to a bygone era whose reality in the past students re-created. Oakeshott showed Burston that 'if the writing of history is guided by a practical attitude towards the events of the past, then it is unlikely that we shall ever reconstruct the past as it actually was . . . Unless we can achieve some degree of detachment from present-day pre-occupations we are unlikely, in reading history, to enter sympathetically into the minds and problems of a past age'.[49]

The practical approach could not, paradoxically, reveal history's practical, present-day uses. History could contribute to the present and its problems only when historians created for themselves through intellectual detachment the mental space to imagine the past in its own terms – 'the past as it actually was, and not the past specifically selected and used for its practical value' – and then later considered possible connections.[50] A detached imagination enabled students to hone in vertically on the past at a particular moment in time and thus enriched the horizontal developmental perspective generated by the line-of-development and practical attitude. In the final analysis, in his words, 'the defence of history as an essential part of a liberal education rests on this ability to penetrate the mind of the past more than we can that of our own age'.[51]

Burston's writings antedated the period that saw empathy rise through its use in the SCHP. With respect to the concept, his significance consists in the procedure of historical explanation that he spelled out and translated directly into a teaching methodology.[52] The history teacher must begin with a general context, but history only lives in the student's mind when that context is filled with individuals who thought and acted with purpose. Burston's philosophically rich considerations emphasized the problems posed by colligating the past into general categories for the historical and idealist conception of history as individual explanation. The intellectual and educational context of the 1970s was one amenable to a deeper historical penetration of people's lives in the past. How this application of analytical philosophy of history sat behind a London approach to this humanistic endeavour can be seen in the writings of Peter Lee.

Lee's competence in the philosophy of history may have been a factor in Burston's decision to recruit him to the IOE in the late 1960s after having taught history at Latymer Upper School, Hammersmith. His interest had been piqued during his days at Oxford as a history undergraduate, where the philosophers whose company he preferred over his less reflective history acquaintances ridiculed history as a futile form of knowledge. A Rhodes Scholar friend introduced him to Dray's work on historical explanation, whereupon he realized that the questions he had been asking on such notions as the possibility of general laws in history lacked a sound philosophical basis, prompting him to read more challenging texts in the philosophy of history.

Lee found one such text in the early 1970s in the Finnish philosopher and successor to Ludwig Wittgenstein's chair at the University of Cambridge, Georg Henrik von Wright. The educational philosopher Leslie Perry held a seminar at King's College London and recommended von Wright to Lee. Perry was a pragmatic thinker whose approach to history attached particular value to identifying the ways that the methods and narratives of so-called objective history, which he located in both covering-law and idealist accounts, inevitably serve practical purposes. He thought that Oakeshott was wrong to claim that there is a difference between objective and practical history; the real issue, rather, is how to contemplate the past from afar before applying a practical use to it. History teachers could work at settling Oakeshott's false division by showing that all interpretations contain normative content.[53]

Like Burston, Perry knew that to approach history in so skilful a way required a fundamental grasp of the nature of historical understanding and explanation. It must be assumed on this basis that Perry pointed Lee in the direction of von Wright. In *Explanation and Understanding*, Wittgenstein's friend and executor broke with the logical positivism of his youth by arguing that human action cannot be explained causally in the subsumption-theoretic covering-law model, but must be understood intentionally in the wants and beliefs developed in a social and cultural context. As he began a piece that became pivotal for Lee, a 'teleological explanation of action [as opposed to causal, scientific explanation] is normally preceded by an act of intentionalist *understanding* of some behavioural data'.[54]

Von Wright gave an example in the outbreak of the First World War.[55] According to him, historians need not regard the assassination of the Austrian archduke as the 'cause' of the conflict, even if they acknowledge that there were many other causes associated with the web of alliances, militarism, imperialism and nationalism. Instead, they should concentrate their reconstructions upon the intermediate links between cause and effect as motivations for further actions; in this case, upon the series of practical inferences that terminated in the Austrian cabinet issuing its ultimatum to Serbia: its designs to maintain Habsburg influence in the Balkans and plans to organize an independent Croatian kingdom to counterbalance Russian influence in the Balkans. The issuing of the ultimatum similarly affected the motivational background for the actions of the Russian government (mobilization), actuating further practical inferences, and thus the war became inevitable 'by force of circumstance'. The individuality of each event is retained in sets of logically distinct practical syllogisms, which combine to explain the causes of the war.

Lee was adequately impressed by von Wright to name a 1978 chapter after the philosopher's book.[56] He imported the schema of practical inferences (von Wright alternated between calling them inferences and syllogisms) to stress that although historians sometimes have to explain the workings of the natural world by reference to covering laws, history is above all the explanation of human actions by reference to people's intentions and reasons for performing an action. With respect to the history discipline, this grounding of historical explanation in the life and viewpoint of historical agents was seen as necessary for historical objectivity. With respect to history education, Lee took it as essential for combating Thompson's invocation of the enormous condescension of posterity in youths who all too readily dismiss historical figures – Chamberlain at Munich, Louis XVI at Versailles, Trotsky at Brest-Litovsk – as cowards or simpletons. Treating actions as motivations for further actions forced students to consider the precise context in which each action was taken, and thus introduced them to the standing presupposition in history that, unless there is contrary evidence, people acted for reasons that from their vantage point at a particular moment in time were good reasons. Such apologia for the primacy of understanding in history were not uncommon in the methodological literature. 'How much easier it is to write for or against Luther than to fathom his soul', wrote Marc Bloch, a historian who lived history at its ugliest. 'We are never sufficiently understanding... If history would only renounce its false archangelic airs, it would help us to cure this weakness. It includes a vast experience of human diversities, a continuous contact with men. Life, like science, has everything to gain from it, if only these contacts be friendly.'[57]

Practical inferences provided Lee with a logical basis for reconstructing an agent's intentions, similar to the kind we perform when we rationalize our actions after an event. Given that we are rarely explicitly conscious of our reasons at the moment of performing an action, or in a state of perpetual calculation, explanation is restricted to the logical sequence made clear after the event. Von Wright referred to this as logical tightness. 'It is only when action is already there and a practical argument is constructed to explain or justify it', he explained, 'that we have a logically conclusive argument. The necessity of the practical inference schema is, one could say, a necessity conceived *ex post actu*.'[58]

Lee took pains to demonstrate the relevance of von Wright's model to history education. Suppose an agent (A) does x to achieve p, seeing his situation (S) in a certain way (S_a), which must be distinguished from the way in which the historian (S_h) or student sees it. The challenge in learning and teaching consists in providing the fullest possible picture of what S_a actually was. If this sounds overly optimistic, it should. As von Wright acknowledged, the intentionalist and antipositivist emphasis on 'understanding' has always had a psychological ring absent from models of scientific explanation.[59] Nevertheless, the poorer the picture of S_a, the more likely students are to think that some other action, x_1 or x_2, visible to them with historical hindsight but perhaps not to A at the time, was more likely to have achieved p, potentially leading them to adopt a condescending view towards the course of action taken, the past and its inhabitants.

Of course, in the absence of a full meeting of past and present minds, and in the absence of agents knowing in any formal sense the objective conditions of their own situation, how is it possible to arrive at reliable practical inferences? According to Lee, when those elements of a situation that evidence suggests became the agent's *reasons* for acting are included, we can follow the practical inference. That is, we know what A's view of his situation was in light of the fact that the evidence tells us he conceived of x as the only possible way of achieving p. In the language of Dray's formulation of rational explanation, the situation is envisaged as one in which x was the appropriate thing to do in the specific circumstances (S_x).[60]

No mere conceptual exercise, this illustrates the strength and danger of history textbooks and teacher presentations: they tend to present S_x, some more than others, in ready-made form. Students are fast-tracked to that stage of the inference without having to have negotiated its earlier and more demanding context-building stages. This partly explains why of all the school subjects, history is the most prone to politicization. The shape S_x takes in the classroom regulates all subsequent evaluations of the various components at play in the explanatory chain. If 'the thing to do' only partially depicts S_a, 'the thing done' will only partially reflect, or plainly distort, the possibilities that A had open for manoeuvre. In other words, the affirmation of the premise 'this was the thing to do' leads of necessity to the affirmation of the conclusion that 'this action was taken to achieve this end' – 'assent to the premises entails action in accordance with them'.[61]

Note that the agent's intentions were not assigned a symbol here. Lee did not succeed in making their nature clear in the practical inference, but stated that the consequence of misinterpreting them is much the same as when S_a is initially misinterpreted or accounts inadequately for the qualifications of p that A had in mind in doing x. The action takes on an arbitrary aspect in the eyes of the student, laying open the charge that the agent acted unintelligently when x_1 or x_2 were available as possible alternatives, and the principle is reiterated that the fullest possible clarification of S_a take primacy in the pedagogical sequence. 'This means', wrote Lee, 'any attempt to give a detailed account of S_a involves the specification of a wide range of alternatives which there are grounds for believing A may have considered. Here historians work on the basis of evidence about A's "ways of thinking", and their evidence of what A knew of other aspects of the situation.'[62] It is where evidence of this kind is lacking that historians oscillate between S_a and S_h, for their stock of knowledge both suggests and circumscribes the range of possibilities open to A. Lee doubted whether students possessed this ability, 'since the less one knows, the wider the range may appear to be, and the more slender are the grounds for eliminating those which are not "on" for the agent'.[63]

In elaborating von Wright's model of practical inferences, Lee had in mind a response to the objectives set down by Coltham and Fines. He stressed that it is not by lack of 'empathy' that historians fail to understand a subject matter of a nature completely alien to them, but because of 'the difficulty of maintaining a complex of suppositions . . . in the face of a world view totally antipathetic to it'.[64] Practical inferences subordinated the imagination to a 'supposing' taking the form of hypotheticals about the connections between agent, situation, action and outcome. This 'hypothetico-deductive' model of supposal was presented as an alternative to Coltham and Fines' excessively intuitionist programme for understanding these connections.[65] Apart from having conflated distinctions of conative, affective and cognitive categories of behaviour, and having loosely distinguished between empathy, sympathy, identification and involvement, their greatest error consisted in reducing the historical imagination to a lower-order mental operation by classifying it as a conative attitude applied at the discretion of the student to the study of historical evidence. Inferring from evidence to see a situation from the viewpoint of people who lived in the past was more likely to involve higher-order thinking – in Piagetian terms, formal operations.

Given that Lee repudiated empathy in articulating this distinctively analytical approach, it should come as a surprise that he was speaking in its favour only a few years later. His adoption of the concept followed pragmatically from the SCHP's success. Lee had developed his model of rational understanding in isolation from the Leeds group that was taking empathy to teachers and students in the trial schools. Following a first encounter with Shemilt in 1978, he implored the group to drop empathy from their programme, foreseeing a barrage of criticism and misunderstanding. Shemilt acknowledged the problem, but voiced regret to his new confrère that it was too late to remove, given the currency that it had attained as a core component of the programme developed by Sylvester.

As the accepted term, empathy began to absorb meanings formerly conveyed in neighbouring and alternative concepts. Most significantly, Lee's concept of rational understanding found a place under empathy's banner and gave rise to the pedagogical formula of 'empathy as achievement', a disciplinary approach unacceptable to some, as we shall discuss next.

Notes

1. David Sylvester, interviewed by Nicola Sheldon, History in Education Project, Institute of Historical Research, University of London, 7 July 2009, 10. In addition to this interview, the more biographical aspects of my discussion of Sylvester, Burston, Lee and Shemilt are drawn from Sheldon's interviews with the latter two. I also benefited from their willingness to answer my questions in private correspondence.

2. F.G. Happold, *The Approach to History* (London: Christophers, 1928), 45–46.

3. M.V.C. Jeffreys, *History in Schools: The Study of Development* (London: Sir Isaac Pitman and Sons, 1939), 16.

4. Ibid., 34.

5. Ibid., 33.

6. D.W. Sylvester, *The Story of Medicine* (London: Edward Arnold, 1965).

7. Department of Education and Science (DES), *Teaching History* (London: HMSO, 1952), 18.

8. P.H.J.H. Gosden and D.W. Sylvester, *History for the Average Child: Suggestions on Teaching History to Pupils of Average and Below Average Ability* (Oxford: Blackwell, 1968), 48.

9. Ibid., 45.

10. Ibid., 43. This quote is from a passage in R.G. Collingwood, *The Idea of History*, rev. edn [1946] Jan van der Dussen (Oxford: Oxford University Press, 1994), 218, but Gosden and Sylvester have substituted the original 'To the historian . . .' for 'To the boy or girl . . .'. This underlines the point that, in Leeds and SCHP thinking, the methods by which the school history student was to work corresponded to those by which the historian was seen to work, viz. 'student as historian'.

11. Roy Wake, 'History as a Separate Discipline: The Case', *Teaching History* 1, 3 (1970), 155.

12. Ibid., 157.

13. Schools Council History 13–16 Project, *A New Look at History* (Edinburgh: Holmes McDougall, 1976), 36–43.

14. Ibid., 13, 44.

15. Ibid., 17; R.G. Collingwood, *An Autobiography* [1939] (Oxford: Clarendon Press, 1978), 110. The SCHP authors cite the 1944 Penguin edition.

16. SCHP, *New Look*, 36–37; Collingwood, *Autobiography*, 110.

17. Peter Lee and Rosalyn Ashby, 'Empathy, Perspective Taking, and Rational Understanding', in O.L. Davis Jr., Elizabeth Yeager and Stuart Foster (eds), *Historical Empathy and Perspective Taking in the Social Studies* (Lanham: Rowman & Littlefield, 2001), 21.

18. Denis Shemilt, *History 13–16 Evaluation Study: Schools Council History 13–16 Project* (Edinburgh: Holmes McDougall, 1980).

19. Peter Lee, 'Historical Literacy and Transformative History', in Lukas Perikleous and Denis Shemilt (eds), *The Future of the Past: Why History Education Matters* (Nicosia, Cyprus: Association for Historical Dialogue and Research, 2011), 138.

20. Shemilt, *Evaluation Study*, 3–4.

21. Ibid., 5.

22. Ibid., 33.

23. Ibid., 37.

24. Denis Shemilt, 'Beauty and the Philosopher: Empathy in History and Classroom', in A.K. Dickinson, P.J. Lee and P.J. Rogers (eds), *Learning History* (London: Heinemann, 1984), 39.
25. Ibid., 39–40.
26. Ibid., 41–4.
27. G.R. Elton, 'What Sort of History Should We Teach?', in Martin Ballard (ed.), *New Movements in the Study and Teaching of History* (London: Temple Smith, 1970), 221–30.
28. Ibid., 230.
29. W.H. Burston, 'Explanation in History and the Teaching of History', *British Journal of Educational Studies* 2, 2 (1954), 112–21.
30. W.H. Burston, *Principles of History Teaching* (London: Methuen, 1963), 15–17; W.H. Walsh, *An Introduction to Philosophy of History*, rev. edn [1951] (London: Hutchinson University Library, 1958), 13–16.
31. Michael Oakeshott, *Experience and its Modes* (Cambridge: Cambridge University Press, 1933), 143, quoted in Burston, 'Explanation', 117, and Burston, *Principles*, 65.
32. C.G. Hempel, The Function of General Laws in History'. *Journal of Philosophy* 39, 2 (1942), 37.
33. Leslie R. Perry, 'Objective and Practical History', *Journal of Philosophy of Education* 1, 1 (1967), 39. Perry addressed the more technical aspects of Popper and Hempel's ideas in 'The Covering Law Theory of Historical Explanation', in W.H. Burston and D. Thompson (eds), *Studies in the Nature and Teaching of History* (New York: Humanities Press, 1967), 27–48.
34. Burston, *Principles*, 65–66, 73–74.
35. Walsh, *Philosophy of History*, 25.
36. Ibid., 25, 59–63.
37. Ibid., 59–60, quoted partly in Burston, *Principles*, 69–70.
38. Burston, 'Explanation', 120.
39. Ibid., 116.
40. W.H. Burston, 'The Place of History in Education', in W.H. Burston and C.W. Green (eds), *Handbook for History Teachers* (London: Methuen, 1962), 7–8; Burston, *Principles*, 71.
41. Burston, 'Explanation', 117; Burston, *Principles*, 89–90.
42. Isaiah Berlin, 'History and Theory: The Concept of Scientific History', *History and Theory* 1, 1 (1960), 15.
43. Ibid., 14–15.
44. Burston, 'Explanation', 114–15; Burston, *Principles*, 22–23.
45. Walsh, *Philosophy of History*, 25.
46. Burston, 'Explanation', 121.
47. Oakeshott, *Experience and its Modes*, 101–3.
48. Burston, 'Place of History', 2.
49. Burston, *Principles*, 27.
50. Ibid.
51. Burston, 'Place of History', 11–12.
52. I have discussed elsewhere the enduring relevance of Burston's model. See Tyson Retz, 'The Structure of Historical Inquiry', *Educational Philosophy and Theory* 49, 6 (2017), 606–17.
53. Perry, 'Objective and Practical History', 35–48.
54. Georg Henrik von Wright, *Explanation and Understanding* (Ithaca: Cornell University Press, 1971), 132.
55. Ibid., 139–43.
56. P.J. Lee, 'Explanation and Understanding in History', in A.K. Dickinson and P.J. Lee (eds), *History Teaching and Historical Understanding* (London: Heinemann, 1978), 72–93.

57. Marc Bloch, *The Historian's Craft,* trans. Peter Putnam (New York: Alfred A. Knopf), 141, 143–44.

58. Von Wright, *Explanation and Understanding,* 117, quoted in Lee, 'Explanation and Understanding', 75.

59. Von Wright, *Explanation and Understanding,* 6.

60. Lee, 'Explanation and Understanding', 82–3; William H. Dray, *Laws and Explanation in History* (Oxford: Oxford University Press, 1957), 118–55.

61. Von Wright, *Explanation and Understanding,* 27.

62. Lee, 'Explanation and Understanding', 84.

63. Ibid.

64. Ibid., 74.

65. A. Gard and P.J. Lee, '"Educational Objectives for the Study of History" Reconsidered', in Dickinson and Lee (eds), *History Teaching and Historical Understanding,* 32–33.

CHAPTER 3

A Conceptual Portmanteau

Empathy emerged as the hallmark of the new history from a conjunction of trends in educational philosophy and psychology, academic history, school history and the philosophy of history.[1] The subsumption of the London approach to rational understanding under the Leeds approach to empathy brought extra complexity to a concept already in dispute.

On the one hand, in the hands of educationalists, empathy had embraced too many meanings for it to have a clear meaning itself. Tony Boddington, who replaced Sylvester as SCHP director in 1975 until Shemilt took the reins in 1978, expressed regret in 1980 that although the majority of teachers subscribed to its educational aims, its entanglement with a sum of cognitive skills and array of affective attitudes, contiguous with an equal number of terms, had left many confused and frustrated. He proposed stripping back the concept so that it served the sole purpose of rationally or intellectually understanding meaningful behaviour in past societies not by means of the various notions on offer for seeing oneself as a member of a strange society, but by means proper to the 'philosophical activity' of surmising what was 'logically possible' under those conditions.[2]

On the other hand, any attempt to eliminate polysemy by returning to empathy's roots might prove equally dubious. Peter Knight argued a decade after Boddington that it was precisely because empathy occupied an ambiguous place in philosophy and psychology that warranted its total rejection in history education. 'The surprise is not that it was the 1970s before those interested in school history incorporated the term into the commonplace explanations of their purposes and methods', he wrote, 'it is that they ever did so.'[3] In other words, any effort to refurnish empathy with a stricter definition

---

Notes for this section begin on page 69.

of understanding past behaviour logically would soon find that it had never held credibility as a means for doing so.

Educationalists could persevere with the task of giving empathy a distinct meaning, or they could reject it by appeal to its poverty as a concept in general. Nobody approached the task historically by examining the concept's role in the emergence of historical thinking. Instead, the disciplinary conception that combined the London and Leeds approaches in the pedagogical formula of 'empathy as achievement' has provided teachers with a model of historical inquiry, but it has left unanswered questions of how the concept contributes to an enriched understanding of historical context, how actions are to be understood in relation to that context, as well as how differences between past and present values, goals and beliefs are to be navigated – the very platform on which empathy was introduced as part of history's reinvigoration as a subject relevant to the present.

History educationalists may not have considered empathy's roots in historical thought, but by linking the concept to Collingwood's doctrine of re-enactment they imported into the educational realm fundamental questions discussed by philosophers of history regarding the processes of historical thinking and the status and composition of historical knowledge. Collingwood's ideas had already penetrated educational circles before he became empathy's spokesperson through the establishment of the SCHP. His influence had become sufficiently widespread by 1972 that Peter Rogers, a lecturer in education at Queen's University Belfast, could produce the first major assessment of Collingwood's philosophy as it concerned the teaching of history.[4]

Rogers challenged the view given wide acceptance by Bruner and Hirst that history exhibited a conceptual autonomy or inner logic from which could be extracted historical concepts applicable to every historical subject matter. Committed to Oakeshott's notion of the historical past, Rogers argued that historical study is directed by concepts belonging to the specific topic of investigation – in the case of nineteenth-century international relations, concepts such as 'balance of power' or 'national interest'; in the case of art history, concepts such as 'form', 'gothic' or 'baroque'. It distorted history to suppose that innate to the discipline were 'forms of knowledge' verifiable by experience, just as it was misguided to suppose that key ideas found in certain historical periods could be built upon in other periods to greater and greater complexity. Rogers believed that the historical past offered a frame of reference, a set of working assumptions, from which analogies could be drawn for understanding present-day experience and states of affairs, but that remained subsidiary to the study of the past for its own sake.

As with Burston, Walsh's principle of colligation served Rogers as the organizational device for discerning the intrinsic relations between events, which in turn determined the content chosen for inclusion in the syllabus. Colligation and practical inferences operate on the basis of historical hindsight having disclosed a logically tight explanatory chain, perceptible only after the chain's connection with present-day webs of reciprocities has been severed. According to Rogers, this necessity of hindsight posed a real danger to the integrity of the historical past by imposing a tidy and precise pattern on 'a reality that was in fact shot through with doubt and uncertainty'. This had the potential to make every aspect of a historical explanation appear the result of an entirely rational and deliberative calculation. To keep at bay this danger of an unhistorical, teleological attitude, hindsight had to be set aside as far as possible in the actual study of historical material by seeking to 'place oneself in the position of the agent one is studying, trying to reconstruct the situation as it bore on him'.[5] Of course, the most emphatic argument for 'reconstruction' of this kind had been put by Collingwood, who in Rogers' words 'held that historical explanation involves "getting inside" the subject of historical inquiry – Julius Caesar or Cromwell – in making their thoughts our thoughts and hence apprehending the full significance of what they did; and this feat is performed by sympathetic intuition – not be reference to, and not by inference from, general considerations'.[6]

That Collingwood relied on a 'thoroughgoing subjectivity' to 'get inside' his subjects was apparent to Rogers in the following quotation from *The Idea of History*: 'When the historian has ascertained the facts there is no further process of enquiring into their causes. When he knows what happened, he already knows why it happened.'[7] The integrity of the historical attitude relied on an ability to see events in their individuality. Rogers rejected the idea that a psychological re-creation of thought by intuition could achieve this goal, save in the most obvious of cases. Nelson's thought at Trafalgar could be intuited by anyone with a basic knowledge of naval tactics, but to attempt the same for Cromwell's actions, say, between Naseby and the King's execution would prove more hazardous. Nor was it clear how 'intuitive explanation' could function without the appropriate and accompanying emotions, excluded from the dictum 'all history is the history of thought'. Collingwood appeared to be proffering a form of study that violated history's empirical standards of inferring and cross-referencing from a variety of sources. 'For in recent years', Rogers opined, 'it has become much more common to modify formal instruction with "creative" or "imaginative" activity . . . this activity is not practised upon, or disciplined by, genuine evidence, and, consequently, is not shaped by its proper use.'[8] To the question 'what grounds have you for these statements?', it could not suffice to answer that their truth had been intuited and for private reasons they were known to be true, for it was precisely these reasons that needed justification. Rogers encouraged educators to reconstruct the past on the 'interplay between conceptual and particular evidence', a recommendation delivered at Collingwood's expense, but, as we shall see, one Collingwood would have fully endorsed.[9]

This interplay between conceptual and particular evidence removed the danger that colligation might pose to the historical past. Since the historian who explains an individual case must also consider the complex social matrices suggested by the evidence, it is never in practice possible to streamline the various components of an explanation into the teleological tunnel Oakeshott warned against. Rather, explanations drawn from the point of view of the agent posed the greatest danger. 'An "explanation" of, say, Cromwell's motives and actions leading to the execution of the King', Rogers wrote, 'could be no more than a mere reflex of predetermined religious or social prejudice'; the action confirms a preconceived idea of the agent's worldview.[10] This Collingwood-inspired approach to reconstruction impeded students from acquiring a steadily expanding conceptual framework through which their sense of relevance sharpened and became more deft at handling the particulars of history.

In this relatively thorough examination of the relation between educational philosophy, the philosophy of history and the teaching of school history, Rogers shied away from all use of the term 'empathy'. It is thus a testament to the extent of empathy's *enracinement* that in a pamphlet for the Historical Association six years later, he interweaved the concept with evidence and context in discussing the importance of reconstruction, which again he proposed as the remedy to colligation's imposition of a pattern upon past realities.[11] Since the significance of a particular fact ascertained from a source is often latent, it needs to be interpreted, and the basis for this interpretation is the context of the norms and assumptions typical of its time. 'All too often the past is judged by *present* standards of appropriateness and rectitude, and the possibility of reconstructing the past as it was – of understanding it – is lost.'[12] In order to understand the past as it was, to penetrate beneath the objective conditions in which an agent acted, students had to comprehend how these conditions were perceived by the agent. 'In a word, "*empathy*" is a vital part of the reconstructive enterprise', to identify with agents in the contextual sense but also in the personal sense of seeing things the way they did. Insofar as this contextual frame reveals itself only thanks to historical distance, and empathizing signifies the attempt to overcome this temporal division, Rogers concluded that reconstruction is an integrative operation whose components – evidence, context and empathy – are inseparable in practice.[13]

The subsumption of rational understanding under empathy was also clearing new space for the concept to be theorized. Shemilt's three portraits of Collingwood's empathizing historian, published in 1984, has already shown how empathy became conceived in terms analogous to Lee's application of von Wright, which extended the idea of re-enactment beyond that described by Collingwood. The so-called black-box problem took the content of an agent's mind as an unknown located syllogistically at the intersection of the agent's situation and action. Shemilt's claim that the historian's task is to somehow penetrate this black back and discover its contents worked under the same assumption expressed by Lee that students were to be introduced to the working presupposition in history that, unless shown otherwise, agents acted for reasons good for them at the time. The intentions that Lee did not assign a symbol in the practical inference schema were for Shemilt the black box's hidden contents, whose discovery in both models ran up against the problem of there being no sure way of obtaining an accurate picture of how the agents perceived their situation, and thus of there being no sure criteria for evaluating the truth of the claims contingent upon that picture.

Lee's writings in the 1980s provide clearer evidence of the marriage of the two strands. Consider the breadth of meanings contained in four statements from his 1984 chapter on the historical imagination: (1) empathy, understanding and imagination are related in complex ways in history; (2) empathy is part of and a necessary condition of historical understanding ... imagination as supposal is criterial for that same understanding; (3) without empathy, there could be no historical understanding of action, which is why acquiring the disposition to empathize is an essential part of learning history; (4) understanding actions in history presupposes empathy as achievement, because it involves seeing an action as appropriate in terms of the agent's goals and intentions, and the agent's view of the situation.[14]

First, Lee announced that empathy, understanding and imagination could no longer be dissociated from one another. Second, empathy became viewed as the basic ingredient that activates the historical imagination, providing the link, third, to empathy functioning as a disposition of supposing by inference from evidence. Yet the notion of empathy as disposition fell flat at the last statement, where Lee described it as the achievement of having successfully reconstructed an action in the light of an agent's circumstances, that is, given his background in von Wright's philosophy, of having accurately followed the relevant set of practical inferences. In a formulation to be refined and repeated in future writings, the concepts were wedded under an ethic of openness and suspending one's own judgement.

Empathy as achievement meant being able to entertain ideas one may not share. Lee argued in the language of Hirst that such an understanding of historical agents had to be a form of knowledge testable against public criteria. There had to be in the exercise of empathy the possibility of 'cashing in' knowledge of the past with knowledge of the present, and vice versa. Here he was guided by Elton's criticism of the idea that a historian should 'read into a period until you hear its people speak'.[15] 'Who ever knew or understood people just because he heard them speak?', Elton had asked. 'The truth is that one must read them, study their creations and think about them until one knows what they are going to say next.'[16]

In this respect, empathy could be regarded as the achievement of knowing what is to be expected in certain historical situations. It offered history's learners vicarious or secondhand experience from which they would form conceptions of the full range of human possibilities while opening up the possibility of holding these conceptions reflexively. Without empathy, they could never achieve such purchase on the world of human potential, for in order to see before them what was possible in the past, they had to hold to the presupposition that people acted for reasons, and thus to a principle of rationality.[17] Lee insisted that if a word such as tolerance were to have any meaning in history, it must be through this kind of openness, 'in a willingness and ability to entertain beliefs and values not necessarily found acceptable for the purpose of understanding'.[18]

How well students kept in mind these beliefs and values while reflecting upon them critically determined how far they achieved empathy. Lee and Ashby went on to establish five levels for evaluating students' achievement in empathy.[19] Considered in relation to Lee's earlier theoretical work, it is noteworthy that the opening discussion on empathy's nature and value filled only two pages. They recognized that empathy was 'still at best a shorthand term for a cluster of related notions', but believed in the formulation of 'empathy as achievement' that they had a sufficient conceptual grounding for conducting empirical work.

Students at the lowest level committed the historical fallacy of assuming that people in the past had the same knowledge of their situation as we have today with historical hindsight, leading them to look upon the past as a catalogue of strange behaviour. The next level exhibited some ability to operate on the basis of historical context, albeit a context composed of a generalized stereotype. Mid-range students took the complexity of past contexts seriously, but were unable to avoid projecting their own experiences onto them. At level four, students demonstrated 'restricted historical empathy' by recognizing that actions usually involved qualifications that need to be worked into and redescribed in the reconstruction of an event. Finally, at the highest level, students achieved 'contextual historical empathy' when there was evidence in their thinking of a clear differentiation between the point of view of a historical agent and that of the historian, between what the agent knew and what we know, between the beliefs, values, goals and habits embedded in a past society and those of our own society. Students were empathizing when they adopted strategies to assimilate 'what had to be done' from their understanding, generated by the historical imagination, of a wider context in which evidence was lacking.

The switch in attention from theory to practice did not, of course, remove the difficulties raised in the theoretical literature. For instance, the challenge at level four consisted in accounting for an agent's qualifications in performing an action. At level five, the achievement of a fully contextualized historical empathy was in fact the accomplishment of closing a practical inference. Students capable of this level of inferential reasoning could see 'these people *must* have believed p^1 and been in circumstance c^1 to have found it possible to believe p in circumstance c, and it is therefore p^1 and c^1 which allows us to understand how they could have done x'.[20] They explained actions by having first understood beliefs in relation to their context.

The description of the five levels demonstrated the extent to which Lee's model of rational understanding – a product of the application of analytical philosophy of history in the Burston IOE tradition – defined empathy as attention was shifting from theory to practice. Collingwood's account of re-experiencing the past may have supplied empathy with its educational raison d'être, but through the convergence of the Leeds and London approaches it was the logic of practical inferences that put flesh on the concept's bones and provided teachers with the formula of empathy as achievement.

★ ★ ★

It is easy to lose sight of empathy's contribution to historical understanding when it is conceived on the scale of practical inferences. While the model may have succeeded in establishing empathy's disciplinary credentials by defining it analytically as the necessary process of inferring connections between situation, agent, action and outcome, it leaves unsaid the precise nature of the historical context that forms the basis of its explanatory procedure. Empathy's developers have been more concerned with the *how* of historical knowing than the *what* that empathy supposedly helps us know.

Against the earlier trend of associating empathy with imagination and identification, Stuart Foster and Elizabeth Yeager laid down a procedure of historical empathy they hoped would finally affirm its place in historical method. This 'considered and active process', they wrote in 1998, consisted of four interrelated phases: (1) introduction of a historical event necessitating the analysis of human action; (2) understanding of historical context and chronology; (3) analysis of a variety of historical evidence and interpretations; and (4) construction of a narrative framework through which historical conclusions are reached. Although Foster and Yeager considered empathy a 'process' rather than an 'achievement', their construction of this specifically historical concept echoed Lee's insistence that, applied to historical evidence, empathy allows historians to bridge gaps in what is known, to infer from given knowledge an explanation of past actions. They extended the concept by bringing under its heading Rogers' discussion of the historical imagination as a complex of context, outcomes and evidence.[21]

Foster reworked these four interrelated phases into four instructional stages for practising history teachers. Contained within the stages were empathy's six fundamental qualities: (1) the ability to understand and explain why people acted the way they did; (2) the ability to appreciate context and chronology; (3) the ability to analyse and evaluate historical evidence; (4) the ability to appreciate the consequences of actions; (5) the ability to distinguish past from present; (6) the willingness to respect the complexity of human action and achievement. He offered a model unit on Neville Chamberlain's 1938 appeasement policy to indicate how these qualities could be cultivated through the kinds of topics typically covered in school history syllabi. Historical empathy was on display when students demonstrated evidence of having thoughtfully understood, appreciated and evaluated Chamberlain's actions in the light of what was possible in the specific historical context.[22]

Some have regarded these attempts to affirm empathy's disciplinary status as limiting the concept's potential to contribute to a fuller historical experience in history classrooms. Christopher Blake spoke for the American social studies tradition of teaching school history in responding to Foster and Yeager that the integrative, holistic and essentially cross-functional nature of the empathetic process prohibited any single discipline from stamping its title upon it: 'Ultimately history cannot claim its particular version of empathy because it cannot offer a static, monolithic paradigm or model of the past by which such a version is defined or operable.'[23] For example, to empathize with a civilian supporter of the Viet Cong in the Vietnam War would require political and cultural insights from the modern era, whereas to empathize with a civilian zealot involved in the Maccabean revolt against the Roman occupation of Judea would require insights into religious and pre-scientific thinking. Since history needs the freedom to harness the necessary epistemic tools from across disciplinary boundaries, it may be appropriate in certain cases to sympathize, imagine and identify in the history classroom – 'to anesthetize empathy from a gamut of possible perspectives and emotions is absurd', Blake remonstrated.[24] He suggested that it is perfectly reasonable, if not invaluable, for instance, that feelings of sympathy and revulsion accompany the study of the victims and perpetrators of the Holocaust. Just as some in psychology regard empathy as the bedrock of all other moral emotions, such feelings do not damage its status in the history classroom; they help us grasp the emotional and cognitive structures we bring with us to a given cultural and temporal setting, which need to be recognized and contextualized before we can hope to 'think with' the subjects encountered there.

In other words, empathy in history, not historical empathy, challenges us in Blake's view to account for the 'here-and-now' in historical understanding, providing the means for viewing ourselves within the historical process, for sensitizing us to our relative contemporaneity and for reflecting on the ways in which human historicity both reveals and obscures our understandings of the past. In its reflexivity, empathy illuminates elements of ourselves otherwise obscured by a strictly empirical method. By giving us a handle on self-understanding, it acts as a prism, as an interpretive key, through which the themes of past and present may enter into dialogue. The view of empathy propounded first in orthodox phenomenology that the search for meaning in the lives of others requires us to 'bracket out' our own experiences, insights and historical legacies is a line of reasoning, implicit in the strictly cognitive, disciplinary approach, that needs to be abandoned in history education. 'The reason we need to sensitize ourselves to our relative contemporaneity in any empathetic activity', Blake concluded, 'is that our understanding of the past is distorted and compromised without a recognition of the perspectives we bring constructively from our present lives into the hermeneutic task of understanding the past of others.'[25]

To redirect empathy along this trajectory would involve acknowledging that it operates in the same intermediate space as that of hermeneutics, whose work, in the words of its greatest twentieth-century exponent, Hans-Georg Gadamer, 'is not to develop a procedure of understanding, but to clarify the conditions in which understanding takes place'.[26] Conceived as an achievement or methodical process, empathy overlooks the possibility of undertaking this reflection; in placing its trust in its own procedure, it forgets its own historicity.

Blake had good reason to draw attention to the vaster range of empathy's dimensions mostly overlooked in the action-explanation conception. Less defensible was the claim that this narrowness results from the disciplinary conception itself. A history of the concept will reveal that it emerged in the history discipline in connection with the problems, questions and tensions he believes afford the concept its educational value. Put differently, the educational worth of empathy can be shown by bringing to the fore the issues it has raised in the history of historical thought.

Educationalists before Blake had recognized empathy's hermeneutical character, but never in fact described as such. Ashby and Lee stressed that rational understanding and empathy were so difficult an intellectual achievement precisely because they involve holding in mind structures of thought that are not one's own.[27] In the piece that saw rational understanding brought under the rubric of empathy, Lee concluded with a discussion of Margaret Donaldson's notion of 'disembedded thinking'.[28] The concept showed that since it is often the validity of past agents' viewpoints that comes into question in historical thinking, a validity that must be assessed independently of one's own viewpoint, so a great deal of historical thinking must be disembedded or prised out of the supportive context of one's own experience.

An educational psychologist, Donaldson had argued that even preschool children have the capacity to reason about patterns of events corresponding to what they know, believe or want to know and want to believe; that is, about patterns of events making 'human sense'. When thinking moves beyond these bounds, so that it is no longer supported by a context of familiarity, it becomes formal, abstract or disembedded, and far more difficult.[29] Lee took this to reveal the complexity of trying to integrate the familiar with the unfamiliar in historical learning. Should teachers make things make historical sense by dressing unfamiliar content in familiar clothing? Or is it rather that historical thinking is necessarily disembedded and counterintuitive? Stepping back from Lee's analysis, is it characterized by what the educational philosopher Shaun Gallagher has called the 'dilemma of Romantic hermeneutics'?[30] In order for understanding to be possible, history students must remain connected to their historical situation, but in order for that understanding to be valid, they must disconnect themselves from that situation to hold in mind the viewpoints of historical agents.

Sam Wineburg's framing of the problem of historical thinking as an 'unnatural act' pivots precisely on this tension. On the one hand, he explains, history's humanizing potential requires being able to locate ourselves in a familiar past, where we can tie our stories to those who came before us, recognize our place in the stream of time and cement our identity in the present. On the other hand, it requires being able to penetrate a strange past where, detached from present-day concerns and needs, distant forms of meaning and modes of thought can expand our conceptions of human experience, its limitations and possibilities, and our place within it. This disciplined study of the past may reveal a relevance in what strikes us initially as its irrelevance.[31]

Troubling our efforts to approach the past in this disinterested manner is the hermeneutical dilemma. Put in Wineburg's words: 'Historical thinking requires us to reconcile two contradictory positions: first, that our established modes of thinking are an inheritance that cannot be sloughed off, and, second, that if we make no attempt to slough them off, we are doomed to a mind-numbing presentism that reads the present into the past.'[32]

A seventeen-year-old Advanced Placement history student and subject of Wineburg's early empirical research brought this dilemma clearly into view. While the student made astute observations from a series of primary readings on the Battle of Lexington, such as the inappropriateness of the term 'battle' for so one-sided an affair, his overall conclusions on the event were guided by a set of assumptions about how normal people behave in such circumstances; in this case, when one faces a stronger adversary, one flees behind walls and engages in guerrilla warfare. He did not pause to reflect 'what a strange group of people, what would make them act this way?', which would have seen him consider such codes of behaviour as duty, honour and dying for a cause. Instead, his existing frames of reference shaped the historical information so that it conformed to the already known.[33] His failure to appreciate that the actions exhibit ways of thinking different from our own prompted Wineburg to ask: 'Given what we know about the entrenched nature of beliefs, how, exactly, do we bracket what we know in order to understand the thinking of people in the past?'[34]

Wineburg identified Gadamer as the most qualified to deal with this problem of how we are to overcome established modes of thought when it is precisely those modes of thought that enable understanding in the first place: 'We, no less than the people we study, are historical beings. Trying to shed what we know in order to glimpse the "real" past is like trying to examine microbes with the naked eye: The instruments we abandon are the ones that enable us to see.'[35] Moreover, he contrasted Gadamer's position directly with the 'classic historicist stance' of Collingwood, whose belief that the historian is able 'to put him- or herself in Julius Caesar's mind, "envisioning . . . the situation in which Caesar stood, and thinking for himself what Caesar thought about the situation and the possible ways of dealing with it"' implied for Wineburg that 'we can somehow "know Caesar" because human ways of thought, in some deep and essential way, transcend time and space'.[36]

This juxtaposition of Gadamer and Collingwood served Wineburg to drive home the message that historical understanding is characterized at its heart by an interplay between the familiar and the strange, between the 'naïve historicism' of attempting to re-think past thoughts in their original form and the unhistorical 'presentism' of applying present standards to the study of the past. To put the dilemma in two oft-quoted literary epigrams, historical thinking is an unnatural act because in it there is a rift between L.P. Hartley's 'The past is a foreign country: they do things differently there' and William Faulkner's 'The past is never dead. It's not even past'.[37] One requires an intrepidness and methodological preparedness that is not necessary for the investigation of a familiar and immediate past.

Historians and philosophers of history know too well that present-day conditions and concerns impress themselves upon the study of the past. For all his censure of practical history, the early Oakeshott still maintained that the historical researcher shapes and fits past experience to his pre-existing premises: 'No historian ever began with a blank consciousness, an isolated idea or a genuinely universal doubt, for none of these is a possible state of mind. He begins always with a system of postulates (largely unexamined) which define the limits of his thought, and with a specific view of the course of events, a view consonant with his postulates.'[38] Similarly, Collingwood's point that historians extract evidence from historical sources by applying certain questions to them stood in direct contrast to the empiricist belief that sources speak for themselves and that historians' task is to let them speak.

Nevertheless, the limits placed on historical knowledge by the fact that we are present-day creatures are easily exaggerated. Keith Jenkins' weighing in on the legitimacy of empathy as a historical concept is a prime example of how they can be taken to exclude the possibility of historical knowledge at all. The idea of an 'empathetically retrievable' past struck him as an absurdity, and he pondered why the philosophically unachievable task of understanding other minds had become so high an educational priority. 'Given that there is no presuppositionless interpretation of the past, and given that interpretations of the past are constructed in the present', Jenkins, a decade before Wineburg employed similar language to describe the 'unnatural act' of historical thinking, wrote that 'the possibility of the historian being able to slough off his present to reach somebody else's past on their terms looks remote'.[39]

Jenkins identified three 'disparate pressures' to explain the ascent of this fanciful concept.[40] First, from the extension of comprehensive schools came the emergence of the educational notions of relevance, needs, involvement and student-based learning. This process of democratization gave students the opportunity to express their 'equally valid/valued opinions' in the form of questions like 'what do you think of the past?', 'what does history mean to you?' and 'what is your explanation?', which for Jenkins invited them to adopt the mindset of historical agents.

Second, within the academy reigned an entrenched idealism flowing over onto the school scene. According to Jenkins, the problem with Collingwood's idealist view that history involves discovering what agents held in mind is that standing between an agent's mind and our own mind is the historian's account. Asked to consider what Thomas Cromwell was thinking, we are in fact 'empathising less with Cromwell's mind than Elton's', the authority through whom we encounter Cromwell and the world he inhabited. Hence Jenkins' overall thesis that history is not so much the 'history of past people's minds', but the 'history of historians' minds'.

Finally, pressure from schooling and idealism combined with a liberal ideology descendant from John Stuart Mill. Central to his idea of freedom was the notion that individuals could do as they desired so long as the exercise of that desire did not curtail the freedom of other individuals. To calculate whether this would occur as a consequence of any action, individuals had to put themselves in other people's positions to see their point of view. This calculation worked under an assumption of rationality and universality of thought, for it could only function to avoid bringing harm to one another if it were capable of rational reciprocation. Transposed to the past, in Jenkins' view, it universalized time and space in a local and time-bound ideology of the calculation of interests per se, bringing people considerably different from ourselves into the pull of our contemporary conceptual frameworks, the very definition of what it means to think ahistorically.

Jenkins' critique has drawn the ire of history educationalists who see in it a denial of the possibility of historical knowledge. To be sure, his view that empathy diverts attention from the real task of coming to grips with our contemporaneity in relation to the past disregards the idea that there may be different levels of historical understanding and better or worse historical explanations.

Even so, Jenkins' objections can be helpful, though in a way that he did not intend. Sceptical as he is to the idealist philosophy of mind and its attendant conceptions of historical method and knowledge, he draws attention to the need to account for the intermediating role of the present in any attempt aspiring to empathetically recapture the past.

Somewhere in the middle is the moderate hermeneutical approach that I shall propose. In attempting to identify and come to terms with the context in which people thought and acted, the opportunity also arises for us to reflect on what we share with them, which makes understanding them possible, as well as the ways in which we differ, which provides us with new content from which to learn.[41] We come to see how the past is both distant and built into the present. Although the present context in which we study history interposes itself and renders impossible any unmediated apprehension of the past, the fact that this past asserts itself against our present-day ways of thinking and behaving as something in need of comprehension supplies the resources for reflecting upon human conditions both past and present.

Notes

1. See Tyson Retz, 'At the Interface: Academic History, School History and the Philosophy of History', *Journal of Curriculum Studies* 48, 4 (2016), 503–17.

2. Tony Boddington, 'Empathy and the Teaching of History', *British Journal of Educational Studies* 28, 1 (1980), 13, 18.

3. Peter Knight, 'Empathy: Concept, Confusion and Consequences in a National Curriculum', *Oxford Review of Education* 15, 1 (1989), 44.

4. Peter Rogers, 'History', in Keith Dixon (ed.), *Philosophy of Education and the Curriculum* (Oxford: Pergamon Press, 1972), 75–134. See also Peter Rogers, 'History: The Past as a Frame of Reference', in Christopher Portal (ed.), *The History Curriculum for Teachers* (London: Falmer Press, 1987), 3–21.

5. Rogers, 'History', 110.

6. Ibid., 111.

7. Ibid.

8. Ibid., 121.

9. Ibid., 112.

10. Ibid., 113.

11. P.J. Rogers, *The New History: Theory into Practice* (London: Historical Association, 1978), 12.

12. Ibid.

13. Ibid., 12–13.

14. P.J. Lee, 'Historical Imagination', in A.K. Dickinson, P.J. Lee and P.J. Rogers (eds), *Learning History* (London: Heinemann, 1984), 89–90.

15. Ibid., 101.

16. G.R. Elton, *The Practice of History* (Sydney: Sydney University Press, 1967), 17.

17. P.J. Lee, 'Why Learn History', in Dickinson, Lee and Rogers (eds), *Learning History*, 10–12.

18. Ibid., 12.

19. Rosalyn Ashby and Peter Lee, 'Children's Concepts of Empathy and Understanding in History', in Christopher Portal (ed.), *The History Curriculum for Teachers* (London: Falmer Press, 1987), 62–88.

20. Ibid., 81.

21. Stuart J. Foster and Elizabeth Anne Yeager, 'The Role of Empathy in the Development of Historical Understanding', *International Journal of Social Education* 13, 1 (1998), 1–2; reprinted with minor alternations in O.L. Davis, Jr., Elizabeth Yeager and Stuart Foster (eds), *Historical Empathy and Perspective Taking in the Social Studies* (Lanham: Rowman & Littlefield, 2001), 13–20.

22. Stuart Foster, 'Using Historical Empathy to Excite Students about the Study of History: Can You Empathize with Neville Chamberlain?' *Social Studies* 90, 1 (1999), 19–23.

23. Christopher Blake, 'Historical Empathy: A Response to Foster and Yeager', *International Journal of Social Education* 13, 1 (1998), 27.

24. Ibid., 28.

25. Ibid., 29.

26. Hans-Georg Gadamer, *Truth and Method,* 2nd rev. edn, trans. Joel Weinsheimer and Donald G. Marshall (New York: Continuum, 2004), 295. First published in German (*Wahrheit und Methode*) in 1960; first published in English in 1975.

27. Ashby and Lee, 'Children's Concepts of Empathy', 63.

28. Lee, 'Historical Imagination', 110.

29. Margaret Donaldson, *Children's Minds* (London: Fontana, 1978), 76.

30. Shaun Gallagher, *Hermeneutics and Education* (Albany: State University of New York Press, 1992), 210.

31. Sam Wineburg, *Historical Thinking and Other Unnatural Acts: Charting the Future of Teaching the Past* (Philadelphia: Temple University Press, 2001), 5–7. For an opposing view, see Jon A. Levisohn, 'Historical Thinking – and its Alleged Unnaturalness', *Educational Philosophy and Theory* 49, 6 (2017), 618–30.

32. Wineburg, *Historical Thinking,* 12.

33. Ibid., 7–9.

34. Ibid., 10.

35. Ibid.

36. Ibid., quoting from R.G. Collingwood, *The Idea of History,* rev. edn [1946] Jan van der Dussen (Oxford: Oxford University Press, 1994), 215.

37. L.P. Hartley, *The Go-Between* (New York: New York Review Books, 1953), 17; William Faulkner, *Requiem for a Nun* (New York: Random House, 1951), 92.

38. Michael Oakeshott, *Experience and its Modes* (Cambridge: Cambridge University Press, 1933), 97.

39. Keith Jenkins, *Re-thinking History* (London: Routledge, 1991), 49. See also Keith Jenkins and Peter Brickley, 'Reflections on the Empathy Debate', *Teaching History* 55 (1989), 18–23.

40. Jenkins, *Re-thinking History,* 51–55.

41. See Tyson Retz, 'A Moderate Hermeneutical Approach to Empathy in History Education', *Educational Philosophy and Theory* 47, 3 (2015), 214–26.

Part II
ORIGINS

You're always thinking what nobody else has remotely in mind.

—Saul Bellow, *Humboldt's Gift*

CHAPTER 4

Empathy and Historicism

What grounds have history educationalists for associating empathy with Collingwood's doctrine of re-enactment? Collingwood never used the term, and he inveighed specifically against psychologistic conceptions of historical thinking.

The strongest reason may be that a good proportion of writers on historical method and the philosophy of history have discussed re-enactment in precisely that way. Peter Johnson, in mentioning Collingwood's praise for the contribution to historical thought of the German philosopher-historian Wilhelm Dilthey, writes that 'Empathy with the past is', for both, 'not a luxury that historians indulge, but a necessity if there is to be genuine historical understanding at all'. Rex Martin contends that the 'essence of empathy' is also the essence of Collingwood's theory, the goal of both being 'to take the point of view of the agent, by regarding his situation and the elements of his thought, and to deliberate on possible courses of action from that point of view'. Alun Munslow invokes 'Collingwood's empathetic rethinking of the past', 'the state of being "in touch with" the thoughts and situation of the historical agent'. 'For many *reconstructionist* historians', Munslow registers in his glossary of terms, 'it is the empathetic linkage of evidence and context that constitutes history.'[1]

Louis Mink observes in Collingwood's philosophy of art that while he 'never mentions "empathy," he clearly is suggesting an explanation of *why* we find it natural to describe music or poetry as "soaring" or "plodding" or to regard Cézanne's still-lifes . . . as suggesting objects "that have been groped over with the hands"'.[2] Dray remarks too that Collingwood sometimes gives the impression that he believed in 'some kind of direct em-

---

Notes for this section begin on page 88.

pathetic understanding', but that re-enactment in the final analysis proved to be a 'great improvement over older doctrines of *verstehen* or empathetic understanding . . . which some critics think it resembles'.[3]

Such a critic is A.R. Louch, who names Collingwood among a group of philosophers culpable of 'mystical and divinatory excesses', supposing what is needed for the explanation of an agent's motives or intentions is 'some unique method, *verstehen,* empathy or sympathy', and in following such a method, 'we are in some mysterious way identifying or entering into the thought processes of those whose careers we investigate'. As von Wright remarked in the book that supported Lee's formulation of practical inferences, the intentionalist and antipositivist emphasis on understanding has always had a 'psychological ring' absent from models of scientific explanation. Without taking full account of the necessity in both empathy and re-enactment to consider alternatives for action as indicated by the evidence, Martin acknowledges that Collingwood's battery of metaphors – 'inside-outside', 'penetration', 're-thinking' – can give rise to the view that his position is intuitionist.[4]

Dray points out in a similar vein that Collingwood's repeated insistence that historical understanding is ratiocinative, not intuitive, is often ignored; it is not only upon a critical study of historical evidence that the investigator sees an agent responding to a problem in a rational manner, 'but upon the critical analysis of the thought that an action allegedly expresses'. Collingwood contended that actions are exhibitions of human thought, but both action and thought still need to hold up against what the evidence reveals about the situation. That human rationality occupies so pivotal a role in his philosophy has led others to flatly reject the notion that empathy and re-enactment share a common bond. To claim that Collingwood proffered a theory of empathy, intuition or even methodology of history, according to Stein Helgeby, violates his description of re-enactment as a theory of reason and of the conditions of historical knowledge.[5]

These examples serve as sufficient grounds for continuing to consider empathy and re-enactment alongside one another in a critical investigation of their origins and function in historical studies. Yet concerned as they are with the connection between empathy and re-enactment, they shed only faint light on the nature of empathy itself. Before turning to Collingwood's theory, there is first the task of determining empathy's function in the history of historical thought. Although it is a term of relatively recent coinage, its significance has been felt from the earliest days of the history discipline.

★ ★ ★

Empathy (*Einfühlung*) emerged in the substantive as a technical term of philosophical analysis in German aesthetics in the late nineteenth century. Of course, its formulation as a philosophical concept was not without precedent. Linguistically it stretched back to the ancient Greek *empátheia,* other terms carried similar meanings in Germany and elsewhere, and questions concerning the way human beings identify with one another and the objects they perceive were, of course, by no means new. A century earlier, Herder had implored the historian to 'feel yourself into everything', the age, the region, the entire history, in the active sense of *sich einfühlen.*[6]

Yet empathy's formulation as a central category for examining the nature of aesthetic experience is typically overlooked in monographs of the German aesthetic tradition. This omission can be explained largely by the fact that empathy developed at the periphery of mainstream philosophical aesthetics, in a tributary known as 'psychological aesthetics'.[7] Robert Vischer and Theodor Lipps, the leaders of this 'empathy school', in Paul Guyer's nomenclature, rejected the prevailing position stretching back to Kant that aesthetic experience involves the pleasurable play of our cognitive powers, but remains detached from cognition itself, and argued instead that aesthetic experience is a form of cognition occurring in symphony with the emotions aroused or experienced in the arts particularly.

Vischer, a professor of art history and aesthetics at Breslau and later Göttingen, and the son of the more renowned Friedrich Theodor Vischer, who himself had developed a form of empathy to break out of the cognitivist confines of Hegelian aesthetics, gave birth to the modern noun in his 1873 doctoral thesis, 'On the Optical Feeling of Form'. In this work, empathy designated the notion that there is a union of subjective response with the perception of objective form; it is a *projection* of the body's emotional and physical characteristics, responding to the objective stimuli, onto the perception of the object, creating, in his words, 'a harmony between the object and the subject, which arises because the object has a harmonious form and a formal effect corresponding to subjective harmony'.[8] His coining of *Einfühlung* constituted the latest addition to a patchwork of ideas and prefixal variations to the noun 'feeling' (*Fühlung*), all of which resist translation into a single English word and all of which carry conceptual distinctions lost in the translation of *Einfühlung* as empathy.[9]

The best-known theorist of empathy, Lipps followed a similar career path but missed Vischer by one year at Breslau, where he filled a chair of philosophy and published large treatises on logic, psychology and aesthetics from the mid-1880s until his death in 1914. He expounded his theories on empathy in writings on aesthetics, which he maintained is the study of the psychology of beauty. Beauty itself he defined as 'the capacity of an object to produce a particular *effect* in me', an effect whose aesthetic value is none other than the pleasure it produces. Pleasure arises when the impressions given to the mind in aesthetic experience produce conditions that facilitate the mind's activities. He borrowed Vischer's equation of empathy as the projection of human emotions onto external objects, whether human or nonhuman, in virtue of harmonies or resemblances between those objects.[10] In close to his own words, my pleasure *in* an external object, insofar as it is an object of pleasure, is not an object but *myself*; it is a pleasure in a self, which, insofar as it is aesthetically enjoyed, is not myself but something *objective*. 'This is what is meant by Empathy', he concluded, 'that the distinction between the self and the object disappears or rather does not yet exist.'[11]

As simulation theorists discuss nowadays, in this state of being 'in' the object, empathy suffers from the problem of *quid juris*. Without an external standard, by what means can the knowledge obtained by empathy be verified? Empathizers might be put in touch with the underlying causal mechanisms of another person's behaviour, but without something *against which* their knowledge of these mechanisms may be tested, they lack a means for justifying whether it constitutes true knowledge of the other person's mental state. We often hear that we cannot recognize a problem because we are still 'in' it; in this same way, to claim true knowledge of another person's mental state requires something against which it can cast its shadow and be seen for what it is.

Lipps' psychological formulation of empathy makes greater sense when it is considered alongside what was seen as the only alternative for conceiving of knowledge of other minds: John Stuart Mill's theory of analogical inference. The 'problem of other minds' was waiting to be noted as far back as Descartes, but only came to prominence with Mill, whose theory held sway until Wittgenstein's concept of language as public property and of the logical impossibility of private language destroyed with it the need for a theory of access to other minds. In his *System of Logic,* published in English in 1843 and in German six years later, Mill undertook to liberate the empirical sciences from the rigidity of syllogistic logic and to develop instead an inductive logic derived from the principles of the natural sciences. Its centrepiece is that there is a causal link between people's mental states and their behaviour. He adhered to a Cartesian conception of mind whereby one's knowledge of one's own mind is direct and infallible, whereas one's knowledge of other minds is indirect, inferential and fallible. In spite of this barrier, Mill thought that human beings are alike and behave in similar ways in similar circumstances. My direct knowledge of my own mind allows me to infer the mental states of others whom I find performing similar actions in similar circumstances. In my own case, it being one o'clock in the afternoon is associated with my feeling of hunger, and this experience then gives rise to my eating a sandwich. When I observe other bodies eating a sandwich at one o'clock in the afternoon, I am entitled to infer that they feel hunger too. Although the inference's evidentiary slim basis does not provide me with indubitable knowledge of another person's mental state, it does provide me with the best explanation of the hidden mental cause of an observable behaviour.

The two approaches sit behind a present-day split in the theory of mind. Mill's concept of analogical inference characterizes the view that the possession and use of a theory provide us with the capacity to attribute mental states to others in order to interpret, explain and predict their behaviour. It holds that understanding others engages us in a detached intellectual process as we move from one inference to another by reference to this theory. By contrast, Lipps' concept of empathy epitomizes the simulationist view that we use solely our own mind as the model for understanding other minds. Theory-theorists are divided on the issue of whether the theory in question is innate and modularized or acquired in the same manner as ordinary scientific theories. As for the simulationists, they differ on whether the simulation in question involves the exercise of conscious imagination and deliberative inference, whether it is explicit but noninferential in nature, or whether it is implicit and subpersonal.

Dan Zahavi has argued that this neat division is an oversimplification of what is best understood as a phenomenological concept, as developed in the 1910s by Edmund Husserl and his student, Edith Stein, whose doctoral thesis *On the Problem of Empathy* contained themes that Husserl expounded in *Ideas II*.[12] Phenomenology is the study of the structure of consciousness as experienced from the first-person perspective. The central feature of experience is its intentionality: it is directed towards something because it is an experience of or about something. For Stein, the problem of empathy stemmed from the fact that the knowledge created by empathetic encounters is 'empty', 'blind' and 'restless'; it implied a mode of knowledge that reaches back to its experience with the other but can never possess it.[13] Husserl was unsure how empathy could extend knowledge, for in projecting the other as a subject analogous to my own self, 'it does not produce something novel over against the self'.[14] He classed his own version of the concept as a 'reproductive intuition', an experience of recollection or special form of memory that reproduces past events as they were earlier perceived, or what was earlier judged on the basis of perceptual evidence. Empathy presented another's experience 'as if' I were experiencing it myself. It 'reproduces' in my experience the kind of experience I take another to have.

Husserl's purpose in adopting the term was to give the feeling involved in it not only an emotive quality but also a cognitive status. This involved removing it from its roots in naturalistic psychology and replanting it in the theory of the human sciences, as espoused by Wilhelm Dilthey, whom Husserl knew. Whereas the other of the naturalistic attitude was an 'invisible soul' ready to be filled by my own projection, the other of the personalistic attitude was a 'spiritual being' in whose life I could participate. Just as words express meaning in a direct intentional manner, such that we do not have to decipher each letter and then add their sense, so this 'ensouled' body could be apprehended as an expression of human meaning. Empathy in the spiritual world captured intentional acts whose meaning could be said to be objective. 'The spiritual meaning apprehended is not private', writes Rudolf Makkreel, leaning on Husserl's original, 'but public and typical, and if I consider myself as a co-participant with others in a common surrounding world I can not only transport myself into their actions, but also follow them out . . . the other's "motives become my quasi-motives", and allow me to intuitively . . . fulfil empathy into insight'.[15] Thus transplanted to the *Geisteswissenschaften,* empathy was transformed into a kind of concrete intuition operating in the service of understanding (*Verstehen*).

Empathy's alliance with understanding in the human sciences created a problem Dilthey particularly sought to reconcile. In this tradition, understanding involved capturing individuality, but empathy could apprehend only what is typical in a shared spiritual world. For empathy to contribute to understanding, it would have to be able to specify distinctiveness on the basis of such commonality.

Writers investigating the relation between empathy and understanding have rightly pointed out that Dilthey rarely used the term *Einfühlung.* The term was not sufficiently established outside the realm of psychological aesthetics in the early part of his career and entered wider usage only later when he had abandoned his strongly psychologistic conception of the human sciences. He used *Einfühlen* to engage with Herder's work, but seldom in a positive manner, preferring instead *Nachfühlen* (re-feel) and *Nacherleben* (re-experience), whose prefix *Nach* indicates a need for critical distance on the part of the person contemplating another's experience.[16]

Dilthey probably concluded that empathy established too direct and intuitive a relation between individuals to be a reliable source of understanding. Like Husserl and Stein, he was unsure how surrendering oneself to the contemplation of an object provided a view from which its individuality and difference could stand out against one's own self. Understanding others requires that I see them as standing independently of me. This need for distance led Dilthey to adopt a more positive stance towards *Mitfühlung,* or sympathy. In contrast to empathy, I do not project myself onto others or identify with them in sympathy; I claim to resonate in harmony with their situation while recognizing our differences.[17] Dilthey's hermeneutics took the structure of the surrounding world (*Umwelt*) as the starting point for understanding individuality in the human sciences. Rather than moving from the self to the object to the surrounding world, the structural outlines of human experience objectively given in the world were seen to form an intelligible whole that provided interpreters with an implicit or at least initial understanding of context.

Dilthey could conceive of structure as the gateway for understanding only after he had undergone his Hegelian turn and adopted the concept of objective spirit around the turn of the century. The psychologism with which he is often charged represented a significant but ultimately passing moment in the development of his thought, during which he held that it was the task of understanding to reproduce the psychological state of mind of the person to whom the object of understanding is attached – what Makkreel terms Dilthey's 're-enactment view'.[18] In two later essays, 'The Rise of Hermeneutics' (1900) and 'The Understanding of Other Persons and Their Manifestations of Life' (1910), Dilthey made clear that understanding originates in the 'manifold forms in which a commonality existing among individuals has objectified itself in the world of the senses', where 'the past is a continuously enduring present for us', which 'contains something that is common to the I and the Thou'. He believed that exegetes in the human sciences held an advantage over those seeking *interpretatio naturae* because their object of understanding was no mere reflection of reality or sensory experience, but 'first and foremost an inner reality, a nexus experienced from within'.[19] The scientific basis of history rested on the capacity of such 're-understanding' of what is singular to be raised to universal objectivity. The notion of 'historical consciousness', much invoked nowadays in discussions of historical culture and learning, for Dilthey referred to the ascendency of the idea that this objective apprehension of what is singular 'enabled modern man to hold the entire past of humanity present within himself . . . [historical consciousness] comprehends all these historical tendencies within a purposive system as a series of possibilities contained within it . . . historical thought itself becomes creative in that it raises human activity in society above the limits of the moment and the situation'.[20]

The possibility of bringing an individual objectification of life to the level of a universally valid objective understanding was governed by the condition that 'in no alien individual objectification can anything appear that is not also contained in the mental life of the one who apprehends it. The same functions and (psychic) constituents are to be found in all individuals. The dispositions of different people differ only in terms of the degree of their intensity.'[21] One could attribute shared qualities to all human beings and still study individual human beings and groups in terms of how they express these qualities in their laws, institutions, customs and so on.

That the world is 'given' to us in this way is what made Dilthey's theory of *Verstehen* a fundamentally historical one. Objective knowledge of singular human existence was to be re-experienced in the 'vital connectedness' of what has been passed down in the historical world and the 'acquired psychic nexus' of our own reality. This process of 'transposition' could occur only 'if the connectedness that exists in one's own lived experience and has been experienced in innumerable cases is always available to accompany the possibilities inherent in its object', whether a human being or a work. 'Then every line of a poem is transformed back into life through the inner nexus of the lived experience from which the poem arose.'[22] Preserving the universal validity of such understanding against 'romantic caprice' and 'sceptical subjectivity' was the task of hermeneutics, which in Dilthey's time concerned itself with the theory of the rules governing the interpretation of written texts. The art of understanding consisted in the exegesis or interpretation of the remains of human reality preserved in the written form.

With this Hegelian turn, Dilthey could proclaim at the beginning of the twentieth century that 'German culture had turned its attention away from literary production to a reunderstanding of the historical world'.[23] As for empathy, its early development in psychological aesthetics penetrated the independent scientific discipline of psychology in the new century, and together with its entry into philosophy through Husserl's phenomenology, the concept's twentieth-century history could be traced along any number of paths ploughed by these two disciplines. But having identified the concept's place alongside understanding in the human sciences, we have unearthed the line of inquiry able to elucidate empathy's specific function, development and transformation in historical studies. In particular, Dilthey's attempts to specify the procedures of humanistic understanding will have us work forward to consider Collingwood and Gadamer's responses to that tradition of methodological hermeneutics.

Yet the emergence of a term hardly means that its forms of signification were previously unknown. It remains to be seen that the concept of empathy, *avant la lettre,* played a formative part in the rise of historical consciousness and the birth of the history discipline. The growth of historicism in nineteenth-century Germany saw the development of a set of ideas that codified history's disciplinary procedures in terms tantamount to those used to describe empathy's function in capturing individuality.

★ ★ ★

Historicism is the doctrine that human ideas and values are historically conditioned and subject to change, and the methodological principle consequent to this position that human phenomena should be studied in relation to their particular historical contexts. It is the view, in Mark Bevir's words, 'that human life is inherently historical: ideas, texts, actions, and practices are historical objects, and explanations of them must be historical' and, in Frank Ankersmit's words, 'that the nature of a thing lies in its history', a view that from the late eighteenth century to the early twentieth century offered a common ground for reflecting on the nature and writing of history.[24] What could be the purpose of historians' activities, both thinkers ask, if they rejected the view that the nature and identity of their subject matter resides in the past? There would be little point in investigating the past if historical objects had meanings discoverable in the present. Before historicism, there was no scientific history in the sense that the historian aimed to acquire knowledge of past objects in their own terms. Historicism ended history's function as *magistra vitae* by cleansing it of value judgements and inaugurated a historical method for reconstructing a past with its own distinct qualities. Rather than fixing their attention on the 'recurrent general', historians set their sights on the unique constellations of meaning expressed in human behaviour and institutions. As Georg Iggers has shown, this required a hermeneutical method able to grasp the individual in the whole and the whole in the individual.[25]

Historicism has not always been used to denote this meaning. Karl Popper is typically identified in his *Poverty of Historicism* as having committed the most egregious distortion. Popper prepared the manuscript in the mid-1930s as a refutation of the 'fascist and communist belief in the Inexorable Laws of Historical Destiny'. He defined historicism as 'an approach to the social sciences which assumes that *historical prediction* is their principle aim, and which assumes that this aim is attainable by discovering the "rhythms" or the "patterns", the "laws" or the "trends" that underlie the evolution of history'.[26] Popper's definition appears idiosyncratic plainly for the fact that historicism has generally been identified, in the directly opposite sense, with the recognition that the unique and complex spontaneity of life renders impossible the reduction of history to general laws in the manner of the natural sciences. However, his criticisms make greater sense when it is known that the historicism against which he was arguing was the translation of the Italian term *storicismo,* as used by Benedetto Croce, which retained a more Hegelian and thus system-building connotation than the German term *Historismus,* which had entered English earlier as 'historism'.[27] Given that Leopold von Ranke, the father figure of historicism and the history discipline, promulgated his methods for studying the past through the term *Historismus,* and not *Historizismus,* the German equivalent of *storicismo* and historicism, certain scholars have opted for historism as insurance against its original sense being confused with Popper's Hegelian-Marxist conception of historicism.[28]

The meaning of historicism conveyed here holds to the three sets of ideas that Iggers identified as having underpinned its rise as the predominant outlook in nineteenth-century German historical thought: (1) a view of the state as an end in itself; (2) the rejection of thinking in normative terms; and (3) the rejection of conceptualized thinking.

First, in contrast to French and English historiography, the political traditions of the state were seen to exist neither culturally in the style of Michelet nor in the history of parliamentary institutions in the style of Burke. German historiography maintained a sharper distinction between the government and the governed, underplaying the pernicious aspects of state power and viewing it instead as a guarantor of human freedom. A nation-centred, politically oriented approach to studying the past developed alongside a concept of state that viewed it as an 'individual', as an end in itself, 'governed by its own principles of life', whose model for historians was the enlightened *Obrigkeitsstaat* of the Hohenzollern monarchy of the Prussian Reform Era. In place of a utilitarian concept of state, existing for the interests and welfare of its population, the state acquired more than merely an empirical existence; it became the representation of a higher spiritual principle, 'an idea of God', in Ranke's words.[29] As Iggers quotes from a study of the German liberals in the Frankfurt Parliament of 1848, they all assumed that a man's personal freedom, as the Lutheran tradition conceived it in spiritual and nonpolitical terms, existed in pre-established harmony with his membership in a community. In criticizing eighteenth-century French liberal thought, they reasoned that freedom in the abstract is meaningless and must be defined in terms of concrete social institutions.[30]

Second, a philosophy of value, congeneric with the concept of state as an individual end in itself, went beyond the baseline historicist assumption that all values arise within the concrete setting of a specific historical situation to assume that whatever arises in history is valuable per se. Historical thinking was non-normative. No individual, no institution, no historical deed could be judged by standards external to the situation in which it arose; it had to be judged in terms of its inherent values. But while there were no transhistorical standards of value available for studying the range of human institutions, historically contingent phenomena could still be said to represent true values insofar as they were regarded as emanations of divine will. The striving for power that German historicism raised to an ethical principle or reason of state manifested in an endeavour to develop the institutions that, as historically rooted in Germany's innate tendencies and traditions, could bring the state the strength and independence it required to prosper in the community of states. Each state cultivated its inimitable spirit and ethics through its institutions, which as embodiments of the specificity of each state's historical experience were intransferable to other states.

Lastly, the idea bringing German historicism squarely into line with empathy, the individual character of the state and its many components could only be grasped, it was believed, if concepts were left aside while casting oneself into the individual character of the subject matter. Just as the universalistic principles of eighteenth-century rationalism and political thought spoke little to what was unique about Germany and its inhabitants, so a historical methodology based on a set of common denominators worked against the discovery of those qualities. The seed of what we identified in Dilthey's conception of *Verstehen* had germinated earlier upon the recognition that history is the area of *willed human actions,* and that this understanding of the vital qualities of individuals' lives is distorted by the application of concepts imported from without. An understanding of human reality was rather to be pursued by a direct confrontation with the subject, by contemplation (*Anschauung*) and by intuition (*Ahnung*).

Clear from these three points is the reactionary character of historicism. Its rise was the result of a general rejection in Germany of the abstract intellectualism of classical, medieval and Renaissance thought, and above all to its expression in the cultural hegemony of eighteenth-century French Reason. The historicist outlook took shape in the revolts of national traditions against Enlightenment culture and its application of a mathematical mentality to the human, moral and political sphere. An enlightened despotism could be seen to lie at the heart of the cosmopolitanism of Voltaire and the *encyclopédistes,* whose philanthropic mission to replace local attachments and superstitions with universal Reason met resistance in movements seeking to affirm traditional liberties in the face of an encroaching Enlightenment state, producing a new ferment of liberal thought. Where universalists had searched the past and found transhistorical norms and values at best, and a suite of abuse, superstition and violence at worse, the historicist outlook defended and rehabilitated history by creating the need for a unified theory of the nation consecrated upon its language, literature, institutions and domestic customs.

Specifically, national histories written in the historicist mode were produced first in the decades following the Napoleonic occupation of the German lands in the years 1806–13, a period during which, as Stefan Berger puts it, 'the hijacking of the Enlightenment's universalism by French nationalism' stimulated a desire for national unity across a territory that lacked a centralized administration and whose peoples lacked a sense of their own unique and shared character, a fragmentation due in large part to the desiccated territorial structure of the Holy Roman Empire.[31] With the growing sense of nationalism came an acceptance of traditional authority and a more exclusive notion of national identity than the model that had intruded from across the Rhine. The distinct logic by which the nation had developed began to be regarded as a subject matter apprehensible only to those whose own development was tied up in that specific national-historical trajectory, leaving each nation, in principle, with a monopoly on the interpretation of its own history as the universalistic basis of extrinsic judgement became largely discredited. With their training in scholarly techniques, this placed historians in the privileged position of being the select few with direct access to the nation's past when history became a professional academic discipline upon the establishment of the University of Berlin in 1809.

History became self-conscious and in a climate of Romanticism established itself as an autonomous vehicle for imaginative reflection. The metaphor of the 'eye of history' that, since the seventeenth century, had symbolized the way in which the auxiliary sciences of chronology and geography helped historians pave a way through the temporal and spatial expanses of history began to reflect the manner in which the past could be understood; that is, a historical method.[32] The image of the historian as seer of that which others could not see relied on an expertise in applying the philological-critical or hermeneutical-philological method of source criticism, which in the production of meticulously researched monographs became the hallmark of objectivity, truth and scientificity.

Barthold Georg Niebuhr, a professor of ancient history at the University of Berlin from 1810 to 1816, and Ranke, whose publications and teachings extended those of Niebuhr at the same institution from 1825 to 1870, insisted that all historical research must rest on *Quellenkritik* – the critical examination of primary sources. This philological tradition, which sprang from Friedrich August Wolf's examination of the language of the Homeric poems in the late eighteenth century and became widespread in history in the nineteenth century, had as its philosophical foundation the assumption that all reality is historical. The pursuit of presenting the past as it actually happened went beyond an empiricism holding to the view that knowledge is restricted to what the senses can perceive. Since the highly individualized formations seen to comprise the historical world could not be reduced to a system or viewed as parts of a grandiose whole in the manner of Hegel, history required intuitive understanding.

The Neapolitan Giambattista Vico and the East Prussian Johann Gottfried von Herder supplied the philosophical basis for this form of historical apprehension. As Isaiah Berlin declared: 'No one stressed the importance of comprehensive historical treatment more boldly or vehemently than Vico; no one argued more eloquently or convincingly than Herder that ideas and outlooks could be understood adequately only in genetic and historical terms, as expressions of the particular stage in the continuing development of the society in which they originated'.[33] Vico 'uncovered a species of knowing not previously clearly discriminated, the embryo that later grew into the ambitious and luxuriant plant of German historicist *Verstehen* – empathetic insight, intuitive sympathy, historical *Einfühlung* . . . a discovery of the first order'.[34] Nurtured by Herder, it was a discovery that set the agenda for the nineteenth century's preoccupation with epistemology and the philosophy of mind.

Central to the line of thought to be developed, Collingwood regarded himself as belonging to this tradition inaugurated by Vico and Herder, which in the nineteenth century encompassed such theorists as Rickert and Dilthey in Germany and Croce in Italy. 'It is difficult, indeed', observes Patrick Gardiner, 'not to see in Vico's particular application of the so-called *verum factum* principle, according to which we can only fully know what we ourselves have made, an anticipation of an idea that lay at the heart of many of Collingwood's contentions regarding the distinctive character of historical knowledge.'[35] Collingwood translated Croce's study of Vico in his early twenties while a fellow of Pembroke College, Oxford, and in *The Idea of History* stated that the 'extraordinary merit of his work' became recognized only two generations later, when at the end of the eighteenth century German scholars rediscovered him and attached great value to his doctrine that 'ideas are propagated not by "diffusion", like articles of commerce, but by the independent discovery by each nation of what it needs at any given stage in its own development'.[36]

Against the almost universally held view that mathematics produced the surest and most distinct forms of knowledge, Vico declared that its claims were the most rigorous and irrefutable only because it is the free creation of our own minds; mathematical propositions are true so far as we ourselves have made them. If the single criterion of truth or validity consisted in whether a proposition could be analysed into 'simple', indivisible constituents, this would instantly have ruled out the greater part of common human existence not reducible to clear and distinct categories. The *verum factum* theory that the true and the made are identical cohered with the old idea that knowledge *per causas* is superior to any other but maintained that genuine knowledge of causes cannot be discriminated alone by logical demonstration; instead, it must consist in knowledge of *certum* – that which constituted the 'certainty' by which human beings lived in their direct experience of the world. Descartes' view that history was of small value given its incapacity to produce schema for arriving at permanently verifiable conclusions warred with Vico's view that, as God's creation, it was in fact the natural, external world that was inaccessible to the human mind, which could therefore be known only from the 'outside'. History, on the other hand, as the study of what human beings have forged through their efforts, struggles, purposes, motives, hopes, fears and attitudes, provided the way to true knowledge by furnishing its inquirers with an 'inside' view of human action, which as a species of self-knowledge, of knowledge obtained by the inquirers' knowledge of themselves as authors of actions endowed with motives, purposes and a continuous social life, revealed in the light of a common human nature binding humanity, was to Vico a view observed through the reconstructive imagination, or what he called *fantasia*. By his own pen, 'human customs are the practices or habits of a human nature that does not change all at once but always retains an impression of some former practice or habit'.[37] This distinction between 'outer' and 'inner' knowledge justified for him the claim that historical studies were autonomous and superior to those of nature, a proclamation that commenced hostilities between *Naturwissenschaft* and *Geisteswissenschaft*.

Vico did not explain how historians come to know the minds of historical agents by invoking the language of empathy, analogical reasoning, intuition or participation in the unity of a World Spirit. His theory of knowing was neither deductive nor inductive; neither founded upon an unmediated perception of the world nor upon an imagination that makes no claim to truth or reality. Rather, it was fundamentally reciprocal in nature, mutually confirmed on account of Vico's belief in the indivisibility of philosophy and philology. Philosophy apprehended truth by distinguishing metaphysical causes of phenomena in the human world; philology found *certum* by identifying empirical causes that determine what in fact occurs. 'Indeed we make bold to affirm', wrote Vico, 'he who mediates this Science makes it for himself by that proof "it had, has and will have to be" . . . this world of nations has certainly been made by man and its guise must therefore be found within the modifications of our own human mind.'[38]

These 'modifications' allowed the historian to convert historical evidence into historical fact and to explain the succession of historical phases by bringing to bear on the evidence the kinds of causes relevant to the task, not in the sense that they constituted *a priori* laws, but in the sense that they brought into communication the vehicles of expression constitutive of the historian's inner state and the facts that are themselves the product of the inner states of human beings living in the past. In the process of mutual confirmation, the philological proofs both confirmed their own authority by reason and at the same time confirmed reason by their own authority.

Half a century later, Herder was similarly animated by a distrust of the classifying sociological assumptions of the Paris establishment and its absolute criteria of progress and universal civilization. For Voltaire, Diderot, Helveticus, Holbach and Condorcet, the prototype for human flourishing was invariably sought in the one timeless universal standard – Athens, Rome, Florence, Paris. As the father of the *Volksgeist,* Herder argued that although cultures are comparable, they are not commensurable. Cultures come into existence by processes good in themselves and are of inestimable value to the societies they support. A principal doctrine of *Sturm und Drang,* the artistic movement of which he was one of the leaders along with Goethe, held that the truth of one's entire inner experience, of all one is, expressed itself in works of art, broadly conceived as encompassing virtually all of one's outward activities, as opposed to that which dissected life into its various parts and saw expressions in correspondingly atomistic, detached and specialized terms. Of central importance to the German historicist tradition that followed, Herder insisted that all expressions of human existence are valid because humans' lives differ. However, that no one life is the same did not imply that expressions were to be found on the level of the individual. Expression existed solely in communication, in 'voices speaking'; it was insensibly transmitted in the 'natural community', which at the same time was a 'collective individuality'.

Herder's hermeneutical or historical-philological theory of interpretation blended methodological empiricism with a quasi-empiricist approach to concept formation. Several lines before imploring the historian to 'feel yourself into everything', he grieved over 'the weakness of general characterizing' and queried whom one has painted when one paints a whole people, age and region of the earth. After all, he wrote, one 'draws them together into nothing but a general word in relation to which each person perhaps thinks and feels what he wants – imperfect means of depiction!, how one can be misunderstood!'[39]

Herder's methodological empiricism consisted in the idea that interpretation must never proceed by way of *a priori* concepts, but must always be guided by, and remain strictly faithful to, exact observations of linguistic evidence – the 'word', though still a generalized word abstracted from its individual reality.[40] His epoch-making break with the Enlightenment belief that thought and concepts are separate and prior to language established modern interpretation theory, linguistics and philosophy of language. By making language the necessary condition of thought (i.e. one cannot think without language), the language of historical subjects became the means by which the scope of their thought could be understood. Since concepts and meanings were seen to convey themselves in the usage of words, interpretation became a matter of studying this usage through a comprehensive examination of historical evidence. But empiricism alone could not overcome the generalization Herder abhorred in enlightened historical scholarship. The apprehension of distinctive individuality rested on his development of a quasi-empiricist theory of conceptualization according to which perceptual and affective sensation remained the source of all our concepts (standard empiricism), but according to which we formulate non-empirical concepts by means of a certain metaphorical extension from the empirically derived ones.

This was, in essence, the innovation that carried with it the methodological necessity of empathy, for understanding the words of those historians study required that they recapture their origin in sensation. Historical interpretation had to go beyond standard empiricism if it were going to produce understandings of past phenomena in individual terms. This meant that a large part of historical interpretation involved the intellectually demanding task of overcoming the radical difference that separated the studier from the studied by imaginatively reconstructing the perceptual and affective sensations embedded in the subject's language, an exercise inseparable from that of gaining a deep familiarity with the subject's historical, geographical and social context. Finally, this attention to word usage had to be supplemented by an attention to authorial psychology – the author's intentions in relation to the source being used as historical evidence, conveyed not explicitly in parts but distributed holistically as expressions of inner experience in the author's language and concepts. *Divination,* a term central to the development of nineteenth-century hermeneutics, for Herder was a process of hypothesis, its source the historical evidence, yet going beyond it, and thus susceptible to review in the light of further evidence.

In emphasizing concrete, historical experience and thereby establishing the conceptual grounds for historical studies, Herder went against the grain of his old friend and teacher, Immanuel Kant. Kant's promise for unique insights into the human condition and views inferred from Newtonian naturalism on absolute space and time, *a priori* knowledge, abstract reason and generalized experience were incompatible with history's promise for unique insights into how such concepts arise and develop, insights not into pure reason but human reason. In its reasoned and conjectural forms, history aspired to the conceptual comprehensiveness of philosophy, yet in its empirical and critical forms, it repudiated the ambitious systematicity and universalistic claims of formal philosophy.[41] Not until they encountered a mutual foe in positivism in the second half of the nineteenth century did some begin to view history and philosophy no longer as opposites, but as potential allies.

Notes

1. Peter Johnson, *Collingwood's* The Idea of History*: A Reader's Guide* (London: Bloomsbury, 2013), 14; Rex Martin, *Historical Explanation: Re-enactment and Practical Inference* (Ithaca: Cornell University Press, 1977), 53; Alun Munslow, *Deconstructing History,* 2nd edn (London: Routledge, 2006), 184, 195.

2. Louis O. Mink, *Mind, History, and Dialectic: The Philosophy of R.G. Collingwood* (Bloomington: Indiana University Press, 1969), 231, quoting from R.G. Collingwood, *The Principles of Art* (Oxford: Clarendon Press, 1938), 144.

3. William H. Dray, *History as Re-enactment: R.G. Collingwood's Idea of History* (Oxford: Clarendon Press, 1995), 137, 32.

4. A.R. Louch, *Explanation and Human Action* (Berkeley: University of California Press, 1969), 3, 201; G.H. von Wright, *Explanation and Understanding* (Ithaca: Cornell University Press, 1971), 6; Martin, *Historical Explanation,* 52.

5. Dray, *History as Re-enactment,* 137; Stein Helgeby, 'Collingwood and Croce', in Aviezer Tucker (ed.), *A Companion to the Philosophy of History and Historiography* (Chichester: Wiley-Blackwell, 2009), 503.

6. Johann Gottfried von Herder, 'This Too a Philosophy of History for the Formation of Humanity' (1774), in *Philosophical Writings*, ed. and trans. Michael N. Forster (Cambridge: Cambridge University Press, 2002), 292.

7. Paul Guyer, *A History of Modern Aesthetics: Volume 2: The Nineteenth Century* (Cambridge: Cambridge University Press, 2014), 378–437.

8. Robert Vischer, 'On the Optical Sense of Form: A Contribution to Aesthetics', in Robert Vischer et al., *Empathy, Form, and Space: Problems in German Aesthetics, 1873–1893*, trans. Harry Francis Mulgrave and Eleftherios Ikonomou (Santa Monica: Getty Center for the History of Art and the Humanities, 1993), 95.

9. A follower of Lipps particularly, Vernon Lee, the pseudonym of Violet Page, coined the term 'empathy' in her 1912 work with Clementina Anstruther-Thomson, *Beauty and Ugliness and Other Studies in Psychological Aesthetics* (London: John Lane).

10. Guyer, *History of Modern Aesthetics*, 397–98, quoting from Lipps' *Ästhetik* (1903).

11. Theodor Lipps, 'Empathy, Inward Imitation, and Sense Feelings' (1903), in E.F. Carritt (ed.), *Philosophies of Beauty: From Socrates to Robert Bridges, Being the Sources of Aesthetic Theory* (Oxford: Clarendon Press, 1931), 253. See also in the same volume Theodor Lipps, 'A Further Consideration of "Empathy"' (1905), 256–58.

12. Dan Zahavi, 'Empathy, Embodiment and Interpersonal Understanding: From Lipps to Schutz', *Inquiry: An Interdisciplinary Journal of Philosophy* 53, 3 (2010), 285–87.

13. Edith Stein, *On the Problem of Empathy* (1917), trans. Waltraut Stein (The Hague: Martinus Nijhoff, 1964), 19.

14. Husserl quoted in Rudolf A. Makkreel, 'How is Empathy Related to Understanding?', in Thomas Nenon and Lester Embree (eds), *Issues in Husserl's Ideas II* (Dordrecht: Kluwer Academic Publishers, 1996), 200.

15. Ibid., 2002.

16. Karsten R. Stueber, *Rediscovering Empathy: Agency, Folk Psychology, and the Human Sciences* (Cambridge, MA: MIT Press, 2006), 223; Marnie Hughes-Warrington, *How Good an Historian Shall I Be? R.G. Collingwood, the Historical Imagination and Education* (Exeter: Imprint Academic, 2003), 51.

17. Makkreel, 'How is Empathy Related to Understanding?', 206, 211; Rudolf A. Makkreel, 'From Simulation to Structural Transposition: A Diltheyan Critique of Empathy and Defense of *Verstehen*', in Hans Herbert Kögler and Karsten R. Stueber (eds), *Empathy and Agency: The Problem of Understanding in the Human Sciences* (Boulder: Westview Press, 2000), 182.

18. Makkreel, 'How is Empathy Related to Understanding?', 204; Makkreel, 'From Simulation to Structural Transposition', 183.

19. Wilhelm Dilthey, 'The Understanding of Other Persons and Their Manifestations of Life' (1910), trans. Rudolf A. Makkreel and William H. Oman, in Rudolf A. Makkreel and Frithjof Rodi (eds), *Selected Works, Volume III: The Formation of the Historical World in the Human Sciences* (Princeton: Princeton University Press, 2002), 229; Wilhelm Dilthey, 'The Rise of Hermeneutics' (1900), trans. Fredric R. Jameson and Rudolf A. Makkreel, in Rudolf A. Makkreel and Frithjof Rodi (eds), *Selected Works, Volume IV: Hermeneutics and the Study of History* (Princeton: Princeton University Press, 1996), 235–36.

20. Dilthey, 'Rise of Hermeneutics', 235, 258.

21. Ibid., 253.

22. Dilthey, 'Understanding of Other Persons', 234.

23. Ibid., 247.

24. Mark Bevir, 'In Defence of Historicism', *Journal of the Philosophy of History* 6, 1 (2012), 111; Frank Ankersmit, 'The Necessity of Historicism', *Journal of the Philosophy of History* 4, 2 (2010), 227–28.

25. Georg G. Iggers, 'Historicism: The History and Meaning of the Term', *Journal of the History of Ideas* 56, 1 (1995), 143, 145.

26. Karl R. Popper, *The Poverty of Historicism* (London: Routledge & Kegan Paul, 1957), 3.

27. Georg G. Iggers, *The German Conception of History: The National Tradition of Historical Thought from Herder to the Present*, rev. edn (Middletown: Wesleyan University Press, 1983), 296–97; Iggers, 'Historicism', 137; Bevir, 'In Defence of Historicism', 111–12.

28. This variation in the use of terms is on show in the two opening chapters of the nineteenth-century volume of *The Oxford History of Historical Writing* (Oxford: Oxford University Press, 2011). Stefan Berger, 'The Invention of European National Traditions in European Romanticism', begins by referring to historism, while immediately following this, Georg Iggers, 'The Intellectual Foundations of Nineteenth-Century "Scientific" History: The German Model', adheres to the more widespread historicism.

29. Iggers, *German Conception*, 7–8.

30. Ibid., 103–4.

31. Berger, 'Invention', 25.

32. Stephen Bann, *Romanticism and the Rise of History* (New York: Twayne Publishers, 1995); Jo Tollebeek, 'Seeing the Past with the Mind's Eye: The Consecration of the Romantic Historian', *Clio* 29, 2 (2000), 167–91.

33. Isaiah Berlin, *Vico and Herder: Two Studies in the History of Ideas* (London: Hogarth Press, 1976), xiv.

34. Isaiah Berlin, 'A Note on Vico's Concept of Knowledge', in Giorgio Tagliacozzo, Hayden V. White, Isaiah Berlin, Max H. Fisch and Elio Gianturco (eds), *Giambattista Vico: An International Symposium* (Baltimore: Johns Hopkins University Press, 1969), 375.

35. Patrick Gardiner, 'Interpretation in History: Collingwood and Historical Understanding', in Anthony O'Hear (ed.), Verstehen *and Humane Understanding* (Cambridge: Cambridge University Press, 1996), 109. See also in the same volume Roger Hausheer, 'Three Major Originators of the Concept of *Verstehen*: Vico, Herder, Schleiermacher', 47–72.

36. Benedetto Croce, *The Philosophy of Giambattista Vico*, trans. R.G. Collingwood (London: Howard Latimer, 1913); Collingwood, *Idea of History*, 71.

37. Giambattista Vico, *The First New Science* [*Scienza Nuova*, 1725], ed. and trans. Leon Pompa (Cambridge: Cambridge University Press, 2002), 66.

38. Quoted in Leon Pompa, *Vico: A Study of the 'New Science'*, 2nd edn (Cambridge: Cambridge University Press, 1990), 144–45.

39. Herder, 'This Too a Philosophy of History', 291.

40. Michael N. Forster (ed.), *Herder: Philosophical Writings* (Cambridge: Cambridge University Press, 2002), vii–xxxv.

41. Donald R. Kelly, *Fortunes of History: Historical Inquiry from Herder to Huizinga* (New Haven: Yale University Press, 2003), 7–9.

CHAPTER 5

Historicism, Neo-Kantianism and Hermeneutics

The reaction to universalism precipitated by Vico and Herder affirmed the autonomy of the historical world and formed the bedrock of the historicist's conception of the methods, standards and purposes of historical knowledge. For the historicists, everything that has happened in history was to be explained within history and by specifically historical methods. This principle excluded two alternatives. First, it excluded naturalism, the positivistic doctrine that historical actions are part of nature and that the sole means for explaining them are the methods of the natural sciences. Although history falls within nature, it is not reducible to it. Historicism thus stressed the fundamental context-dependency of social-historical phenomena. To find the identity of social-historical phenomena in the natural world was seen to *hypostasize* them, as if their identity were independent of the circumstances that affected them. Second, historicism excluded metaphysics from historical explanation, that is, explaining historical phenomena by reference to goals and processes outside of history, such as the ends of providence. This exclusion extended to metaphysical dualism: historicism considered the mental and the physical to be inseparable. In addition to these two negative dimensions, a third, positive dimension of historicism consisted in the claim that history is a science no less capable of attaining objective knowledge than its naturalistic counterparts.[1] While historicists dressed these principles in different clothing, what defined them as a group was their conviction that history suffered from a problem of legitimation whose resolution consisted in securing its independent scientific status.

Notes for this section begin on page 103.

Placing more recent historiographical developments in perspective, Donald Kelly has called this reaction to naturalism the 'linguistic turn' of the late eighteenth century.[2] Two scholarly movements of the Romantic period intersected and brought language to the centre of attention. One was what Edgar Quintet, Michelet's colleague and translator of Herder, referred to as the 'oriental renaissance' springing from the discovery of Sanskrit, which underlay the resurgence of classical philology in German universities and that Friedrich von Schlegel predicted would prove no less grand and no less extensive in its influence than the Italian Renaissance. The second movement was Romantic hermeneutics, that older tradition of the theory or science of textual interpretation that in the climate of the new age was reinvigorated by an unsatisfiable longing for completeness.

What distinguished Romantic hermeneutics from its theological and rationalist predecessors? Jean Grondin attributes the transition to the disjuncture created by the reception of Kant's *Critique of Pure Reason* (1781/1787) between phenomena and things in themselves.[3] Kant proposed that the *a priori* truths deduced from the principle of reason (*nihil est sine ratione*) organize and direct themselves in ways valid only for knowledge of the world of phenomena, that is, objects as they appear to us and are framed by us, while things in themselves dissolve into unintelligibility. While Kant celebrated the capabilities of pure reason, whose accomplishment was the constitution of nature and science, his critique left the legacy of reducing the status of pure reason. As Collingwood noted in relation to his 'rhetorical pessimism' and 'exaggerated gloom about the past' that human history is above all a spectacle of 'folly, ambition, greed, and wickedness', 'if history is the process in which man *becomes* rational, he cannot *be* rational at the beginning of it; therefore the force which serves as mainspring of the process cannot be human reason but must be the opposite of reason, that is, passion: intellectual ignorance and moral baseness'.[4]

After Kant, since a text appeared to us in the world of phenomena, attempting to understand became regarded as an approach to the world that involved a subjective interpretation or viewpoint, which meant that the method for understanding had to begin with the interpreting subject. Faced with objects of interpretation that were themselves the products of their creators' subjective processes, the break with the belief in a purely rational access to the world rendered these subjects increasingly speechless and spurred the need for a whole of spirit in terms of which individual utterances could be comprehended. Thus Friedrich Ast in 1808 expressed what later became known as the hermeneutic circle: the fundamental law of all understanding and knowing consisted in discovering the spirit of the whole in the individual while grasping the individual in terms of the whole. If in this process I and Thou could be brought into communication, nothing precluded the possibility of bridging the gap between past and present. By moving from word to meaning, from *Wort* to *Geist* and perhaps to *Zeitgeist* and *Volksgeist,* intertextual and paratextual interpretation supplied the means for sharing a common meaning over large expanses of time.

Ast's insights into the circularity of understanding were not enough to earn him the title of the father of modern hermeneutics. Since Dilthey, the first historian of hermeneutics, this honour has been reserved for Friedrich Daniel Schleiermacher, the theologian and translator of Plato whose immediate contribution to historicism came through his lectures at Berlin on the 'historical Jesus' and hermeneutics in the years 1809–32, and thereafter through the writings of his devoted student, Friedrich Lücke, and Dilthey's biographical compositions in the 1860s. Schleiermacher revolutionized hermeneutics by adding a second dimension to the traditional philologico-grammatical approach of treating texts as finished artefacts whose interpretation involved analysing the grammatical and syntactical structures in which the web of meanings connected to words was to be ascertained and clarified. In addition to this activity, the *Kunstlehre des Verstehens,* or methodology or art of understanding demanded the psychological-technical operation of penetrating the act of production that lay behind the specimen of speech or writing in front of us. 'Technical' referred to the need on the part of interpreters to understand the special art (*technē*) the author employed in constructing the text. 'Psychological' referred to the need to replace the syntactical view of language with one concentrated on what the words were really trying to say, for understanding the *verbum interius* of every utterance.

Rather than words and speech themselves, Schleiermacher took thought to be the productive element behind language that interpreters thus needed methods to penetrate. A century later, Gadamer could quite rightly claim that he laid the foundations of modern hermeneutics on the idea that to interpret a text is to understand it in some way better than the person who wrote it. Understanding consisted in the *reconstruction of original production*; 'in its changing interpretation', Gadamer wrote, 'the whole history of modern hermeneutics can be read'.[5]

Yet this divining a better understanding implied no need for transhistorical flights of imagination or empathy, nor did interpreters require entry into a quasi-Platonic realm of immutable meanings where they could contemplate face-to-face the author's timeless message.[6] Rather, the infinite task or interpretive ideal involved establishing anew the original meaning of the text and, with interpreters coming to the task with their own concepts, categories and capacity for understanding, reconstructing the original meaning while simultaneously enriching and extending it. They had to be able to reconstruct the text from the ground up, just as if they were its author; in so doing, they extended its original meaning.

Kelly suggests that Romantic hermeneutics supplied the epistemological foundation of Romantic historicism and linguistic studies.[7] Its basic premise was that understanding historical texts is mediated by a metaphysical unity connecting text to interpreter. But this would appear to contravene the principle that historicism excluded metaphysics from its theory of historical understanding and knowledge. If a metaphysical unity did indeed tie historical exegetes to the texts they studied, the historical individualities that Ranke and his followers sought to grasp could be apprehended individually only insofar as they were imbued with a spiritual conception of the whole.

Historicism rejected metaphysics not on the basis of a shared spiritual world enabling interpretation, but in protest at Hegel's *a priori* imposition of the meaning of history on a past yet to be discovered in the archive. Hegel arrived at the University of Berlin in 1818 and together with the philosophical school he led, which carried on the tradition of natural-law philosophy stretching back to G.W. Leibniz and Christian Wolff, supplied the philosophy of historical metaphysics against which the historicists directed their energies. Hegel argued that the subject matter of philosophy, the objects into which it inquires, is timeless. Yet its diverse history had shown that as a purely rational enterprise, its many attempts to come to know the true nature of its objects had failed. Any separate part of the truth, any claim or assertion taken on its own, was incomplete, yet no part could be considered unnecessary. The rational and the historical need not deny each other of their truth claims. Rather, they could complement each other in the pursuit of truth, synchronically, in the exposition of philosophy as it is now known to be, and, diachronically, the history of philosophy revealed the structure truth will have when the historical process by which it comes to be has been completed. According to Hegel, in each stage of development, the history of philosophy finds society held together by a single principle, one that expresses itself in all aspects of culture – *Geist,* that collective mind in which all individuals participate, whether conscious of it or not. A consequence of this position held a status whose influence on idealist philosophy of history cannot be understated. This is the idea that philosophy is built upon *unacknowledged presuppositions* that are to be understood historically. At every moment in time, certain tacitly accepted conceptions of the nature of mind, world, human agency and so on lie behind and condition the explicit arguments made by philosophers. Philosophy is the historical study of the connections between the two.[8]

The historical school shared in this conviction that behind all phenomena exists a metaphysical reality and that historical study involves apprehending it. The key difference was that for the historicists, the source for apprehending this reality was the individual concrete realities of lived experience in the past. Hegel's panlogistic conception of the universe laid down a set of presuppositions about the constitution of historical development that for them transcended the limits of experience definitive of a proper science. The vitality and complexity of individual human experience exhibited too much room for spontaneity and uniqueness than could be expressed through the strictures of teleological explanation.[9] Hegel wanted the historical philosopher to achieve a conceptual grasp of the whole, a systematic knowledge of how spirit realizes itself in the different epochs of world history. The aim of the Rankean historian, by contrast, was fundamentally intuitive and on a separate plane from intellectual discourse. The historian's ultimate end was not to know the whole of world history, but to intuit the particular, to feel the individual in its unbounded depth.[10]

This variety of historical reflection could be empirical without being empiricist. It was empirical because the school raised its methodological charter in protest at Hegel's *a priori* construction of the meaning of history, but it was not empiricist because it knew full well that historical knowledge was not simply a matter of taking a good look at the evidence; on the contrary, it demanded some process for moving beyond bare facts and linguistic literalness.

If, then, a 'theory' of history is one applied from without in order to structure and illuminate historical material, the historicists were without doubt nontheoretical. The historicists opposed Hegel for the simple reason that the individual essence of past particulars could never be apprehended by the historian who colligates them to construct a historical narrative if they are overlain by a predetermined theoretical system that is foreign to them. But although they rebelled against Hegel with his historical philosophy explicitly in mind, they carried with them implicitly the substratum of idealist philosophy of history. For Ranke, the notion that the historian apprehends the essence of the universal dwelling in every particular presupposed the existence of a supervening and unchallenged religious whole. 'It is not necessary for us to prove at length that the eternal dwells in the individual', he proclaimed. 'This is the religious foundation on which our efforts rest.'[11]

Indeed, the idealist philosophy of history that underpinned the rise of history as a distinct discipline and form of knowledge gave the impression that history was free from theory. Wilhelm von Humboldt's classic formulation of the theory of idealist historicism rooted its object of apprehension in events themselves and not in the world at large. In his 1821 address to the Prussian Academy of Sciences, 'On the Historian's Task', he set out to convince his audience they should allow the ideas that are the object of their researches to emerge from events themselves because philosophy, that is, Hegel, had come to impose a goal or teleology on events. As the first theorist of the *Ideenlehre* or doctrine of ideas, Humboldt placed the character and meaning of past phenomena in the ideas that act themselves out in the human world of action and experience. And since 'no event is separated completely from the general nexus of things', an understanding of individual events could now be said to furnish general knowledge, once the sole ken of philosophy. As for how historians achieve this understanding, he believed that there existed 'an original, antecedent congruity' between them and their object of inquiry.[12] His theory of *Verstehen* was neither a projection of the subject nor a borrowing from the object; it was both simultaneously. But unlike the subject-object unification to be posited in psychological aesthetics decades later, Humboldt's historical method recognized that an understanding of the specific presupposed a knowledge of the pre-existent idea relevant to the inquiry, determined through exact and critical examination of the events, under which the specific could be comprehended.

This is the historical basis of the claim advanced earlier that the concept of colligation, which as a generalizing mechanism spawns the need for the reconstruction of individual experience, belongs to the idealist conception of history. As Humboldt put it, 'through a study of the creative forces of world history, the historian conceives for himself a general picture of the form of the connection of all events, and it is within this realm that the ideas discussed above are contained. They are not being projected into history, but are the essence of history itself'.[13] In the manner of Ast's spirit and Ranke's God, Humboldt's ideas underpinned the idealist belief that the illumination of the part revealed the whole residing in it.

Adhering to this methodological charter, Ranke could champion the application of critical methods to historical research on the conviction that in each empirical fact uncovered in the archive is the appearance of the infinite. Considered outside its context in idealist philosophy of history, it is easy to see how this view has led many to think that he was a philosophical *naïf* unconcerned with the theory of his craft and the intellectual ancestor of positivistic historiography.[14]

Much of this confusion has stemmed from the difficulty of translating his famous dictum 'wie es eigentlich gewesen'. The key word in this phrase, *eigentlich,* usually translated as 'actually', for Ranke in the nineteenth century meant 'characteristic' or 'essential'.[15] 'The past as it *essentially* occurred', rather than orienting historians simply towards a crude facticity, encouraged them to navigate a course between what was essential and what was factual. Since the essential was regarded as dwelling within the fact, in practice this philosophical idealism exhibited itself in the many anecdotes Ranke included in his writings. In his *History of the Popes* (1834), for example, the repeated allusions to the 'idea' of the papacy served not to influence the interpretation of the factual account, but to reveal the entire idea of the event being recounted in the one episodic description.[16] In Germany, the source for a critique of the Rankean tradition never presented itself in the image of the unreflective historian labouring under the illusion that the accumulation of facts equates with the establishment of historical truth. The actual philosophy underlying the idealist account of the historical process presented the critic with a more pressing item of investigation.

'What we need is a Kant', exclaimed Johann Gustav Droysen, a colleague and rival of Ranke, by which he meant that the scientific domain of history needed to be epistemologically justified, defined and organized.[17] Droysen's call for a *Historik* was a statement of personal ambition that over the course of a series of lectures on the methodology of history from the late 1850s to the early 1880s brought the historicist tradition directly into contact with the hermeneutical tradition that had developed and diffused alongside it. His education in philology at the University of Berlin in the 1820s certainly lent itself to the development of a composite approach. These were the years Ranke lectured on world history, Humboldt delivered his address on the historian's task, Hegel expounded his philosophy of history and Böckh, following his teacher Schleiermacher, set forth the methods of philological hermeneutics. From Böckh, whose chief interest was the interpretation and reconstruction of ancient texts, Droysen learnt the basis of the hermeneutic tradition and applied it to history: the concept of understanding, the hermeneutic circle and the varieties of criticism and interpretation.[18] What Böckh did for philology, Droysen set out to do for history.

Droysen unified history and hermeneutics by arguing that human actions – those expressions of human individuality so central to the historicist tradition – were to be understood as though they were texts in need of interpretation, and so the method for understanding texts became the method for understanding human action itself. Droysen rejected Ranke's view that with impartiality and neutrality, the whole picture of a person appears to the historian who thereby weaves a narrative of the past as it really was. Droysen shifted attention to the subjective factors taken for granted by idealist historicism. 'Objectively, phenomena do not separate themselves according to space and time', he declared, 'it is our apprehension that thus distinguishes them.'[19] No facts exist independently of the historian's understanding of them. All understanding is partial and perspectival, shaped by historians' interests, methods and goals, and by the culture in which they live. Rather than attempting to overcome their own place in time and space, Droysen urged historians to write from their moral and political standpoints. As a leading figure of the Prussian school of historiography calling for Prussian hegemony in matters of state, this was no mere surrender to epistemological finitude, but was part of a larger attempt to eliminate the distinction between scholarship and partisanship for political ends.[20]

Through the hermeneutical operation Droysen hoped to transcend the fragmentary literalness of written sources and to restore to history a cognizable ethical purposiveness he found lacking in the Rankean historical vision. For Ranke, the relation between whole and part was mutually confirmed in the affirmation of their sharing a common essence; for Droysen, the whole-part dialectic was a progressive continuum that determined the context of facts and arbitrated the attribution of their historical significance in a theoretically justifiable interpretation of the facts of events.[21] 'All empirical investigation governs itself according to the data to which it is directed', he wrote, 'and it can only direct itself to such data as are immediately present and susceptible of being cognized through the senses.'[22] To see the truth of the 'moral forces' actualized in the actions investigated by historians is to understand them as words being spoken to us, which we translate into our own terms. 'The possibility of this understanding arises from the kinship of our nature with that of the utterances lying before us in the historical material.'[23] The historian became the totality of an 'I' who 'fills out' the individual utterance of a historical agent whose own totality feeds back into the understanding of the individual utterance.[24] Droysen's hermeneutic circle was a cumulative network of reciprocal dependence, not to be executed by any conceptual set of procedures, but rather learnt in the course of a self-correcting process whereby preconceptual insights accumulate to complement, qualify and correct one another.

Droysen's appeal for a Kant did not see him use the conceptual apparatus of Kantian philosophy in developing his historical hermeneutics. Yet from the 1860s until the demise of historicism in the 1920s, the movement to establish the epistemological basis of history took place within the context of the programme set by the revival of Kantian philosophy in German universities, whose exponents, like the historicists, disapproved of Hegel's absolute idealism for its system-building, metaphysics and *a priori* constructions, and who like the historicists struggled against positivism to assert the autonomy of their discipline by securing its scientific status.[25] Otto Liebmann's exhortation 'we need to go back to Kant', though its exact significance in the history of philosophy is debated, contained the clear meaning to those who made it their motto that there was a need to reconcile the two philosophical traditions of materialism and idealism.

The physiological and mechanistic theories of the materialists were seen to endanger morality, religion and the Prussian regime. Many considered themselves free thinkers, champions of political liberty, and believed in the independence of the soul. Conversely, the idealism of the Romantic era had thought organically and in historic-individualizing terms, preventing philosophy from acquiring a scientific status by privileging the singular, contingent and inimitable over the universally valid.[26] Kant's purpose in attempting to reconcile empiricism and transcendentalism had been to discover within consciousness the foundations that make science possible. With the alliance of historicism and neo-Kantianism, the provision of a secure foundation for history offered the possibility of a critical philosophy capable of rescuing philosophy from obsolescence by reconceiving it as a second-order science charged with investigating the logic of the first-order sciences.

Unsurprisingly, then, the first expositor of neo-Kantian philosophy of history was a historian of philosophy, Wilhelm Windelband, the founder of the Southwest or Baden school of neo-Kantianism and *Doktorvater* of Heinrich Rickert, who together influenced the methodological thought of historians and social scientists at the turn of the twentieth century, including Max Weber and Georg Simmel. Windelband understood that in spite of their mutual aspirations for disciplinary and methodological autonomy, the marriage of historicism and neo-Kantianism was a highly combustible union. As described earlier, historicism emerged as a reaction against the universalistic claims of Enlightenment thought: the principle of individuality entailed a philosophy of value holding that all values are specific to, and only valid for, their particular age and culture. The reconstructive imagination, empathy, intuition and understanding were methodologically central for the historicists because the construction of a national identity capable of supporting nationhood required the historically located features unique to the German people to be rendered perceptible to the historian who wrote history in the service of this political objective. At the opposite pole, the neo-Kantians, true to their Enlightenment heritage, strove to uphold the authority of reason, which they maintained was the source of the universal and necessary principles underpinning human institutions and practices. To historicize reason was to relativize reason and the fundamental principles arrived at through its exercise.

Windelband approached this problem by stressing that while it is an axiom of philosophy that the validity of a proposition is ahistorical, knowledge of the principles of reason come only through historical investigation. Kant had dismissed historical knowledge as contingent, arbitrary and inconsequential because, in his time, before Niebuhr and Ranke, it was still the province of *belles lettres*; a century later, the critical methods of the professional historian could supply the empirical material from which philosophers extract the normative content upon which they base their attempts to formulate universal propositions. Windelband could thus claim to have secured the normative dimension of philosophical thinking against the hypostasis of the ahistorical approach, which placed norms in a transcendental realm existing beyond the phenomenal realm of history, and the historical dimension of thinking against the relativism of judging norms as internal to specific contexts, and hence against the growing loss of faith in ultimate values. Historicism succumbed to relativism, he argued, when the normative is conflated with the factual, when causal and genetic questions about the origins of knowledge are conflated with questions about its logic and truth value. What more recent philosophers of history refer to as the 'genetic fallacy' holds that simply because a value or norm arose under certain circumstances does not mean that it is valid solely under them.[27] Although the famous speech in which he distinguished between the 'nomothetic' natural sciences and 'idiographic' historical sciences contained little that had not been reflected upon at least since Vico's *verum factum* principle and theory of 'inside' and 'outside' knowledge, it produced a shift in historical thought by ascribing value to these two different cognitive interests: in the nomothetic domain, value was ascribed to knowledge of the general properties of reality; in the idiographic domain, value was ascribed to knowledge of its concrete and unique properties.[28]

A more systematic exponent of Kant's transcendental philosophy, Rickert argued that while Windelband succeeded in making values the object of which idiographic inquiry forms a complete picture, he failed to account for the conceptual preconditions that make possible knowledge of the object as distinct to historiography. Kant had defined transcendental philosophy as the study of 'our manner of cognition of objects insofar as this is to be possible a priori', and the neo-Kantians' renewed concern with the epistemological preconditions for knowledge was central to their self-understanding as transcendental philosophers.[29] Robert D'Amico has categorized Rickert's 'historiographical concepts' as the first species of historicism concerned with identifying the concept of the object that makes objective historical knowledge possible.[30] Just as forms of intuition of space, time and causality offered the world perceptible to natural science, Rickert argued against Mill's common methodology of the natural and human sciences that the individualizing method of what he termed the 'cultural sciences' (*Kulturwissenschaft*) fixed the historian's attention not on the universal laws of nature to explain causal relations, but on the values that subsisted in such conjunctions of human activity.[31]

This argument that the object of knowledge is a norm contained two steps. The first of these was the identification of cognition with true judgement. Ranke's historicism and Comte's positivism were infected with the pre-Kantian epistemology that conceived of truth as the correspondence of a representation with a thing in itself. Against this view that cognition involves merely having representations, Rickert emphasized that cognition involves affirming or denying the truth of representations. The Rankean doctrine that the historian's impartiality and neutrality give history its scientific status was a falsehood propagated under the illusion that judgement can be suspended because it is somehow separate from cognition. Second, since for Rickert there was no escaping questions of value and truth, the activities of affirming and denying, like all activities, were to be governed by norms and rules that set the standard by which our representations are judged.

What was to be the source of such rules? The object of knowledge itself. Truth is when our actual judgements conform to the standard set by the object of our investigation. Arnold Brecht has called this standard the 'transcendental Ought' integral to the rise of 'scientific value relativism' in the early twentieth century.[32] Max Weber, Rickert's friend and one-time colleague, thought that the immense diversity of human norms could be organized as heuristic 'ideal types' that bring order to such diversity and guide the social scientist provisionally in the scientific study of social reality. But while Weber believed that the presentation of the operative effect of cultural values through these classifications and typologies made possible an objective social science, he did not share Rickert's faith in there being any such possibility of an objective cognition of social reality, for he regarded all scientific analysis as perspectival.

Rickert's attempt to provide history with an epistemological foundation came at the expense of following the lead of Schleiermacher, Droysen and Dilthey in dealing with questions of meaning, significance and the logic of interpretation. Of course, Kantian philosophy was not incompatible with hermeneutics. After all, it was Kant's separation of phenomena and things in themselves that stimulated the Romantic hermeneutic break with rationalism by assigning subjectivity a new, constitutive role in cognitive processes. In the late nineteenth century, the subjectivizing tendencies of Kantian critique intersected with the emergence of historicism, which confronted hermeneutics with the problem of theorizing the objectivity of the human sciences.

Yet in other ways, the neo-Kantian preoccupation with epistemology and verifiability obstructed hermeneutics from making a worthwhile contribution to this project. Dilthey's hermeneutic turn occurred only after his Hegelian turn and discovery of the importance of absolute spirit in opening the possibility of understanding sociohistorical reality. Dilthey had in fact begun his career concerned almost exclusively with hermeneutics, having won in 1860 the Schleiermacher Foundation prize for his essay 'The Hermeneutic System of Schleiermacher in Comparison with Earlier Protestant Hermeneutics', completed a Latin dissertation on Schleiermacher's ethics in 1864, and published the first volume of his Schleiermacher biography in 1867. Nevertheless, the revitalization of Kant's attempt to develop a system of reason created the conditions for a refurbishment of Hegel's philosophy.[33] Windelband proclaimed this 'revival of Hegelianism' in a speech in 1910, its core thesis being that Kant's critique of reason needed a historical basis and that the copious development in the study of 'rational values' needed a 'spiritual basis of life' and 'total meaning of reality'; in short, it needed what Dilthey called a *Weltanschauungen*, or worldview.

Dilthey had been the forerunner in combining Kantian and Hegelian philosophy, captured in the alternative title, 'Critique of Historical Reason', to his most renowned work, *Introduction to the Human Sciences* (1883). For him, the problem with Hegel's philosophy consisted in the contradiction between the historical consciousness of the relativity of all historical reality and the metaphysical conclusion of an absolute system. How could this claim be maintained, he asked, in the midst of the diverse system of worlds, the multiplicity of forms of development that take place upon them, the limitless future hidden in the womb of this universe, incessantly marching forward to new structures?

Dilthey's response was to historicize Hegel's metaphysics. Hegel's world, dominated by spirit, became sociohistorical reality, in itself neither rational nor irrational, but in some way significant. But this significance was no longer based upon the world itself; it became a product of our attitude towards the world and our understanding of it. We do not import meaning into life from the world; on the contrary, we open ourselves to the possibility that meaning and significance come into being only in human life and its history. The 'great objective forces' of human history – the objective spirit of Hegelian philosophy – became the substance to which individuals must cling if they are to understand human life on the basis of themselves. Dilthey was the only productive refurbisher of Hegelian philosophy, precisely because he gave in to it.[34]

Dilthey's turn to Hegel represented a shift in his thought from epistemology to metaphysics. The earlier Dilthey of the critique of historical reason belonged to the forty-year period of his life during which he abandoned hermeneutics and devoted himself fully to explicating his conception of descriptive psychology, which he hoped would provide the historical school's evaluation of phenomena with a philosophical foundation for their explanation. 'Lacking a healthy relationship to epistemology and psychology', he began the critique, 'this school has not attained an explanatory method.'[35] Although he was a more complex adherent than Windelband and Rickert of neo-Kantianism – an epistemological movement par excellence – he maintained that the core problem of philosophy concerned the possibility of knowledge and its solution consisted in limiting knowledge to experience. Before his Hegelian turn, injecting blood into the veins of the anaemic rationalist subject required a phenomenological method grounded in an awareness of the different varieties of human experience and whose purpose was to provide a historical description of human beings' past efforts to acquire knowledge. The lived 'inner' cognition of the connected elements of a functional unity or whole comprised the unique content of the human sciences that descriptive psychology directed itself to apprehending.

Given his early mastery of Schleiermacher's techniques, it is unclear why Dilthey left himself so vulnerable to the charge of psychologism – the view that all phenomena can be explained by reference to psychological processes – by not rooting this conception in the language of the hermeneutic circle, which may have forced him to consider more systematically the nature of the relation between the historian, part and whole in historical thinking. Through the key principle of 'phenomenality', he laid claim to the idea that all objects, including persons, exist for a subject as 'facts of consciousness' and that, consequently, all evidence for the existence of the external world, including the evidence for explaining human actions in the past, derives only from perceptions and their existence within the subject. Lacking a conception of what binds human beings in the reciprocations of language and life, he postulated a kind of identity in mental life between subject and object, knower and known, similar in principle to the correspondence empathy theories being put forward contemporaneously in psychological aesthetics.

Several decades later, on the other side of the English Channel, Collingwood, looking back admiringly on Dilthey's contribution to historical thought, did not use the term 'empathy' to describe this attempt to have the object of historical understanding live in the historian who at once lives in the object. However, he believed that the turn to psychology to shore up history's epistemological and methodological legitimacy was a turn *away from the past* as the provider of such a support. Although Collingwood considered the past to be 'incapsulated' in the present, through his doctrine of 're-enactment', he attempted to show how in being re-thought by historians in the present, the past comes to be viewed as something distinct from their own experience and the world in which its traces remain. Historical knowledge is so valuable to human civilization precisely because it is knowledge that the present cannot provide.

Notes

1. Frederick Beiser, 'Historicism', in Brian Leiter and Michael Rosen (eds), *The Oxford Handbook of Continental Philosophy* (Oxford: Oxford University Press, 2007), 157–59.

2. Donald R. Kelly, 'Mythhistory in the Age of Ranke', in Georg G. Iggers and James M. Powell (eds), *Leopold von Ranke and the Shaping of the History Discipline* (Syracuse: Syracuse University Press, 1990), 7–8.

3. Jean Grondin, *Introduction to Philosophical Hermeneutics*, trans. Joel Weinsheimer (New Haven: Yale University Press, 1994), 64.

4. R.G. Collingwood, *The Idea of History*, rev. edn [1946] Jan van der Dussen (Oxford: Oxford University Press, 1994), 101–2.

5. Hans-Georg Gadamer, *Truth and Method*, 2nd rev. edn, trans. Joel Weinsheimer and Donald G. Marshall (New York: Continuum, 2004), 191.

6. Roger Hausheer, 'Three Major Originators of the Concept of *Verstehen*: Vico, Herder, Schleiermacher', in Anthony O'Hear (ed.), *Verstehen and Humane Understanding* (Cambridge: Cambridge University Press, 1996), 69.

7. Kelly, 'Mythhistory', 9.

8. Michael Rosen, 'The History of Philosophy as Philosophy', in Leiter and Rosen (eds), *Continental Philosophy,* 125–26.

9. In this respect, Hegel and Marx were not historicists, as is often believed. Although they wanted history to be a science and were opposed to naturalism, they went against historicism by putting their metaphysical systems before concrete individual experience. Ranke addressed Hegel directly in two essays: 'The Pitfalls of a Philosophy of History' (1840s) and 'On Progress in History' (1854), in Leopold von Ranke, *The Theory and Practice of History,* eds Georg G. Iggers and Konrad von Moltke (Indianapolis: Bobbs-Merrill Company, 1973), 47–56.

10. Frederick C. Beiser, *The German Historicist Tradition* (Oxford: Oxford University Press, 2011), 265. Although the anti-Hegelian sentiment of Ranke and the historical school played a crucial role in their forging their own identity, it is important to note that Ranke's arguments against Hegel were in many ways misconceived. Hegel too believed that the philosopher should derive the universal from the particular rather than attempt to deduce the particular from the universal. He also thought that philosophers should examine their subject matter for its own sake and according to its own internal standards. Nevertheless, Hegel often violated his own principles in practice by setting up conceptual divisions before considering his subject matter, which was the core of Ranke's argument against the philosophical school.

11. Leopold von Ranke, 'On the Character of Historical Science' (1830s), in Iggers and von Moltke (eds), *Theory and Practice,* 38.

12. Wilhelm von Humboldt, 'On the Historian's Task' (1821), *History and Theory* 6, 1 (1967), 65, 71.

13. Ibid., 65.

14. Georg G. Iggers, 'The Image of Ranke in American and German Historical Thought', *History and Theory* 2, 1 (1962), 17–40.

15. Iggers and von Moltke (eds), introduction to *Theory and Practice,* xix.

16. Ibid., lx–lxi.

17. Droysen (1843) quoted in Beiser, *Historicist Tradition,* 289.

18. Ibid., 294–95.

19. Johann Gustav Droysen, *Outline of the Principles of History* (1867), trans. E. Benjamin Andrews (Boston: Ginn and Company, 1893), §1.

20. Robert Southard, *Droysen and the Prussian School of History* (Lexington: University Press of Kentucky, 1995).

21. Michael J. Maclean, 'Johann Gustav Droysen and the Development of Historical Hermeneutics', *History and Theory* 21, 3 (1982), 356.

22. Droysen, *Principles of History,* §5.

23. Ibid., §9.

24. Ibid., §10.

25. Beiser, *Historicist Tradition,* 365–75.

26. Klaus Christian Köhnke, *The Rise of Neo-Kantianism: German Academic Philosophy between Idealism and Positivism,* trans. R.J. Hollingdale (Cambridge: Cambridge University Press, 1991), 138; Thomas E. Willey, *Back to Kant: The Revival of Kantianism in German Social and Historical Thought 1860–1914* (Detroit: Wayne State University Press, 1978), 26.

27. Beiser, *Historicist Tradition,* 366–87.

28. Wilhelm Windelband and Guy Oakes, 'History and Natural Science', *History and Theory* 19, 2 (1980), 165–68, introduces a reprint of Windelband's speech, 'Rectorial Address, Strasbourg, 1894', 169–85.

29. Immanuel Kant, *Critique of Pure Reason* (1781/1787), eds and trans. Paul Guyer and Allen W. Wood (Cambridge: Cambridge University Press, 1998), B5.

30. Robert D'Amico, 'Historicism', in Aviezer Tucker (ed.), *A Companion to the Philosophy of History and Historiography* (Chichester: Wiley-Blackwell, 2009), 245.

31. Heinrich Rickert, *The Limits of Concept Formation in Natural Science: A Logical Introduction to the Historical Sciences* (1902), ed. and trans. Guy Oakes (Cambridge: Cambridge University Press, 1986).

32. Arnold Brecht, *Political Theory: The Foundations of Twentieth-Century Political Thought* (Princeton: Princeton University Press, 1959), 209–10.

33. Karl Löwith, *From Hegel to Nietzsche: The Revolution in Nineteenth-Century Thought*, trans. David E. Green (New York: Holt, Rinehart and Winston, 1964), 121–25.

34. Ibid., 124.

35. Wilhelm Dilthey, preface to *Introduction to the Human Sciences*, volume I of his *Selected Works*, eds Rudolf A. Makkreel and Frithjof Rodi (Princeton: Princeton University Press, 1989), 48.

CHAPTER 6

Collingwood and the Continent

Intellectually isolated at the University of Oxford, Robin George Collingwood liked his intellectual influences to come from a different time and place.[1] 'Multilingual, polymathic, hydratalented and omniskilled', writes the philosopher of mind, Colin McGinn, 'he did not want to be tied down to one way of looking at things. In particular, he did not want to be confined to the present: historical knowledge had to be integral to philosophy, as it was for Hegel.'[2]

In spite of his reluctance, 'in accordance with a method of writing which I inherit from a long line of English philosophers', to credit his influences directly, it is well established that the Italian representatives of Hegel made the deepest impression on his thought.[3] 'Collingwood wanted allies of a kind not forthcoming in England', as James Connelly remarks. 'He wanted to create a philosophy which took the claims of history as a form of human experience seriously . . . he approved of the Italians because they approved of history (and practised history) and he took from them what he recognized as valuable in explaining his own experiences as a historian.'[4]

Unlike in Germany, where the questions contained in Hegelian philosophy had become increasingly obscure as the nineteenth century wore on, and where a deliberate refurbishment of it was needed to provide neo-Kantian philosophy with a historical basis, Hegel's thought had survived the nineteenth century relatively intact in Italy. In 1907, three years before Windelband announced the revival of Hegelianism in its native land, Benedetto Croce had declared the theory of the 'objective spirit' – the same theory that had sustained Dilthey's hermeneutic conversion – the 'living' portion of Hegelian philosophy, to the extent that its systematic absolute claim could be reduced to a historical claim.

Notes for this section begin on page 118.

This living portion of Hegel had a profound effect on the direction of Italian *storicismo* developed by Croce. Whereas German historicism emerged in direct opposition to Hegelian philosophy and Enlightenment universalism, the Italian variety attached itself to Hegel's all-embracing system. What Croce eventually termed 'absolute historicism' in 1939 described the process whereby the human world grows out of itself. History is all there is: the ultimate reality, the grounding for faith, the object of knowledge. History is not, as the German historical school maintained against Hegel's philosophical school, a reality consisting of a series of historically differentiated and incommensurable individualities.[5]

Collingwood wrote to Croce in 1928 that he had learnt from him 'to regard philosophy as primarily the methodology of history'.[6] For Croce, this consisted in the mutual implication of individual or historical judgement and universal or philosophical judgement, 'a judgement whose subject is the individual while its predicate is the universal', in Collingwood's words.[7] Against the German view – found in Rickert's neo-Kantianism, for example – that reality consists of bare particulars to which the mind adds an element of the universal, Croce sought to illuminate the historical particular as 'nothing but the incarnation of the universal'. Collingwood's survey of the history of historical thought in *The Idea of History* culminated on this point:

> History is thus no longer conceived as mere intuition of the individual; it does not simply apprehend the individual . . . it judges the individual, and hence the universality, the a priori character, which belongs indefeasibly to all thought, is present in history in the form of the predicate of the historical judgement. What makes the historian a thinker is the fact that he thinks out the meanings of these predicates, and finds these meanings embodied in the individuals he contemplates. But this thinking-out of the meaning of a concept is philosophy; hence philosophy is an integral part of historical thinking itself; the individual judgement of history is a judgement only because it contains in itself, as one of its elements, philosophical thinking.[8]

Philosophy is history because the universal inheres in the individual; history is philosophy because this universal is true only as realized in the individual. Philosophy is the 'methodological moment' during which predicate-concepts are thought out of the historical evidence in which they are contained. As a result:

> All history is contemporary history: not in the ordinary sense of the word . . . but in the strict sense: the consciousness of one's own activity as one actually performs it. History is thus the self-knowledge of the living mind. For even when the events which the historian studies are events that happened in a distant past, the condition of their being historically known is that they should 'vibrate in the historian's mind', that is to say, that the evidence for them should be here and now before him and intelligible to him. For history is not contained in books or documents; it lives only, as a present interest and pursuit, in the

mind of the historian when he criticizes and interprets those documents, and by so doing relives for himself the states of mind into which he inquires.[9]

Early on in his career, around 1920, these Crocean influences expressed themselves in Collingwood's first principle of the philosophy of history: 'the past which an historian studies is not a dead past, but a past which in some sense is still living in the present'. This was the idea, he explained in his *Autobiography*, that history is not concerned with 'events', but with 'processes': 'things which do not begin and end but turn into one another . . . if a process P_1 turns into a process P_2, there is no dividing line at which P_1 stops and P_2 begins; P_1 never stops, it goes on in the changed form P_2, and P_2 never begins, it has previously been going on in the form P_1'.[10]

In an essay for his friend Guido de Ruggiero, Collingwood pitted this idea against the realist supposition that subject and object are things standing simultaneously apart as separate items, yet brought into mutual relation in the act of knowing.[11] Reality is not something that *is* but *happens*, Collingwood maintained in this essay 'Libellus de Generatione'; 'the reality of mind is the process of its experience, its life and nothing else'. Realism, with its conception of reality as static, could not account for *becoming* and so could not account for the possibility of historical knowledge. Within this idea of becoming:

> Identity . . . means that the past phase of the process is preserved in the present phase . . . The present affirms the past. Difference means that the past moment is transcended, is superseded, is no longer in existence; the present negates the past. The categories of identity and difference are thus, as interpreted in the world of becoming, the categories of affirmation and negation, positivity and negativity . . . The past is entirely misunderstood if it is regarded either as pure negativity, that is as having been left utterly behind and in no sense preserved, or as pure positivity, that is as surviving entirely unchanged in the present.[12]

Collingwood was 'against false divisions', as Simon Blackburn remarks. The 'past lives in the present and there is no understanding of either on its own, any more than there is understanding myself as opposed to others, or others as opposed to myself', this last part being a principle central to Blackburn's own concept of self.[13] In *Speculum Mentis,* Collingwood's only book of the 1920s, he sought to provide a taxonomy of knowledge in the unity of experience between art, religion, science, history and philosophy: 'The parts of a whole exist in mutual support, and the aspects of an objective reality become more comprehensible when seen in their interrelations.' 'History', furthermore, 'is the knowledge of an infinite whole whose parts, repeating the plan of the whole in their structure, are only known by reference to their context.'[14]

This theory of processes developed into the last of three propositions devised during a trip to Die, in southern France, in 1928: (1) all history is the history of thought; (2) historical knowledge is the re-enactment in the historian's mind of the thought whose history he is studying; and (3) historical knowledge is the re-enactment of a past thought incapsulated in a context of present thoughts that, by contradicting it, confine it to a plane different from theirs.[15]

Propositions (1) and (2) indicate the close relation between history *a parte objecti*, historical fact, and history *a parte subjecti*, historical thought.[16] What Collingwood began to call 'incapsulation' in the third proposition had caused him the greatest difficulty in his studies of historical method. He knew that a past thought, as a past agent thought it and as the historian re-thinks it, was certainly one and the same thought; the historian must re-think it as it once was if it is to qualify as *historical* knowledge. Yet he understood at the same time that they were two separate, numerically distinct thoughts, and so they could not match each other perfectly in content. Collingwood had not resolved the problem of identity and difference between a past thought and the re-enactment of that thought incapsulated in the present.

The solution, Collingwood came to realize, lay in the *context*. There is a conceptual identity between the two thoughts, just as it is possible to hear the same symphony twice, dine in the same restaurant twice or know the same binomial theorem invented by Newton. 'The past event, ideal though it is, must be actual in the historian's re-enactment of it. In this sense, and in this sense only', he explained in the Die manuscript, 'the ideality of the object of history [its quality of being an object of thought without being present to actual perception] is compatible with actuality and indeed inseparable from actuality.'[17] But in the process of acquiring this actuality – that is, in its being re-thought by the historian in a fresh context – the thought undergoes a change disqualifying it from being regarded as a copy of the one thought in the past. 'We understand what Newton thought by thinking – not copies of his thought – a silly and meaningless phrase – but his thoughts themselves over again.' The present-day life in which historical thinking takes place always gives the past thought 'a new quality, the quality of being one element within a whole of thought that goes beyond it, instead of being a whole of thought outside of which there is nothing'. The historian 'must enter into it [a past frame of mind], reconstitute it with his own mind, and at the same time objectify this very reconstitution, so as to prevent it from mastering his own mind and running away with him'.[18] By seeing this contrast between the re-thought thoughts of the past and our thoughts in the present, historical thinkers gain a fuller conception of mind and its possibilities for deliberate and purposive action in practical life. This is the political philosophy at the heart of Collingwood's philosophy of history, intended to check a growing irrationalism he observed in European culture.

At home, the dialectical character of this relation between re-enactment and incapsulation separated Collingwood from his contemporary, Michael

Oakeshott. Collingwood applauded Oakeshott's *Experience and its Modes* (1933) as representing 'the high-water mark of English thought upon history' and the 'complete transcendence of the positivism in which that thought has been involved'.[19] Rather than viewing historical knowledge as the mere addition of new facts to those already known, Oakeshott conceived it as the transformation of the historian's already known ideas and postulates in the light of those newly discovered. He regarded history as a 'mode of experience' that arrests the past at a certain point to form a fixed postulate or category for historical representation. This arrested past is a 'historical' or dead past – a 'past for its own sake' – that, though dead, presents itself to the historian in the form of present-day evidence and facts. There is no movement between past and present worlds – according to Oakeshott, the movement in experience occurs only within the present world of ideas because it is there that the past world of ideas manifests itself in the evidence the historian studies.[20]

In spite of his praise, Collingwood objected that Oakeshott provided no reason why history should exist if the knowledge it produced flows purely from the present. The past *is* incapsulated in the present, for Collingwood, but in *re*-thinking that past it becomes known *as past*. 'The fact that it is also present does not prevent it from being past', he responded to Oakeshott:

> any more than, when I perceive a distant object, where perceiving means not only sensation but thought, the fact that I perceive it here prevents it from being there . . . the historian thinks of his object as there, or rather then, away from him in time; and, because history is knowledge and not mere immediate experience, he can experience it both as then and as now: now in the immediacy of historical experience, but then in its mediacy.[21]

Arnold Toynbee's voluminous *A Study of History* represented, meanwhile, a reaffirmation of historical positivism by not heeding to the processes principle that 'a civilisation may develop into new forms while yet remaining itself'. Toynbee's assumption that in changing, a civilization ceases to be itself and becomes a new one presupposed a naturalistic boundary separating what is within each civilization from what is outside it: 'This is the kind of individuality which is possessed by a stone or any other material body.'[22] Collingwood replied that Western civilization, for example, was not to be understood as relating to Hellenic civilization in an external way. The relation is an internal one that has been sustained by apprehending the mental life of the former civilization and developing that wealth of experience in new directions. Individual human beings do not stand alone in their environment; they absorb this environment itself. The re-thinking of past thought does not confine itself to mere mental contents; it *draws in* this *wider context* as providing the *conditions* in which the thought could take place.

Rik Peters has argued that Collingwood formed his views on the relation between re-enactment and incapsulation by observing a debate between

Croce and another neo-Hegelian Italian, Giovanni Gentile.[23] Croce maintained in his first *Logic* (1905) that since history contains concepts, history presupposes philosophy. Philosophy, as the source of concepts, is logically prior to the intuition of the historical particular. After an exchange of letters with Gentile over the next four years, Croce revised this position: philosophy now presupposes history. According to this view, a philosophical judgement is developed in the mind of an individual philosopher as an answer to a question, which presupposes in its turn an individual judgement, historical in nature. Gentile held all along that in reconstructing the thought of a past philosopher, we construct our own philosophy simultaneously. Through his theory of 'mind as pure act', developed between 1909 and 1911, past reality could be re-activated as thought in action – the action being the thinking of a thought by a past agent in acting a certain way and our re-thinking of that thought in the present.

In a review of Gentile's contribution to a *Festschrift* for Ernst Cassirer in 1937, 'The Transcending of Time in History', Collingwood expressed his approval of Gentile's actual idealism:

> What is indubitably historical is the life of the human mind; now, for Gentile, mind is the only reality, nature is only a construction of ideas, a product of human thought, existing and therefore developing with the development of the thought that constructs it . . . Time is transcended in history because the historian, in discovering the thought of a past agent, re-thinks that thought for himself. It is known, therefore, not as a past thought, contemplated as it were from a distance through the historian's time-telescope, but as a present thought living now in the historian's mind. Thus, by being historically known, it undergoes a resurrection out of the limbo of the dead past, triumphs over time, and survives in the present. This is an important idea, and I believe a true one.[24]

Collingwood may well have said that he had made it his own idea. Gentile made a distinction between two phases of this dialectical process, also evident in the above description of re-enactment. In the first phase, we repeat the past thought by re-thinking it as our own thought, thus actualizing or making a reality of it. In the second phase, this actuality is transcended by a new act of thinking in which the past thought receives a new objectivity: our thinking in action absorbs it and forms an organic whole with it. Thus, although Collingwood played down his satisfaction with Croce and Gentile in a letter to de Ruggiero in 1926, the parallels between Gentile's theory and Collingwood's attempt to reconcile the problem of identity and difference in re-enactment and incapsulation suggest a greater debt.

In emulating the Italians, Collingwood shifted the focus of Oxford philosophers away from German idealism. To de Ruggiero he wrote in 1921: 'I find myself rather inclined to react against the English idealists because they imported so much of what was bad in Hegelianism to England; and I find their present successors a real nuisance and my chief enemies.'[25] The development of Collingwood's position regarding idealism and realism was a complicated affair; to describe the idealists as his chief enemies in the early 1920s was certainly at variance with the unmistakeably idealistic views on history expounded, for example, in the Die manuscript later that decade. Collingwood declared his respect for Germany as 'the home of historical criticism', 'the mother-country of modern historical method' and 'of philosophical reflexion upon it'. Dilthey, Simmel, Windelband and Rickert had laid the foundations of a 'flourishing school of thought', and by degrees provided an incentive for French, English and Italian thinkers to turn their attention to the theory of historical knowledge.[26]

Ultimately, however, Collingwood charged the German movement with having sacrificed inquiry into the objective features of the historical process for questions of exclusively epistemological purport; 'its real interest is in the historian's subjective mental processes', a consequence of its 'general prejudice against metaphysics', a prejudice 'partly neo-Kantian and partly positivistic'. The root of its error consisted in regarding the subjective and the objective as two separate things, 'heterogeneous in their essence, however intimately related'.[27] As he came to comprehend in reconciling re-enactment and incapsulation, thinking historically (*a parte subjecti*) ought to be regarded as homogeneous with the object of history itself (*a parte objecti*). The objective past is a process of thought that, re-thought in the present, confines it to its past context.

Nevertheless, Collingwood's criticisms of the German tradition have not deterred writers from considering his affinities with it. Richard Murphy argues that his ambition to reunify in a complete and undivided life the different forms of human experience that Western civilization had partitioned into specialist branches of knowledge places him within the framework of Romanticism and historicism. David Boucher observes that 'Collingwood has become accepted by modern hermeneutic thinkers as a major force in the field'. Mark Bevir writes that he was 'a lone voice in Oxford drawing on an elder idealism to address hermeneutic themes' and the progenitor of an 'Anglophone hermeneutics' that challenged attempts in the mid-twentieth century to develop a positivist and naturalist analysis of historical explanation. John Hogan cites Collingwood's 'seminal influence on the development of hermeneutics in the twentieth century' and suggests that his philosophy of history 'provides deep insights into the linkage between the two interpretive operations: the hermeneutical movement from the text forward to the present and the historical movement from the text backward to the event', which 'converge to form a single theme'. Collingwood's philosophy of history was not concerned with patterns, trends or explanation theories. It was a hermeneutic – a critical endeavour whose focal point was the historicity of mind; the endeavour of historically constituted minds to come to know the nature of this constitution by studying minds in the past likewise historically constituted. Boucher concurs that 'a formidable array of intellectual giants in the theory of hermeneutics can be invoked to testify their indebtedness' – Bultmann, Gadamer, Pannenberg, Lonergan and Ricœur – all of whom, it can be added, responded in the twentieth century to the problems set down by the pioneers of hermeneutics – Schleiermacher, Droysen and Dilthey – in the previous century. Munslow, in his glossary of terms, goes so far as to say that Dilthey's extension of the hermeneutic circle to include drawing parallels between the intentions of the author of the evidence and the historian's own experiences 'formed the basis' of Collingwood's notion of empathy.[28]

But by far the weightiest recommendation for studying Collingwood in the light of German historical thought has been put forward by Gadamer, at whose instigation *An Autobiography* was translated into German and published in 1955, and for which he wrote the introduction. Collingwood expressed his historical philosophy, in Gadamer's words, 'with incomparable clarity', placing it 'among the classics of English prose'. The Anglo-Saxon tradition since Hume 'has produced a type with whom he cannot be classified'. For the English reader, 'it is a novel about the passion for thinking, about the interpenetration of thought and living'. But for the German reader, in Gadamer's estimation, 'the appearance of the *Autobiography* means a whole lot more':

> In a surprising and puzzling way this foreign writer is no foreigner and when he begins to speak to us in German he is almost like someone coming home, like someone who, though living and working abroad, never forgot his spiritual home. His homeland is the large expanse of German romanticism and of the historical school – Hegel, Schelling, Humboldt, Ranke, Droysen, Schleiermacher and Dilthey . . . Collingwood is at home in this tradition, to which Italian Hegelianism and in particular Croce is intimately related, in a way which is much more than the adoption of something alien. It is useless to look among his compatriots for one who could have led him to historical philosophizing, for it is not simply idealistic thought but precisely its historical turn that is important.[29]

Gadamer found in Collingwood the basis for a repudiation of neo-Kantian 'problem history', an approach to the history of philosophy that considered problems to be eternal and unchanging, against which the various attempts to solve them throughout history formed the subject matter of inquiry. 'Problems' were viewed as the constant and fundamental questions to which human beings at successive stages of their development have attempted to find answers. Problems themselves had no histories; they were the starting point from which historical variation was registered in the shifts of thinking regarding them.

Against this view, Collingwood raised the question of whether 'constant' problems could be more than mere abstractions without a criterion of historical truth, and responded firmly in the negative. Gadamer agreed with Collingwood that the true meaning of a proposition was not to be discovered by taking it as an answer to 'whatsoever arbitrary question', that is, a question purported to be pertinent to all people at all times, but by discovering the real question to which it was offered as an answer. For both men, this meant that the truth of a proposition is inseparable from its function as an answer, an answer to a question arising out of a specific historical situation, not taken from a storehouse of extrahistorical problems in contrast to which the various answers proposed in the human past can be evaluated for their validity. To say 'it is historically true', according to Collingwood's 'radically historical' thinking and 'exotic form of historicism', is identical to saying 'this is its meaning'.[30]

Elsewhere, reflecting upon his debt to Hegel's legacy, Gadamer credited Collingwood fully for the service this logic of question and answer provided in formulating his own theory of hermeneutics. 'That one only "understands" a statement when one understands it as an answer to a question is compellingly evident.' Gadamer made no secret of the role this idea played in his own formation:

> What convinced me about Collingwood's logic of question and answer was not its methodological usefulness, which is ultimately trivial, but its validity (that transcends all methodological usage) according to which question and answer are utterly entangled with one another. For what then is a question? Surely something that one has to understand and that one does understand only when one understands the question itself in terms of something, that is, as an answer; and in doing so one limits the dogmatic claim of any proposition. The logic of question and answer proved itself a dialectic of question and answer in which question and answer are constantly exchanged and are dissolved in the movement of understanding.[31]

But while it is beyond doubt that this question-and-answer complex, on his own testimony, permeated Gadamer's thinking, it is the factor ultimately distinguishing Collingwood from the German tradition among whose progeny Gadamer counted him. Thus, before considering in greater detail the intellectual threads stretching between Oxford and Heidelberg, it is necessary to clarify what separated Collingwood from the general current of Teutonic historical thought. With this explanation, the differences between empathy and re-enactment begin to become visible.

★ ★ ★

Collingwood, it has been stressed, never used the term 'empathy', either in reference to his own doctrines or in discussing those of others. Nevertheless, he did engage in a prolonged polemic against psychology, from which empathy originated and with which it has remained most readily associated to the present day.

Psychology went amiss, Collingwood described in his late book *An Essay on Metaphysics* (1940), when it ceased to see itself as a science of feeling and began to see itself as a science of thought.[32] It arose in the sixteenth century from the recognition that 'feeling is not a kind of thinking', that in feeling coldness, seeing redness or hearing shrillness we are not cognizing an object, but simply having a feeling, a feeling no doubt connected to things in our environment, but itself containing no knowledge of these things. For Collingwood, feeling could not be a kind of thinking because thinking is always a self-critical activity. 'The business of thinking includes the discovery and correction of its own errors.'[33] Psychology fulfilled its function when it filled the gap between the sciences of bodily function and the sciences of mind.

When, however, a 'materialistic or mechanistic biology' combined with a 'materialistic epistemology' in the eighteenth century, the intellectual activities or operations of thought previously the subject matter of the criteriological sciences – logic and ethics – became looked upon as 'aggregations and complexes of feelings and thus special cases of sensation and emotion'. Theoretical reason or knowledge became 'only a pattern of sensations; practical reason or will, only a pattern of appetites'.[34] Crucially, this new psychological science of thought removed the criterion of truth and falsehood by reference to which the self-critical sciences of thought had attempted to offer an account of the criteria used in their own self-criticism. Having mistaken 'feelings' for 'thoughts', which are neither true nor false, but simply 'are', it did not occur to the psychologist to discuss the functions by which thought distinguishes itself in the things it thinks about. The rise of this 'pseudo-science' in the nineteenth century thus threatened scientific method and accuracy, concerned as they ought to have been with discussing an object of investigation in terms of its relation to the criteria used in investigating it.

In the sometimes intemperate tenor of his later works, William James' *Varieties of Religious Experience* (1902) served as a case in point. James left his subject matter 'completely unilluminated', wrote Collingwood in his *Autobiography*, 'not because the book was a bad example of psychology, but because it was a good example of psychology'.[35] By placing religion in the 'psyche' or inner realm of personal experience, James excluded from his vision the great part of religious experience exhibited throughout history in human institutions and practices. In Roman Britain, his own field of historical expertise, this 'fashionable scientific fraud of the age' had produced a hypothesis that a 'Celtic temperament', rather than the 'survival of certain workshop practices' (theory of processes and incapsulation), was behind the revival of Celtic art three centuries after the cultural steamroller of the Romans had flattened Celtic tastes and replaced them with their own. 'With [occult] entities of that kind', he rued, 'we have left behind us the daylight, and even the twilight, of history, and have entered a darkness peopled by all the monsters of *Rassentheorie* and Jungian psychology. In that darkness we find not history but the negation of history; not the solution of historical problems, but only a heady drink which gives us the illusion of having solved them.'[36]

The opening pages of *The Idea of History* affirm in a far more modulated tone why Collingwood opposed psychologism in historical thinking. The reasons he provided are now familiar. 'The philosophizing mind never simply thinks about an object, it always, while thinking about any object, thinks also about its own thought about that object.'[37] History is an act of thinking about an act of thinking. Its object is this act of thinking in the past, which in being re-thought in the present, makes it stand out against the present thought, which in turn allows both to be critically evaluated. Philosophy and history are thought of the 'second degree', *thought about thought*. Psychology, on the other hand, is thought of the 'first degree', *thought by itself*. Psychology regards thought as something separate from its object, as a special kind of mental event that happens in the world, which nevertheless can be investigated independently of that world. 'The whole psychological analysis of historical thought', in the final analysis, 'would be exactly the same if there were no such thing as a past at all.'[38] Its object is in the immediate or here-and-now experience of the person experiencing it, not in something given from the past in relation to which present thinking reflects upon it.

This flow of consciousness studied by psychology, consisting of sensations and feelings, could in its particular details and general characteristics be made the object of human thought, but it 'need not be, and indeed cannot be, re-enacted in the thinking about it. In so far as we think about its particular details', Collingwood explained:

> we are remembering experiences of our own and entering with sympathy and imagination into those of others; but in such cases we do not re-enact the experiences which we remember or with which we sympathize; we are merely contemplating them as objects external to our present selves, aided perhaps by the presence in ourselves of other experiences like them. In so far as we think about its general characteristics, we are engaging in the science of psychology. In neither case are we thinking historically.[39]

Collingwood charged Dilthey with having conflated psychological thinking and historical thinking into one process.[40] The neo-Kantian tradition as a whole strove to ground history in an epistemology capable of legitimating its study of concrete individualities. That it never realized this goal, Collingwood reasoned, was due in no small part to its failure to consider isolated historical facts within an integrated process of historical development, that is, within a historical metaphysics, a weakness characteristic of late nineteenth-century German historical thought. Specifically, when Dilthey claimed that historians come to know the past from the materials they study by reliving in their own minds the spiritual activity that originally produced them, he may have put forward an account of the historian's subjective mental processes, but he left unanswered how this process constituted knowledge of the past. Dilthey described only how it is by virtue of the historian's own spiritual life, and in proportion to the richness of that life, that he infuses life into the dead materials of the past. Collingwood viewed this process of arriving at historical knowledge as 'an inward experience (*Erlebnis*) of its own object' – or, rather, a conception of the historian as living in his object.[41]

The knowledge generated from this process, Collingwood went on to explain, could not be considered as knowledge of the past, just as the knowledge 'I *am*' could not be considered as knowledge of myself. Dilthey recognized this too. To *be* Julius Caesar or Napoleon, since 'life' for them was immediate experience rather than reflection or knowledge, is *being* Julius Caesar or Napoleon, not having knowledge of them. Dilthey sought the solution to this problem by recourse to psychology. By means of psychological analysis, individuals come to know themselves; they understand the structure of their own personalities. Correspondingly, historians who relive the past in their own minds, in order to know that past, must understand the structure of what they are reliving. By reliving it, they are enlarging and incorporating into their experience the experiences of other people in the past. But since Dilthey believed that whatever is so incorporated from the past becomes integrated into the structure of the historian's personality, what historical understanding really involved was a psychological analysis of selves. This led Dilthey in his late essays on the history of philosophy to reduce it to the study of the psychology of philosophers, Collingwood wrote, 'on the principle that there are certain fundamental types of mental structure, and that each type has a certain necessary attitude to, and conception of, the world'.[42] A theory intended to shore up the status of historical knowledge failed to illuminate the historical nature of its object. A science erected on naturalistic principles, psychology illuminated universal mental categories under which individuals could be seen as historical actualizations of those categories, which, themselves being necessary to history, stood outside it.

Collingwood treated Dilthey as the archetype of the German tradition's over concern with processes of knowing (epistemology) and under concern with what is known (metaphysics). Dilthey's concept of reliving the past may have described a procedure for discerning its fundamental structures living within us, but it took place more as an examination of one's own mental constitution in the present than as a discovery of a past form of life. There was no real need for a concept of history concerned with the past at all. To be sure, Collingwood also believed that all history is contemporary history, for it is re-enacted in the present and thus a product of and contribution to that present-day environment. But whereas Dilthey's psychological form of historical understanding blended past and present-day structures seamlessly in the one transhistorical entity, Collingwood's dialectical re-enactment untangled them and brought into view a past distinct from the present.

The way in which this untangling of past and present occurs is elucidated in the next two chapters: first, through the clarification of Collingwood's position *vis-à-vis* the Romantic hermeneutical tradition that furnished historicism with its empathy-dependent methodology; and, second, through the evaluation of his theories from the standpoint of their place in the twentieth-century hermeneutical tradition that sought to neutralize historicism's psychological excesses by accounting for the here and now of historical understanding. Collingwood introduced in re-enactment the possibility that a past thought, in being re-thought by the historian in the fresh context that is the present moment, could assert itself in contrast to the present-day modes of thought in which the past thought is incapsulated. In this way, Collingwood could uphold the historicist principle indispensable to history that the meaning of a past object resides in its past while attending to the fact that history is a form of knowledge fashioned by present-day questions and concerns. Re-enactment is not a passive surrender to apprehension and intuition, but the labour of critical thinking.

Notes

1. Collingwood entered Oxford in 1908 on a Classics scholarship. He rose thereafter to a hybrid lectureship in philosophy and Roman history, then to the Waynflete Chair of Professor in Metaphysical Philosophy from 1935 to 1941, when poor health forced him into retirement.

2. Colin McGinn, 'Homage to Education', *London Review of Books* 12, 15 (1990), 16–17.

3. Collingwood, letter to Benedetto Croce, 20 April 1938, quoted in James Connelly, *Metaphysics, Method and Politics: The Political Philosophy of R.G. Collingwood* (Exeter: Imprint Academic, 2003), 47.

4. James Connelly, 'Art Thou the Man: Croce, Gentile or de Ruggiero?', in David Boucher, James Connelly and Tariq Modood (eds), *Philosophy, History and Civilisation: Interdisciplinary Perspectives on R.G. Collingwood* (Cardiff: University of Wales Press, 1995), 101.

5. David. D Roberts, *Benedetto Croce and the Uses of Historicism* (Berkeley: University of California Press, 1987), 4.

6. Collingwood, letter to Croce, 5 January 1928, quoted in B.A. Haddock, 'Vico, Collingwood and the Character of Historical Philosophy', in Boucher, Connelly and Modood (eds), *Philosophy, History and Civilisation*, 132.

7. R.G. Collingwood, *The Idea of History*, rev. edn [1946] Jan van der Dussen (Oxford: Oxford University Press, 1994), 196.

8. Ibid.

9. Ibid., 202.

10. R.G. Collingwood, *An Autobiography* (Oxford: Clarendon Press, 1978), 97–98.

11. Of the three Italians discussed here, de Ruggiero was the only one Collingwood mentioned in his *Autobiography*. Whereas he played the acolyte with Croce and displayed hostility to Gentile after his conversion to Fascism, his relationship with de Ruggiero was marked by mutual respect and collaboration.

12. Collingwood quoted in Connelly, 'Art Thou the Man', 109–10. Collingwood composed '*Libellus de Generatione*: An Essay in Absolute Empiricism' between 20 and 23 July 1920, and sent it to de Ruggiero, to whom it was dedicated. A photocopy of the essay is stored in the Bodleian Library, Oxford.

13. Simon Blackburn, 'Against False Divisions', *Times Literary Supplement,* 6 April 1990, 370. On needing others for self-knowledge, see Simon Blackburn, *Mirror, Mirror: The Uses and Abuses of Self-Love* (Princeton: Princeton University Press, 2014).

14. R.G. Collingwood, *Speculum Mentis, or the Map of Knowledge* (Oxford: Clarendon Press, 1924), 47, 231.

15. Collingwood gives this account of his trip to Die in *Autobiography,* 110–14. The 'Die manuscript', as it is often called, was undiscovered at the time of the first edition of *The Idea of History*. It is included in the revised edition as 'Outlines of a Philosophy of History'.

16. Collingwood, 'Outlines of a Philosophy of History', in *The Idea of History,* 429. Collingwood remarked later that his thinking on this formula had been muddied by the equivocality of the word 'thought', which can mean both *noēsis* (the act of thinking) and *noēma* (the object of thought). In lecture notes prepared in 1936, he expressed this peculiar relation in the argument that history should be viewed as *noēseōs noēsis,* an act of thinking about an act of thinking.

17. Ibid., 441–42.

18. Ibid., 450, 448, 442. Collingwood uses the example of William the Conqueror in the Battle of Hastings (448). William's tactics, for him, constituted an actual whole comprising everything he knew about fighting battles. For historians, on the other hand, William's tactics constitute a thought or plan that can be re-thought only as one part of a series of other parts that form the whole they call the history of the Battle of Hastings. This is their actual historical knowledge forming the whole of their present thought, just as William's tactical plan formed the whole of his thought.

19. Collingwood, *Idea of History,* 159.

20. Ibid., 151–54.

21. Ibid., 158.

22. Ibid., 161–62.

23. Rik Peters, 'Croce, Gentile and Collingwood on the Relation between History and Philosophy', in Boucher, Connelly and Modood (eds), *Philosophy, History and Civilisation,* 152–67.

24. R.G. Collingwood, 'Philosophy and History: Essays Presented to Ernst Cassirer by Raymond Klibansky; H.J. Paton', *English Historical Review* 52, 205 (1937), 143.

25. Collingwood, letter to de Ruggiero, 20 March 1921, quoted in Connelly, 'Art Thou the Man', 100.

26. Collingwood, *Idea of History,* 165; Collingwood, 'Philosophy and History', 142.

27. Collingwood, *Idea of History,* 184, 190.

28. Richard Murphy, *Collingwood and the Crisis of Western Civilisation: Art, Metaphysics and Dialectic* (Exeter: Imprint Academic, 2008); David Boucher, *Texts in Context: Revisionist Methods for Studying the History of Ideas* (Dordrecht: Martinus Nijhoff, 1985), 24; Mark Bevir, 'Introduction: Historical Understanding and the Human Sciences', *Journal of the Philosophy of History* 1, 3 (2007), 264, 266; John P. Hogan, *Collingwood and Theological Hermeneutics* (Lanham: University Press of America, 1989), 1, 3, 21; David Boucher, 'The Life, Times and Legacy of R.G. Collingwood', in Boucher, Connelly and Modood (eds), *Philosophy, History and Civilisation,* 17; Alun Munslow, *Deconstructing History,* 2nd edn (London: Routledge, 2006), 198.

29. Hans-Georg Gadamer, 'Introduction to *Denken*: The German Translation of *An Autobiography*', trans. G. Barden and N. McCormick, *Collingwood Journal* (Spring 1992), 9–14.

30. Ibid.

31. Hans-Georg Gadamer, 'The Heritage of Hegel', in his *Reason in the Age of Science,* trans. Frederick D. Lawrence (Cambridge, MA: MIT Press, 1981), 46–47.

32. R.G. Collingwood, *An Essay on Metaphysics,* rev. edn [1940] Rex Martin (Oxford: Clarendon Press, 1998), 101–21.
33. Ibid., 109–10.
34. Ibid., 113–14.
35. Collingwood, *Autobiography,* 93.
36. Ibid., 95, 139–40.
37. Collingwood, *Idea of History,* 1.
38. Ibid., 2.
39. Ibid., 302–3.
40. Ibid., 171–76.
41. Ibid., 172.
42. Ibid., 173.

CHAPTER 7

Questions, Answers and Presuppositions

How far psychology infused Dilthey's hermeneutics remains an open question. For Collingwood's part, although he was aware that Dilthey continued to publish 'scattered essays' until 1910, his treatment of the 'lonely and neglected genius' appears to have been based on his 1883 *Introduction to the Human Sciences,* well before his Hegelian and hermeneutic turn. Collingwood may never have mounted his attack had he known the position Dilthey would come to take on empathy and sympathy. As the early phenomenologists also believed, Dilthey concluded that empathy established too direct and intuitive a relation between individuals for it to be a reliable medium for understanding. To understand an object requires something within that object to stand over against the self, so that it can be grasped as something independent of the self.

A similar idea was expressed in twentieth-century analytical philosophy of history: only after the connections linking separate events cease to subsist in the present context and confine themselves to a closed and self-sufficient historical context can they offer themselves to the practical inferences schema of reconstructing an agent's intentions. Both traditions agree: while appearing to be a means for understanding the distinct context in which actions were taken, empathy removes the distinction between past and present that allows this context to present itself as something to be studied in its own right.

Collingwood's postulates against psychology and immediate experience have made this point sufficiently clear. Immediate experience offers nothing that can be re-enacted by the historian in thinking about a thought. Insofar as we think about the particular details and general characteristics of immedi-

---

Notes for this section begin on page 141.

ate experience in the belief that we are thinking historically, we contemplate them without having to reflect upon their function in the lives of people whose actions tie them to specific historical contexts. As Collingwood put it in his last book, *The New Leviathan,* the source of the content that historians ponder is other people's lives in the past: 'To think historically is to explore a world consisting of things other than myself, each of them an individual or unique agent, in an individual or unique situation, doing an individual or unique action which he has to do because, charactered and circumstanced as he is, he can do no other.'[1]

But this privileging of the past world has nothing to do with uncritically accepting what is uncovered in its exploration. Collingwood made plain his belief in *An Essay on Metaphysics* that the mere apprehension or intuition of an item confronting us is a kind of 'low-grade thinking' requiring no effort on the part of the thinker to consider what other people may have thought of it. 'High-grade thinking', on the other hand, 'means thinking energetically instead of idly: thinking hard instead of allowing your mind to drift.'[2] Against Samuel Alexander's suggestion that 'there are only facts, and minds recognizing the facts when they are brought up against them', he argued that there is never anything like 'compresence' with an object: 'There is at first a whole nest of problems all tangled up together. Then by degrees the tangle is reduced to order.'[3] Scientific thinking and civilization depended on systematic and orderly thinking; empathy and its cognates entailed a level of passive receptivity that to him was at the centre of a growing irrationalism in European culture, leaving all in its path to renounce the importance of truth and the need to think and act in a systematic and methodical way.

Nevertheless, in spite of having argued specifically against intuitionist and uncritical approaches to philosophy and history, the misconception still circulates that re-enactment is a concept of empathy. Tellingly, the making of this claim typically follows from the assertion that re-enactment belongs to the philosophy of mind of German idealism and Romantic hermeneutics. It supposes that the doctrine consists in a unidirectional recapturing of past mental contents, in which are said to reside the pristine meanings of past texts as intended by their authors.

A case in point is Quentin Skinner's view of re-enactment.[4] While being the foremost advocate for a Collingwoodian approach to the history of political thought, Skinner has been a vocal critic of the doctrine he believes belongs to the epistemologically naïve hermeneutics of recovering the contents of past mental events. Critics of this approach, he writes, 'have complained that the traditional idea of hermeneutics asks for the impossible if it asks us, in Collingwood's phrase, to think other people's thoughts after them'. We should never hope, as re-enactment suggests, 'to abolish the historical distance between ourselves and our forebears, speaking as though we can spirit away the influence of everything that has intervened, empathetically reliving their experience and retelling it as it was once lived'.[5]

At pains to distinguish his own method from this empathy-dependent conception of uncovering an author's intentions, Skinner insists that nothing he puts forward 'presupposes the discredited hermeneutic ambition of stepping empathetically into other people's shoes and attempting (in R.G. Collingwood's unfortunate phrase) to think their thoughts after them'. The historical reconstruction of an agent's intentions requires no such 'conjuring trick' because, 'as Wittgenstein established long ago in criticising the concept of a private language, the intentions with which anyone performs a successful act of communication must, *ex hypothesi,* be publicly legible'.[6]

As is well known, Skinner's linguistic contextualism treats speech acts as evidence of what authors were *doing* with their words. Just as publicly inscribed language allows us to grasp what people are trying to say to us in the everyday sense, so in historical documents the language used is the gateway for an intertextual understanding of the intentions with which authors wrote. The problem with re-enactment, as he conceives it, is that it wants to gain access to a private world of language and meaning, these being the productive force in a text's creation. In so endeavouring to retrieve this meaning, the task of re-enactment consists in the same ambition to understand past authors in ways that they were unable to understand themselves. According to Skinner, the logocentrism of this unidirectional movement back to the event of textual production relegates the doctrine to the most primitive stage in the development of hermeneutics.

Skinner rejects re-enactment on the same grounds that he rejects historicism's empathy-dependent hermeneutics. No such communion with the past is necessary. The ordinary techniques of historical scholarship suffice because the texts historians study are composed of language that expresses the nature of the contribution their authors made to a pre-existing context it was their purpose to affect. It is by studying texts as actions intended to redefine an aspect of this anterior context that yields insight into the purposes for which they were written, not by reconstructing the act of production.

In spite of these criticisms, Skinner invokes Collingwood at key moments in the explication of his methodology. Collingwood's ideas began to be vigorously discussed in the 1960s by a group of philosophers and intellectual historians – among them John Passmore and John Pocock in Australasia, and Peter Laslett, John Dunn and Skinner himself at the University of Cambridge – who sought to define a methodology that accounted for the historicity of political theory and intellectual history in general. For Pocock, this took the form of distinguishing the various levels of abstraction at which different writers work; for Passmore, of recovering the intentions and underlying purposes of authors; and for Dunn, of defending the 'realist' aspiration to recover and describe past intellectual projects in the terms in which their creators conceived them. Skinner has explained how sitting behind this common methodological programme, not least his own, was Collingwood's commitment to recovering the precise questions to which the texts historians study were intended as answers.[7] As Kenneth McIntyre has observed, Skinner applied Austin's speech-act theory to historical texts through Collingwood's logic of question and answer.[8]

In his seminal and programmatic 1969 article 'Meaning and Understanding in the History of Ideas', Skinner mobilized the logic of question and answer to help repudiate the textualist approach and expound his contextualist approach. Textualism is the doctrine that every text is a self-sufficient object of inquiry and understanding. As a way of coming to understand the meaning of historical texts, it is logically tied to the belief that this meaning consists of the 'timeless elements', 'universal ideals' and 'dateless wisdom' that historical texts continue to convey. The priority of the paradigm governing the inquiry sets the investigator; where often there is none, coherence is found in a body of work or in the development of an idea among different writers in different periods. The significance of a work may then be discussed in terms completely removed from what it meant for the author who produced it. The retrospective significance of the work outweighs concerns regarding its meaning for the persons attached to it. Such 'mythologies of prolepsis' conflate the 'necessary asymmetry between the significance an observer may justifiably claim to find in a given statement or action, and the meaning of that action itself'.[9] Meaning belongs to the past; significance is attributed from the present to the past.

To grasp this meaning belonging to the past involves investigating a special kind of historical context, one understood as composed of questions to which the statements made in historical documents were intended as answers. Histories that account for the development of ideas by charting their various appearances in the works of various thinkers – social contract, progress, equality, sovereignty, justice, natural law, Utopia and so on – may bring to light certain problems of the day, but they cannot explain what part the idea played in the thought of the thinker who mentioned it, or the place, typical or atypical, the idea may have taken in the intellectual climate of the period in which it appeared. What we cannot learn from such histories, 'to cite Collingwood's very important point' in Skinner's estimation, 'is what questions the use of the expression was thought to answer, and so what reasons there were for continuing to employ it'.[10] Identifying these questions leads to the discovery that there is no determinate idea to which various writers contributed, only a variety of statements made by a variety of agents with a variety of intentions. There is no history of the idea to be written, but rather a history concentrated on the various agents who invoked the idea and on the varying situations in which they intended it as an answer to a question. The persistence of such ideational expressions tells historians nothing about the persistence of the questions that the expressions may have been intended to answer. 'The only history to be written is thus a history of the various statements made with the given expression.'[11]

This refutation of historically investigating timeless truths does not, however, prevent contextualism from unearthing past meanings relevant to the present day. Much in the way that Collingwood aligned historical knowledge with self-knowledge and political action, Skinner conceives it as offering a grasp on the various functions human action can have on the world. To demand of history that it help solve perennial problems is to commit not merely a methodological error; it is to commit the moral error of presuming an 'essential sameness' unable to grasp the 'essential variety of viable moral assumptions and political commitments'.[12] To presume sameness in a common set of problems facing all humanity at all times is to maintain that humans have no capacity through their actions to affect the conditions in which they live, for if the problems have remained the same, what humans have done in the face of them must have had small effect. For Skinner and Collingwood, by contrast, the past offers a key to self-knowledge and awareness because in each question to which humans have responded in the past lies a source for considering the ways in which they have and have not been able to affect their circumstances. Self-knowledge is knowing what has been possible in given contexts.

The significance of Skinner's treatment of Collingwood is that it entails the possibility of taking a Collingwoodian approach without subscribing to his most famous doctrine: re-enactment. To Skinner, the logic of question and answer is indispensable to intellectual historians. To treat historical statements as answers to questions is to see what their authors were doing with their words, when 'doing something with words' is understood as intervening in or contributing to an ongoing debate that redefines in some manner the basis upon which that debate takes place. But due in part to Collingwood's failure to elucidate the connection between re-enactment and the logic of question and answer, Skinner denies that this operation has anything to do with re-enacting past thoughts. According to him, re-enactment and empathy are one and the same specimen. Both are attached to the delusion of nineteenth-century hermeneutics that the historian can obliterate historical distance and relive the past in its purest and most private forms.

It is fair to criticize empathy on these grounds, but the same cannot be said for re-enactment. Without doubt, the notion of empathetically reliving the past was connected to the Romantic hermeneutic programme of psychological interpretation. As a concept in psychological aesthetics and phenomenology, too, empathy was predicated on the belief that the factors standing between a knowing subject and object of interpretation cease to form a barrier in the event of their mutual unification. But Collingwood never spoke in these terms. In fact, his repudiation of psychology as the science of immediate experience points to the precise opposite: reliving the past in re-enactment works specifically at the interface of past and present, strange and familiar, knower and known. Collingwood did not try to overcome historical distance; for him, historical distance served as the productive ground enabling historical understanding. He worked with the problem of how the past can be incapsulated in the present and still be known historically by distinguishing the past context to which a past thought belongs and the present context in which it is re-thought and held up to analysis and criticism. It is because thought transcends its immediate environment, survives and revives in new contexts that the historian can re-think it. There is no reason to believe from what Collingwood said about past and present contexts in *The Idea of History* that he saw any need for historians to 'place themselves' in the past context:

> The peculiarity of thought is that, in addition to occurring here and now in this context, it can sustain itself through a change of context and revive in a different one . . . the immediacy of the first occasion can never again be experienced: the shock of its novelty, the liberation from perplexing problems, the triumph of achieving a desired result . . .
>
> It has been said that anything torn from its context is thereby mutilated and falsified; and that in consequence, to know any one thing, we must know its context, which implies knowing the whole universe . . . On such a doctrine Euclid's act of thinking on a given occasion that these angles are equal would be what it was only in relation to the total context of his then experience, including such things as being in a good temper and having a slave stand behind his right shoulder: without knowing all these we cannot know what he meant.
>
> . . . even thought itself, in its immediacy as the unique act of thought with its unique context in the life of an individual thinker, is not the object of historical knowledge. It cannot be re-enacted; if it could, time itself would be cancelled and the historian would be the person about whom he thinks, living over again in all respects the same. The historian cannot apprehend the individual act of thought in its individuality, just as it actually happened.[13]

A separate yet complementary interpretation of re-enactment emerges from Collingwood's manuscript *The Principles of History*, the book he intended to be his final pronouncement on the philosophy of history. Although the concept of re-enactment made no explicit appearance in the text, as Dray and van der Dussen observe, it might reasonably be regarded as implicit in the presentation and discussion of his historical examples.[14] These examples feature mainly in the section 'Evidence and Language', which if taken as illustrations of re-enactment at work implicitly present the idea as a kind of reading of historical documents.

Here re-enactment can be regarded as a kind of reading thanks to the way in which language expresses the thought embodied in action. '*Res Gestae*', or the doings or deeds historians study, 'are not mere action, they are rational action, action which embodies thought. To embody thought is to express it. To express thought is to be language.'[15] Since actions exhibit thought and since historians read the language that expresses that thought, this shared language provides a direct line to discovering the thought behind *Res Gestae,* which is to discover what the creators of historical documents meant by or intended by them. To simply know that Diocletian issued an Edict of Prices or Louis XIV revoked the Edict of Nantes does not qualify as historical knowledge. These 'dry bones of historical knowledge' are rather to be considered as the means for gaining historical knowledge of the situation that the statements contained within them were issued to affect. The 'special business of the historian' is then to 'interpret it as implying he envisaged the situation in which he found himself in a certain manner, was discontented with it for certain reasons, and proposed to amend it in a certain way'.[16] Historical documents such as these become evidence only by virtue of the historian's autonomy: the statements of which they are composed are not evidence in themselves; the evidence with which the historian works is 'his own autonomous statement of the fact that they are made'.[17] Against the view of re-enactment as passive and uncritical, the historian's 'evidence is always an experience of his own, an act which he has performed by his own powers and is conscious of having performed by his own powers: the aesthetic act of reading a certain text in a language he knows, and assigning to it a certain sense'.[18]

All this throws considerable doubt on the notion that Collingwood proffered a naïve theory of empathy concerned with recovering the pristine meaning of the past. Returning to his account of context in *The Idea of History,* he made plain that the experiential context in which an act of thought occurred is not an object of historical inquiry. A past agent's experiential context is part of the situation in which he conceived himself, but it is not the context pertaining to the problem or question he tried to answer.[19] Two people can think the same thought without sharing the same experiential context. By 'context', then, Collingwood meant not the milieu of actual experience, but the terms of the problem or question to which past activities were directed as answers. This context becomes a shared context congenial to re-enactment when the questions guiding the historical inquiry reflect the questions that guided the past discussion being investigated. So long as there is this correspondence, a past thought can be said to exist in a new context without losing its identity, and having been considered in the light of new evidence and knowledge in this new context, it can be said to constitute new historical knowledge.[20] Collingwood called this 'thought in its mediation'.

In formulating the theory of re-enactment, Collingwood emphasized that thinking historically is not visceral and immediate, but critical, ratiocinative and inferential. On their own, however, re-enactment and question-and-answer logic leave unarticulated the nature of the object towards which historical thinking and questioning direct themselves. A third element – the 'absolute presuppositions' that govern the possibilities and limitations of human thought, belief and action – must be added to elaborate his full programme for historical inquiry, as well as to establish its hermeneutical significance and implications.

★ ★ ★

Empathy posits the unification of subject and object in the contemplation of a shared experiential context. Re-enactment and question-and-answer logic seek no such fusion and instead work at the productive interface of past and present contexts. To insist that the past must be left to assert its own meaning against the present context is to state that the questions that animated past actions and speech acts must take precedence over and above any we might have regarding them. On the one hand, there is a need to account for the role of our questions; on the other hand, there is a need to distinguish the context of past questions.

Beginning with the latter, Collingwood became attentive to the inadequacy of the method of his 'realist' colleagues when he discovered that they routinely attributed to past philosophers views not to be found expressed in their writings. Collingwood could at first forgive historical inaccuracy. They 'professed philosophy, not history'. Their business as philosophical critics consisted in showing whether a given doctrine was sound or unsound, and 'their historical blunders on the question of whether a certain author held that doctrine, however distressing to myself, did not affect the philosophical issue'.[21]

Historical error did not affect the philosophical issue because the realists considered the known to be independent of the knowing it. Knowing was a matter of intuiting or apprehending objects whose value consisted in whether it were true or false. The question of the purpose that a philosophical argument had in being put forward did not concern them because what mattered was the analytical soundness of the argument itself.

Collingwood became dissatisfied with this approach when he began to teach philosophy in the early 1910s. Having continued his historical and archaeological studies during these years, he had learnt in this 'laboratory of historical thought' what Bacon and Descartes had confirmed three hundred years earlier, 'that knowledge comes only by answering questions, and that these questions must be the right questions and asked in the right order'.[22] This discovery led him to adopt in his teaching the procedure, 'more by example than by precept', of striving to understand what an author expounded with regard to a particular doctrine before attempting to criticize it. 'Let us see whether that is what Kant really said' and 'What is Aristotle saying and what does he mean by it?', held priority over the question 'Is it true?'[23]

This idea behind his revolt against philosophic convention took concrete form when the outbreak of war brought academic life to a standstill. Working for the Admiralty Intelligence Division, Collingwood passed the Albert Memorial every day while crossing Kensington Gardens on his way to the Royal Geographical Society, where a section of the Admiralty was based. The monument, to his eyes, was a monstrosity. Searching for an explanation as to how something so unattractive could come to be, he meditated on the intentions of its originator, Sir Gilbert Scott:

> To say that Scott was a bad architect was to burke the problem with a tautology; to say that there was no accounting for tastes was to evade it by *suggestio falsi*. What relation was there . . . between what he had done and what he had tried to do? Had he tried to produce a beautiful thing; a thing, I meant, which we should have thought beautiful? If so, he had of course failed. But had he perhaps been trying to produce something different? If so, he might possibly have succeeded. If I found the monument merely loathsome, was that perhaps my fault? Was I looking in it for qualities that it did not possess, and either ignoring or despising those it did?[24]

Collingwood did not divulge his conclusions after putting the monument to this first test of question and answer. The experience had a more enduring significance. First, he concluded that a particularized and detailed proposition must be the answer not to a general question, but to a question as particularized and detailed as itself. In the old rivalry between the human and natural sciences, he was not as hostile to the latter as his Vichian inside theory of knowledge might lead to believe. One does not offer a truer account of the world, nor must one exist to the exclusion of the other; rather, both respond to different questions in the one world. Second, from this principle of 'correlativity', according to which a proposition is a distinct answer to a distinct question, he claimed that no two propositions can contradict one another unless they are answers to the same question. The meaning of a proposition, like Skinner's contextualism after him, is relative to the question it answers. Finally, this meant that the truth of proposition must be relative to the question it answers as well.[25]

As for the nature of our questions, Collingwood maintained that the degree to which history could claim to be a science was in direct proportion to the degree to which historians could elicit evidence from their sources. The autonomy of history meant not to him what it had meant for the nineteenth-century historicists concerned with establishing history's disciplinary status; it meant through their questioning of historical sources, historians decide what happened in the past.

That the questions historians take to sources determine the nature of the evidence yielded controverts *de novo* the argument that Collingwood propounded a theory of empathetic recapture of the past. Historians work under the condition of being their own authorities. The 'scissors-and-paste' history of the Greco-Roman world and Middle Ages excerpted and combined the testimonies of various authorities to produce a narrative. The notion of authority began to lose currency in the seventeenth century, and a source became treated as a statement *sub judice,* valueless until the historian judges it. This 'critical history', the apotheosis of which was the historical consciousness of nineteenth-century historicism, descended from Vico's view that 'the important question about any statement contained in a source is not whether it is true or false, but what it means'. But although it proved a great advance on scissors-and-paste history, critical history did not go far enough in putting its sources 'to the torture'.[26]

Collingwood's 'scientific historian' had a model to follow in Francis Bacon's precept for natural science that it must 'put Nature to the question'.[27] No longer passive receptors of what a source has to tell them, scientific historians read it with a question in mind, having already decided what they want to find out from it. With this question in mind, they elicit an answer from parts of the source with which it is not prima facie concerned. Fundamentally, the investigative procedure corresponds to that of the detective attempting to solve a crime.

Through the story of the murder of John Doe, Collingwood described this procedure as the process of turning the statements made by people connected to the victim into statements that on the detective's own authority reveal the killer's identity. Interrogating his suspects, he asks 'what does this statement mean?', which, in addition to the question 'what did the person who made it mean by it?', involves asking 'what light is thrown on the question in which I am interested by the fact that this person made this statement, meaning by it what he did mean?' The detective goes about answering the question 'who killed John Doe?' not only by inquiring into the meaning of his suspects' statements, but more importantly by what they were intending in making them. Thus the conceptual point that question and answer are correlative results in the empirical point that evidence comes to hand solely in relation to a certain question. When a person who the detective knows could not have committed the crime steps forward and volunteers 'I killed John Doe', the meaning of this statement itself is obviously useless; nevertheless, it becomes evidence for helping find the real culprit when the detective autonomously states 'this person tells me that she killed John Doe' and infers accordingly that she is attempting to shield somebody.[28] What counts as evidence is that which can be re-enacted by historians in their own minds. This is the process of inferring from sources evidence withheld in their testimony.

In direct opposition to the view that Collingwood espoused a kind of divinatory hermeneutics, the historian as detective underscores the empirical character of his method. Whereas to some he has been seen to be in league with the mystical excesses of his speculative predecessors, to others his emphasis on evidence and inference has been offered as proof that he cannot be brought under any such classification. Indeed, Jan van der Dussen has argued that Collingwood was 'both too rational and empirical' to support Gadamer's pronouncements on the German complexion of his thought.[29] Put differently, the rational, inferential and evidentiary nature of re-enactment acquitted him of the charge of hermeneutical naïveté, but then these features would seem to preclude him from being considered a thinker of the hermeneutical mould.

In order to treat Collingwood within the historicist-hermeneutic tradition outlined by Gadamer, it must therefore be shown that an empirical method is not incompatible with hermeneutics. Van der Dussen underestimates the extent to which this method can be empirical without being empiricist. This was a key feature of the analysis of Ranke and his followers in the historical school. Although they applied themselves to the empirical task of discerning in the archival traces of the past the concrete realities that followers of Hegel's philosophical school conceptualized from the armchair, they were not empiricists because they knew that the true nature of these past realities did not present itself immediately to the cognition of the inquiring historian. The whole reason why empathy, intuition, *Verstehen* and their cognates were integral to the historicist method is because they required a way of going beyond the mere perception of literal meaning.

Herder's methodological empiricism introduced the methodological necessity of empathy as a means of extending beyond words and recapturing their origins in an author's inner experience (*Divination*). For Humboldt, the historical method of the new century offered the only way of capturing the 'essence' of concrete realities. Ranke followed suit, believing that in every fact uncovered in the archive came a revelation of the infinite. In this process, Droysen's historical hermeneutics attempted to account for the role of the subjective interpreter, whose inner life breathed life into the dead historical fact in a circular network of mutual dependence. This subjectivizing tendency reached its zenith at the end of the nineteenth century, when under the animus of Kant's earlier project to reconcile empiricism and transcendentalism, neo-Kantian philosophers of history endeavoured to set knowledge of a bygone past on a secure epistemological footing. Hegel's metaphysics had to be rehabilitated before it could be asked anew what was the precise nature of the object historians go beyond themselves to discover.

As accounts of how knowledge of the past is produced and verified in the encounter with extant traces of the past, they were all *empirical*. Yet concerned as they were with what is required for enlivening these traces and rendering their content knowable in the present, they were not *empiricist*. An empiricist maintains that the sole grounds for knowledge consists in what offers itself to sensory perception. Nothing 'beyond' what is perceived is a candidate for knowledge. Elton's appeal for a 'return to essentials' in historical scholarship exemplifies how this strictly empiricist approach clashes with an empirical hermeneutics. 'Hermeneutics', according to him, 'is the science which invents meaning; historical study depends on discovering meaning without inventing it. Hermeneutics seeks to reduce variety to cohesiveness, while history accepts the probability of unpredictable variety.'[30] Its use by historians enables them to impose meaning on their materials when they should be extracting meaning and significance from them.

For the empiricist, this extraction of meaning occurs in much the same way as Collingwood's adversaries in the psychological and realist camps conceptualized knowledge as deriving from the direct apprehension or intuition of reality and the content of other selves. Hermeneutical historians, contends this empiricist, impose meaning on the past by filtering this content through their present-day frames of references, which paint the past in a presentist hue.

A chief concern of hermeneutics is this problem of the foregrounding of knowledge. The Romantic tradition is with good reason regarded as naïve, mostly for the fact that it failed to consider the epistemological significance of prior understanding in its belief that the present moment could be transcended in the apprehension of a past productive moment. It was for this reason that empathy was its flagship method. But with the shift to a more ontologically grounded hermeneutics in the twentieth century, as we shall see in the next chapter, it could hardly be claimed that interpreters operated in ignorance of everything intermediating the encounter between past and present. To be methodologically adroit is to navigate this territory fully aware that the evidence contained in historical material belongs and is tied to the past environment from which it sprang, and therefore needs to be represented in relation to that past environment. In the final analysis, just as the ordinary, empirical methods of historical research sit behind Skinner's contextualism, so the empirical character of Collingwood's question-and-answer historian does not exclude him from hermeneutical examination.

★ ★ ★

The thrust of empathy and re-enactment is a description of the processes of knowing historically. But the shift in attention to the exact nature of the historical context that this species of knowing tries to uncover is less an epistemological question than a metaphysical one concerned with the object of historical knowledge. Collingwood was dissatisfied with the neo-Kantian tradition for zeroing in on questions of subjectivity at the expense of casting light on the precise content that historical reconstruction represents as historical knowledge. It can now be affirmed this was a dissatisfaction with a tradition that concerned itself almost exclusively with epistemology. Kant established the need to go beyond the one-sidedness of rationalism and empiricism to a recognition of the interdependence and mutual implication of the subject and the object in cognition. On this basis, Romantic hermeneutics developed in the nineteenth century and the concept of the hermeneutic circle was formulated along epistemological lines as proposing a kind of access to past mental states. Collingwood himself supplied a historical epistemology through dialectical re-enactment. Historians could claim knowledge of the past because, in re-thinking a past thought, the past context to which it belonged could be seen in contrast to the present context through which it offered itself to analysis and criticism.

But studying alone the processes of knowing historically was insufficient. As Dilthey realized in returning to hermeneutics through Hegel's metaphysics at the end of his career, what he needed in order to provide history with a full account of itself was a historical metaphysics – an account of the object of knowledge into which it investigates and holds up to analysis and criticism. Without this account of what knowledge of past thought is knowledge *of,* a philosophy of history remained only half-fulfilled. Collingwood may have provided in re-enactment an account of the processes by which historical knowledge is produced, but by itself it left only a vague impression of its object – 'thought'. The view that re-enactment belongs to a naïve hermeneutics of recovery is mistaken not only because it overlooks the concept of thought in its mediation, but also because it neglects to consider the larger project for history and philosophy entailed by his methodology for a historical metaphysics.

Question-and-answer logic and the theory of absolute presuppositions were the foundation of Collingwood's metaphysics. The first of these illuminated a distinct object of investigation for the scientific detective-historian by portraying the procedure as an attempt to identify the hidden meaning of a source's testimony. This is to return to the 'black-box' idea elucidated by Denis Shemilt that the 'Collingwoodian empathizing historian' investigates the unstated assumptions people held in the past. With the shift to Collingwood's historical metaphysics, the historian's task becomes identifying the predicate from which a question-and-answer complex arose, through which it could be treated as a problem specific to that context.

In *An Essay on Metaphysics,* Collingwood set out to reform metaphysics by charging it with this task. He repudiated the traditional Aristotelian conception of metaphysics for having left this predicate in a state of abstract obscurity, for 'groping blindly for what is not in fact there'.[31] Following

Kant's view that 'being is not a predicate' and grounding of metaphysics in the objects of experience, he declared that the science required 'a definite subject-matter to think about', with 'special problems of its own that arise out of the special peculiarities of the subject-matter'.[32] The purpose of metaphysics as a historical discipline would be to identify and describe the absolute presuppositions that governed thought, belief and action in past epochs.

Collingwood conceived absolute presuppositions as the historically shifting foundations or groundforms of knowledge without which thinking would be impossible and knowledge meaningless. Yet in spite of their supreme function, it was not until 1938, in *An Autobiography,* that Collingwood used the term for the first time to define the work of the metaphysician:

> metaphysics . . . is no futile attempt at knowing what lies behind the limits of experience, but is primarily at any given time an attempt to discover what the people of that time believe about the world's general nature; such beliefs being the presuppositions of all their 'physics', that is, their inquiries into its detail. Secondarily, it is the attempt to discover the corresponding presuppositions of other peoples and other times, and to follow the historical process by which one set of presuppositions has turned into another.[33]

These presuppositions are absolute in the sense that they 'are not answers to questions but only *presuppositions of questions,* and therefore the distinction between what is true and what is false does not apply to them, but only the distinction between what is presupposed and what is not presupposed'.[34] The thinkers whose theories historians investigate held in mind presuppositions that gave rise to the questions to which they sought answers in their inquiries.

An Essay on Metaphysics, written immediately afterwards on board a Dutch cargo ship on a routine tour of the Dutch East Indies and published in 1940, saw this idea worked into a full-fledged doctrine.[35] 'Whenever anybody states a thought in words', Collingwood began, 'there are a great many more thoughts in his mind than are expressed in his statement. Among these there are some which stand in a peculiar relation to the thought he has stated: they are not merely its context, they are its presuppositions.'[36] Through the 'orderly and systematic thinking' definitive of a Baconian science, the historical metaphysician aims to 'disentangle' this knot of thoughts by reducing it to 'a system or series of thoughts in which thinking the thoughts is at the same time thinking the connexions between them'.[37] Collingwood stated his thesis on the nature of these relations in a series of propositions and definitions:

> *Prop. 1.* Every statement is made in answer to a question.
>
> *Def. 1.* That which is stated (i.e. that which can be true or false) is a proposition; stating it is called propounding it.
>
> *Prop. 2.* Every question involves a presupposition.

Def. 2. To say that a question 'does not arise' is to say that it involves a presupposition not in fact being made.

Def. 3. That something causes a certain question to arise is the 'logical efficacy' of that thing.

Def. 4. To assume is to suppose by an act of free choice.

Prop. 3. The logical efficacy of a supposition does not depend on the truth of what is supposed, or even on its being thought true, but only on its being supposed.

Prop. 4. A presupposition is either relative or absolute.

Def. 5. A relative presupposition is one that stands relatively to one question as its presupposition and relatively to another as its answer.

Def. 6. An absolute presupposition is one that stands, relatively to all questions to which it is related, as a presupposition, never as an answer.

Prop. 5. Absolute presuppositions are not propositions.[38]

An example should help clarify what Collingwood had in mind. It is an *absolute presupposition* of contemporary Western medicine that bodily illnesses have physical causes. When I experience a stomach ache, recollect that I ate seafood for lunch and thereby propound 'the seafood has given me a stomach ache', I state this as a *proposition*. Propositions, unlike absolute presuppositions, are testable against other propositions; the present one could be challenged by my wife's contention that my habit of eating too hurriedly is the cause of my stomach ache. Moreover, *propositions are answers to questions*. 'The seafood has given me a stomach ache' is my answer to the question of its physical cause. The absolute presupposition 'bodily illnesses have physical causes' does not enter the question-answer complex; rather, it provides the framework in which the whole inquiry into my stomach ache takes place. Had I presupposed absolutely or unquestioningly something besides 'bodily illnesses have physical causes', say, 'bodily illnesses have supernatural causes' or 'bodily illnesses are the result of immoral behaviour', different questions would have arisen, which would have led me to propound different propositions on the cause of my stomach ache. This is what Collingwood meant when he stated that questions 'arise' relative to the absolute presuppositions governing an inquiry. The historical metaphysician identifies these absolute presuppositions and, in so doing, reveals the basis upon which thought and action make sense.[39]

Since they are the logically ultimate foundations of a given science or universe of discourse, it may be expected that Collingwood placed a premium on expounding the role of absolute presuppositions in re-enactment and the logic of question and answer. Their relation to the logic of question and answer can be easily discerned. Behind the questions to which statements are answers are presuppositions; relative, if they can be propounded as propositions and thereby tested against other propositions; absolute, if they are so grounded in the foundation of the inquiry that no means exists for their verification – they can only give rise to further presuppositions relative to them, which together were termed a constellation of presuppositions.

The case for re-enactment is less transparent. Collingwood did not consider the two theories in a way that may have illuminated how absolute presuppositions are recovered in the re-thinking of past thoughts. There has nevertheless been a tendency to interpret re-enactment as arriving at knowledge of absolute presuppositions, the source of which is T.M. Knox, the editor of Collingwood's two posthumous works, *The Idea of Nature* and *The Idea of History*. Citing 'documentary evidence that in 1936 he still believed in the possibility of metaphysics as a separate study, distinct altogether from history', Knox propagated the view that Collingwood had undergone a 'radical conversion' by 1938, after which he embraced a 'historicism not unlike Croce's', according to which 'philosophy as a separate discipline is liquidated by being converted into history'.[40] On this interpretation, since the practice of philosophy became identifying absolute presuppositions and since the practice of history had long been the re-enactment of past thought, re-thinking past thoughts could be regarded as the method for recovering absolute presuppositions.

However, this argument for the seamless integration of re-enactment and the theory of absolute presuppositions hits a stumbling block when it is recalled that Collingwood conceived re-enactment as a means for producing knowledge of the *purposive* and *intentional* thoughts of past agents, which must exclude knowledge of their *unconsciously held* absolute presuppositions.[41] Indeed, the whole reason why re-enactment attained such a status in analytical philosophy of history from the 1950s consisted in the way that it provided a basis for erecting a liberal, humanistic and intentionalist philosophy of history that its proponents hoped could defend history's methodological autonomy against Hempel's scientific determinism. As for absolute presuppositions, Collingwood was unambiguous that their logical efficacy lay in how they governed thought and action at a preconscious level. Again in the context of a rebuke of psychology and its realist epistemology, he wrote:

> Introspection can do no more than bring into the focus of consciousness something of which we are already aware. But in our less scientific moments, when knowledge appears to us in the guise of mere apprehension, intuiting that which simply confronts us, we are not even aware that whatever we state to ourselves or others is stated in answer to a question, still less that every such question rests on presuppositions, and least of all that among these presuppositions some are absolute presuppositions. In this kind of thinking, absolute presuppositions are certainly at work; but they are doing their work in darkness, the light of consciousness never falling on them.

Or a few pages later, in discussing how absolute presuppositions change:

> The absolute presuppositions of any given society, at any phase of its history, form a structure which is subject to 'strains' . . . If the strains are too great, the structure collapses and is replaced by another, which will be a modification of the old with the destructive strain removed; a modification not consciously devised but created by a process of unconscious thought.[42]

As Connelly has clarified against earlier misunderstandings, by unconscious Collingwood was not suggesting that absolute presuppositions inhabit the hidden psychic recesses of Freudian psychology. 'Unconscious' is better understood as 'unaware'. Collingwood's point was that presupposing has a logical structure; in Connelly's words, 'we are unaware of our presuppositions in so far as we do not realise to what our statements logically commit us'.[43] The principle to be stressed following from this is that historical and philosophical inquiry enables us to know better something we, so to speak, already know. Put differently, we come to know explicitly that which is operative implicitly in the present. As early as *Speculum Mentis,* Collingwood explained that the distinction between explicit and implicit requires careful clarification. For example, although a 'moral agent' must remain explicitly aware of the difference between right and wrong in order to be a moral agent, an observer studying his experience may find it impossible to give an account of it without stating principles and distinctions that the agent himself did not recognize:

> Thus an artist constructs his work on principles which are really operative in the construction, but are not explicitly recognized by himself: in art they are implicit, to become explicit only in the criticism of art. Similarly theology makes explicit certain principles which are implicitly, but never explicitly, present in the religious consciousness; and in general what we call philosophy reveals explicitly the principles which are implicit in what we call everyday experience.[44]

A decade later, in *An Essay on Philosophical Method,* 'what we are trying to do is not to discover something of which until now we have been ignorant, but to know better something which in some sense we knew already'.[45] The late attempt to reform metaphysics as the historical science of discovering absolute presuppositions belonged to a prolonged effort to bring into focus the foundations of thought and action implicit in each epoch's self-understanding.

With regard to empathetic understanding, Collingwood's theory of absolute presuppositions marked a shift from an inadequate epistemologically preoccupied individual-to-individual conception to a metaphysical one concerned with exposing the conditions in which it was possible for past agents to hold their beliefs as true and to act upon them accordingly. This is the historical context that empathy's exponents have wanted to identify, but never fully illuminated.

But how can historians provide satisfactory accounts of absolute presuppositions when they are defined by the idea that they are never propounded and therefore unavailable to be verified as true or false? 'To inquire into the truth of a presupposition', after all, 'is to assume that it is not an absolute presupposition but a relative presupposition.'[46] As absolute, they presuppose nothing; nothing is logically prior to them, meaning that the entire network of knowledge claims by reference to which we determine truth and falsity already presuppose them.

The answer lies in making a distinction between the content of an absolute presupposition, which as logically ultimate can be neither true nor false, and the descriptive formulation of an absolute presupposition, which can be accurate or inaccurate, and thus true or false in the light of evidence. In contrast to natural scientists who presuppose them in the basic conceptions of their inquiries – for example, 'some events have causes' (Newtonian), 'all events have causes' (Kantian) or 'no events have causes' (Einsteinian) – the historical metaphysician's business is to propound the proposition that this one or that one was presupposed in such universes of discourse.[47]

What Collingwood called the 'metaphysical rubric' offered a formula for conducting this business: 'in such and such a phase of scientific thought it is (or was) absolutely presupposed that . . .'. Since metaphysical inquiry was to be historical, history's rubric, 'the evidence at our disposal obliges us to conclude that . . .', could be prefixed to the metaphysical rubric to indicate a procedure for the historical investigation of absolute presuppositions.[48] History demands proof, and the only way to prove that a man presupposed something absolutely is to analyse the records of his thought and find out. Yet for all Collingwood's finely tuned deliberations on historical method elsewhere, he did not elaborate for the metaphysician of absolute presuppositions what is involved in this analysis of historical records; it is 'analysis pure and simple'.[49]

Nor did Collingwood, the archaeologist and historian of Roman Britain, provide examples of the kinds of absolute presuppositions historians outside the history of science, his sole interest in *An Essay on Metaphysics,* have occasion to describe. This is to be expected from a doctrine whose purpose was to replace ontological pure being with concrete knowledge of the foundations of scientific paradigms. Another factor is the late arrival of the doctrine in his philosophy. Having formulated it at the end of his career, he lacked the language in his earlier writings to refer to the absolute presuppositions of his subjects. This does not mean that he was without the conceptual resources to proceed in this manner or that earlier versions did not exist. Connelly has produced evidence from a selection of mainly lesser-known works indicating a role for them at least as far back as his 1919 address to the John Ruskin centenary conference exhibition.[50] The resemblance of *Ruskin's Philosophy* to that of *An Essay on Metaphysics* is unmistakable:

there are certain principles which the man takes as fundamental and incontrovertible . . . These principles form, as it were, the nucleus of his whole mental life: they are the centre from which all his activities radiate. You may think of them as a kind of ring of solid thought . . . to which everything the man does is attached . . . But for the most part we do not know that we possess it: still less do we know what are the convictions which constitute it. The fact seems to be that a man's deepest convictions are precisely those which he never puts into words . . . only the philosopher makes it his business to probe into the mind and lay bare that recess in which the ultimate beliefs lie hidden.[51]

Collingwood's account in *The Idea of History* of three stages of development in the history of historical thinking has been cited as evidence of an attempt to describe the absolute presuppositions of each in terms of its dominant intellectual tradition.[52] His point was that these traditions worked, and continue to work, from theories of knowledge inimical to the production of historical knowledge: Greek mathematical thinking failed to locate its objects in time and space, which is what makes them knowable; medieval theological thinking considered its objects to be singular and infinite, whereas the events of the past are finite and plural; natural scientific thinking determined truth on the basis of observation and experiment, whereas the past is inaccessible and our ideas about it can never be verified.

However, even with the presence of absolute presuppositions in intellectual traditions, there is no sign that Collingwood worked backwards from propositions to the presuppositions that underlay them, as question-and-answer logic would have him proceed. Rather than taking this route, he composed the survey by offering accounts of the relative presuppositions that arose from particular conjunctions of absolute presuppositions. Thus Adrian Oldfield believes the theory is most fruitful when its procedure is reversed, so that the historian begins with an absolute presupposition and proceeds to identify and describe its attendant relative presuppositions. He invokes the imagery of a river, its mouth and source to illustrate the difference. If we stand at the mouth of the river, we have only to walk along its bank to discover its source, but if we stand at its source, while some courses will be ruled out, there appears to us a variety of courses that might have led to it.[53] The view is that of a 'situational analysis', whereby absolute presuppositions supply the context for understanding past actions as conditionally appropriate or adequate to the situation as an agent perceived it.[54]

Collingwood was comfortable with the conceptual relativity of this theory. To those who agonize over a loss of meaning in human life if all our values are little more than historical accidents, he reassures us that all we should hope to do is to live up to the best principles that we have found in our history, grasping something of their provenance and mortality, the better to gain wisdom and act with a knowledge of what is possible in our circumstanced lives.[55] Rather than despair at history's incapacity to supply life with unchanging forms of meaning, Collingwood's metaphysics places meaning in humankind's capacity to act knowingly and purposively within this dynamic structure. This is a historical activity requiring a willingness to learn from the past.

Yet the relativity of the theory of absolute presuppositions appears to create an insurmountable epistemological barrier. Stephen Toulmin has had this to say:

> Being 'enculturated' by our upbringings as we are, we think and act in terms of intellectual and moral presuppositions characteristic of our own culture; these presuppositions determine not only what kinds of conduct we consider right and wrong, but also what kind of phenomena we regard as puzzling or self-explanatory, what sound or established picture of the world we use to interpret our experience, what types of scientific argument and evidence we find cogent or plausible . . . The only safe position (the relativist declares) is to concede final authority within any milieu to the particular intellectual standards current in it, while denying those standards any relevance and authority outside their original contexts.[56]

Presuppositional systems are self-sufficient and self-contained, inside of which propositions have meaning, but outside of which the seeker of historical understanding lacks the appropriate epistemological furniture. By Toulmin's analysis of Collingwood's position in *An Essay on Metaphysics*, 'propositions and concepts can be rationally appraised only "relative to" one particular constellation of absolute presuppositions, viz. that within which they are operative; and, once we leave the scope of one particular framework, we leave also the scope of rational comparison and judgement'.[57]

In so preserving the self-sufficiency of past systems of thought, Collingwood ruined any chance of genuine historical knowledge. Since the thinking that takes place in every epoch does so within its own constellation of presuppositions, inquirers who do not share the presuppositions of their subjects cannot know their thoughts. Self-enclosed presuppositional systems, while enabling understanding and knowledge within them, constitute impenetrable barriers to understanding and knowledge across time. We can have historical knowledge only of those whose presuppositions we share, which is to say we can have no historical knowledge at all.

Shifting our attention back to the hermeneutical complexion of Collingwood's thought, Toulmin's analysis could be said to highlight the lack of consideration that Collingwood, for all his pronouncements on the need to account for the presuppositions held by people who lived in the past, gave to evaluating the role that our own presuppositions play in thinking historically. Put differently, there is in Collingwood an appeal to study the groundforms of knowledge that shaped past thoughts and actions, but an inattentiveness to the ways in which our present-day historical makeup bears upon that study.

This was Gadamer's position in offering a critique of re-enactment. For all his praise of question-and-answer, Gadamer found the Oxford philosopher-historian deficient on the question of how the past is understood from the standpoint of the present. Collingwood succumbed in his view to the historicist pitfall of limiting the meaning of a text to its author's intention. This one-sidedness Collingwood shared with the tradition of hermeneutics alongside which historicism developed in the nineteenth century. 'Traditional hermeneutics', Gadamer wrote in *Truth and Method*, 'has inappropriately narrowed the horizon to which understanding belongs.'[58] Reposed in an agent's intentions, Collingwood's horizon could not account for 'the dimension of hermeneutical mediation which is passed through in every act of understanding'.[59]

Nor did Gadamer approve fully of Collingwood's application of the logic of question and answer to his reconstructionist historical method: 'Historicism tempts us to regard such reduction as a scientific virtue and to regard understanding as a kind of reconstruction which in effect repeats the process whereby the text came into being.'[60] Rather, he took the doctrine to connote an openness to what he termed the '*horizon of the question*, within which the sense of the text is determined', but as a meaning in movement (sense) lies both behind and beyond the text.[61] Two paths lay before Gadamer early on in his career: Hegel's 'integration of past thought into one's own thought' or Schleiermacher's 'psychological reconstruction of past thought'.[62] Taking the Hegelian route, he came to believe that history has an effect (*Wirkungsgeschichte*) on human beings in ways that they mostly do not recognize. 'In fact', he wrote, 'history does not belong to us; we belong to it.'[63]

Gadamer held too incomplete a picture of Collingwood's writings to notice their first-order affinities. He may have remarked that history's hold on human life functions at the level of the absolute presuppositions that enable and set limits on what can be thought, said and done at different stages of human development and within different paradigms of scientific discourse. Nor could he reflect on Collingwood's project to make these unstated principles of human life the object of historical and metaphysical inquiry. His appraisals of Collingwood drew solely from *An Autobiography* and *The Idea of History*. Having explored further regions of Collingwood's thought, the true nature of their conjunction can now be specified.

Notes

1. R.G. Collingwood, *The New Leviathan, or Man, Society, Civilisation and Barbarism*, rev. edn [1942] David Boucher (Oxford: Clarendon Press, 1992), §18.52. Collingwood's books of a later date were compiled posthumously.

2. R.G. Collingwood, *An Essay on Metaphysics,* rev. edn [1940] Rex Martin (Oxford: Clarendon Press, 1998), 36.

3. Ibid., 177–78.

4. I have examined elsewhere Skinner's repudiation of re-enactment alongside his overall endorsement of a Collingwoodian approach. See Tyson Retz, 'Why Re-enactment is Not Empathy, Once and for All', *Journal of the Philosophy of History* 11, 3 (2017), 306–23.

5. Quentin Skinner, 'The Rise of, Challenge to and Prospects for a Collingwoodian Approach to the History of Political Thought', in Dario Castiglione and Iain Hampsher-Monk (eds), *The History of Political Thought in National Context* (Cambridge: Cambridge University Press, 2001), 185.

6. Quentin Skinner, *Visions of Politics, Volume 1: Regarding Method* (Cambridge: Cambridge University Press, 2002), 120.

7. Skinner, 'Collingwoodian Approach', 176–77.

8. Kenneth B. McIntyre. 'Historicity as Methodology or Hermeneutics: Collingwood's Influence on Skinner and Gadamer', *Journal of the Philosophy of History* 2, 2 (2008), 152.

9. Quentin Skinner, 'Meaning and Understanding in the History of Ideas', *History and Theory* 8, 1 (1969), 23.

10. Ibid., 38.

11. Ibid., 39.

12. Ibid., 52.

13. R.G. Collingwood, *The Idea of History,* rev. edn [1946] Jan van der Dussen (Oxford: Oxford University Press, 1994), 297, 298, 303.

14. W.H. Dray and W.J. van der Dussen, introduction to R.G. Collingwood, *The Principles of History: and Other Writings in Philosophy of History,* W.H. Dray and W.J. van der Dussen (eds) (New York: Oxford University Press, 1999), lxvi.

15. Collingwood, *Principles of History,* 50.

16. Ibid.

17. Ibid., 54.

18. Ibid.

19. Christopher Fear, 'The Question-and-Answer Logic of Historical Context', *History of the Human Sciences* 26, 3 (2013), 71.

20. Collingwood, *Idea of History,* 301.

21. Collingwood, *An Autobiography* (Oxford: Clarendon Press, 1978), 23.

22. Ibid., 25.

23. Ibid., 27.

24. Ibid., 29–30.

25. Ibid., 31–33.

26. Collingwood, *Idea of History,* 257–60, 270.

27. Ibid., 269.

28. Ibid., 275–76.

29. W.J. van der Dussen, *History as a Science: The Philosophy of R.G. Collingwood* (The Hague: Martinus Nijhoff, 1981), 3.

30. G.R. Elton, *Return to Essentials: Some Reflections on the Present State of Historical Study* (Cambridge: Cambridge University Press, 1991), 30.

31. Collingwood, *Metaphysics,* 3–20, 62.

32. Ibid., 15.

33. Collingwood, *Autobiography,* 65–66.

34. Ibid., 66.

35. Collingwood suffered a small stroke in 1938. His doctors recommended this journey by sea to restore his health. Any improvement was short-lived: a series of strokes forced him to resign his chair in 1941 and he died of pneumonia in 1943, aged 53.

36. Collingwood, *Metaphysics*, 21.
37. Ibid., 22–23.
38. Ibid., 23–33.
39. No shortage of comparisons to other doctrines have been offered for illuminating the nature of absolute presuppositions. Louis Mink, *Mind, History, and Dialectic: The Philosophy of R.G. Collingwood* (Bloomington: Indiana University Press, 1969), 146, calls them '*a priori* conceptual systems', similar to Kant's 'categories of understanding', which provide 'the general structure of experience'. Timothy C. Lord, 'R.G. Collingwood: A Continental Philosopher?', *Clio* 23, 3 (2000), 333–34, notes 'remarkable similarities' with Kuhn's 'conception of paradigm changes in the history of science' and with Foucault's conception of the *archive* 'as a determiner of what can be thought, said, or stated in a manner similar to that in which absolute presuppositions determine relative presuppositions'. Rom Harré and Michael Krausz, *Varieties of Relativism* (Oxford: Blackwell, 1996), 85, suggest that they function like Wittgenstein's 'boundary propositions', expressing 'the grammar of the discourses that sustain a form of life'. Similarly, Marnie Hughes-Warrington, *How Good an Historian Shall I Be? R.G. Collingwood, the Historical Imagination and Education* (Exeter: Imprint Academic, 2003), 89, invokes the imagery of Wittgenstein's forms of life as being grounded in a dynamic and changing 'riverbed', rather than an immobile 'bedrock' in the style Kant tried to expose.
40. T.M. Knox, editor's preface to R.G. Collingwood, *The Idea of History* (Oxford: Clarendon Press, 1946), x–xi.
41. David Boucher, *The Social and Political Thought of R.G. Collingwood* (Cambridge: Cambridge University Press, 1989), 117; Rex Martin, 'Collingwood's Claim that Metaphysics is a Historical Discipline', David Boucher, James Connelly and Tariq Modood (eds), *Philosophy, History and Civilisation: Interdisciplinary Perspectives on R.G. Collingwood* (Cardiff: University of Wales Press, 1995), 211.
42. Collingwood, *Metaphysics*, 43, 48.
43. James Connelly, *Metaphysics, Method and Politics: The Political Philosophy of R.G. Collingwood* (Exeter: Imprint Academic, 2003), 105
44. R.G. Collingwood, *Speculum Mentis, or the Map of Knowledge* (Oxford: Clarendon Press, 1924), 85.
45. R.G. Collingwood, *An Essay on Philosophical Method* (Oxford: Clarendon Press, 1933), 11.
46. Collingwood, *Metaphysics*, 53–54.
47. Ibid., 33, 49–57.
48. Ibid., 55–56 (emphases removed).
49. Ibid., 40.
50. Connelly, *Metaphysics, Method and Politics*, 115–41. This tribute to Ruskin nineteen years after his death took place at Coniston, in the Lake District, where until beginning at Rugby School at the age of thirteen, Collingwood was educated at home under the Ruskinian vision of his father, William Gershom Collingwood, Ruskin's biographer, unpaid secretary, lifelong admirer and devoted disciple. See Fred Inglis, *History Man: The Life of R.G. Collingwood* (Princeton: Princeton University Press, 2009), Chapter 1.
51. R.G. Collingwood, *Ruskin's Philosophy: An Address Delivered at the Ruskin Centenary Conference, Coniston, August 8th, 1919* (Chichester: Quentin Nelson, 1971), 6–8 (first published in 1922).
52. Adrian Oldfield, 'Metaphysics and History in Collingwood's Thought', in Boucher, Connelly and Modood (eds), *Philosophy, History and Civilisation*, 195–200.
53. Ibid., 196.
54. Karl Popper, *Objective Knowledge: An Evolutionary Approach* (Oxford: Clarendon Press, 1972), 178–79, described situational analysis as a conjectural explanation of a human action that appeals to the situation in which agents find themselves. Creative actions can never

be fully explained, but they can be made rationally understandable, that is, seen as adequate to the situation as an agent saw it, through an idealized reconstruction of the problem situation as it was viewed by the agent. Peter Skagestad, *Making Sense of History: The Philosophies of Popper and Collingwood* (Oslo: Universitetsforlaget, 1975) has compared Collingwood's analysis of absolute presuppositions with Popper's analysis of historical knowledge.

55. Inglis, *History Man*, 214.

56. Stephen Toulmin, *Human Understanding, Volume 1* (Oxford: Clarendon Press, 1972), 66–67.

57. Ibid., 73–74.

58. Hans-Georg Gadamer, *Truth and Method*, 2nd rev. edn, trans. Joel Weinsheimer and Donald G. Marshall (New York: Continuum, 2004), 251.

59. Hans-Georg Gadamer, 'Hermeneutics and Historicism' (1965), in *Truth and Method* (supplement 1), 516.

60. Gadamer, *Truth and Method*, 366.

61. Ibid., 363.

62. Hans-Georg Gadamer, 'The Heritage of Hegel', in his *Reason in the Age of Science*, trans. Frederick D. Lawrence (Cambridge, MA: MIT Press, 1981), 40.

63. Gadamer, *Truth and Method*, 278.

CHAPTER 8

Horizons of Context

At the time when Collingwood was in the south of France propounding the three propositions that came to anchor his philosophy of history, Gadamer was writing his *Habilitationsschrift* under the supervision of Martin Heidegger, one of the foremost philosophers of the twentieth century. Eleven years his senior, Collingwood was an established philosopher, historian, archaeologist and Oxford don. Gadamer's elevation to academic prominence followed a less certain path.

Hans-Georg Gadamer was the son of the distinguished pharmacist Johannes Gadamer, an unyielding man of conservative and Bismarckian temperament, elected rector of the University of Marburg in 1922. After having his doctoral thesis accepted that same year at the same institution, following which he became infected with polio, Hans-Georg turned his attention to earning the respect of Heidegger, attending his seminars at the University of Freiburg and accompanying him back to Marburg when Heidegger was appointed there to an associate professorship in 1923. The rector's son assisted Husserl's former *Assistent* in settling into his new surrounds, running errands for him and serving in his turn as the fêted phenomenologist's unpaid departmental hand. Yet despite their close association, Gadamer failed to convince Heidegger of his talents. 'If you cannot summon sufficient toughness toward yourself', he wrote the young man in 1924, 'nothing will come of you.'[1]

Understandably discouraged, Gadamer resolved to reorient his studies towards a career in teaching classical philology. During the course of study for his teaching certificate, he prided himself on reading only books at least two thousand years old. According to his biographer Jean Grondin, this 'flight to the Greeks' sharpened his hermeneutic bent by cultivating in him a 'sensitivity to the rhetorical dimension of meaning, to the *vouloir-dire* to be

---

Notes for this section begin on page 167.

heard behind what is explicit'.[2] More immediately, it won him Heidegger's esteem: when he sat his teacher's examination in late 1927, Heidegger was one of three present to assess him – the next day, he invited Gadamer to do his *Habilitation* with him.[3]

In his evaluation of the thesis 'Interpretations of Plato's *Philebus*', submitted in 1928 and revised and published in 1931 as *Plato's Dialectical Ethics*, Heidegger lauded Gadamer for taking 'the right path of concrete interpretation' to the study of philosophy.[4] In his doctoral thesis, also on Plato, Gadamer had already adopted a critical posture towards what he later found Collingwood expressing in his 'brilliant and telling critique' of the Oxford realists; that is, the idea, promulgated in Germany by the neo-Kantians, that philosophical problems could be studied divorced of their context. As Robert Pippin has observed, Gadamer's programme began as a reaction against the anaemic philosophizing of the neo-Kantians and their 'great problems' approach to the history of philosophy.[5] He made plain what he thought of that approach in the introduction to his 1922 thesis:

> This is the general problem involved in doing history of problems, namely that it removes a problem from its unique historical context and yet thinks it has comprehended its full content. Actually, though, its content is decisively determined by the context in which the problem emerged, and it is just this uniqueness which cannot be abstracted without loss . . . It is a fundamentally false endeavor to try to point out, from within the standpoint of the our present problematic, contradictions or mistaken inferences in Plato's thought, and to explain them by appeal to deficiency in the abstractive capacity of Plato's thought.[6]

In Grondin's words, and conveying the message of Gadamer's later hermeneutics, 'Plato's perspective ought rather to be conceived as something completely different from ours, one that is perfectly alien to our time, from which we have a good deal to learn'.[7] As we have seen with Collingwood, and now with Gadamer, this involves investigating a historical subject matter determined by the *problem context* in which it emerged.

Well before he discovered Collingwood around the time of the Second World War, Gadamer had taken the view that it is not problems themselves, but the attempts to solve them that have their histories. The distinctly local context in which he came to this conclusion keeps in check the claim that Collingwood exerted a direct and formative influence on the development of his hermeneutics. Collingwood appeared more as a kindred spirit of the German tradition of historical thought than as a thinker to be emulated for having superseded it. Collingwood is completely absent from Grondin's account of Gadamer's century-long life, and it is for good reason that Heidegger, his concept of *Dasein* (literally, 'being there') and his magnum opus, *Being and Time* (1927), take pride of place in the biography before Gadamer himself appears. Nor did Gadamer in his own biography *Philosophical Apprenticeships* feel compelled to mention Collingwood among the portraits of the main protagonists in his intellectual evolution.[8] In terms of Gadamer's intellectual allegiances, Jürgen Habermas, another dignitary in twentieth-century German intellectual life, may have put it best when he described Gadamer's hermeneutics as 'an urbanization of the Heideggerian countryside', by which he meant – at the expense of reducing Heidegger to something provincial – Gadamer translated Heidegger's motifs into the social language of humanity in the age of science and technology.[9]

Notwithstanding these qualifications on the Heideggerian complexion of Gadamer's work, it has been firmly established that Collingwood played an instrumental role in bringing his hermeneutical outlook to its full fruition. To Gadamer, the dialectic of question and answer was the 'hermeneutical *Urphänomen*: No assertion is possible that cannot be understood as an answer to a question, and assertions can only be understood in this way'.[10] The thrust of his hermeneutics is this: by what questions were the texts we study driven?

Scholars have not failed to notice the significance of Collingwood and Gadamer's agreement. John Hogan has suggested that Collingwood provides 'clarifying insights' into the functioning of Gadamer's concept of historically effected consciousness. Kenneth McIntyre has drawn parallels between both men's desire to reunify the radical division in human consciousness associated with modernity. Chinatsu Kobayashi and Mathieu Marion have considered re-enactment and Gadamer's 'fusion of horizons' from the perspective of temporal distance and its implications for historical understanding. Dimitrios Vardoulakis has evaluated these concepts and looked to supplement deficiencies in one with insights from the other.[11]

Philosophers indebted to Gadamer have also made reference to the Collingwoodian dimension of his thought. For Alasdair MacIntyre, Collingwood and Gadamer illuminated the importance for philosophy of having a shared respect for past standards of argument. In order to 'constitute ourselves members of a community able to engage with others in a dialectical inquiry', the questions we pose must 'invite a type of answer that is open to evaluation in respect of the quality of arguments that would have to be advanced in order to sustain it', a type of questioning 'Collingwood called the logic of question and answer'. According to Paul Ricœur, Collingwood announced Heidegger's distinction between a 'bygone past' (*Vergangenheit*) and a 'having-been' (*Gewesenheit*) in his conceptions of a natural past, superseded and dead, and a past event, incapsulated in the present. The transmission of tradition in Gadamer's history of effect similarly turns temporal distance from an empty space to be traversed into the productive field in which understanding takes place.[12]

In terms of textual evidence, these appraisals rest on Gadamer's eight-page discussion of Collingwood in *Truth and Method* as well as the shorter critique of Collingwood's historicism in his 1965 essay 'Hermeneutics and Historicism'. Published originally in 1960 (*Wahrheit und Methode*), with translations from later German editions appearing in English and French in the mid-1970s, Gadamer devoted a whole decade to his *summa* of hermeneutics while an associate professor at the University of Heidelberg.[13] If the section on Collingwood is relatively brief, this is offset by the pivotal position it occupies in the development of Gadamer's argument.

Composed of three parts, the book's thesis is that 'truth' and 'method' coexist in the human sciences in an uneasy and unstable tension. The scientifically methodical procedure that monopolized truth in nineteenth-century hermeneutics and historicism could not, Gadamer believed, yield a definitive grasp of its object. Understanding can never be fully grounded because we always come too late to the task of conceptualizing and objectifying what we in a sense already understand. Understanding in the humanistic disciplines should consist not in attaining a subjective relation to a given object, but in integrating the 'horizon' to which it belongs into that of the present situation, which in turn requires integrating the present horizon into that of the past. The backward movement from present to past describes the shift in our thinking needed to accommodate the object; the forward movement from past to present describes the extension of that object into the language of today without which it could not be thought about.

Part One identifies Kant's aesthetics as having excessively subjectified the discovery of truth in artistic experience by associating it with the mastery of reflection over its object. In Part Two, this accentuation of subjective experience is taken to be behind the belief in nineteenth-century historicism and hermeneutics that interpreters could detach themselves from their present-day circumstances to recapture original meaning in its own terms. By rehabilitating the concepts of prejudice, tradition and temporal distance, Gadamer attempts to replace a crude psychologism in nineteenth-century thought with a fusion of past and present horizons, rather than trying to overcome temporal constraints, one enabled by human historicity. Finally, he develops in Part Three a linguistically grounded concept of understanding that takes language to be something not personal to the subject, but something common to a community that unites I and Thou. The disinterested and contemplative interpreter who reconstructs the *mens authoris* behind a text shifted to one interested, concerned and open to reaching an agreement with the meaning of the text itself.

Gadamer discusses Collingwood at the end of Part Two, after having delivered his verdict on the inadequacies of the historicist-hermeneutic conception of historical consciousness and before turning to the Platonic dialogues in Part Three to find its corrective. By locating the meaning of past events in the intentions of the agents involved in them, Gadamer viewed re-enactment as repeating the errors of an outdated hermeneutics. But by fixing the interpreter's gaze on the distinct subject matter raised by the text, the logic of question and answer stood as a point of agreement upon which the new hermeneutics of the twentieth century had begun to establish itself.

★ ★ ★

It is vital to be clear about the manner in which this new hermeneutics of the twentieth century differed from its predecessor, for I am making claims about the hermeneutical significance of Collingwood's theories by evaluating Gadamer's reception of them. Placing in perspective much of our discussion of the empathy-dependent method of nineteenth-century German historicism, Michael Ermarth has examined the distinction between the 'traditional' or 'methodological' hermeneutics developed by Schleiermacher, Droysen and Dilthey, and the 'philosophical' hermeneutics initiated by Heidegger and made by Gadamer his own. He writes that a major difference between the two:

> concerns the notion of *Verstehen* as empathetic re-construction, re-enactment, or re-experiencing. The old hermeneutics held meaning to be primarily a matter of the interpreter's reconstituting the genesis, development, and derivation of the originator's ideas and mental contents. The new hermeneutic, on the other hand is far more radical. It does not view hermeneutics as being concerned solely with establishing or re-cognizing past meanings but rather puts forward ontological claims concerning the relation between past meaning and the 'happening' of history itself.[14]

Such descriptions of the nineteenth-century tradition are by now familiar. Schleiermacher cast aside the distinction between induction and deduction, illuminating instead the circular structure of understanding as it occurs in the interplay between part, whole and the interpreter's preliminary sense of the context in which part and whole belong. Droysen took this subjective element of the hermeneutic circle to be proof that history is inevitably constituted from the vantage point of present-day 'ethical collectivities', within which there is relative objectivity, but never of the unmediated kind sought by Ranke. Dilthey, finally, in attempting to found the *Geisteswissenschaften* on a sure epistemological footing, extended the circle to include a continuity between ordinary sense perception as given in concrete experience (*Erlebnis*) and the methodical cognition of the human sciences.

Beyond the exegesis of canonical texts and historical traces, and indeed beyond considerations of correct method and epistemological justification, this widening of the interpretive circle continued in the twentieth century to encompass 'the question of questions', that of 'the Being of being'. Ricœur has accounted for this transition from the methodologically disposed hermeneutics of the nineteenth century to the ontologically conscious hermeneutics of the twentieth. Hermeneutics, in his words:

> had to disengage itself from the psychological problems of transfer into another's life, and come to grips with the more ontological problems involved in comprehending 'being-in-the-world'. Here we see the influence of the early Heidegger . . . Here comprehension is no longer a psychological concept; it is dissociated from any idea of empathy, any perception of an alien consciousness; it is interpreted in ontological terms as one of the components of *Dasein,* which is no longer a consciousness but a being-in-the-world, a being which faces the question of being within the context of specific situations and plans, against a background of finiteness and mortality. Thus 'depsychologized', comprehension is brought nearer the primordial problem of language.[15]

In *Being and Time,* published the year Gadamer won Heidegger over at his teacher's examination, the latter observed that Dilthey's fondness for methodology and epistemology, characteristic of his century, blinded him to the wider ontological dimensions of his project. *Verstehen* is not a way of investigating the world, held Heidegger, it is a way of being in the world. The phenomenon of 'understanding the "psychical life of Others" . . . none too happily designated as *"empathy" ("Einfühlung")*', is one according to which 'The Other would be a duplicate of the Self'.[16] Heidegger's terms for understanding were not those of his subjects, not because they were unaware of their own meaning, but because they could not articulate the 'being' presupposed in all thought and utterance. The real question for genuine thinking and understanding is not what they thought, but what thinking and understanding reveal themselves to be through them. In every act of thinking, something new comes into being different from its derivation.

In a series of lectures Gadamer attended at the University of Freiburg in 1923, only months before he returned to Marburg with the new appointee, Heidegger had in fact already instigated the break with the older variety of hermeneutics. 'In hermeneutics', he told his audience, 'what is developed for *Dasein* is a possibility of its becoming and being for itself in the manner of an understanding of itself'.[17] Whereas hermeneutics previously concerned itself with specifying the relations that bind the structures of interpretive interdependence, as well as the rules that govern interpretation within this structure, it became with Heidegger the means by which the 'already given' nature of our structures of understanding discloses itself in the investigation of that which is to be understood. Within the hermeneutic circle, as he put it in his larger work:

> is hidden a positive possibility of the most primordial kind of knowing. To be sure, we genuinely take hold of this possibility only when, in our interpretation, we have understood that our first, last, and constant task is never to allow our fore-having, fore-sight, and fore-conception to be presented to us by fancies

and popular conceptions, but rather to make the scientific theme secure by working out these fore-structures in terms of the things themselves.[18]

Since we always find ourselves *in* the world, we find ourselves *along with* that which is to be understood. Structures of understanding are thus already given over to the subject matter we try to understand. This new hermeneutics is the attempt to make explicit this 'situatedness', which, prior as it is to any specific event of understanding, is presupposed in the attempt at its own explication.

Gadamer took Heidegger's ontologically fundamental hermeneutics to imply a universality that for him became encapsulated in the term 'philosophical hermeneutics'. In a suite of essays intended to clarify and extend positions taken in his major work, collected under the title *Philosophical Hermeneutics,* Gadamer was at pains to distinguish this approach from its forebears. 'Philosophical hermeneutics', he began one piece, 'takes as its task the opening up of the hermeneutical dimension in its full scope, showing its fundamental significance for our entire understanding of the world and thus for all the various forms in which this understanding manifests itself.'[19] 'The problem is really universal', he reflected in another, 'science always stands under definite conditions of methodological abstraction', the successes of which 'rest on the fact that other possibilities for questioning are concealed by abstraction'. Methodology alone 'does not guarantee in any way the productivity of its application . . . there is such a thing as methodological sterility, that is, the application of a method to something not really worth knowing, to something that has not been made an object of investigation on the basis of a genuine question'.[20] 'What I am describing', he concluded, 'is the mode of the whole human experience of the world':

> I call this experience hermeneutical, for the process we are describing is repeated continually throughout our familiar experience. There is always a world already interpreted, already organized in its basic relations, into which experience steps as something new, upsetting what has led our expectations and undergoing reorganization itself in the upheaval. Misunderstanding and strangeness are not the first factors, so that misunderstanding can be regarded as the specific task of hermeneutics [as it was for Schleiermacher]. Just the reverse is the case. Only the support of familiar and common understanding makes possible the venture into the alien, and thus the broadening and enrichment of our own experience of the world.[21]

What was Gadamer's conception of method that led him to repudiate it so thoroughly? As Joel Weinsheimer has explained, method must be understood as the 'paradigmatic expression of the condition that gave rise to epistemology'.[22] Like Collingwood, Gadamer shifted attention from epistemology to metaphysics, which for him signified an explication of the ontological structures of understanding. He concentrated on the categories of being through which we understand, not the methods by which knowledge can be said to be scientifically validated.

From Descartes to Husserl, the search for the foundations of knowledge remained a prime occupation in philosophy. Gadamer believed that method and epistemology were a response to *Fremdheit*: the condition of no longer being at home in the world. In the natural sciences, man's alienation from nature came to manifest itself in the epistemology of self-consciousness, whose method consisted in taking as certain only 'clear and distinct perceptions'. Coming from the same background, the human sciences of the nineteenth century removed past creations from the familiar, self-evident and primordial domain of the present, and gave them up to research as data from which the past was to be represented. Method derived from this awareness that the intelligibility of objects no longer belonged self-evidently to the present.[23] In this context, empathy emerged from a psychologistic epistemology as a method of *transfer* to a past mental state. According to Gadamer, the longer hermeneutics concerned itself with method, the longer it would perpetuate the false division in human consciousness between past and present, I and others, self and world.

Gadamer's resistance to method assumes a more concrete character in the context of the so-called crisis of historicism of the early twentieth century in Germany. Historical research in the historicist tradition operated from the single-point Cartesian and Kantian conception of subjectivity that after the 'catastrophe of 1918' came under attack for its logical and metaphysical assumptions of diachronic succession, order, continuity, totality and progress. Friedrich Nietzsche's second essay of his *Untimely Meditations* (1874), 'On the Uses and Disadvantages of History for Life', had already captured the mood of senescence and passivity in the 'race of eunuchs' watching over 'the great historical world-harem': those disciples of Ranke labouring in the archive. In a 1939 lecture course, Heidegger credited Nietzsche with having shown historicism to be the final stage of the self-conscious, autonomous *cogito* of Cartesian metaphysics, that which had furnished historicism with its values of objectivity, methodological clarity and scientific truth.[24]

Within this framework, Windelband, Rickert and Dilthey had attempted to affirm the objectivity of historical research against the idealist metaphysics of Hegel's Christological revelation of *Geist*, Humboldt's *Ideen,* Ranke's God and Droysen's moral powers. In the upheaval of the new century, however, the belief in a rigorously methodical access to truth, by embodying the universal validity of scientific consciousness, appeared to contradict the lived experience of the previous decades as well as finite historical consciousness. 'By attempting to fit history within the recalcitrant frame of science', writes Charles Bambach, 'historicists had denied the hermeneutic experience that first made history possible.'[25] Gadamer inherited from Heidegger the belief that human historicity and objective science were irreconcilable. The question for them was not the way out of the subject-object *aporia* the neo-Kantians had sought, but the destruction of that form of thinking altogether.

Two clarifications can be made from this. First, unlike Collingwood, whose prime interest was historical understanding and knowledge, Gadamer was not a philosopher of history in the sense that he directed his energies to illuminating the processes and nature of historical understanding and knowledge per se. His point was that *all* understanding – not only historical understanding – is historically effected. Historicism, the doctrine that the meaning of an object resides in its past, warred in his thought with historicity, the condition of our living in history and thus of our being historically constituted. Since we understand only thanks to our belonging to a historical tradition, there is no vantage point from which something inhering in that tradition could be grasped independently and represented historically in its own terms. Second, and in the same vein, Gadamer intended philosophical hermeneutics to be a corrective to the epistemological naïveté of historicism and its concept of historical consciousness. It was not an extension of Dilthey's programme for the human sciences; it aligned itself specifically against the idea that thinking and understanding in the humanistic disciplines is methodically executed.

With greater economy than in the notoriously tortuous *Truth and Method,* Gadamer made plain these points in his 1957 lectures at the University of Louvain, published later under the title 'The Problem of Historical Consciousness'. In many ways a summary of the arguments expounded in the larger work, Gadamer set out to call into question the conception of knowledge that seeks to grasp a historical phenomenon in its singularity. 'Historical consciousness is interested in knowing not how men, people, or states develop *in general,* but, quite on the contrary, how *this* man, *this* people, or *this* state became what it is; how each of these *particulars* could come to pass and end up specifically *there*.'[26] As the mode of consciousness from which the historical school sprang, it is commonly described as having a 'historical sense', by which is designated the historian's ability to conquer the 'natural naïveté' that makes the less trained judge the past by present-day standards and frames of reference, and instead understand it from within its own genetic context. 'Historical consciousness no longer listens sanctimoniously to the voice that reaches out from the past but, in reflecting on it, replaces it within the context where it took root in order to see the significance and relative value proper to it.'[27]

The 'problem of historical consciousness' was therefore the problem of historicist method in the human sciences. Schleiermacher's circular movement between the divination of the meaning of the whole and its articulation in the parts was not so much a result of inquiry as it was a *deficiency* of inquiry.

He needed a 'genial gift for empathy' in order to decipher a *lost* meaning, a meaning whose *absence* in the present necessitated its *retrieval* from the past.[28] Historicism supposed that temporal distance is a space to be traversed, an exploit achieved by empathy, which in many ways symbolized the 'triumph of the philological method'.[29] Having brought the I and Thou into reciprocal accord, the task for historical consciousness in Dilthey's method was raised to gaining a victory over its own relativity; that is, to obtaining objective knowledge of the psychical conditions behind past forms of life. But while Dilthey recognized that the hidden meaning to be deciphered inhered in the historicity of his subjects, he neglected to address in equal measure how the features constitutive of his own historical situation impinged on that inquiry. He believed he had achieved a truly historical view of the world, 'but at bottom', in Gadamer's view, 'what his historical reflections were able to justify was nothing other than the grandiose and epical self-effacement practiced by Ranke'.[30] Thus Gadamer affirmed in *Truth and Method* that Dilthey, in extending Romantic hermeneutics into a historical method, 'is only the interpreter of the historical school'; he formulated 'what Ranke and Droysen really think' and, in the final analysis, 'the foundation for the study of history is hermeneutics'.[31]

In the book, Gadamer moves fluidly from a repudiation of nineteenth-century historical consciousness to an advancement of Collingwood's question-and-answer account of historical understanding. Historical consciousness consisted in knowing that the otherness of the past demanded not the instantiation of a general law, but something historically unique. Yet by attempting to transcend its own situatedness to know the other, it indulged in the 'dialectical illusion' of 'perfect enlightenment'. In so deceiving itself, historical consciousness was not genuinely open to the past. Its method for reading texts historically 'smoothed them out' beforehand, so that the criteria of the historian's own knowledge were never called into question by the contents of the text itself. Gadamer's historically effected or hermeneutical consciousness, on the other hand, culminated not in methodological sureness, but in a readiness to experience the truth claims of the other.[32] Plato's model of the dialectic supplied the 'logical structure of openness' that characterized this hermeneutical consciousness. It was a logic of question and answer:

> The essence of the question is to have sense. Now sense involves a sense of direction. Hence the sense of the question is the only direction from which the answer can be given if it is to make sense. A question places what is questioned in a particular perspective. When a question arises, it breaks open the being of the object, as it were.[33]

Gadamer found in the Platonic dialogues 'a profound recognition of the *priority of the question* in all knowledge and discourse that really reveals something of an object'.³⁴ It showed that the real nature of a 'sudden idea' is less that a solution to a problem occurs to us than that a question occurs to us that reveals the problem in a new light, and thereby makes an answer possible. Hence a question 'occurs', 'arises' or 'presents itself' to us more than we 'raise' or 'present' it ourselves. 'Asking the right questions', 'preserving an orientation toward openness' and 'entering into dialogue with a text' meant *allowing oneself to be conducted by the subject matter,* which was the art of strengthening others' arguments before dismantling them.³⁵

'Despite Plato', Gadamer continues, 'the only person I find a link with here is R.G. Collingwood.' Through his doctrine that we 'understand a text only when we have understood it as an answer to a question', Collingwood expressed an 'axiom of all hermeneutics' – the 'fore-conception of completeness'.³⁶ This was evident in his attack on the Oxford realists, whose philosophical 'shadow boxing' had them search for answers to their philosophical problems in texts written as responses to questions entirely different from theirs, and who then complained when the answers found were to them inadequate. Gadamer took Collingwood to be remonstrating against their lack of openness to the question *put by* the text, which at the same signified a lack of willingness to investigate the context *behind* the text. The principle of the fore-conception of completeness designated an indispensable assumption on the part of interpreters that the text's truth and meaning lie within this context. In so expressing it, Collingwood hit the nerve of historical knowledge: 'The historical method requires that the logic of question and answer be applied to historical tradition. We will understand historical events only if we reconstruct the question to which the historical actions of the persons involved were the answer.'³⁷

Gadamer's praise for Collingwood ends there. Since he 'unfortunately never elaborated it [the logic of question and answer] systematically', his philosophy had to be judged according to its centrepiece – the theory of re-enactment – which, in a manner strikingly similar to Skinner after him, Gadamer associated with the nineteenth century's epistemologically preoccupied and empathy-dependent hermeneutics.³⁸

Collingwood's failure to elucidate the relation between the two theories led Gadamer to surmise that re-enactment was the method of the logic of question and answer. As established in the previous chapter, this cannot be the case, because re-enactment is the attempt to recover an agent's consciously held intentions in acting, while the logic of question and answer attempts to recover an agent's tacitly held absolute presuppositions. Re-enactment might yield 'inside' and not 'outside' knowledge of past exhibitions of thought, but the ideational context that gave rise to them remains unknown.

Karsten Stueber has summarized Gadamer's criticisms of re-enactment. First, he found the concept to be epistemologically deficient.³⁹ A condition for the possibility of knowing something, according to Gadamer, is that its meaning be meaningful for us. By evoking a naturalistic cognitive ideal, where to understand a process is to be able to reproduce it artificially, re-enactment failed to satisfy this condition.[40] Gadamer discerned in re-enactment no break with the positivist and detached conception of understanding that reared empathy's deployment in psychological aesthetics and theory of the human sciences. The problem he identified might better be stated as a failure on Collingwood's part to provide an account of re-enactment that incorporated his metaphysics.

Second, Gadamer found the concept to be ontologically misguided. By making the fixed standard of historical interpretation the thoughts and intentions of historical agents, it misidentified the ontological location of meaning. Gadamer had gleaned from his historical studies that the events of history do not generally manifest agreement with the subjective ideas of the persons involved in them, no more than the meaning of a text remains confined to what its author originally intended. Indeed, 'reconstructing what the author really had in mind is a limited undertaking'.[41] Hermeneutical understanding involved no attempt to reveal a psychological entity; it meant striving to recognize the objective content of the text (*die Sache selbst*), which was to understand it as an answer to a particular question. It implied a dialogue with the text, not with its author. The meaning that emerged could be understood as a kind of agreement reached between the interpreter and the text, and although there could be no real 'fusion of horizons', the effort to integrate the past horizon of the text with the present horizon of the interpreter through the logic of openness raised the possibility of bringing them into mutual and productive dialogue. The psychologistic attempt to see through the other's eyes shared none of these characteristics. It meant we have ceased trying to reach agreement. By concealing its own standpoint, it gave itself no firm ground where this could take place.

These deficiencies led Collingwood to fall on either one side of past and present horizons. He never occupied the hermeneutical middle ground where past and present meet and new understanding emerges. This one-sidedness showed in two examples of the doctrine provided in *The Idea of History* and *Autobiography*.[42] On the present-day horizon, Gadamer regarded Collingwood's re-enactment of the *Theaetetus* as subsuming the context of Plato's thought under the present context of the historian. Collingwood's purpose in this passage is mostly negative. Against the realist conception of thought, which takes knowledge to be mainly sensation, and against subjective idealism, for which knowledge is the subject's own thought process, he argued that since thought 'can sustain itself through a change of context and revive in a different one', that is, since it can be re-thought in a different context without losing its identity, the immediate context in which Plato thought is inconsequential to re-enactment. 'We shall never know how the flowers smelt in the garden of Epicurus, or how Nietzsche felt the wind in his hair as he walked on the mountains.'⁴³ As we have seen, this is the principal reason why empathy had no place in Collingwood's anti-psychologistic conception of historical thinking and knowledge. Yet Gadamer perceived an inconsistency. 'One should like to remind Collingwood here of the critique of statements in his own "logic of question and answer"', put forward in the *Autobiography*. 'Is not the re-enactment of Plato's idea, in fact, successful only if we grasp the true Platonic context . . . And who will be able to grasp this context if they do not explicitly hold in abeyance the preconceptions of modern sensualism?'⁴⁴ This was evidence that Collingwood did not appreciate the level of hermeneutical mediation passed through in every act of understanding.

Conversely, Collingwood's concern with Nelson's plans at the Battle of Trafalgar symbolized the inadequacy of his conception of human historicity. Collingwood claimed that re-enacting the tactical plan Nelson set himself at Trafalgar sees the naval historian 'argue back from the solution to the problem'. Hence an agent's intentions can be re-enacted only if they were successfully executed. 'It is not worth while arguing about Villeneuve's plan', Collingwood stated in his *Autobiography*. 'He did not succeed in carrying it out, and therefore no one will ever know what it was. We can only guess. And guessing is not history.'⁴⁵ For Gadamer, this was to conflate two substantially different questions: first, the question of the meaning of an event; and, second, the question of whether the event went to plan. Gadamer had learnt again from history that its course has been determined as much by unintended consequences as by the actualization of people's intentions: 'The infinite web of motivations that constitute history only occasionally and briefly acquires the clarity of what a single individual has planned.'⁴⁶ The question the historian must set about discovering relates not to the mental experiences of the agent, but rather the meaning of the event itself.

Gadamer's arguments against re-enactment went to show that Collingwood failed to recognize the in-between nature of historical understanding. To question the truth of his position and the significance of his position is to address two separate issues. Having dealt in the previous chapter with the issue of Collingwood's mistaken association with the nineteenth century's empathy-dependent hermeneutics, the truth of Gadamer's position can be ascertained briefly. Like Skinner after him, Gadamer overlooked in re-enactment the importance of the doctrine of thought in its mediation. He failed to grasp that the passage in which Collingwood argued that the immediate, experiential context of Plato's thought is inconsequential to re-enactment is in fact directed against the same psychologistic epistemology he himself sought to displace by the shift to ontology in philosophical hermeneutics.

Collingwood was clear that 'the immediacy of the first occasion can never again be experienced'.[47] Re-enactment always takes place in the fresh context of the present day and so is determined by the questions that interest us in studying the past subject matter. A past thought re-thought in the present context always assumes the character of a present thought, a product of its time and purposes, against which the past thought can be critically evaluated.

The act of following a past agent's process of argument is not in conflict with this act of criticism. Shortly before the extract to which Gadamer referred in the *Autobiography*, Collingwood was unequivocal that 'getting inside other people's heads' and 'looking at their situation through their eyes' is simultaneously 'thinking for yourself whether the way in which they tackled it was the right way'.[48] In the story of John Doe, the meaning of a suspect's statement was not the same meaning as that discovered by the scientific detective-historian. The question of interest concerned what light was thrown on the subject matter by the fact that the suspect made the statement, meaning by it what he did mean.[49] Ascertaining the objective meaning of the statement – that is, identifying its objective content – on this account proceeded hand-in-hand with investigating what a suspect intended *in making* the statement.

As a thinker foreign to the hermeneutical tradition, it is perhaps unreasonable to expect Collingwood to have expounded his theories on how we understand the past while being situated in the present in a way that Gadamer, the twentieth-century spokesperson for that tradition, would have judged satisfactory. 'What remains problematic', as Dimitrios Vardoulakis puts it, 'is Collingwood's vacillation between a hermeneutic position in most of his writings and historicism in his theory of re-enactment.'[50] Which variety of hermeneutics? Vardoulakis's statement can be improved by adding that Collingwood appears to fluctuate between a Romantic-historicist hermeneutics in re-enactment (when the critical aspect of thought in its mediation is overlooked) and an ontologically oriented hermeneutics in the theory of absolute presuppositions. Whereas the more recent variety accounted duly for historicity and the need to ground historical phenomena in their anterior context, the older variety, focused solely on past thoughts and intentions, believed itself to have apprehended them directly. The significance of Gadamer's critique is that it provides the opportunity to supplement Collingwood's theories with principles from his hermeneutics.

Gadamer's differences with Collingwood are captured in a recent debate between theorists of social cognition. In a chain of articles defending and extending positions taken in his book *Rediscovering Empathy*, Stueber has upheld Collingwood's view that re-enactment is the prime epistemic method for understanding other people's actions.[51] In what boils down to a dispute between empathy and narrative, 'reenactive empathy', according to Stueber, comprehends the *indexicality* or 'I-concept' of rational thought: another person's reasons for acting can be understood as such only when, through imaginative perspective taking, I understand that they could be my reasons for acting. Reenactive empathy is the gateway supplying the content for a normative evaluation of a past agent's actions in the light of a first-person practical deliberation. This is the critical aspect of re-enactment. The historian decides what content enters the historical narrative based on a critical evaluation of rational agency — the beliefs, desires and intentions behind agents' reasons for acting in specific situations.

On the narrative side, Shaun Gallagher has called this a simulation theory of social cognition that misses the point that all understanding occurs against the backdrop of a prior understanding of the subject matter.[52] Gallagher's approach is essentially Gadamerian.[53] Just as Gadamer sought in the fusion of horizons to fill the space left vacant by the failure of historicists such as Collingwood to recognize this feature of understanding, so Gallagher sees in the concept of 'narrative competency' a more viable means than empathetic re-enactment for bridging the gap between different ways of thinking. 'With respect to empathy', he writes, 'putting myself in the other person's shoes will be difficult if the other person does not wear shoes.'[54] If empathy is supposed to help us understand people different from ourselves, if the past is a foreign country, 'how does knowing what *we* would do help us know what someone else would do?'[55]

According to Gallagher, our interactions with people tend to be framed along the lines of what we already know about their lives and specific circumstances. We do not, generally speaking, reduce our understandings of others to our own experiences. Rather, we form our understandings by remaining open to what they have experienced in their own lives and in their own context, in terms of a diversity of narratives that have informed our understanding. 'Narrative competency' is the skill of being able to use these frames of reference as a 'way into' interpreting new actions and behaviour. The structure of the narrative framework shifts as new interpretations are integrated, and it is because we hold this background firmly in mind that we are able to take other people's perspectives.

The debate between empathy and narrative creates similar confusions to those generated by Gadamer's treatment of Collingwood. Just as Gadamer did not observe the critical aspect of re-enactment, so the narrativist challenge to re-enactment overlooks the fact that it does not entail a passive surrender of one's own cognitive system to that of another. Collingwood's emphasis on the critical and inferential aspects of re-enactment places him closer to Gadamer's hermeneutics than to simulation theories that disregard the repercussions of the re-enactor's own historicity. If this point was made earlier to separate Collingwood from an empathy-dependent hermeneutics, its purpose here is to illustrate that the emphasis on narrative tells us nothing of what supplies a narrative with its content. A narrative is a cake composed of individual ingredients. Re-enactment is epistemically central to the historical process because it is a device with which the historian turns sources into evidence. In this way, its function is to supply individual content (parts) to larger narratives (wholes). That we approach an investigation already with a sense of the whole, that narrative structures are already in place, is not to be denied. As an alternative doctrine, however, leaves us with little idea of what fills a historical narrative. The debate is in fact about two aspects of the hermeneutic circle.

Among historians, David Harlan has contrasted the approach to intellectual history that attempts to recover original meaning with Gadamer's description of interpretive traditions. In *The Degradation of American History*, Harlan argued that the attempt to make history scientific and objective has, since its professionalization, led to its demise as a vehicle for moral reflection. He introduced Gadamer as the author of 'devastating critique' of the Romantic hermeneutical project behind the new contextualist orthodoxy in intellectual history, steered from the 1960s by Skinner and exemplified in his 1975 article 'Hermeneutics and the Role of History'.[56] Gadamer's work becomes important for historians at the point where hermeneutics ceases to concern itself with authorial intentions. 'So the author vanishes, his or her intentions disappear, and the text begins to suggest possibilities its authors may never have imagined.'[57] Gadamer's 'rehabilitation of prejudice' made clear that it is futile trying to cast aside one's inherited preconceptions to enter into a past mental universe, since these preconceptions are what enable understanding in the first place. Following from this, he highlighted that the text to be interpreted is embedded within a particular historical tradition, not the tradition in which it was written, which can never be reconstructed, but the tradition of interpretation that has grown up around the text since it was written.[58]

Indeed, as Joyce Appleby noted in responding to Harlan, included among the major feats of historical scholarship are reconstructions of interpretive traditions: 'When Pocock set out to capture the "Machiavellian moment" in England, he was reconstructing one of the many traditions inspired by Machiavelli's writings.'[59] David Armitage has similarly stated that the historian's task consists in puncturing myths by investigating where they came from and what motives lay behind them. In practice, this is the investigation of interpretive traditions. For example, 'the idea that the international realm is "Hobbesian" comes from the 1920s; the myth of the Westphalian state goes back to the early nineteenth century; and the very idea of the "international" emerged only in the 1780s'.[60] Hobsbawm pointed out three decades ago that historians had not adequately studied what he termed 'invented traditions' – those, like the seemingly ancient pageantry of the British monarchy, that appear to be old, but are in fact of relatively recent origin. Inventing traditions is a process of formalization and ritualization that establishes continuity with an often fictitious past, typically by imposing repetition. It is a process that has accelerated as the rapid transformations of human life associated with modernity have weakened or destroyed older patterns of social stability.[61] 'History divests the lived past of its legitimacy', as Pierre Nora exclaimed. 'The thrust of history, the ambition of the historian, is not to exalt what actually happened but to annihilate it', to transform what is absolute, sacred and symbolic in collective life into something relative, temporal and incomplete.[62] In Gadamer's language, invented traditions are a product of modern historical consciousness. It is because we 'no longer listen sanctimoniously to the voice that reaches out from the past' that there is a hollow for them to fill.

However, as Appleby acknowledged, Gadamer's argument could be a double-edged sword.[63] Positively, if traditions foreground understanding and provide the conditions making it possible, negatively, they are barriers to understanding other traditions. On the one hand, no longer concerned with finding a method for penetrating the productive act, historians set about appraising a text with respect to the tradition of interpretation that has grown up around it, to which they contribute by interpreting it anew. On the other hand, the very notion of an interpretive tradition implies a conceptual self-sufficiency scarcely distinguishable from the individual paradigms of political discourse studied by the contextualists. As with Toulmin's analysis of absolute presuppositions, a tradition is a self-contained system of thought and language within which propositions and concepts have meaning only relative to it. To speak of a tradition is to invoke the language and ways of thinking (Collingwood's foundations of scientific discourse) that give it stability as the prime unit of meaning production. Why, then, Appleby asked, is it possible to recover the tradition of interpretation attached to a text, but not the tradition in which it was originally produced?

Gadamer is misunderstood if he is seen to be offering an argument against all attempts to understand the original context. His disapproval was for the tradition of historicist hermeneutics that conceived of it as a kind of isolated mental event. He knew full well that interpretive traditions had to be verified against what the original texts say themselves – this is the question-and-answer task of discovering the conditions that made possible their theses and arguments as rational forms of belief. His experience as Heidegger's assistant is a case in point. Gadamer's first duty involved obtaining copies of Thomas Aquinas, whose interpretation of Aristotle as a systematizer and dispenser of ready-made solutions to problems had in Heidegger's view deformed the entire image of Greek philosophy. Aristotle's concept of order was a Thomistic construction, and so the only way of expunging this false interpretive tradition was to return to Aristotle himself. 'With one stroke', Gadamer wrote, 'Aristotle was no longer read with the eyes of Aquinas; rather, he bore witness to the origin of Greek thought as such.'[64]

Thus in general historical research prides itself on destroying or extending established narratives and interpretive traditions by bringing to bear on them fresh analyses of primary sources. Only by returning to these original sources and investigating the traditions that gave rise to them can an orthodoxy that has grown out of them be overturned.

★ ★ ★

'It is a grave misunderstanding', Gadamer warned, 'to assume that emphasis on the essential factor of tradition which enters into all understanding implies an uncritical acceptance of tradition and sociopolitical conservatism.'[65]

Even so, any discussion of Gadamer's project to affirm the 'authority of tradition' must contend with the criticism that it is too accepting of the social consensus that some argue ought to be submitted to ideology critique – a mode of analysis that measures received social truths against actual social conditions. In what is known as the Habermas-Gadamer debate, beginning in 1967, Habermas claimed that by giving priority to tradition, Gadamer had damaged the emancipatory potential of reason and reflection. Whereas for Gadamer tradition was the locus of understanding, insofar as one understands only in relation to what has been handed down from the past, for Habermas, philosophical hermeneutics ignored the Enlightenment insight that tradition is the storehouse and perpetuator of myth, oppression and distortion.[66]

The publication in 1986 of a book by the German historian Andreas Hillgruber allowed Habermas to continue his attack against the Gadamerian hermeneutical project, this time in its specifically historiographical emanation in the so-called *Historikerstreit*. Hillgruber argued that the historian, in identifying himself with the concrete conditions of the German population in the East during the winter of 1944–45, could come to only one conclusion: the Wehrmacht's bitter fighting, even though it prolonged Nazi rule and consequently facilitated the continued destruction of the Jews, was justified in the face of an impending Red Army set on exacting the highest possible revenge. As Amos Goldberg has described, Hillgruber's 'conservative empathy' in vindicating the Wehrmacht's value system on the Eastern Front belonged to a postwar conservative project to restore a sense of national historical continuity and tradition by having Germans identify with their difficult past. This identification with a national collectivity differed from the kind of 'liberal empathy' put to work a few years later by the American historian Christopher Browning in his canonical explanation of how 'ordinary men' could become the mass killers responsible for executing the horrors of the Holocaust. Both varieties could be condemned. Liberal empathy turned perpetrators into rational agents acting within historical structures outside their control; conservative empathy presented perpetrators as moral agents doing bad deeds for the collective good.[67]

The difficulty of being receptive to a past that excluded women from political and intellectual life has raised similar concerns among feminists. They tend to support a 'hermeneutics of suspicion' in the style of Marx or Nietzsche, where the purpose of interpreting a text is to reveal a different side of the reality it purports to present. The voice from the past to which Gadamer implores us to listen in his 'hermeneutics of trust', they maintain, transmits through a rarefied academic and social universe, never deviating to absorb the resonances emitting from outside that masculine milieu.[68]

Gadamer made no secret of the one-sidedness of philosophical hermeneutics. This he acknowledged in the foreword to the second German edition of *Truth and Method,* published in 1965. He wrote: 'I shall not deny – among all the elements of understanding – I have emphasized the assimilation of what is past and of tradition. Like many of my critics, Heidegger too would probably feel a lack of ultimate radicality in the conclusions I draw.'[69] Following the publication of the first edition five years earlier, Heidegger left his former student in suspense waiting for a reply to the book. When it came, he made clear that Gadamer's preservation of the language of tradition with respect to the *Geisteswissenschaften* represented too weak a response to the age's technological crisis.[70] Heidegger bade farewell to the field of hermeneutic thought, resigning it to Gadamer, but pessimistic about its future: '"Hermeneutic philosophy" is Gadamer's business; it makes a good counterweight to "analytic philosophy" and linguistics. Over the long run, the "Ge-stell" will gain the upper hand within the moribund "*Geisteswissenschaften*" too.'[71]

But it was a one-sidedness that Gadamer deemed necessary in order to correct an imbalance perpetuated by the Cartesian-Kantian belief that the humanistic inquirer could reflect himself over tradition. Modern man, instead of thinking that he has risen above his own historical situatedness in adopting a reflexive posture towards the past, needed an awareness of human finitude – 'what is feasible, what is possible, what is correct, here and now'.[72] In spite of the fact that historicism grew out of a Romantic backlash against rationalism and natural-law philosophy, Gadamer alleged that it had retained its prejudices: 'And there is one prejudice of the Enlightenment that defines its essence: the fundamental prejudice of the Enlightenment is the prejudice against prejudice itself, which denies tradition its power.'[73] Against the view that prejudice is blind belief insulated from the domain of reason, he attempted to restore to the concept its pre-Enlightenment connotation of prejudgement, as a judgement 'rendered before all the elements that determine a situation have been finally examined', or simply as the condition in which we first experience something. Kant's motto of the Enlightenment, 'Have the courage to make use of your *own* understanding', refracted through Romanticism onto historicism, gave Schleiermacher the confidence that he understood past authors better than they understood themselves, and in Dilthey produced a psychologism that precipitated the shift in Gadamer's century to a universal, ontological hermeneutics.[74]

This theme of finitude and tradition permeated Collingwood's philosophy too. 'This tradition', as Collingwood's biographer Fred Inglis observes, 'teaches that a good life may be lived only in terms of those virtues which an individual truly possesses and is capable of. The trouble with the word "tradition" is that it has, damnably, been so monopolised by the political Right, which contrasts the stability of tradition with the crazy enthusiasms of revolutionary struggle.'[75]

As Michael Kissell has written, 'absolute presuppositions lying at the foundation of human civilization are the basic elements of tradition' and the 'life of tradition is its creative re-enactment in response to the needs of an ever-changing life'.[76] Collingwood's 'progressive traditionalism' consisted in living dialectically with these basic elements, that is, as he wrote in *The New Leviathan,* 'in constant endeavour to convert every occasion of non-agreement into an occasion of agreement'.[77] The past thought historians were to re-enact in their own minds went a step beyond the old insofar as it was an agreement with the past reached in the present. With respect to absolute presuppositions, their historical investigation exposed logical fallacies in the thought of thinkers who demand proofs, refutations or justifications of absolute presuppositions, when in fact their logical efficacy is that, as the foundation upon which thought is built, they give rise to the questions societies ask. The logic of question and answer could therefore be understood as an attempt to explicate the principles of valid thinking and action apposite to particular societies. It expounded a theory of the type of life valued by a society, towards which it aims, by determining what has been given to it through the circumstanced activities of its forebears. Unlike the individual-to-individual view of empathy that grew out of a psychologistic epistemology, it asked historians to investigate common and shared forms of life in the past.

This is the concept of tradition that Alasdair MacIntyre commended in expounding the importance of shared standards of argument in dialectical inquiry. With Vico, Hegel and Collingwood, and against the main current of contemporary analytical philosophy, he argued in *After Virtue* that it is only within the context of a 'living tradition' that claims about truth and rationality can hope to be justified. In moral philosophy, the subject matter is 'nowhere to be found except as embodied in the historical lives of particular social groups and so possessing the distinctive characteristics of historical existence'.[78]

As for Gadamer, he helped show that we come to understand the past context not by stepping outside our own historical situation into an extra-historical realm of timeless judgement, but by recognizing that 'our historical situation is itself partly constituted by the possibility of appealing beyond and even against that situation'.[79] A living tradition is a historically extended, socially embodied argument about the goods the pursuit of which gives that tradition its particular character and purpose. So when an institution such as a university is a bearer of a tradition of practices, its common life will most vitally be constituted by an ongoing argument about what a university is or ought to be.[80] We can appeal beyond a tradition while living in it precisely because it is an argument about the practices that have through history brought it to its present state and given it its current complexion.

To argue with tradition in such a way is inevitably to be critical of it. Being open to the past is not to surrender to it; it is to recognize that the past context into which we inquire to understand the lives of people who lived in the past is one that we share by way of an inheritance. A historical hermeneutics is fully conscious of the unity of everything handed down from the past in a living tradition and the attempt in historical research to grasp its elements and articulate their properties. For Collingwood, this was to render the implicit explicit. For Gadamer, it was a form of understanding tempered to the thing itself: '*the object itself* must determine the method of its own access' and 'every hermeneutical understanding begins and ends with the thing itself'.[81] Every 'application' of understanding is a constitutive moment:

> The object of our application determines from the beginning and in its totality the real and concrete content of hermeneutical understating. Application is not a calibration of some generality given in advance in order to unravel afterwards a particular situation. In attending to a text, for example, the interpreter does not try to apply a general criterion to a particular case; on the contrary, he is interested in the fundamentally original significance of the writing under his consideration.[82]

To be conducted by the subject matter is to remain alert to the possibility of the text putting questions to the interpreter, rather than trying to obtain a unilateral control over the object such that it cannot 'talk back'.[83] 'That just bolts the door against new insight', as Charles Taylor remarked in *A Secular Age*. As 'Gadamer has shown so well . . . It is by allowing ourselves to be challenged by the ways . . . [past people and events] fail to fit into our recognized range of meanings, that we can begin to discern how this range has to be broken open and transformed if we are to understand them'.[84]

In this way, Gadamer steered clear of interpretive conservatism. Although in privileging the past 'the text can present itself in all its otherness and thus assert its own truth against our own fore-meanings', this encounter 'stirs up' our fore-meanings and makes us aware of the prejudices that tacitly direct our judgement. Coming to an understanding with the text requires that we put our prejudices at risk by giving those of the other priority in the interpretive exchange. To understand is always to understand differently. We understand anew when the fore-meanings that constitute our present horizon integrate with a meaning contained within another. This is how historical thinking takes account of its own historicity.[85] We grasp the nature of our own historical existence by allowing the truth claims of those who we study from the past to stand up against our own.

★ ★ ★

By what right is Collingwood's doctrine of re-enactment described as a theory of empathy? Few grounds have been found in Part II for a positive response. In spite of having his theory routinely associated with the nineteenth century's empathy-dependent hermeneutics of recovery, Collingwood's attention to the questioning activity that transforms past thought into present-day historical knowledge aligns him more closely with the twentieth-century hermeneutics spearheaded by Gadamer. Both Collingwood and Gadamer reacted against the time-negating psychologism of nineteenth-century historical thought by accounting for the ways in which historical understanding is necessarily a product of present-day questions and concerns. But they did so in a manner that did not diminish the historicist principle indispensable to history that historical knowledge is constructed upon meanings that belong to past contexts or constellations of presuppositions different from our own. Question-and-answer logic ensured that the inquirer's questioning of a past occurrence remained directed towards the question constituted in the event, not one prepared or given in advance. Historical inquiry is dialectical insofar as it is the constant attempt to come to an agreement between a past meaning in its historical context – when that meaning is understood as an action taken to affect some aspect of a pre-existing ideational situation – and what that meaning, with all that it tells us about different ways of conceiving of the world, signifies to us now in our present-day context.

The educational history in Part I and intellectual history in Part II have supplied themes with implications that remain to be seen back in the school scene. It became clear in the years following empathy's introduction to school history education that questions concerning the subject's teaching encompassed far more than history's conceptual structure. Empathy became symbolic of a perceived crisis in British culture and education, and raised the ire of the country's highest figure. In an ensuing battle of skills versus content, the concept-based approach gained the higher ground, expanding beyond its native United Kingdom and finding a new home in a Canadian model of historical thinking used globally in teacher training and curriculum and textbook design. At the same time, a conception of historical consciousness derived from Germany's historical hermeneutics has entered educational phraseology and brought to renewed light that old question of the connection between past, present and future, as well as of the uses of history for life.

Notes

1. Heidegger quoted in Jean Grondin, *Hans-Georg Gadamer: A Biography,* trans. Joel Weinsheimer (New Haven: Yale University Press, 2003), 117.
2. Ibid., 123.
3. Ibid., 91–127; Lawrence Schmidt, 'Hans-Georg Gadamer: A Biographical Sketch', in Jeff Malpas, Ulrich Arnswald and Jens Kertscher (eds), *Gadamer's Century: Essays in Honor of Hans-Georg Gadamer* (Cambridge, MA: MIT Press, 2002), 3–4.
4. Gadamer personal files, Universitätsarchiv Marburg, quoted in Grondin, *Gadamer,* 138.
5. Robert B. Pippin, 'Gadamer's Hegel', in Robert J. Dostal (ed.), *The Cambridge Companion to Gadamer* (Cambridge: Cambridge University Press, 2002), 225.
6. 'Das Wesen der Lust nach den platonischen Dialogen' [The Essence of Pleasure according to Plato's Dialogues], quoted in Grondin, *Gadamer,* 84.
7. Grondin, *Gadamer,* 84.
8. Hans-Georg Gadamer, *Philosophical Apprenticeships,* trans. Robert B. Sullivan (Cambridge, MA: MIT Press, 1985) (first published in 1977 under the title *Philosophische Lehrjahre*).
9. Habermas quoted in Grondin, *Gadamer,* 6.
10. Hans-Georg Gadamer, 'The Universality of the Hermeneutical Problem' (1966), in his *Philosophical Hermeneutics,* ed. and trans. David E. Linge (Berkeley: University of California Press, 1976), 11.
11. John P. Hogan, *Collingwood and Theological Hermeneutics* (Lanham: University Press of America, 1989), 4; Kenneth B. McIntyre, 'Historicity as Methodology or Hermeneutics: Collingwood's Influence on Skinner and Gadamer', *Journal of the Philosophy of History* 2, 2 (2008), 166; Chinatsu Kobayashi and Mathieu Marion, 'Gadamer and Collingwood on Temporal Distance and Understanding', *History and Theory* 50, 4 (2011), 81–103; Dimitrios Vardoulakis, 'The Vicissitude of Completeness: Gadamer's Criticism of Collingwood', *International Journal of Philosophical Studies* 12, 1 (2004), 3–19.
12. Alasdair MacIntyre, 'On Not Having the Last Word: Thoughts on Our Debts to Gadamer' and Paul Ricœur, 'Temporal Distance and Death in History', in Jeff Malpas, Ulrich Arnswald and Jens Kertscher (eds), *Gadamer's Century: Essays in Honor of Hans-Georg Gadamer* (Cambridge, MA: MIT Press, 2002), 162 and 249–51 respectively.
13. Unlike Heidegger the dedicated National Socialist, Gadamer kept a distance from politics in the 1930s, describing himself as a liberal centrist. In January 1939, he was appointed as ordinary professor at the University of Leipzig, which to his pleasure he discovered was a 'thoroughly unpolitical university'. During the war, he managed to maintain an oppositional position without becoming a frontline member of the resistance. The autonomy with which he conducted himself politically and intellectually earned him the respect of the Leipzig professoriate and the rectorship in 1946. Weighed down in this role by the growing politicization of the university during the period of Soviet denazification, he sought a position in the western zone. In 1947, he accepted an invitation from the University of Frankfurt, where he stayed until he received a call to the University of Heidelberg two years later. His arrival in the southwest was the realization of a long-held wish to return to quieter surrounds where he

could concentrate anew on his philosophical work. Grondin, *Gadamer,* esp. 153, 157, 195–99, 224–26, 240, 264, 273.

14. Michael Ermarth, 'The Transformation of Hermeneutics: 19th Century Ancients and 20th Century Moderns', *Monist* 64, 2 (1981), 177.

15. Paul Ricœur, *Main Trends in Philosophy* (New York: Holmes & Meier, 1979), 266–67.

16. Martin Heidegger, *Being and Time,* trans. John Macquarrie and Edward Robinson (New York: Harper & Row, 1962), 161–62.

17. Published in English as Martin Heidegger, *Ontology: The Hermeneutics of Facticity,* trans. John van Buren (Bloomington: Indiana University Press, 1999), 11.

18. Heidegger, *Being and Time,* 195.

19. Hans-Georg Gadamer, 'On the Scope and Function of Hermeneutical Reflection' (1967), in *Philosophical Hermeneutics,* 18.

20. Gadamer, 'Universality of the Hermeneutical Problem', 10–11.

21. Ibid., 15.

22. Joel C. Weinsheimer, *Gadamer's Hermeneutics: A Reading of* Truth and Method (New Haven: Yale University Press, 1985), 4.

23. Gadamer, *Truth and Method,* 56.

24. Friedrich Nietzsche, *Untimely Meditations,* trans. R.J. Hollingdale (Cambridge: Cambridge University Press, 1983), 84; Martin Heidegger, *Nietzsche,* vols 1–4, trans. David Farrell Krell (New York: Harper & Row, 1979–87).

25. Charles R. Bambach, *Heidegger, Dilthey, and the Crisis of Historicism* (Ithaca: Cornell University Press, 1995), 16.

26. Hans-Georg Gadamer, 'The Problem of Historical Consciousness', in Paul Rabinow and William M. Sullivan (eds), *Interpretive Social Science: A Second Look* (Berkeley: University of California Press, 1987), 95.

27. Ibid., 90.

28. Ibid., 133–34. Gadamer uses the phrase 'Schleiermacher's genial gift for empathy', in 'Heritage of Hegel', in his *Reason in the Age of Science,* trans. Frederick D. Lawrence (Cambridge, MA: MIT Press, 1981), 40. There is a continuity here with the Enlightenment prejudice against history that it served as a route to knowledge only in cases where the present did not.

29. Gadamer, 'Problem of Historical Consciousness', 107, 136.

30. Ibid., 100.

31. Gadamer, *Truth and Method,* 196–97 (emphases removed).

32. Ibid., 354–55.

33. Ibid., 356 (emphases removed).

34. Ibid., 357.

35. Ibid., 360–62.

36. Ibid., 363–64.

37. Ibid., 364.

38. Ibid., 363.

39. Karsten R. Stueber, 'The Psychological Basis of Historical Explanation: Reenactment, Simulation, and the Fusion of Horizons', *History and Theory* 41, 1 (2002), 35.

40. Gadamer, *Truth and Method,* 366.

41. Ibid., 365–66.

42. Vardoulakis, 'The Vicissitude of Completeness', 14.

43. Collingwood, *Idea of History,* 296–97.

44. Gadamer, 'Hermeneutics and Historicism', 515–16.

45. R.G. Collingwood, *An Autobiography* (Oxford: Clarendon Press, 1978), 70.

46. Gadamer, *Truth and Method,* 365.

47. R.G. Collingwood, *The Idea of History,* rev. edn [1946] Jan van der Dussen (Oxford: Oxford University Press, 1994), 298.
48. Collingwood, *Autobiography,* 58.
49. Collingwood, *Idea of History,* 275.
50. Vardoulakis, 'Vicissitude of Completeness', 6.
51. In addition to his works already cited, see Karsten Stueber, 'Reasons, Generalizations, Empathy, and Narratives: The Epistemic Structure of Action Explanation', *History and Theory* 47, 1 (2008), 31–43; 'Theories Explain, and So Do Historical Narratives: But There are Differences', *Journal of the Philosophy of History* 2, 2 (2008), 237–43; 'Intentionalism, Intentional Realism, and Empathy', *Journal of the Philosophy of History* 3, 3 (2009), 290–307; with Mark Bevir, 'Empathy, Rationality, and Explanation', *Journal of the Philosophy of History* 5, 2 (2011), 147–62; 'Understanding versus Explanation? How to Think about the Distinction between the Human and the Natural Sciences', *Inquiry* 55, 1 (2012), 17–32; 'Varieties of Empathy, Neuroscience and the Narrativist Challenge to the Contemporary Theory of Mind Debate', *Emotion Review* 4, 1 (2012), 55–63; 'Empathy versus Narrative: What Exactly is the Debate about? Response to My Critics', *Emotion Review* 4, 1 (2012), 68–69.
52. See Shaun Gallagher, 'Simulation Trouble', *Social Neuroscience* 2, 3–4 (2007), 353–65; 'Narrative Competence and the Massive Hermeneutical Background', in Paul Fairfield (ed.), *Education, Dialogue and Hermeneutics* (London: Continuum, 2010), 21–38; 'In Defense of Phenomenological Approaches to Social Cognition: Interacting with the Critics', *Review of Philosophy and Psychology* 3, 2 (2012), 187–212; 'Three Questions for Stueber', *Emotion Review* 4, 1 (2012), 64–65; 'An Education in Narratives', *Educational Philosophy and Theory* 46, 6 (2014), 600–9.
53. See Shaun Gallagher, *Hermeneutics and Education* (Albany: State University of New York Press, 1992).
54. Gallagher, 'Education in Narratives', 606.
55. Gallagher, 'Questions for Stueber', 64.
56. David Harlan, *The Degradation of American History* (Chicago: University of Chicago Press, 1997), 4–7, 583–89; Quentin Skinner, 'Hermeneutics and the Role of History', *New Literary History* 7, 1 (1975), 214. It is probably in response to such claims that contextualism is built upon the pillar of Romantic hermeneutics that Skinner has since emphasized that recovering intentions is achieved by the ordinary procedures of the historical method and not by a species of empathy.
57. David Harlan, 'Intellectual History and the Return of Literature', *American Historical Review* 94, 3 (1989), 587.
58. Harlan, *Degradation,* 9–10; Harlan, 'Intellectual History', 587–88.
59. Joyce Appleby, 'One Good Turn Deserves Another: Moving beyond the Linguistic; A Response to David Harlan', *American Historical Review* 94, 5 (1989), 1329.
60. David Armitage, 'Horizons of History: Space, Time, and the Future of the Past', *History Australia* 12, 1 (2015), 214–15.
61. Eric Hobsbawm, 'Introduction: Inventing Traditions', in Eric Hobsbawm and Terence Ranger (eds), *The Invention of Tradition* (Cambridge: Cambridge University Press, 1983), 1–5.
62. Pierre Nora, *Realms of Memory: The Construction of the French Past,* trans. Arthur Goldhammer (New York: Columbia University Press, 1996), 3.
63. Appleby, 'One Good Turn', 1329.
64. Gadamer quoted in Grondin, *Gadamer,* 114.
65. Gadamer, 'Problem of Historical Consciousness', 87.
66. The Gadamer-Habermas debate was conducted in German-language volumes and periodicals. Paul Ricœur, 'Ethics and Culture: Habermas and Gadamer in Dialogue', *Philosophy Today* 17, 2 (1973), 153–65 produced the first commentary available in English. Jack

Mendelson, 'The Habermas-Gadamer Debate', *New German Critique* 18 (Fall 1979), 44–73 produced another early treatment.

67. Andreas Hillgruber, *Zweierlei Untergang: Die Zerschlagung des Deutschen Reiches und das Ende des europäischen Judentums* (Berlin: Siedler, 1986); Amos Goldberg, 'Empathy, Ethics, and Politics in Holocaust Historiography', in Aleida Assmann and Ines Detmers (eds), *Empathy and its Limits* (New York: Palgrave Macmillan, 2015), 53–59; Christopher R. Browning, *Ordinary Men: Reserve Police Battalion 101 and the Final Solution in Poland* (New York: Aaron Usher Books, 1992).

68. Lorraine Code, 'Introduction: Why Feminists Do Not Read Gadamer', in Lorraine Code (ed.), *Feminist Interpretations of Hans-Georg Gadamer* (University Park: Pennsylvania State University Press, 2003), 1–36; Marie Fleming, 'Gadamer's Conversation: Does the Other Have a Say?', in Code (ed.), *Feminist Interpretations*, 129.

69. Gadamer, *Truth and Method*, xxxiv.

70. Grondin, *Gadamer*, 292.

71. Heidegger, letter to O. Pöggeler, 5 January 1973, quoted in Grondin, *Gadamer*, 292–93.

72. Gadamer, *Truth and Method*, xxxiv.

73. Ibid., 272–73.

74. Ibid., 273–74. Kant's motto appears at the beginning of his 1784 essay 'What is Enlightenment?'

75. Fred Inglis, *History Man: The Life of R.G. Collingwood* (Princeton: Princeton University Press, 2009), 28.

76. Michael A. Kissell, 'Progressive Traditionalism as the Spirit of Collingwood's Philosophy', *History and Theory* 29, 4 (1990), 54.

77. R.G. Collingwood, *The New Leviathan, or Man, Society, Civilisation and Barbarism*, rev. edn [1942] David Boucher (Oxford: Clarendon Press, 1992), §39.15.

78. Alasdair MacIntyre, postscript to the second edition of *After Virtue* (Notre Dame: University of Notre Dame Press, 1983), 265.

79. MacIntyre, 'On Not Having the Last Word', 158.

80. MacIntyre, *After Virtue*, 222.

81. Gadamer, 'Problem of Historical Consciousness', 93, 139.

82. Ibid., 125–26.

83. Charles Taylor, 'Understanding the Other: A Gadamerian View on Conceptual Schemes', in Malpas, Arnswald and Kertscher (eds), *Gadamer's Century*, 279–97.

84. Charles Taylor, *A Secular Age* (Cambridge, MA: Belknap Press, 2007), 286.

85. Gadamer, *Truth and Method*, 271–72, 299.

Part III
CONSEQUENCES

> The first thing I saw was a piece where it said the English had been beaten in some battle or other. There's a nice thing to go teaching children! The parents won't stand for *that* kind of thing, I can tell you!
> —George Orwell, *A Clergyman's Daughter*

CHAPTER 9

Competing Conceptions

Collingwood's biographer remarked that 'much was made in a minor pedagogic movement of the 1970s' of his idea of 'putting oneself imaginatively into some past period'.[1] Part I of this book should have shown that this movement was more than minor. Indeed, nearly two decades after empathy was introduced by the Leeds-based Schools Council History Project, even Colin Dexter's lugubrious Inspector Morse could complain to his colleague: 'But they don't go in for facts in History these days. They go in for empathy, Lewis. Whatever that is.'[2]

Empathy became a key concept in the method of teaching school history, we observed, due to the emphasis placed on replicating in the school subject the modes of inquiry of the trained historian. David Sylvester has confirmed that the SCHP's mission was to teach a kind of history in schools 'as similar as possible to history as philosophers conceived it and as the best professionals practise it'.[3] Roy Wake, the person responsible for installing Sylvester as the first SCHP director, commented upon its establishment that whereas the universities had in his view failed to train graduates in the techniques of historical scholarship, the situation was more encouraging in the colleges of education where new teachers were receiving 'a proper historical training'.[4] Although historians such as Bloch, Carr, Elton and Kitson Clark had produced a small but important literature on the theory and method of historical practice, it was texts in the philosophy of history that provided educational reformers with an outline of history's conceptual structure and so a model for the subject's teaching. History's established and prestigious place in the university meant that it seldom needed to justify its disciplinary status and methodological integrity; in the school there was no such defer-

---

Notes for this section begin on page 189.

ence and the guardians of the subject looked to philosophers of history to distinguish it from others.

Peter Lee suggested in 1983 that the philosophy of history served two functions in history teaching. First, it offered itself to teachers and researchers as an aid for discerning the distinct structure of the subject and, second, it gave them an analytical basis for evaluating students' thinking and performance.[5] Within the philosophy of history were seen to lie the concepts, logic and forms of knowledge that the discipline-specific and method-centred educational theories of Bloom, Bruner and Hirst had called upon them to articulate and operationalize for classroom practice. At a time when the roll-out of comprehensive schools was bringing students of mixed academic abilities under the one roof, a curriculum modelled on the concepts and procedures that historians were regarded as taking to the past was considered a surer route to revitalizing the school subject than the traditional content-focused curriculum.

This situation changed when the announcement of the development of a National Curriculum for England and Wales reintroduced the old question of what students were to learn in history. The reformist agenda had concentrated on the procedures of historical investigation said to constitute an induction into a historical form of knowledge. The content through which students received this initiation was a matter of less importance, and indeed dissatisfaction with the Gradgrind approach to studying facts had provided a large part of the impetus for school history reform. Margaret Thatcher saw no need to overcomplicate matters. 'Though not an historian myself', she recounted later in her autobiography, 'I had a very clear – and I had naïvely imagined uncontroversial – idea of what history was. History is an account of what happened in the past. Learning history, therefore, requires knowledge of events.' The so-called new history being taught in the schools that had adopted the SCHP programme, 'with its emphasis on concepts rather than chronology and empathy rather than facts, was at the root of so much that was going wrong'.[6] Empathy not only violated history's empirical standards and time-honoured adherence to facts, its inclusion sat at the heart of a perceived crisis in British culture. In the Final Report of the National Curriculum History Working Group (HWG), tabled in April 1990, the concept was completely absent.[7]

The debates that attended the development of the national curriculum in the 1980s threw into relief fundamentally different conceptions of the purposes of a historical education. Educationalists hoped that the HWG would embed the SCHP approach and combat the mostly negative political reaction to it.[8] Yet the group entrusted with the task of framing a core curriculum worked from a standpoint that did not see them share the reformists' enthusiasm for using the philosophy of history as a guide for history's teaching. Burston went so far as to take history's logic of explanation as the logic of its pedagogy, and we have seen that he was not alone in converting philosophical ideas into educational procedures. The movement as a whole attempted to translate the epistemology of the discipline into the pedagogy of the school subject. However, when asked to develop a core curriculum, HWG members from a range of backgrounds expressed a surprising unanimity on the direction that school history should take. Empathy, a prize possession of the reformists' philosophical outlook, was not part of it.

It was in England that empathy entered the history educational scene and it is there that our focus must return as we examine the way in which its formulation as a concept predicated on Collingwood's philosophy of history played out in day-to-day educational practice as well as in professional, political and academic debate. In empathy were questions concerning the nature of history that determined how different groups ascribed value to a historical education.

★ ★ ★

The theory of re-enactment that furnished empathy with its theoretical basis in the SCHP can be described as belonging to an intentionalist philosophy of history. The backlash against Hempel's attempt to bring historical explanation into the orbit of the natural scientific method provoked attempts among analytical philosophers of history to fortify the intentionalist argument in the years following the Second World War.[9] In attempting to establish a rigorous and testable methodology of historical explanation, Hempel's positivism set a new standard for a scholarly field long guided by the metaphysical and speculative theories of philosophers in the Italian, German and British idealists traditions, from Vico and Herder in the eighteenth century, to Hegel, Dilthey and Bradley in the nineteenth century, to Croce, Collingwood and Oakeshott in the twentieth century. Their imprints have appeared throughout this account of empathy's role in historical understanding.

Analytical philosophy of history came to mean one thing: an endorsement or repudiation of what Dray termed Hempel's covering-law account of scientific explanation. Kerwin Lee Klein has described a dynamic whereby analytical philosophers of history mostly rejected the model of scientific explanation, judging it a form of methodological determinism and an accomplice to the intellectual threats of behaviourism, functionalism and, by the 1960s, structuralism, while attempting to shore up with analytical rigour older varieties of humanism and metaphysics, which they had associated with imprecise thinking and communist politics. They represented themselves as saviours of freedom between two varieties of determinism, one metaphysical and the other methodological, and arguments proliferated about the autonomy or *sui generis* character of historical understanding and knowledge.[10]

An intentionalist approach appealed to those who wished to assert history's autonomy against the natural sciences. Its exponents stressed that historical explanation consists in the historical reconstruction of the intentions of human agents in the past, not in subsuming human behaviour under pregiven laws and categories purported to be operative at all times and all places. At the university level, an entire course in historical method could be reduced to two founding texts: Hempel's essay and Collingwood's *The Idea of History*. 'All history is the history of thought' translated into a way of doing history that made the intentions, purposes and motives of past agents the source for understanding and explaining their actions and the events in which they were executed. History was about human actions and, rejecting the Cartesian distinction between the mental and the physical, human thought was considered inseparable from those actions.

Just as intentionalism provided a basis for affirming history's autonomy against science's claims to methodological universalism, so it became attractive to history educationalists working to revive the school subject once transformations in educational thought began to regard the school subjects as an induction into distinct forms of knowledge. The debate in the philosophy of history between positivism and intentionalism provided the resources for history to be defined as a distinct school subject. A philosophy of history affirming history's autonomy offered itself to an educational paradigm eager to distil the disciplinary essence of the school subject, as a specifically historical way of investigating the world. To this end, Burston, Sylvester, Lee and Shemilt leant on the writings of Collingwood, Oakeshott, Walsh, Dray and von Wright. This latter group had set down the principles educationalists repurposed as tenets of school history teaching.

Her Majesty's Inspectorate (HMI) was an important vehicle for disseminating the SCHP philosophy to the schools. It had been the main point of contact since its establishment in 1839 between the schools across England and the politicians and civil servants in Westminster and Whitehall. Its function was essentially mediatory, acting as a vital cog in an education system that operated as a partnership between central and local government and the teaching profession. It had a discursive power diffused through conversations and reports, and centred upon its elite status, professional networks and operational significance as the only body that united disparate sites and practices across the country.

Two reports particularly indicate the extent to which SCHP thinking penetrated HMI. First, *Curriculum 11–16,* a collection of working papers written by a group of HM Inspectors in 1977, began by observing that teachers feel the loneliness of their profession and thus welcome partnership and the opportunity to consider the case for a core curriculum. The history paper affirmed in the first paragraph that historians are 'interested in human intent, and so in some evaluation of human success and failure'. History was to cultivate a series of 'historical attitudes', an 'awareness of the nature of evidence', a 'sense of change and continuity', an 'interest in cause' and a 'degree of empathy', stated as an 'ability to enter into some informed appreciation of the predicaments and points of view of other people – the development, in fact, of a historical imagination'. This ability belonged in turn to the ethical and moral domain and was offered support by a passage from Collingwood on self-knowledge being the product of knowing what man has done in the past.[11]

Second, the 1985 HMI booklet *History in the Primary and Secondary Years* transformed these four attitudes into 'skills' that history teaching enables students to develop. To evidence, change and continuity, cause and empathy were added 'an ability to pose historical questions' and a 'sense of chronology and time'.[12] Apart from the posing of historical questions, these were the concepts Lee had declared two years earlier 'provide the structural basis for the discipline'.[13] Empathy remained 'the ability to enter into some informed appreciation of the predicaments and points of view of other people in the past', but this time it did not merely correspond with the historical imagination; rather, it depended 'on an imaginative interpretation of historical evidence'. Discussions, simulations, role plays and drama might pose the question, for example, 'why William of Normandy still decided to cross the Channel in the autumn of 1066, despite the threat of equinoctial gales, knowing that he might face a powerful and effective Saxon army but unaware of its forced march from the North'.[14]

Students by the age of eight were expected to be able to write or draw 'what they think it felt like' after having a historical story told to them; by twelve, they imaginatively reconstructed a past situation using several pieces of historical evidence; by fourteen, they considered the viewpoints of 'people for whom they may not feel sympathy'; by sixteen, students identified 'the extent of the choice available to a person in a given situation in the past' as well as 'the values and attitudes on which human actions have been based in the past'. Suggestions for assessment transposed this language to a particular case, from a sketch of the 'likely feelings' of the persons described in a work of historical fiction to a written or oral presentation of the options available to William I during his conquest.[15]

David Sylvester and John Slater, an Oxford-trained historian and HM Inspector from 1968 to 1987, played a leading hand in producing these government documents. Sylvester accepted a position in HMI in 1975, having concluded his tenure as SCHP director and with his lectureship at Leeds facing an uncertain future. He reports taking pride in the fact that, among a team of roughly eight history specialists, he was the only one to have taught in a comprehensive school, and confirms his heavy involvement in the 'red book' *Curriculum 11–16,* as well as his roles as editor or secretary in others. He produced in 1976 a table of skills that went on to be used in subsequent HMI course material, not least in *History in the Primary and Secondary Years,* where it provided the objectives for student progress in empathy and the other historical skills. Just as Sylvester could claim the SCHP conception of history as his own, so his vision guided HMI directives, though he still faced opposition from certain Inspectors on the 'Collingwoodian idea' of empathy.[16]

Slater exercised his influenced less as an expositor of concepts than as an advocate of the SCHP programme within the HMI. He succeeded Wake as HM Staff Inspector for History in 1974, and over the course of his career advised eight secretaries of state for education and science, including Thatcher, Shirley Williams and Sir Keith Joseph.[17] Those who worked alongside him have testified that he remained close to the SCHP while in this role and was the main force behind the application of its ideas in HMI publications.[18] He referred to it in a special professorial lecture delivered at the Institute of Education (IOE) in 1988 as 'the most significant and beneficent influence on the learning of history and the raising of its standard to emerge this century . . . It proclaims the crucial distinction between knowing the past and thinking historically'.[19] A colleague summarized his approach as 'the apotheosis of that period of many syllabuses, many approaches'. This was to credit him with trailblazing a middle ground occupied on either side by proponents of a skills-based and knowledge-based curriculum in an English education system defined by its regional differences.[20]

Slater gave particular credit to Keith Joseph, holder of the education portfolio from 1981 to 1986, for being the first in that position to offer a measured defence of the role of history in schools.[21] Joseph maintained that the inclusion of greater breadth in the curriculum through subjects such as geography and economics should not come at the expense of weakening history's position as an independent subject. But he stopped well short of the idea that history's purpose in the schools was to train students to be historians. 'Of course there is much that is common between the two', he told an audience at the Historical Association in 1984. 'But the objectives of school history are wider and different.' Highest among these objectives was to enable students to view the past with 'sympathetic understanding' rather than with the misunderstanding of anachronistic attitudes. 'How difficult it is to think ourselves into a pre-Copernican moral world', Joseph recognized. History teaching had to convey to students that it was possible for intelligent and noble men to hold beliefs and commitments that to us seem contradictory, that one could believe in the humanity of all men and in the institution of slavery, and that liberty is a less significant value than order. The school was not a place for extending the frontiers of historical knowledge and understanding; it was where students were to be awakened to the possible legitimacy of other points of view.[22]

Thatcherite education policy was driven by the belief that Britain's unique enterprise culture had become imperilled by a left-leaning and 'progressive' educational establishment, represented by such bodies as the Department of Education and Science (DES), HMI, the National Union of Teachers, Local Education Authorities (LEAs) and the Schools Council, the last of which Joseph abolished in 1984. As in other countries, a publicly administered and funded system of education had long unglued the bond between schools and families. Thatcherism emphasized that it was within the family that the individual virtues on which the public benefit relies were to be cultivated. Schools had come to be regarded as wholly distinct in purpose from the family rather than as an extension of it. Those who looked upon schools not as surrogate to parents but as instruments of social policy destroyed their function as an extension of the family. Each school, like each family, ought to have a distinctive personality and respect for its own traditions. On that basis, the head of each school ought to be left to select the curriculum, rules of conduct, and staff and students appropriate to it.[23]

Why, then, did a government committed to giving schools the capacity to conduct their own affairs impose a national curriculum on them? The answer is that Britain's cultural decline was seen in part to be the result of declining academic standards in its schools. If the educational theories that fermented inside the expanded departments of education had fuelled the comprehensive revolution and made student-centred teaching the new orthodoxy, a counter-revolution was needed to reinvigorate the young with the enterprising disposition that had helped make Britain great.

A month before addressing the Historical Association, Joseph laid out his plan for raising academic standards in schools in a speech at the North of England Education Conference.[24] James Callaghan's 1976 speech at Ruskin College in Oxford had already launched the 'great debate' about the need for and means of achieving what he called 'a basic curriculum with universal standards'.[25] Shirley Williams followed with a Green Paper proposing a nationally mandated core curriculum to occupy half the school timetable. Thatcher came to power in 1979 having previously opposed the idea of a national curriculum on the grounds that it entailed a level of state centralization more befitting of the French than the English. But evidence of educational failure, contained mainly in reports issued by the Centre for Policy Studies (CPS), made the case that change was necessary.[26] With the backing of his boss, Joseph announced to his listeners that a higher standard of student achievement required all parties to agree on a set of clear curricular objectives, as well as a system of examination calibrated to assess what students knew, understood and could do in relation to them. His 1985 White Paper *Better Schools* gave weight to these plans and provided a blueprint for the future reforms.[27]

There had been pressure for two decades to merge the O-Level (Ordinary Level of the General Certificate of Education) with the CSE (Certificate of Secondary Education) examinations. Williams had ordered an inquiry that recommended they be abolished and replaced by a common examination to be taken at the age of sixteen, the GCSE (General Certificate of Secondary Education). Joseph worried that the introduction of the GCSE would result in a further dilution of academic standards, with its emphasis on differentiation, continuous assessment and the 'sacred cows of coursework', which would count for 20 per cent of a student's final mark. The authority it granted teachers to assess their own students militated against the drive towards standardization. Whatever its weaknesses, Joseph decided in the spring of 1984 that it should proceed; the first GCSE was sat in the summer of 1988.[28]

It was ironic that a government and minister committed to undoing the damage caused in their eyes by the destruction of the grammar schools introduced the GCSE. Joseph had intended to bring higher standards to bear on the education of students with fewer academic talents. In practice, the new examination destroyed the distinction between grammar and secondary modern students, which had survived after the demise of the secondary modern schools in the distinction between the O-Level and CSE examinations, thus completing the ascendency of the comprehensive system. Teachers believed that with the GCSE they were being given a common examination; in fact, they were given a common examining system, with differentiated examination papers. During the second reading of the Education Reform Bill in the House of Lords in 1987, Joseph expressed his dismay at the way the GCSE had turned out. 'The examinations were written by the same old educational establishment who continued to make the new scheme serve the old orthodoxy, indeed to entrench it', as one onlooker described it. 'Within the host of apparently innocent words (whose meaning was a mystery) setting forth the virtues of the brave new requirements – empathy, oracy, school-based assessment, skills, breadth, balance, differentiation, relevance – lay hidden the same old orthodoxy of progressive education.'[29]

The GCSE included empathy because it was based on the previous examinations designed by the SCHP. SCHP syllabi were offered for several years by three examining groups: the London and East Anglian Group, the Midland Examining Group and the Southern Examining Group. A 1988 primer for the new examination noted that since the SCHP syllabi had been converted to the GCSE 'in virtually unchanged form', history teachers were more likely than teachers of other subjects to observe a continuity between the past and present examinations. Since the SCHP developed an O-Level examination based upon its principles, it had a substantial influence on the form of the GCSE history examination. Indeed, the greatest single development ensuring the primacy of the SCHP approach was the establishment of the GCSE.[30] Its architects could boast two years after its establishment that their programme had already been adopted by the Southern Regional Examinations Board (SREB) and the Oxford Local Examinations Board in the 16+ GCE and CSE examinations. They knew that its success depended on how well teachers were able to work with its materials within the context and limitations of the system of examination, and thus on the degree of its collaboration with examining boards.[31]

At the grassroots level, teachers, examiners and inspectors have discussed how important the Project's professional networks were for bringing its principles into the mainstream. Bob Wolfson reported in 1980 that there had been an enormous increase in contact among neighbouring schools through the cluster group meetings that assembled teachers to share ideas and resources for teaching the SCHP course *What is History?*[32] Roughly 40 per cent of English schools were taking the course; 512 schools had embarked or were embarking on its examination course, which amounted to around 18,000 of that year's candidates.[33] Chris Culpin recalls fondly how a Suffolk LEA advisor embraced the project and arranged monthly meetings for schools embarking on the course. 'It was very convenient . . . you would turn up, have a cup of tea, sit around, somewhere to go to develop materials . . . I know talking to other teachers and advisers that that was the case across large swathes of England.' Ian Dawson suggests that these networks grew most considerably between 1979 and 1985. Teachers at that stage 'were not frenzied about league tables because they did not exist, and examinations could trial types of questions . . . and meetings were being held at which examiners would discuss the effectiveness of questions'. Scott Harrison points out the project's adoption by the Bristol-based Southern Universities Joint Board, which counted initially on having 25 schools under its purview, was 'so successful, it had clearly totally overwhelmed them'. John Clare recollects a 'Damascus road experience' upon hearing Shemilt speak at a network meeting. 'I realised that I had been up through O-level, A level and I had studied history at Oxford, and I did not have a clue about history, about the study of history, I did not know what I was talking about.'[34]

Those being trained as history teachers were less likely to have received the SCHP message as an epiphany. With teacher training based increasingly in the universities, the teacher educators responsible for raising them were more likely than teachers already in the field to have encountered the SCHP and its philosophy of history, and thus brought it to bear on the development of the new generation of teachers. Empirical work conducted in the mid- and late-1980s confirms that the large majority of PGCE (Postgraduate Certificate in Education) students thought favourably of the source- and skills-based approach, even if many expressed doubt in their ability to teach one of its concepts, namely empathy. A study into the syllabi of twenty-one school history departments at the end of the decade revealed that all but five referred directly to the teaching of historical skills as a priority.[35]

The SCHP made such a mark on the teaching profession that empathy continued to feature in GCSE textbooks and guides, in spite of having been omitted from the *National Criteria* for the new examination. Released by the DES in 1985, the criteria for history were intended to underscore the equal importance of content and skills. The document in fact placed greater emphasis on the skills that history should develop than on the content that it should inculcate. However, unlike their SCHP forerunners, the committee members chose 'perspective' over empathy to label the activity of looking at the past through the eyes of its inhabitants. Students were 'to show an ability to look at events and issues from the perspective of people in the past' and this was 'to understand the importance of looking for motives'.[36] Nowhere in the criteria was there mention of 'entering into' past predicaments and points of view. The language shifted to having students study historical evidence to identify what motivated people to act the ways they did.

Still the authors of GCSE manuals persisted with calling this empathy. In a 1987 teaching guide, *Teaching GCSE History,* Booth, Culpin and Macintosh acknowledged that the term 'empathy' did not feature in the criteria, but still insisted that 'historical empathy' best summed up the activity of looking at events and issues from the perspective of people in the past. There was no longer any point in discussing whether empathy could be done: 'the national criteria are perfectly plain . . . and all history examinations at GCSE are required to test it'. The substantial amount of empirical work undertaken on teaching and assessing the concept had, in their appraisal, resulted in a more utilitarian view of the concept being taken as 'a tool to illuminate motivation', which had 'downgraded the emphasis placed upon imagination'.[37]

A 1989 guide by Ian Colwill and Maureen Burns, *Coursework in GCSE History: Planning and Assessment,* simply adjoined empathy to the criteria's description of perspective, 'Understanding the Perspectives of People in the Past – Empathy'. They recognized the danger in using the term, for instances of its misuse were legion, but insisted that the idea behind the concept posed no controversy. As they put it, an incontrovertible element of historical understanding involves being able to understand that values and beliefs change over time and, in consequence, people in the past were motivated to act according to values and beliefs different from those motivating people to act in the present day. Since this understanding was taken to be the 'essence of empathy' and so basic to the historian's task, they wondered why empathy had become so contentious an issue.[38] Teachers' resources produced by educational authorities in the years surrounding the introduction of the GCSE confirm that the concept had a wide currency.[39]

The more utilitarian view of empathy as perspective was accentuated in a pamphlet produced in 1986 by a working party convened by the SREB in the Department of Education at the University of Cambridge, *Empathy in History: From Definition to Assessment*. Its authors stressed that the concept referred not to an enlivening of the imagination, but rather to an understanding of motivated action through the taking of past perspectives. They began by placing the national criteria's assessment objective for perspective under the title of historical empathy and proceeded to plot a three-stage course for its development, from 'everyday empathy' (the student applies present-day feelings and attitudes to the past), to 'stereotype historical empathy' (the student identifies the predominant view held at the time, such as the 'Elizabethan worldview') and finally to 'differentiated historical empathy' (the student recognizes that different groups and individuals held different points of view). The most accomplished students could assimilate these three forms – they explained how people lived different lives within a common worldview while reflecting on their own experience to enrich their understandings of the past. Curiously, the first and only book by a philosopher of history recommended for further reading by the working party was Collingwood's *The Idea of History*, even though its prime ambition in producing the pamphlet was to expunge the concept of historical imagination that was so central to Collingwood's work.[40]

Empathy's inclusion in the GCSE within the SREB jurisdiction provoked a response that became a *cause célèbre* in the press and raised the attention of academic historians to events transpiring behind school walls. Chris McGovern, the head of history at Lewes Priory comprehensive school in East Sussex, along with his deputy, Anthony Freeman, were dismissed from their posts in 1987 after balking at the new examination and preparing their students for the Scottish O-Level equivalent, which they believed was a more rigorous examination. McGovern had conducted an experiment with sixty students confirming that the skills component of the new examination was so central, they could pass without demonstrating factual knowledge of the events under question. 'Was I dealing with a group of child prodigies?', he gibed in one piece. 'Clearly not. But, in history at least, academic ability has been redefined to make it seem as though this could be the case.' A separate piece described how the 'national criteria for GCSE were hijacked by the new history'. The Conservative peer Baroness Cox characterized the teachers' dismissal as a situation 'more akin to East Germany than East Sussex' in a debate she initiated in the House of Lords on their behalf, during which twenty MPs united to demand their reinstatement.[41] The GCSE had cemented empathy's place in the new history teaching and made it the hallmark of a nation fretful about losing its historical moorings.

The shift to the GCSE was the first step in a broader move towards centralization in education policy, and what had formerly been small-scale disputes and controversies erupted onto the national stage. Kenneth Baker's appointment to the education portfolio in May 1986 intensified these centralist tendencies. Historically educated himself, Baker agreed with his predecessor Joseph that students ought to leave school with enough knowledge of Britain's past to be able to understand and appreciate contemporary British life. Influenced by both neoliberal and neoconservative elements of the New Right, he was an eclectic policy maker not prone to the indecision often attributed to Joseph's intellectually complex background and temperament. Baker was resolute in his conviction that a radical overhaul of a curriculum in which history would be a 'foundation' subject could only be achieved by state centralization. This put him at odds with Thatcher, whose neoliberal propensities favoured a minimum core curriculum as recommended by the CPS.[42]

HMI responded swiftly to the changed mood at the DES. Roger Hennessey, a relative outsider to the history section, having served mostly in social studies, replaced Slater as Staff Inspector in 1987. His appointment came as a surprise inside HMI circles: Sylvester had been expected to succeed Slater. Hennessey was of the same mind as Baker that an undue attention on skills had done the young a disservice.[43] It came as no surprise, then, that the first publication he oversaw, *History from 5 to 16,* was markedly different in tone and emphasis from previous HMI publications. The new-look team declared that the purpose of history education was to 'transmit cultural heritage to new generations' through a syllabus respectful of chronology.[44] History was defined as a body of knowledge to be presented in the order in which it unfolded. Concepts such as 'change and continuity' and 'causation' were regarded as too abstract to support a syllabus without this content. Moreover, the authors took pains to ensure that no hint of the term 'empathy' remained in describing the need to consider past situations from the standpoints of those who lived at the time. 'Such reconstructions must be based on evidence – they should not be uncontrolled flights of imagination.'[45]

Baker established two groups to carry forward the report's recommendations. Privately, he asked a group of academic historians to develop a British history syllabus. Publicly, Baker appointed roughly a dozen experts to a National Curriculum History Working Group. Its task consisted in taking advice and settling upon a set of attainment targets and programmes of study, which it announced in its Interim Report in August 1989 and in its Final Report the following April. A high level of political interferences dogged its activities. Thatcher exercised her veto over Baker to ensure that there was no direct SCHP representation. 'His initial names included the author of the definitive work on the "New History"' (David Sylvester), she recounted later. 'Ken saw my point and made some changes.'[46]

An article in *The Guardian* remarked that it was 'unusual for distinguished academics to become so involved in an issue affecting schools'.[47] These were Baker's academic historians who had just urged the government to adopt its GCSE course, 'The Making of the United Kingdom'. They were headed by Robert Skidelsky, the acclaimed biographer of John Maynard Keynes, Professor of International Studies at the University of Warwick and a Social Democrat life peer who would join the Conservative Party in 1992 when the Social Democrats dissolved. Skidelsky had become implicated in the debate surrounding the GCSE and the National Curriculum as a result of his close association with the Lewes Priory school, which his two sons attended. He defended the ousted teachers' case in articles in both *The Independent* and the *Times Educational Supplement*.[48] The GCSE empathy requirement was in his view an example of how a valid historical concept had been abused for political ends. 'Collingwood (in *The Idea of History*)', he wrote, 'argued that historians only understand the past when they succeed in "penetrating to the thought of the agents whose acts they are studying" . . . However, none of this has much to do with the kind of "empathy assignments" set in GCSE history.'[49]

Instead of Collingwood's principle being applied to the study of 'actual historical events and the recorded thoughts of real historical actors', empathy exercises asked students to penetrate the thought of 'imaginary "ordinary" people' – an active Suffragette, a Jew in Hitler's Germany, a Palestinian. This, Skidelsky believed, held open the way for teachers to 'manipulate students' feelings by depriving them of essential knowledge'.[50] In so depicting empathy, he managed to invert the claim of the new history advocates that the traditional approach was passive and uncritical. Skidelsky wrote the alternative syllabus with McGovern and Freeman. They could cite the support of three eminent historians, Lord Beloff, Lord Bullock and Sir Geoffrey Elton.[51]

The Times stated that the HWG Final Report appeared to have balanced the interests of those who held a traditional view of history with those who advocated a 'more "empathetic" approach'. Yet those who thought that knowledge should be prioritized over skills felt they had lost the battle. 'Now the historians', the article continued, 'including professors Ralph Davis, Sir Geoffrey Elton, Jack Scarisbrick, Robert Skidelsky, Norman Stone, John Vincent and Dr Iain Smith have joined their colleagues in the Lords to put an end to the empathy.'[52]

This group held firmly to the belief that doing history was a far more simple matter than its educational representatives had made it out to be.

'What is history?', began Stone in a piece emblematic of the group's stance. 'This may be a difficult question for philosophers. But for historians it is quite easy.' It was fitting that Stone made a connection between what he saw as school history's unnecessary complexity and the philosophy of history. An outsider to school educational circles, he was probably unaware just how instrumental it had been in the development of a subject built on the principle that every discipline has its own distinct conceptual structure and forms of knowledge. As for empathy, Stone mourned the fact that it had been handled as an 'imaginative trick' rather than as a method for understanding past ages. It was time to assert British culture more confidently. 'We should require a sound knowledge of British history rather than a rag-bag of "empathy" about countries far away.'[53]

These academic historians saw it as their task to wrest history back from an educational establishment that had distorted its essence. Educationalists were well represented in the HWG. Baker appointed two teachers (Carol White and Robert Guyver) and gained further teacher representation with the co-option of a well-known author of school history textbooks and an expert teacher on assessment (Chris Culpin and Tim Lomas). Two teacher-trainers were employed (Anne Low-Beer and Gareth Jones), one of whom (Low-Beer) had been a vocal critic of empathy. Two members came from LEA backgrounds (Henry Hobhouse and Peter Livsey) and the services of two academics were acquired (John Roberts, replaced by Peter Marshall after Roberts resigned in uncontroversial circumstances, and Alice Prochaska). Hennessey was included as an 'observer', a term disguising his highly influential role on the work of the group. Finally, the HWG was chaired by Commander Michael Saunders-Watson, Chairman of the Heritage Education Trust, formerly President of the Historic Houses Association and a landed castle owner from Northamptonshire.[54]

The HWG intended to deliver a fusion of 'traditional' and 'new' history. The debate between the two varieties rested on a spurious content-versus-skills division. As Jones wrote later, 'no historical skills can be exercised in the abstract without reference to specific content'.[55] Jones occupied a vital coordinating role between the HWG and its Welsh counterpart, the History Committee for Wales. He sat on the HWG having edited a volume by historians from university departments of education that announced their intention to develop new solutions to old problems of historical learning and teaching. Jones celebrated the educational research done to enhance teachers' understanding of history's conceptual structure, but questioned its utility in the absence of a continued emphasis on teachers' content knowledge and methods of instruction.[56]

Downing Street received the HWG's attempt to synthesize the old and new approaches as falling too far on the side of the new. Thatcher was appalled by the lack of chronology prescribed in its programmes of study. A press campaign ensued that fuelled the belief that the Final Report was the work of an educational establishment determined to downplay Britain's considerable past achievements. Part of this campaign saw the facts-versus-empathy battle reach a national audience, even though empathy was absent from the Report. This antagonism stood in contrast to the generally positive view held by historians and educationalists. Historians were pleased that the HWG stressed the intellectual value of a disciplined study of the past; educationalists welcomed its insistence that this involved an introduction to historical method.[57]

Of course, not all historians were satisfied. The national reaction saw a wide range of academics contribute to the debate; enough, indeed, for the *Teachers' Weekly* to proclaim 'Academics Enter History Row'. Skidelsky formed with McGovern and Freeman the History Curriculum Association (HCA). In a large advertisement in the *Times Educational Supplement* in May 1990, the HCA announced that it would campaign for the inclusion of a knowledge attainment target absent from the HWG's recommendations. The advertisement contained a list of names of high-profile historians, who it was claimed supported the campaign. In fact, the advertisement prompted several of them to renounce any association with the HCA, unhappy that in seeking to have a stronger emphasis placed on knowledge, it failed to credit the HWG with having specified that the exercise of skills is possible only on the basis of acquired historical knowledge.[58]

During the period of consultation between the interim and final reports, Thatcher and her new education minister, John MacGregor, had manoeuvred to have historical knowledge, not skills, be the basis upon which students were to be assessed. The HWG did not budge, pointing out in reply that, unlike mathematics and the sciences, historical knowledge is not cumulative; accordingly, there can be no hierarchy of factual information to be related to the different stages of learning and tested as such.[59] The Final Report made plain that although students must acquire historical knowledge, it was their understanding of historical information that needed to be assessed: 'Without understanding, history is reduced to parrot learning and assessment to a parlour memory game.'[60] Acquiring historical knowledge provided material to think about through the exercise of historical skills.

As was to be expected given the controversy surrounding it, empathy was not mentioned. But as the concept that designated the need to understand the particular character of the historical context being investigated, it was implicit in attainment target one, 'understanding history in its setting'. Based on the concept of causation, students were to 'recognise that explanations are rarely straightforward and that the causes, motives and intentions of human beings need careful assessment'. The 'cause' of an event was to be found in 'what motivated people to act as they did'.[61] Without doubt, empathy was apparent in all but name to those familiar with how it had been articulated as a way of studying this context over the past two decades.

★ ★ ★

The first National Curriculum for History was established by regulation in March 1991. Developments in the two decades since have come with a sense of *déjà vu*. John Major's Conservative government (1990–97) initiated the Dearing Review in 1994 to overhaul the entire curriculum to ensure more standardization across the subjects. McGovern, who became a member of its History Task Group, dissented from the majority by arguing that it was the work of a government that had shirked its obligation to provide Britain's youth with a core narrative by pandering to the left's concerns about diversity and inclusion.

The situation worsened for those who held McGovern's view under the New Labour governments (1997–2010). They addressed the recurring concern about embedding a set of British values in the history curriculum by highlighting that the national narrative was a multiperspectival narrative. As Chancellor of Exchequer, Gordon Brown, the future Prime Minister and Scot with a PhD in history, acknowledged at events in 2004 and 2006 the difficulty of defining the boundaries of civic duty and the nature of a civic society that transcended cultural and ethnic differences. He reaffirmed the view that it is possible to be British and Cornish or at the same time be both British and Pakistani. Lastly, the election of the Conservative-Liberal Democrat Coalition government in 2010 saw the arguments of the Thatcher era return full circle. Under the Secretary of State for Education, Michael Gove, a former journalist with *The Times* and neoconservative inspired more by E.D. Hirsch's notion of core knowledge than by Hirst's forms of knowledge, the stage was set for another round of public disputes about the composition and purposes of the history curriculum, in which the historians Simon Schama, Niall Ferguson and Richard Evans were chief combatants.[62]

Of course, skirmishes between traditionalists, innovators and politicians over the shape of the history curriculum have by no means been confined to Britain. In Canada, Peter Seixas has observed that policy makers in history, unlike their counterparts in maths and science, lack a common measurement framework by which to evaluate and compare different approaches to history teaching worldwide. 'History education is messier, and it must be so, above all, because it is drenched in politics.'[63] But in spite of the attempts to usurp the critical, reflective, reflexive and multiperspectival dimensions of historical inquiry in favour of what typically amounts to a politically expedient and self-affirming monoculturalism, there is always a disjuncture between political intent and educational practice in history education, in part because the decisions teachers make about what to teach and how to teach it are influenced by their own political orientations and conceptions of the purposes of historical learning. A 1990s study of the attitudes of seventy-one American student-teachers of history made this point abundantly clear. It revealed that 45 per cent of them saw themselves as 'relativist reformers', 22 per cent as 'eclectic', 18 per cent as 'scientific historians' and 11 per cent as 'story-tellers'.[64]

But in an environment where educators have looked to find a structure by which students' progression in historical learning might be articulated and evaluated, it has remained necessary to clarify the forms of historical inquiry that can guide school teaching. Seixas looked to Peter Lee to find the structural, disciplinary or second-order concepts that he laid down as a foundation for his six-part and globally implemented model of historical thinking. At the same time, with increasing international collaboration among researchers in history education, the hermeneutically based German tradition of history didactics has become a focal point in ways that we shall now consider.

Notes

1. Fred Inglis, *History Man: The Life of R.G. Collingwood* (Princeton: Princeton University Press, 2009), 215.
2. Colin Dexter, *The Jewel That was Ours* (London: Macmillan, 1991), 49.
3. David Sylvester, 'Change and Continuity in History Teaching 1900–93', in Hilary Bourdillon (ed.), *Teaching History* (London: Routledge, 1994), 16.
4. R. Wake, 'History as a Separate Discipline: The Case'. *Teaching History* 1, 3 (1970), 156.
5. Peter Lee, 'History Teaching and Philosophy of History', *History and Theory* 22, 4 (1983), 20.
6. Margaret Thatcher, *The Downing Street Years* (London: HarperCollins, 1993), 596.
7. DES, *National Curriculum History Working Group: Final Report* (London: HMSO, 1990).
8. Martin Roberts, 'History in the School Curriculum 1972–1990; A Possible Dialectical Sequence: Thesis, Antithesis, Synthesis?', *Curriculum Journal* 1, 1 (1990), 65–75.
9. Kerwin Lee Klein, *From History to Theory* (Berkeley: University of California Press, 2011), 35–58.
10. Ibid., 51.
11. DES, *Curriculum 11–16. Working Papers by HM Inspectorate: A Contribution to Current Debate* (London: HMSO, 1977), 1, 49–50.
12. DES, *History in the Primary and Secondary Years: An HMI View* (London: HMSO, 1985), 2–4.
13. Lee, 'History Teaching and Philosophy of History', 25.
14. DES, *History in the Primary and Secondary Years*, 3.
15. Ibid., 19, 26.
16. Sylvester, HiEP (History in Education Project, Institute of Historical Research, University of London) interview, 23, 25.
17. Richard Peterson, 'Obituary, John Slater', *The Guardian,* 22 June 2015.

18. Sylvester, HiEP interview, 25; Ian Dawson, HiEP interview, 9 June 2009, 13; Chris Culpin, HiEP interview, 22 September 2009, 9.

19. John Slater, *The Politics of History Teaching: A Humanity Dehumanized?* (London: Institute of Education, 1989), 2–3. Slater was a Visiting Professor at the IOE from 1988 to 1990.

20. Roger Hennessey, HiEP interview, 11 November 2009, 4.

21. Slater, *The Politics of History Teaching,* 3; John Slater, 'History in the National Curriculum: The Final Report of the History Working Group', in Richard Aldrich (ed.), *History in the National Curriculum* (London: Kogan Page, 1991), 8–9.

22. Keith Joseph, 'Why Teach History in School?', *Historian* 2 (Spring 1984), 10–12.

23. Shirley Robin Letwin, *The Anatomy of Thatcherism* (London: Fontana, 1992), 228–37.

24. Keith Joseph, 'Speech by the Rt Hon Sir Keith Joseph, Secretary of State for Education and Science, at the North of England Education Conference, Sheffield, on Friday 6 January 1984', *Oxford Review of Education* 10, 2 (1984), 137–46.

25. James Callaghan, *Time and Chance* (London: Collins, 1987), 411.

26. See, for example, Max Wilkinson, *Lessons from Europe: A Comparison of British and West European Schooling* (London: Centre for Policy Studies, 1977).

27. Andrew Denham and Mark Garnett, *Keith Joseph* (Chesham: Acumen, 2002), 388, 399; David Cannadine, Jenny Keating and Nicola Sheldon. *The Right Kind of History: Teaching the Past in Twentieth-Century England* (Basingstoke: Palgrave Macmillan, 2011), 178–85.

28. Caroline Gipps, 'GCSE: Some Background' and Henry Macintosh, 'The Sacred Cows of Coursework', in Caroline Gipps (ed.), *The GCSE: An Uncommon Examination* (London: Institute of Education, 1986), 11–20 and 21–29 respectively; Cannadine, Keating and Sheldon, *Right Kind of History,* 185–86.

29. Shirley Robin Letwin, *The Anatomy of Thatcherism* (London: Fontana, 1992), 257.

30. Michael Kingdon and Gordon Stobart, *GCSE Examined* (London: Falmer Press, 1988), 91; Little, 'National Curriculum in History', 323; Jenny Keating and Nicola Sheldon, 'History in Education: Trends and Themes in History Teaching, 1900–2010', in Ian Davies (ed.), *Debates in History Teaching* (London: Routledge, 2011), 11.

31. SCHP, *A New Look at History* (Edinburgh: Holmes McDougall, 1976), 49–84.

32. Bob Wolfson, 'Schools Council History 13–16 Project: An Upper School's Experience', *Teaching History* 27 (June 1980), 30.

33. Ibid. (SCHP addendum).

34. Culpin, HiEP interview, 9; Dawson, HiEP interview, 12–13; Scott Harrison, HiEP interview, 6 May 2009, 11; John D. Clare, HiEP interview, 7 April 2010, 9.

35. Bronwen Swinnerton and Isobel Jenkins, *Secondary School History Teaching in England and Wales: A Review of Empirical Research, 1960–1998* (Leeds: Centre for Studies in Science and Mathematics Education, University of Leeds, in Association with the Historical Association, 1999), 23–24, 35–36.

36. DES, *GCSE: The National Criteria – History* (London: HMSO, 1985), 1, 3.

37. Martin Booth, Christopher Culpin and Henry Macintosh, *Teaching GCSE History* (London: Hodder & Stoughton, 1987), 12, 24, 68.

38. Ian Colwill and Maureen Burns, *Coursework in GCSE History: Planning and Assessment* (London: Hodder & Stoughton, 1989), 41.

39. For example, Secondary Examinations Council, *History: GCSE, A Guide for Teachers* (Milton Keynes: Open University Press, 1986); Nicolas Tate, *GCSE Coursework: History, A Teachers' Guide to Organisation and Assessment* (Basingstoke: Macmillan Educational, 1987).

40. SREB, *Empathy in History: From Definition to Assessment* (Eastleigh: SREB, 1986), 1–15, 63.

41. Melanie Phillips, 'Education System Imposes Ideas in Authoritarian Way', *The Guardian,* 29 June 1990, 27; Chris McGovern, 'Hitting the Target, Losing the Battle', *The Guardian,* 22 May 1990, 27; Caroline St John-Brooks, 'Battling to Stop the "Hijack" of a GCSE Subject;

Teaching of New History', *Sunday Times,* 13 November 1988, 8; 'Peers to Take up History Teachers' Sackings', *The Independent,* 22 July 1989, 2.

42. Robert Phillips, *History Teaching, Nationhood and the State: A Study in Educational Politics* (London: Cassell, 1998), 49–52.

43. Ibid., 47.

44. DES, *History from 5 to 16* (London: HMSO, 1988), 1, 10.

45. Ibid., 7.

46. Thatcher, *Downing Street Years,* 596.

47. David Gow, 'Historians Urge New Syllabus', *The Guardian,* 25 May 1989, 4.

48. Robert Skidelsky, 'History as Social Engineering', *The Independent,* 1 March 1988, 15; 'Mutiny at the Priory', *Times Educational Supplement* 3789 (1989), 1–3.

49. Skidelsky, 'History as Social Engineering', 15.

50. Ibid.

51. Gow, 'Historians Urge New Syllabus', 4.

52. Sam Kiley, 'History Battle Joined by Peers', *The Times,* 19 March 1990, 22.

53. Norman Stone, 'Put Nuts and Bolts Back into History', *Sunday Times,* 13 March 1988, 34.

54. DES, *History Working Group,* 193; Phillips, *History Teaching,* 54–5.

55. Gareth Jones, 'The Debate over the National Curriculum for History in England and Wales, 1989–90: The Role of the Press', *Curriculum Journal* 11, 3 (2000), 300.

56. Gareth Jones, 'Traditional and New History Teaching: Towards a Synthesis', in Gareth Jones and Lionel Ward (eds), *New History Old Problems: Studies in History Teaching* (Swansea: University College of Swansea Faculty of Education, 1978), 137–54.

57. Little, 'National Curriculum in History', 331; Jones, 'Debate over the National Curriculum', 301–08.

58. Phillips, *History Teaching,* 85–6.

59. Cannadine, Keating and Sheldon, *Right Kind of History,* 194–5.

60. DES, *History Working Group,* 7.

61. Ibid., 116, 120.

62. Robert Guyver, 'The History Working Group and beyond: A Case Study in the UK's History Quarrels', in Tony Taylor and Robert Guyver (eds), *History Wars and the Classroom: Global Perspectives* (Charlotte: Information Age Publishing, 2012), 171–3; Robert Guyver, 'Michael Gove's History Wars 2010–2014: The Rise, Fall and Transformation of a Neoconservative Dream', *Agora* 49, 4 (2014), 4–11.

63. Peter Seixas, preface to Taylor and Guyver (eds), *History Wars and the Classroom,* xxi.

64. Ronald R. Evans, 'Educational Ideologies and the Teaching of History', in Gaea Leinhardt, Isabel L. Beck and Catherine Stainton (eds), *Teaching and Learning in History* (Hillsdale: Lawrence Erlbaum, 1994), 171–207.

CHAPTER 10

Historical Thinking and Historical Consciousness

Empathy's scandalous biography and omission from the National Curriculum for History forced the concept into hiding under a different terminology. It became the 'concept that dares not speak its name', and only in recent years have Peter Lee and Denis Shemilt asked whether empathy should 'come out of the closet'.[1]

Lee had helped put it there. His salutary pronouncements in 1983 that 'empathy is a necessary condition for historical understanding' and part of the 'structural basis of the discipline' were followed by treatments of structural concepts that omitted mention of empathy entirely.[2] The noble task of spotting intelligence and rationality in past actions was now to be achieved by understanding the *reasons* for which people who lived in the past did what they did.[3] A project launched in 1993 that aimed to chart students' progression in handling historical evidence measured how successfully students articulated these reasons through the concept of rational understanding.[4] This was the term Lee had adopted years earlier from von Wright's model of practical inferences, which, we recall, he continued to promulgate under the title of empathy when that became the recognized term as a result of the SCHP's successes.

The systematic analysis of history as a distinct form of knowledge by analytical philosophers of history enabled history educationalists to reify historical thinking into a set of concepts that teachers could use to induct students into the history discipline. Although the difference between 'analytical' and 'continental' philosophy is prone to oversimplification and exaggeration, the heart of the opposition is the methodological focus on *analysis* versus *syn-*

Notes for this section begin on page 209.

thesis. Analytical philosophers tend to try to solve delineated philosophical problems by reducing them to their parts and to the relations in which these parts stand. For example, logical positivism is the doctrine that the world is the sum of its empirical facts organized into a systematic code that mirrors those facts as closely as possible to how they really are. Hempel's logical positivism worked on a model of logical deduction from general laws, which led intentionalist philosophers of history to attempt to preserve history's autonomy by a similar kind of methodological reductionism. In contrast, continental philosophers tend to address philosophical questions in a synthetic or integrative manner. They consider philosophical problems to be parts of larger entities and as properly understood only when their systems of reciprocities have been established. This final chapter explains how these two traditions have converged to produce a hybrid variety of historical thought steering research directions in twenty-first-century history education.

W.H. Burston loomed behind Lee's efforts to specify the structural, procedural, disciplinary or what are most commonly referred to as 'second-order' concepts. The elder's insistence that history teaching must be based on the distinct logic of historical explanation made colligation the principal category for organizing historical content into a cognizable whole that could then be broken down into its individual parts and reconstructed as such. Burston taught that whereas the historian's method is to work from the part to the whole, history teachers must lay out before the student the general movement of which an event is part before proceeding to an explanation of the event itself. This was the 'theme method' he designed to counter the Whiggish line-of-development approach. Lee commended Burston for the pioneering role he played in bringing history teaching into dialogue with the philosophy of history, but argued against him that there is an activity prior to colligation upon which it rests: the identification of agents' intentions and purposes. If teachers were to colligate events according to their shared purposes, Lee reasoned, they must know what those purposes were. 'The central tasks facing children if they are to understand, and teachers if they are to explain', he wrote, 'lie one step further back, and something more akin to Dray's or G.H. von Wright's account of historical explanation must come first.'[5]

At the time of writing these words, what came first was still empathy, later to be conveyed through its cognate terms. Burston's colligatory concepts or themes – Renaissance, Reformation, Industrial Revolution – were substantive, content-based arrangements of events. They had nothing to do with the actual procedures historians use to reconstruct the past, or with the standards to which they appeal for making claims about the past. The question of how students obtain historical content remained poorly articulated. As means for grasping the beliefs, values and goals behind past actions, empathy and colligation stood at opposite ends of the spectrum of historical explanation. Unlike Burston, who believed that the history teacher ought to proceed in the reverse order to that of the professional historian, Lee argued that teachers and students, like historians, need to capture the intentional and purposive dimension of past actions in order to organize them into larger explanatory matrices. Empathy offered itself as the device by which students collected the raw material of historical understanding and explanation. Other second-order candidates included 'evidence', 'cause', 'change' and 'time', to which in recent years have been added 'explanation' and 'accounts'. Lee did not equivocate as to their importance: 'Teaching history must in the end come down to developing children's understanding of structural second-order concepts.'[6]

Different national traditions of history education continue to be defined by different concepts, methodologies and research interests.[7] Nevertheless, the systematic analysis of history as a distinct form of knowledge in the intentionalist-analytical tradition of the philosophy of history has had a far-reaching effect on shaping practice internationally. Penney Clark has noted that Peter Seixas' conceptual framework for historical thinking, used globally today in the development of school history curricula and textbooks, is grounded in the 'seminal work' of a number of UK researchers active in the 1980s.[8] Seixas himself has confirmed that the 'British work has influenced numerous North American studies, which share the focus on second-order concepts', concepts he has affirmed 'look very much like' the historical thinking concepts he has developed over the past two decades.[9]

Added to the fact that he carried forward Lee's programme and made second-order concepts part of the vernacular of practising history teachers, Seixas' work is significant for the fact that he introduced the concept of historical consciousness into the field of English-speaking history education research. As a result, there now sits alongside anglophone historical thinking concepts a broader theoretical programme with roots in the German hermeneutical tradition. Both traditions of historical thought vie for the attention of teachers, researchers and curriculum writers in a variety of national contexts.

★ ★ ★

An American by birth, Seixas taught social studies for fourteen years in schools in Philadelphia and Vancouver before accepting a position as Assistant Professor in the Faculty of Education at the University of British Columbia in 1990. With a PhD in history from the University of California at Los Angeles, he embarked upon his career in history education research believing that he was inventing a new field. He soon discovered not only the rich, established tradition in the United Kingdom, but also a small group of

North American researchers broadly concerned as he was with translating to the classroom the practices, procedures and ways of thinking of professional historians, among whom Sam Wineburg and his work on the reading of historical texts was the exemplar. Accordingly, a major theme of Seixas' early publications concerned the question of the extent to which those working in the field of history education could claim a set of core components of historical thinking when historians themselves, no longer trained in the same methods, concepts and language, lacked agreement on the features common to historical practice. Part of his response involved considering how historical thinking fitted within a strong tradition of social sciences teaching in North America.[10] Upon being awarded a Canada Research Chair in 2001, Seixas established the Centre for the Study of Historical Consciousness (CSHC), the first of its kind in an English-speaking country to sponsor research into the full range of individual, collective, cognitive, cultural and temporal factors that affect the way in which history is understood, learnt and taught in public, private and institutional settings.

Seixas met Lee in 1993 at the annual meeting of the Organization of American Historians in Anaheim, California. Seixas was Chair of the Committee on Teaching, and invited Lee to speak. He had not yet specified the elements that he would later suggest constitute the basis of historical thinking and package for teachers, curriculum and textbook writers as such. But the project must have been set in train, for on the sidelines of the conference, Lee advised him to exclude empathy from his model. This was the same advice Lee had offered Shemilt fifteen years earlier, to which the Leeds educationalist responded that it was too late to remove. The decade just past in which empathy was held up for mockery could only have reinforced Lee's view that its purpose was more judiciously communicated through an alternative term. Seixas was drawn to the notion of rational, evidence-based understanding across temporal difference. There was too strong a likelihood that empathy would give rise to the belief among teachers that they were being encouraged to cultivate affective or emotional bonds with historical agents.

It was not until Seixas was forced to specify his own concepts in materials for teachers a decade later that he stopped using the term. In his programmatic 1996 article 'Conceptualizing the Growth of Historical Understanding', empathy still played an essential part in historical understanding. He began by noting that the forms-of-knowledge-inspired work of Lee and Shemilt required a stronger sense of history's structure than he was prepared to grant it: 'I use the term "structure" with reserve, and what I propose as a "structure" of history is perhaps no more than a set of closely related core issues that must be confronted in order to foster growth in historical knowledge.'[11] These 'core issues' were organized under the headings of 'significance', 'epistemology and evidence', 'continuity and change', 'progress and decline', 'the confrontation with difference: empathy and moral judgment' and 'historical agency'.[12]

Empathy raised the fundamentally hermeneutical problem of negotiating 'affinity and distance', of the confrontation with difference that tempts history students to impose their frameworks of meaning on others – what Wineburg characterized as the 'presentism' behind the 'unnatural act' of historical thinking. Whereas in England empathy supplied the means for reconstructing the past context in which agents thought and acted, this empathetic understanding or negotiation was more broadly conceived as a basis for making moral judgements in history. 'Moral judgments require empathetic understanding', wrote Seixas. According to him, 'we want to (and generally do) avoid a relativistic historicism that abjures historical judgments because the past is such a "foreign country"'. Our ability to make moral judgements in history rests upon the extent to which we can hold in mind the 'notion of a historically transcendent human commonality', while being open to the possibility that past agents 'differ from us in ways so profound that we perpetually risk misunderstanding them'.[13] Seixas described empathy in a familiar hermeneutical tenor: we understand in the context of a tradition that has been handed down from the past, but historical understanding seems to want that tradition to be put aside in order to grasp what is different about the past.

Even though Seixas endowed empathy with this pivotal role in historical meaning-making, the concept did not feature in his subsequent framework. In partnership with the Historica Foundation, a national nonprofit organization whose goal is to disseminate Canadian history in both popular and educational forums, the Benchmarks of Historical Thinking Project, later renamed the Historical Thinking Project, was launched at the CSHC in 2006.[14] Six 'structural' concepts continued to provide the basis for historical thinking, but what 'is sometimes called "historical empathy"' now appeared under the heading of 'historical perspectives'.[15] Nor did empathy, formerly regarded as necessary for making historical judgements, feature in the description of the concept of 'moral dimension'.[16] The problems and challenges included under the hermeneutically conceived core issue of the 'confrontation with difference' now spread across two new concepts – 'historical perspective' and the 'moral dimension'.

Both concepts relied on a thorough and evidence-based understanding of historical context, and called on students to recognize affinity and difference between past and present contexts. The major difference between the two consisted in the purpose for which the historical context was to be studied. Taking historical perspectives helped students explain why people in the past acted the way they did, whereas understanding the moral dimension helped students judge those actions. As for the relation between past and present contexts, taking historical perspectives related present to past in learning to recognize presentism in historical accounts – students were to see how present-day beliefs and mentalities can be applied to people in the past. Conversely, understanding the moral dimension related past to present in learning to use judgements of past actions to inform judgements of moral and policy issues in the present.

The decision to approach the task of explaining past actions through perspectives rather than empathy was not without precedent. As we have seen, the 1985 GCSE *National Criteria* went against the grain of a teaching profession who mostly accepted empathy and repackaged its focus on determining the context of motivated action in the language of perspective taking. An ability to look at events from the perspective of the people involved in them allowed students to identify their motives, which was central to the intentionalist philosophy of history behind the English approach. Seixas aligned himself with the view that reconstructing the thoughts expressed in human action is central to the historical process. 'Texts come not to convey information, to tell stories, or even to set the record straight', he explained in agreement with Wineburg's discussion of the relation between text and context. 'Texts emerge as "speech acts", social interactions set down on paper that can be understood only by trying to reconstruct the social context in which they occurred. The comprehension of the text reaches beyond words and phrases to embrace intention, motive, purpose, and plan – the same set of concepts we use to decipher human action.'[17]

This is in fact the Austinian theory behind Skinner's idea that an illocutionary force is equivalent to the intention an author had in writing a text, as discussed in Chapter 7. It is equivalent because it is not the pristine origin of the intention itself that Skinner's method wants to recapture in the manner of Romantic hermeneutics, but the intention expressed in what an author or agent was doing in writing a text or performing an action. By invoking it, Seixas implied the need for a Collingwoodian and Skinnerian contextualism: it is not past beliefs themselves that constitute the context to be reconstructed in taking historical perspectives and judging the past; rather, the context to be identified is the system of presuppositions that allowed past agents to hold these beliefs as true and to act upon them accordingly.

In practice, however, the historical thinking model does not have students extend this far back. Its showpiece teaching resource asks students to explain, for example, why Canadian Prime Minister Lester B. Pearson was 'so rude so publicly' to Charles de Gaulle when he rebuked him on public radio during a state visit to Canada in 1967.[18] The 'immediate context' for reconstructing Pearson's perspective is given as consisting of a speech de Gaulle concluded the previous day in Montreal with the exclamation 'vive le Québec libre!', the rallying cry of Quebec separatists during a period of intense Quebec nationalism, which is offered as the 'context' for understanding Pearson's outrage. The chain of reasoning by which students are to evaluate Pearson's scolding of the French President is thus set as follows: there was a Quebec separatist movement (context); Pearson believed that Canada should remain united; de Gaulle threw fuel onto the separatist flame; therefore, Pearson publicly rebuked him and de Gaulle cut short his visit.

The conditions that *made possible* this series of events never enter the inference. De Gaulle's speech should not be understood as the 'immediate context', but rather as the action that preceded and led Pearson to rebuke de Gaulle on radio. De Gaulle's action was a breach of diplomatic protocol, but this in itself does not explain Pearson's response to it. To speak of contexts as actions that lead to other actions says nothing of the conditions underlying their relations.

As for the general context, the fact that there was a Quebec separatist movement does not explain why Pearson was opposed to it. The separatist movement was rather the object of his belief that Canada should remain united. Why should Canada remain united? On what basis did statesmen in the twentieth century wish to safeguard the sovereignty of the territory over which they governed? If the question driving the inquiry is to understand how Pearson could be impudent to de Gaulle, the context to be illuminated must reach back to the ideational setting in which it was possible for him to hold as true and worth defending the belief that Quebec should remain sovereign Canadian territory. Beliefs are propositional attitudes, and propositions spring from presuppositions. Collingwood's twin theories of question-and-answer and absolute presuppositions have made this clear. Illuminating the context that gave rise to the beliefs that guided human action is hard won; it is not the matter of stating the existence of a preceding action, movement or event.

Another difficulty in taking historical perspectives concerns the way that students work with or without sufficient historical evidence. 'Evidence' itself is the second of Seixas' six concepts. There it is recognized that evidence is the product of analysing historical sources or, we might specify, of asking particular questions of a historical source in the style of the detective-historian.[19] It is not clear, however, how students extract evidence from the sources they study in taking historical perspectives. It is made clear that to imagine without consulting evidence is guessing, a practice foreign to the historian and thus to the history classroom.[20] But there is no discussion of the questions that history students might ask to reveal the thoughts and feelings of the people whose perspectives they try to take.

The example unpacked for teachers and students is instead one in which the author was obliged to fill in herself what her main protagonist thought and felt with insights from her own first-person experience. In the story of a girl who grew up amid the religious tensions of eighteenth-century North America, students are told that the historical novelist 'employed a mix of psychological common-sense (i.e. assumptions of timeless human experience) and sensitivity to historical and cultural differences over time'. Open about the fact that the gulf between past and present meant that the author could not fully comprehend the motives that drove the girl to act, the author interweaved chapters describing her own research process with chapters telling the narrative of the girl's life. This method of interweaving the author's own experiences into the narrative is presented as having allowed 'her to better negotiate the distance between past and present', while recognizing the limitations of what can be known about the mental universe in which her protagonist operated.[21] With this method taken to be the exemplar of historical perspective taking, it follows that classroom activities in the concept include reading and writing historical fiction. The fundamental principle that the evidence on which students base their understandings and explanations of past perspectives is the product of a questioning activity does not feature in the concept's elucidation.

Stepping back, it becomes apparent the Seixas model represents a departure from the Collingwood-inspired concept of empathy as re-enactment. Among English history educationalists, empathy was a central component in the attempt to establish a conceptual foundation for the history subject. They argued that by illuminating the situation context in which actions were taken, the empathetic reconstruction of past agents' motives and intentions counteracted the determinism or necessity of natural scientific explanations of cause and effect. For Seixas, although perspective taking was also the attempt to explain historical actions from this past vantage point, it was not attached to a programme of asserting history's distinct structure or autonomous disciplinary status. Seixas was animated by history's potential to equip young people with an ability to evaluate and contest the competing narratives of the past heaped upon them by mass culture and their state-administered education systems. He also believed that empathetic understanding and perspective taking could never avoid a layer of reasoning on the basis of human universals. There is thus a tension in his work between his commitment to the civic and democratizing purposes of history education on the one hand, and the notion implicit in historical thinking concepts that they comprise the central elements of the history discipline on the other hand. One represents a normative, moral and ethical commitment; the other makes claims about the distinct structure of the historical mode of inquiry.

Refracted through the Seixas model, empathy's function in historical inquiry becomes opaque. An example of this is provided by the Australian case, where empathy and perspective taking were included as two separate concepts in the development of a national history curriculum that drew from Seixas' model. The Australian case brings to light the confusion that can arise when educationalists borrow from different traditions of historical thought; in this case, a largely reductionist intentionalist-analytical philosophy of history from which second-order educational concepts were extracted, and the historicist-hermeneutical tradition that tends to synthesize parts into wholes while illuminating their mutual dependencies. There is no problem with conceptual hybridity per se; educationalists are free to mine the variety of intellectual resources available to them. The danger is that practical problems are bound to ensue when conceptual distinctions belonging to separate paradigms of historical thought become muddled in educational usage.[22]

Work began on the Australian Curriculum in 2008 when the Minister for Education under the first Rudd government, Julia Gillard, created the National Curriculum Board (later renamed the Australian Curriculum, Assessment and Reporting Authority). Stuart Macintyre, the Australian historian who chaired the Keating government's Civics Expert Group in the 1990s, was selected to begin the process as the lead writer of a history framing paper. The shape of the curriculum was to follow the contours of the disciplines that form the bases of the school subjects.[23] This emphasis on the disciplinary foundation of knowledge production allowed the architects of the history curriculum to bypass the recurrent and sterile debate between factual knowledge and conceptual understanding. The shaping paper made plain that there can be no historical understanding without a mastery of the methods of historical inquiry. Factual knowledge was to be the building block of historical understanding, for without knowledge of chronology, geography, institutional arrangements, material circumstances and belief systems, no study of a past period, however well intended, could lead to understanding.[24]

'Historical understanding' was chosen after a process of consultation. Macintyre had originally used 'historical thinking', which he drew from Seixas' work.[25] The concepts included to develop historical understanding were at heart those of the Historical Thinking Project. Historical significance, evidence, continuity and change, and cause and consequence translated directly from the Benchmarks. Unlike that model, however, historical perspectives and historical empathy appeared as separate concepts:

> *Historical perspectives:* The cognitive act of understanding the different social, cultural and intellectual contexts that shaped people's lives and actions in the past. This involves an understanding of the dangers of anachronism and an appreciation of diverse perspectives on the past.
>
> *Historical empathy and moral judgement:* The capacity to enter into the world of the past with an informed imagination and ethical responsibility. The discipline of history constrains the practitioner from imposing personal preferences on

the evidence but all meaningful historical accounts involve explicit or implicit moral judgement, and historians require an awareness of their own values and the impact of these values on their historical understanding.[26]

In concord with Seixas' Benchmarks, 'historical perspectives' was the concept that labelled the cognitive act of understanding the context in which past actions were taken. But in that model, historical perspectives had replaced historical empathy. It is difficult to determine in the Australian case what the cognitive act of understanding the context in which people lived and acted (historical perspectives) could involve if not the act of entering into the world of the past with an informed imagination (historical empathy) and vice versa. An *informed* imagination is one presumably disciplined by evidence, which must also be the basis of the *cognitive act* of investigating the historical context.

A better way of putting this is that by historical perspectives is meant the illumination of the *ideational context* in which past agents acted, and by historical empathy and moral judgement is meant the use of the *moral imagination* to judge past actions and beliefs. How the two interrelate is a focal point of hermeneutics. Schleiermacher's empathy, Ranke's disinterestedness, Droysen's activism and Gadamer's fusion each posit varying ethical commitments to the historian's subject matter. In history education, hermeneutics has been discussed primarily through the concept of historical consciousness, whose basis in the empathy-dependent hermeneutics of nineteenth-century historicism has been established and evaluated. The picture that emerges from the Australian example is that empathy was conceived along the lines of Seixas' earlier work, where in discovering affinity and difference in the past, the concept drew attention to the problem of presentism and the need in history to judge the past by its own standards.

The German notion of historical consciousness sets a broader theoretical framework than that with which English history educationalists worked to establish the subject's conceptual basis. Just as philosophers discuss the possibility of a *rapprochement* between the analytical and continental traditions, a challenge facing teachers, curriculum writers and history education researchers consists in making sense of the variety of influences that have come to shape the way in which history education is theorized and practised. No influence has been more powerful than Jörn Rüsen's hermeneutical history didactics.

* * *

Born in 1938, Rüsen studied history, philosophy, German literature and education at the University of Cologne, where he completed a doctorate in philosophy in 1966 on Droysen's *Historik* or theory of historiography. Frank Ankersmit, the Dutch professor of intellectual history and historical theory at the University of Groningen, has described him as 'probably the most influential contemporary German philosopher of history'.[27] Although Rüsen had written five books, numerous articles and edited several volumes of essays on the philosophy of history when Ankersmit wrote these words in 1988, he remained relatively unknown in the English-speaking world. Allan Megill, the American intellectual historian, pointed out shortly afterwards that the specialized character and diverse foci of Rüsen's essays could make it difficult for readers to discern the general outline of his theoretical project.[28] He has written on the history of historiography, the structure and development of historical consciousness, the development of historical culture and identity, and the history of human rights.

The scope of Rüsen's oeuvre need not obscure its guiding vision. His principal concern has been with the status of history as an academic discipline and its practical, mainly pedagogical, implications. His writings pivot on the problematical relationship between history as a form of cognition and history as an instrument of identity formation. His central claim is that historiography can reach its full potential as a positive force in human affairs and become 'living' (*lebendige*) history only when this relationship is framed in a way that meets the standards of reason arrived at by consensus, a position sharing parallels with Habermas' concern with how rational knowledge becomes constituted out of a world of praxis.[29] For Rüsen, the question of historiography's uses for life must be theoretically guided by the mutually agreed methods, procedures and forms of representation of the history discipline. He has appealed not for a new scientific departure in historical method, but rather for an explication and clarification of the ordinary, traditional methods of historical scholarship, obscured by the century-long lapse of time from when they were formulated, during which the intrusion of new, auxiliary fields and disciplines have threatened to dissolve or marginalize history. The standards and criteria of historical scholarship are themselves goals of learning, for they are the means by which historical knowledge is acquired, structured and exhibited in a coherent and credible manner. Historiography and historical didactics converge on this conjunction, 'paradigm' or 'disciplinary matrix', terms he borrowed from Kuhn's *The Structure of Scientific Revolutions* (1962).[30]

Beginning with *Für eine erneuerte Historik (For a Renewed Historics)* in 1976 and followed by the three-volume *Grundzüge einer Historik (Fundamentals of a Historics)*, Rüsen argued that five fundamentals of historical knowledge bind this conjunction: first, a universal human interest in the past; second, the role of historical consciousness in orienting human beings in time; third, our ideas of the past; fourth, methods of empirical research; and, fifth, the forms in which the findings of historical research are presented. The first two are rooted in the practice of life (*Lebenspraxis*), which take shape according to time, place and circumstances. The other three belong to history as a professional discipline, with its own standards of verification no less self-evident than those of the natural sciences. Their relation in the disciplinary matrix has the character of a hermeneutic circle in that each feeds from and regenerates the next, but it is a circle with a clear starting point. Rüsen's argument is that historical thinking, no less than scientific thinking, proceeds from elementary thinking in the practice of life to a methodologization of experience, norms and ideas, not vice versa.

The first of Rüsen's trilogy, *Historische Vernunft* (1983), considered the first two fundamentals partly through a Collingwoodian analysis of the objectivity of historical knowledge. Just as Collingwood believed that the questions historians take to the past arise from the system of presuppositions that define their present epoch, Rüsen granted that history contains an element of partisanship in that historians work in a particular context for a particular purpose. But just as Collingwood stressed that the function of these questions is such that they orient historians to a past world of meaning outside themselves, Rüsen argued that historiography expands our intellectual horizons when merely subjective points of view are overcome and the intersubjectivity of life-worlds emerges as an objective form of consensus. What begins as partisan must, if it is to be communicable outside its original context, end up as objective knowledge. Against individualizing historicism, history relies on and connects with human universals.

In the second volume, *Rekonstruktion der Vergangenheit* (1986), Rüsen offered an account of the next two fundamentals through a study of the concept of narrative explanation. History gives us a sense of our own identity, he suggested, by passing through three phases. First, historians attempt to identify themselves with the people who thought and acted in the past (the hermeneutical phase). In undertaking this, they become aware of a discrepancy between how these people perceived their world and how that world really was (the analytical phase). Finally, historians must achieve a dialectical synthesis between these two phases; that is, they must fill the gap between what they take to be the reality of the past world they investigate and the way in which that reality was perceived by those who lived, thought and acted in it. They must be explicit during each phase about the questions they take to the past (heuristics), analyse historical sources with the help of auxiliary sciences (criticism) and construct the synthesis from what the sources have taught them about the past (interpretation).[31]

Finally, in *Lebendige Geschichte* (1989), Rüsen focused on the fifth fundamental of historical knowledge: the narrative forms in which the findings of empirical research are presented. In contrast to Hayden White, who looked for what historical narrative shares in common with literary forms of narrative, Rüsen searched for a specifically historical typology of narration.³² What distinguishes historical narration is that it has the function of orientating practical life within the framework of time. It is the process of making sense of the experience of time. Since different forms of historical narration make sense of the experience of time in different ways, to be historically conscious is to possess the narrative competence to distinguish and work within and across the different forms.³³ As Rüsen explained in his most widely known essay among researchers in history education:

> Once the narrative form of the procedures of historical consciousness and its function as a means of temporal orientation are clear, it is possible to characterize the specific and essential competence of historical consciousness as 'narrative competence'. Such competence can be defined as the ability of human consciousness to carry out procedures which make sense of the past, effecting a temporal orientation in present practical life by means of the recollection of past actuality.³⁴

This is how the history discipline intersects with history didactics. The narrative forms in which history is written are those through which students learn to experience time. Ambitiously, historical consciousness is seen to give 'structure to historical knowledge as the medium for understanding present time and for anticipating the future. It is a complex combination that contains an apprehension of the past regulated by the need to understand the present and expect the future'.³⁵ Moreover, historical consciousness is a prerequisite for moral reasoning. The moral values that guided action in a given past situation must be related to that situation, but at the same time evaluated 'in terms of our code of applicable moral values'.³⁶ There is a mediation between the values held in present life and those contained in the action-oriented actuality of the past. It is in this way that Rüsen's model permits the grouping of empathy (past action in its context) and moral judgement (judgement of past action according to past and present values) that featured in Seixas' early work and the design of the Australian curriculum based on that example.

Rüsen identified four types of narrative forms, a progression through which postulates the development of historical consciousness. First, 'traditional' narratives furnish us with the origins of present systems of life and affirm their permanence over time and in our pregiven frameworks of self-understanding. Second, 'exemplary' narratives demonstrate general rules of conduct considered to be true for all times. Third, 'critical' narratives foreground deviations that contest the present forms of life and the patterns of continuity they presuppose. Fourth, 'genetic' narratives take continuity to be transformation; the continuation of life-forms depends upon their being constantly modified and renewed in an ongoing process of self-definition.³⁷ The four types are not mutually exclusive – elements of each are found in all historical writing – nevertheless, they are distinguishable from each other in the way that they orient life within time.

Research into history education in Germany has traditionally been conducted as a specialized field within the history discipline (*Geschichtsdidaktik*) rather than by educationalists, who usually limit their investigations to educational processes in a curricular context. Ankersmit has observed that the disciplinary character of German historical reflection derives from the fact that the foundations of German philosophy of history were laid not by philosophers, but by historians such as Gervinus, Ranke and Droysen.[38] This is not to deny that philosophers such as Vico and Herder supplied the German historical school with its theoretical foundation, but to note that the theoretical positions put forward by the historicists *qua* historians were practically guided.

Since the late 1970s, historical didactics has considered itself to be the study of historical consciousness within society, which is to say that it investigates historical thinking and learning wherever they may occur.[39] Rüsen sees historical consciousness as 'the general category that deals not only with the learning and teaching of history'; its analysis 'covers historical studies as well as the use and function of history in private and public life'.[40] He is not the only *Geschichtsdidaktiker* to have used the concept – Karl-Ernst Jeismann defined it in 1977 as 'a complex interaction of interpretations of the past, percpetions of the present and expectations towards the future' – but he has been the central figure in expounding the theory that researchers have used in recent years in curricular and assessment design.[41] Andreas Körber has made progress in the last decade in operationalizing historical consciousness as a set of four dimensions of 'historical competence'.[42] The first three dimensions – questioning, methodology and orientation – work back and forth between analytical or deconstructive and synthetic or constructive aspects. The fourth dimension, not reducible to a single term, encompasses all of what the British called second-order concepts, as well as first-order substantive concepts like 'nation', 'people' or 'culture'. That all this comprises just one of four dimensions demonstrates the model's expansive scope.

Seixas imported Rüsen's concept of historical consciousness and in so doing widened the theoretical boundaries within which English-speaking history education researchers currently operate.[43] When Herbert Gutman, the American labour historian, wrote of historical consciousness in contemporary America in the late 1980s, it was a lament about the fact that the insights of the new labour and social historians had not entered into most Americans' understanding of their past, with no discussion of the theories or concepts behind it.[44] Rüsen's name may have been familiar among readers of *History and Theory* and *History and Memory*, in which he had published half a dozen articles, but this readership has always existed at the periphery of a discipline whose legacy of rejecting theory remains part of its self-conception.

The catalyst came in 1995. Seixas was invited to participate in a symposium on the 'Structure, Logic and Function of Historical Consciousness' at Bielefeld University, where Rüsen was the director of a research group entitled *Historische Sinnbildung* (roughly 'Historical Meaning-Making'). In 1999, he attended two meetings of the research group Traditions of Historical Consciousness, the first in Hanover and the second in Potsdam, at which Wineburg, Lee and Rüsen's colleagues and students were present. These encounters were sufficiently propitious that Seixas convened a symposium at the CSHC in 2001 entitled 'Canadian Historical Consciousness in an International Context: Theoretical Perspectives', from which grew his 2004 volume, *Theorizing Historical Consciousness*. The symposium was in many ways intended as an opportunity for Rüsen to acquaint Canadian, British, American and Australian researchers with the uses of the term. Among the many productive debates, his confrontation with Lee was a particular highlight.

Lee's work in analytical philosophy of history had given him the second-order concepts that underpinned his empirical investigations into students' progression in historical understanding. The main reason why Seixas looked to Lee in developing his historical thinking concepts was that Lee's theoretical models were supported by empirical evidence of how students advance in their use and comprehension of disciplinary concepts. What this work left largely unexplored was students' sense-making of the past – what Lee in the English tradition associated with the gap between Oakeshott's historical and practical past. Therefore: 'Historical consciousness is a valuable concept because it offers the prospect of integrating the wide range of ways in which human beings position themselves in time and take account of their past.'[45]

But what Rüsen's concept failed to do, according to Lee, was distinguish between students' advancing through stages of historical consciousness and their mastering of the second-order, disciplinary concepts. Rüsen's typology for the development of historical consciousness, undergirded by the disciplinary matrix that organizes the relationship between *Lebenspraxis* and the history discipline into a five-part cognitive process, could not in Lee's view be used to illuminate the ways that students relate evidence to different kinds of claims, accounts or explanations. He found support in his research that students able to operate at Rüsen's highest 'genetic' level were not necessarily the students most able to reflect explicitly on the means by which they arrived at their conclusions. They did not necessarily offer the best evidentially supported accounts.[46]

In Vancouver, analytical philosophy of history clashed with historical hermeneutics. The first had been used to distil historical thinking into a group of concepts through which students' progression could be charted and evaluated; the other had served as the basis for an integrative model that emphasized the interdependency and indivisibility of all such concepts.

Understandably, certain confusions have entered into such a free-flowing and heterogeneous discourse. Of considerable interest to those who promote the educational value of historical consciousness ought to be the concept's own origins in hermeneutics. Seixas has chosen to define it as inclusively as possible, as offered by the journal *History and Memory*, as 'the area in which collective memory, the writing of history, and other modes of shaping images of the past in the public mind merge'.[47] While this definition might be consistent with how Rüsen views it operating in every domain of public and private life, a problem emerges when Gadamer is taken to be its spokesperson. In his 1957 lectures, Gadamer wrote that the appearance of historical consciousness is 'likely the most important revolution among those we have undergone since the beginning of the modern epoch', the achievement of which is 'the full awareness of the historicity of everything present and the relativity of all opinions'. Moreover:

> Modern consciousness – precisely as historical consciousness – takes a reflexive position concerning all that is handed down by tradition. Historical consciousness no longer listens sanctimoniously to the voice that reaches out from the past but, in reflection on it, replaces it within the context where it took root in order to see the significance and relative value proper to it.[48]

According to Seixas, who quotes these passages in introducing the concept, historical consciousness thus 'becomes a specific form of memory characterized by modernity and informed by the tools developed by professional historical scholarship'.[49] Aware of its own historicity, it reaches back to the past to know it in a way that it could not have been known by those who lived in it.

These are Gadamer's own words and a clear articulation of the concept's links with modernity's all-conquering scientific attitude. What they do not take into account when used to elucidate the concept for educational purposes is that it was this conception of historical consciousness that Gadamer made it his life's project to dismantle. He offered an account of the historical consciousness of his predecessors only to illustrate its naïveté and to replace it with his concept of historically effected consciousness. Historicism's empathy-dependent hermeneutics worked from the assumption that its critical methods afforded historians the ability to grasp the past in its individuality, which according to Gadamer meant they were not genuinely open to the past; specifically, they were not open to the *question put by the past itself*. In response to Dilthey's methodological hermeneutics of historical consciousness, Gadamer's ontological hermeneutics of historically effected consciousness made no attempt to obtain a unilateral control of the past context in which everything filling tradition took root.

The aim of historically effected consciousness is not to discover the merely context-dependent value of everything handed down from the past;

it is to allow oneself to be conducted by its specific subject matter. By what questions were the texts we study driven is the historical question that yields the productive ground for formulating the questions we take to the past. Gadamer mounted a radical critique of historicism and its belief in superior insight, but he did not throw the baby out with the bathwater. In his logic of openness is retained the indispensable principle that, if history is to remain the study of the past, the past puts questions to us that must be understood as having arisen from a historical context different from our own – from a different constellation of presuppositions, as Collingwood would put it.

The thought by which history education researchers have been animated in Rüsen's work owes a greater debt to Droysen than to Gadamer's post-methodological hermeneutics. Like other social democrats deeply marked by the German catastrophe, Rüsen sought to restore the critical dimension of the Enlightenment paradigm that was muted by historicism's predilection for empathy and understanding. Just as historicism robbed Droysen of a moral standpoint from which to write history, Rüsen the scholar of Droysen could not accept a Heideggerian and Gadamerian hermeneutic circle that dissolved the division between discipline and life-world, between *Fachwissenschaft* and *Lebenspraxis*. Historiography does arise from the life-world's need to orient itself and affirm its identity (national or otherwise), but the fruits of historical research do not loop back into the life-world *in toto*. They produce a 'theoretical surplus' beyond the needs of acting subjects. This surplus is the distinctive rational achievement of historical research, having a universal aspect that transcends the particularity of individual experience in the life-world. Because it has this universal element, historical consciousness can bind past, present and future in ways that context-specific and individualizing historicism cannot.[50]

In so restoring the Enlightenment commitment to universals, Rüsen articulated a version of the idea that there exists a 'grand narrative', 'single' or 'universal' history.[51] His 'historical anthropology' may therefore be more aptly termed '*trans*historical anthropology', for it supposes that universal concepts – progress, decline, individuality, process, structure and so on – are applicable to every historical period. A chief task of his historical science and historical didactics has been to thematize the whole of history through the lens of such universal concepts.[52] Yet in spite of this return to the Enlightenment paradigm, Rüsen remains caught on the horns of the historicist dilemma. To narrate the historical whole requires historians to abstract from individual experience a basic identity, but in positing an identity whose fundamental modifications are now known, they will have articulated a substratum insulated from the vicissitudes of historical time, and so deprived historiography of the possibility of generating new, true and important knowledge.

As with the narrativist challenge to empathy evaluated earlier, a weakness in Rüsen's model is that it does it not specify what supplies a historical narrative with its content. A concern for the past arises from the practical needs of life, and this entry point into the disciplinary matrix then leads to an engagement with the functions, methods and norms of the history discipline. The narrative structure of historical explanation describes the process whereby historiography produces meaning by orienting humanity in time and in relation to universal concepts operative in every epoch, but it does not throw light on the nature of the historical object in which is located the past meaning historians attempt to reconstruct. Put in familiar terms, by eliding the issue of how historians turn sources into evidence through a specifically historical questioning activity, it does not identify the ingredients from the past that fill historical narratives. The enduring significance of historicism consists in its doctrine that the meaning of an object resides in its past. Of course, historians decide for themselves whether the movements they study are a 'decline' in political morality or a 'bourgeois' revolution. Namier did not refuse to colligate eighteenth-century English politics as a series of 'party rivalries' because the agents concerned applied no concept of 'party' to themselves; it was that their activities failed to conform to our conception of what a political party is.[53]

But our ability to make these kinds of colligatory decisions implies that we know the meaning of the activities in the past context. Although it is our conception of what constitutes a political party that ultimately determines whether we find it appropriate to refer to the activities of eighteenth-century English politicians as party rivalries, to arrive at this decision assumes that we have sufficient knowledge of the precise character of the activities in the first place. The past meaning that we attempt to reconstruct can be represented only by means of the linguistic and conceptual resources available to us in the present, but it is a representation composed of content attached to the construction of that meaning in the past.

That history came into being by defining itself as an inquiry into past worlds of meaning is the whole reason historians needed a gift for empathy, and why Collingwood believed where there is no thought, there is no history.

Notes

1. Peter Lee and Denis Shemilt, 'The Concept that Dares Not Speak its Name: Should Empathy Come out of the Closet?' *Teaching History* 143 (2011), 39–49.
2. Peter Lee, 'History Teaching and Philosophy of History', *History and Theory* 22, 4 (1983), 25, 36.
3. Peter Lee, 'Historical Knowledge and the National Curriculum', in Richard Aldrich (ed.), *History in the National Curriculum* (London: Kogan Page, 1991), 53.

4. Peter Lee, Alaric Dickinson and Rosalyn Ashby, 'Researching Children's Ideas about History', in James F. Voss and Mario Carretero (eds), *International Review of History Education, Volume 2: Learning and Reasoning in History* (London: Woburn Press, 1998), 227–51; Peter Lee and Rosalyn Ashby, 'Progression in Historical Understanding among Students Ages 7–14', in Peter N. Stearns, Peter Seixas and Sam Wineburg (eds), *Knowing, Teaching, and Learning History: National and International Perspectives* (New York: New York University Press, 2000), 199–222.

5. Lee, 'History Teaching and Philosophy of History', 20, 31–32.

6. Ibid., 25; See also Lee and Ashby, 'Progression in Historical Understanding', 199.

7. See, for example, the introduction to Manuel Köster, Holger Thünemann and Meik Zülsdorf-Kersting (eds), *Researching History Education: International Perspectives and Disciplinary Traditions* (Schwalbach am Taunus: Wochenschau Verlag, 2014), 6.

8. Penney Clark, 'History Education Research in Canada: A Late Bloomer', in Köster, Thünemann and Zülsdorf-Kersting (eds), *Researching History Education,* 85.

9. Peter Seixas (ed.), introduction to Part II, 'History Education and Historical Consciousness', *Theorizing Historical Consciousness* (Toronto: University of Toronto Press, 2004), 104–5; Peter Seixas, 'A Model of Historical Thinking', *Educational Philosophy and Theory* 49, 6 (2017), 597.

10. Peter Seixas, 'Parallel Crises: History and the Social Studies Curriculum in the USA', *Journal of Curriculum Studies* 25, 3 (1993), 235–50.

11. Peter Seixas, 'Conceptualizing the Growth of Historical Understanding', in David R. Olson and Nancy Torrance (eds), *The Handbook of Education and Human Development* (Oxford: Blackwell, 1996), 765.

12. Ibid., 768–77.

13. Ibid., 776.

14. Carla Peck and Peter Seixas, 'Benchmarks of Historical Thinking: First Steps', *Canadian Journal of Education* 31, 4 (2008), 1017–18.

15. Peter Seixas, 'Benchmarks of Historical Thinking: A Framework for Assessment in Canada', Centre for the Study of Historical Consciousness, University of British Columbia, 18 August 2006, 10.

16. Ibid., 11.

17. Samuel S. Wineburg, 'On the Reading of Historical Texts: Notes on the Breach between School and Academy', *American Educational Research Journal* 28, 3 (1991), 500; quoted in Peter Seixas, 'Student Teachers Thinking Historically', *Theory and Research in Social Education* 26, 3 (1998), 312–13.

18. Peter Seixas and Tom Morton, *The Big Six Historical Thinking Concepts* (Toronto: Nelson Education, 2013), 145.

19. Ibid., 43.

20. Ibid., 138.

21. Ibid., 140–41.

22. Peter Seixas, 'Translation and its Discontents: Key Concepts in English and German History Education', *Journal of Curriculum Studies* 48, 4 (2016), 427–39, has discussed where he sees lie the challenges as well as the possibilities for future research collaboration between the two traditions. Andreas Körber, 'Translation and its Discontents II: A German Perspective', *Journal of Curriculum Studies* 48, 4 (2016), 440–56, responded with a cautious assessment of the complexity of transposing theories and terminologies from one to the other.

23. National Curriculum Board (NCB), *The Shape of the Australian Curriculum* (Canberra: ACARA, 2009).

24. NCB, *Shape of the Australian Curriculum: History* (Canberra: ACARA, 2009), 5.

25. Stuart Macintyre, 'The Challenge for History in the National Curriculum', Keynote Address, Australian Curriculum Studies Association Conference, Canberra, 2 October 2009.

26. NCB, *Shape of the Australian Curriculum: History*, 6. Unlike those who regarded empathy as the central structural concept in history along the lines spelled out by Collingwood in his doctrine of re-enactment, Tony Taylor, 'Trying to Connect: Moving from Bad History to Historical Literacy in Schools', *Australian Cultural History* 23 (2003), 184, with whom Macintyre worked in preparing the shaping paper, took empathy to be 'less about logic and structure [i.e. causation and motivation] and more about feelings'. This helps explain why, in the Australian case, empathy was separated from the cognitive act of understanding the past context and placed instead in the moral domain of historical consciousness, even if in certain places it is described in the more traditional way. See Tony Taylor and Carmel Young, *Making History: A Guide for the Teaching and Learning of History in Australian Schools* (Melbourne: Curriculum Corporation, 2003), 4, 55–57.

27. F.R. Ankersmit, 'Review Essay *Rekonstruktion der Vergangenheit: Grundzüge einer Historik II*', *History and Theory* 27, 1 (1988), 84.

28. Allan Megill, 'Jörn Rüsen's Theory of Historiography between Modernism and Rhetoric of Inquiry', *History and Theory* 33, 1(1994), 39–40.

29. Ibid., 52–53; Robert Anchor, 'Review Essay *Lebendige Geschichte: Grundzüge einer Historik III*', *History and Theory* 30, 3(1991), 347–49.

30. Megill, 'Rüsen's Theory of Historiography', 40, 46, points out that American social scientists used Kuhn to underwrite the authority of their disciplinary communities by focusing on the structural component of the paradigm notion, whereas in Germany the postwar need to move from one paradigm to a new one led social scientists to emphasize the processes behind paradigm change. This explains in part why Rüsen extended the history discipline paradigm beyond its authorized orientations and procedures to encompass its external relations with the social community in general.

31. Ankersmit, 'Review Essay', 91–92.

32. Megill, 'Rüsen's Theory of Historiography', 40–2.

33. Anchor, 'Review Essay', 352.

34. Jörn Rüsen, 'The Development of Narrative Competence in Historical Learning: An Ontogenetic Hypothesis Concerning Moral Consciousness', *History and Memory* 1, 2 (1989), 41; slightly modified versions in Jörn Rüsen, *Studies in Metahistory* (Pretoria: Human Sciences Research Council, 1993), 63–84; Jörn Rüsen, *History: Narration – Interpretation – Orientation* (New York: Berghahn Books, 2005), 21–39; and Seixas (ed.), *Theorizing Historical Consciousness*, 63–85.

35. Jörn Rüsen, 'The Didactics of History in West Germany: Towards a New Self-Awareness of Historical Studies', *History and Theory* 26, 3(1987), 284.

36. Rüsen, 'Development of Narrative Competence', 38.

37. Ibid., 44–50.

38. Ankersmit, 'Review Essay', 85.

39. Sebastian Bracke et al., 'History Education Research in Germany: Empirical Attempts at Mapping Historical Thinking and Learning', in Köster, Thünemann and Zülsdorf-Kersting (eds), *Researching History Education*, 9.

40. Rüsen, 'Didactics of History', 284.

41. Jeismann paraphrased in Bracke et al., 'History Education Research in Germany', 23.

42. Andreas Körber, 'German History Didactics', in Helle Bjerg, Claudia Lenz and Erik Thorstensen (eds), *Historicizing the Uses of the Past: Scandinavian Perspectives on History, Culture, Historical Consciousness and Didactics of History Related to World War II* (New Brunswick: Transcript, 2011), 145–64.

43. Seixas, 'Translation and its Discontents', 428.

44. Herbert Gutman, 'Historical Consciousness in Contemporary America', in Ira Berlin (ed.), *Power and Culture: Essays on the American Working Class by Herbert G. Gutman* (New York: Pantheon Books, 1987), 395–412.

45. Peter Lee, 'Understanding History', in Seixas (ed.), *Theorizing Historical Consciousness*, 142.
46. Ibid., 140–43.
47. Peters Seixas, introduction to *Theorizing Historical Consciousness*, 10.
48. Gadamer, 'Problem of Historical Consciousness', 89, quoted in Seixas, introduction to *Theorizing Historical Consciousness*, 9; Peter Seixas, 'Collective Memory, History Education, and Historical Consciousness', *Historically Speaking* 7, 2 (2005), 17.
49. Seixas, 'Collective Memory', 17.
50. Megill, 'Rüsen's Theory of Historiography', 51–2.
51. Rüsen has confronted the issue of the alleged Eurocentrism of this universalist programme in his edited volume, *Western Historical Thinking: An Intercultural Debate* (New York: Berghahn Books, 2002).
52. Ankersmit, 'Review Essay', 91; Megill, 'Rüsen's Theory of Historiography', 53–54.
53. W.H. Dray, *On History and Philosophers of History* (Leiden: E.J. Brill, 1989), 52.

Conclusion

The rise of psychology, as well as the shift from metaphysics to epistemology in philosophical reflection upon history, created a space for empathy to offer itself to historical method. This discovery that empathy derived from epistemological concerns about history's status as a form of knowledge has been found to be methodologically inadequate. Collingwood's logic of question and answer, together with his attempt to reform metaphysics as the historical science of absolute presuppositions, were offered as specifying the historical context that empathetic inquiry ought to investigate. Gadamer's incorporation of this aspect of Collingwood's thought complemented and supplemented Collingwood's diffuse hermeneutical reflections. It is right to conceive of Collingwood's theories hermeneutically, but not in the nineteenth-century, epistemologically preoccupied and empathy-dependent tradition. Collingwood and Gadamer were at one in their mistrust of this tradition, which underpinned the rise of historicism and history as a professional academic discipline in nineteenth-century Germany, and responded to it by means of a Hegelian philosophy in opposition to which historicism initially developed.

It is striking that empathy came forward in history education, the history discipline and the philosophy of history in essentially epistemological traditions. In the 1950s and 1960s, the leading theorists in educational psychology and philosophy combined in their call for educationalists to establish a conceptual basis for each of the school subjects – to specify the characteristics that lent them their status as distinct forms of knowledge, thinking and experience. Bruner and Hirst's appeal for educationalists to identify the basic structure of the school subjects cast history's prospects in a more propitious light than had shone under the predominantly Piagetian research framework, which, instead of distilling history into a set of concepts by means of which students could articulate their competence in the subject, emphasized what students were unable to achieve in the subject. Second-order, disciplinary, procedural or historical thinking concepts offered teachers and students the means for conceptual articulation in the subject. Through them, learning could be objectified and thus publicly registered and tested. History's epistemology was reified into a pedagogy. A distinctly historical way of thinking about the past became available to those who approached the subject through the forms of knowledge considered to be the foundation of history's epistemological structure.

In undertaking this project of disciplinary distillation, history educationalists were well served by the rise of analytical philosophy of history. Hempel's thesis was almost universally rejected, but the style of philosophy was not. To meet the challenge of the positivistic sciences, philosophers of history expunged older varieties of humanism and metaphysics in an attempt to fortify history with a structure robust enough to repel such attacks. Colligation, rational explanation, re-enactment and empathy were terms with longer histories that, in the new paradigm, needed to be filled with analytical content. Empathy found its way into the school history classroom on the tail of this movement, when the element seen to bind this structure consisted in giving individual content to the general categories through which the past is viewed. A traditionally dull school subject was revitalized by a structure of historical inquiry that placed at its centre reconstructing, reliving or re-enacting the thoughts and experiences of those who lived in the past.

The irony of this attention to the *sui generis* character of historical investigation was that it occurred at a time when the theories and methods of academic historians were becoming increasingly varied and open to outside influences. While philosophers of history and history educationalists narrowed in on what made history particularly historical, those who wrote history were widening their field of vision with insights from geography, sociology, and cultural and literary theory. Young historians of the 1950s and 1960s may have discussed the theories of Hempel, Dray and Collingwood in their theory and method seminars, but they were animated more by the possibilities of an enlarged theoretical and methodological repertory than by questions regarding history's status as a form of knowledge. Chosen by those who study it, history in the university could assume its disciplinary status and procedures of investigation; history in the school, taught to a larger cohort of students with no prior inclination for or familiarity with the subject, was more self-conscious of the factors that granted the subject its distinct identity.

There was, however, no such self-assurance in the tradition of historical thought from which empathy emerged as the historical method for penetrating the past. A need to shore up the legitimacy of historical knowledge stimulated an ambition among theorists to claim for history the title of the science of individual understanding. Historicism had its origins in an eighteenth-century revolt against enlightened mathematism, atomistic thinking, generalization and its claim to provide universal knowledge, but it came to typify an approach to investigating the past only when all *a priori* metaphysical assumptions about the meaning of history had been extirpated and a psychologistic epistemology promised the historian access to a past in its own terms. In a century that conceived the methods of the natural sciences as exemplary, second-order reflection upon history – its methods, standards and procedures of investigation – held higher priority than first-order, metaphysical speculation about the laws, ends, patterns or meaning of history itself. Historicism and neo-Kantianism were epistemological movements. *Einfühlung, Verstehen* and *Transposition* grew in the esteem of the practitioners and theorists of a new discipline that, against philosophy and later science's claim to universal truths, proposed a way of yielding concrete insights into the dynamic and contingent nature of human experience, institutions and practices.

Midway through the twentieth century, with post-Hempelian philosophy of history firmly entrenched, Collingwood was interpreted along epistemological lines to be offering in re-enactment an elucidation of the processes by which historians can claim to have knowledge of the past. There was some justification for doing so. Studied before the discovery of his 1928 manuscript, and in isolation from his life's project to bring about a *rapprochement* between history and philosophy, re-enactment did appear to be concerned more with the how of knowing historically than the what. With his writings on metaphysics left largely aside, it was easily assumed that re-enactment belonged to an outdated and empathy-dependent hermeneutics of reproducing past mental events.

By bringing to the centre of attention the twin theories of question-and-answer and absolute presuppositions, the focus has shifted from epistemology to metaphysics. Re-enactment could so easily be termed empathy because it seemed to be proposing a form of individual-to-individual union or reciprocation of thought. Supplemented by the two theories Collingwood formulated as the basis for his reform of metaphysics, the case for re-enactment following these contours loses its cogency. Although we have seen that the three theories do not fit tightly together – they do not, it must be stressed, constitute a coherent or self-sufficient philosophical outlook – the importance Collingwood placed on investigating the ever-shifting groundforms of knowledge or foundations of discourse makes plain that he conceived the historical process in far broader terms than the gaining of access to past mental contents. The traditional Aristotelian conception of metaphysics as the study of being *qua* being proposed no determinate object for the metaphysician to illuminate. Metaphysics needed to become the historical science of delineating the historically changing categories of human thought and experience upon which 'being' is based. With metaphysics brought to the fore, historians investigate a past context that gave rise to the thoughts, actions and events that yield them their subject matter. By arguing that this should form the basis of empathetic inquiry in history, I have suggested that history students ought to do the same.

It is less easy to speak of metaphysics in the context of Gadamer's thought. Like most post-Heideggerian philosophers, Gadamer preferred the term 'ontology' – precisely the variety of metaphysics Collingwood repudiated. He developed his ontological or philosophical hermeneutics in direct response to the inadequacies of the nineteenth century's psychologistic conception of the human sciences, a tradition confident in its belief that through empathetic transposition, it could know the past in ways superior to those who inhabited it. The task in the new century consisted not in gaining such ascendancy over the past, but in integrating or coming to terms with a past from which we have a great deal to learn. Gadamer's ontological hermeneutics was a metaphysics of belonging to tradition, language and being, mindful of the limits of a metaphysics of subjectivity buttressed by the historicist, Romantic hermeneutical and scientistic project of dominating other beings. Whereas Collingwood's commitment to scientific knowledge saw him illuminate an object that metaphysics could make the centrepiece of its research, Gadamer sought to correct the nineteenth-century misconception that an event of human understanding could stand outside the tradition in which it takes place. In pursuing their respective aims, both men responded to a psychologistic epistemology through a metaphysics of interconnectedness between past and present. The fact that Hegel was being rehabilitated just as they were beginning their careers was a major factor in their taking this approach.

Nevertheless, Gadamer's ontological metaphysics of belonging painted a more opaque picture of the object of understanding than Collingwood's historical metaphysics provided in the theory of absolute presuppositions. Gadamer preferred not to speak of an 'object' of understanding, so eager was he to steer hermeneutics clear of its old concerns with the methods of recovery and towards a conception of humanistic understanding that accounted for the pregiven in every act. By describing the manner in which Collingwood's logic of question and answer influenced Gadamer in the development of his hermeneutics, I have suggested that there remained for Gadamer a need to return to the original context in which the texts we study were produced. This took a very different form to Collingwood's intentionalism. Insofar as Gadamer placed the meaning of texts in the texts themselves and not in what their authors were intending in producing them, he stood in a tradition far outside the historicists' ideal of understanding texts in their own terms. His radical critique of historicism took this as its focal point.

Yet his hermeneutics of trust retained the sense that it is to the past that we must look if we wish to gain new insight into the range of questions with which the human sciences deal. Put more strongly, it is by a distinct past object that we must allow ourselves to be conducted if we are to learn anything from the past. Gadamer took from Collingwood the logic of question and answer to support his view that interpreters must remain open to the foreignness of what the past has to tell us. A fusion of horizons could only occur if there were separate horizons between past and present to integrate. A historical text may be overlain with meanings that different interpretive traditions have applied to it, ones bearing little resemblance to what the text meant at the time of its production. But without allowing ourselves to be conducted by a subject matter belonging to a past context different from the present context in which we attempt to understand it, there was small chance we would identify anything capable of standing up against our present-day situation and asserting itself as an object in need of comprehension. Empathetic unification dissolved the lines of demarcation that made this integration an activity to be undertaken; a dialectic of question and answer foregrounded a past context to be treated in its own right as something to learn from.

★ ★ ★

What, then, remains to be done with the concept of empathy as it is used by history teachers, teacher educators, and curriculum writers and theorists? The history educationalists who launched the concept were aware that it could lead to confusion, but trusted nevertheless that it could be given a meaning, one that earned its inclusion in the method of teaching school history when its place in the method of the history discipline was affirmed. Drawn from the philosophy of history and developed in an educational setting, it was unlikely that empathy would convey the range of meanings and purposes that Collingwood had ascribed to re-enactment. Any concept, not only empathy, is going to deviate from its intellectual, historical and philosophical lineages as it is repurposed as an applied, educational concept. The longer empathy occupied a place in school history, the less those researching it felt obliged to align it with the doctrine of re-enactment from which it originated. With its origins in an interwar philosophy of history mostly forgotten, psychology has offered itself as the more appropriate framework for investigating its function in historical teaching and learning.

Against this trend of psychological research, I have returned to the source of empathy's origins in the history discipline, the philosophy of history and school history. But whatever light I have thrown on the concept's development, transformation and deployment within these fields, a basic problem still faces the history educator who continues to use empathy to label the investigation of historical context. History educationalists may have been confident that they could give empathy a specifically historical meaning, but for those in the field teaching the subject to know precisely what that meaning is, and how to use this knowledge in the classroom, requires a level of training and professional development not even the most enthusiastic educational reformist would think is possible. This is less a commentary on the effectiveness of teacher training and development, and more a recognition of the currency everyday conceptions of empathy carry among teachers and the community at large. Rather than being the name for a way of knowing rooted in the very self-conception of the history discipline, empathy is most commonly associated with feeling for people who lived in the past. We have seen how alternatives such as perspective taking have been used to give the activity denoted by empathy a more transparently cognitive dimension, in the face of an everyday conception of empathy as feeling.

Looking back on these efforts, it is striking to note that the investigation of historical context that empathy was taken to label has not been called precisely that – investigating historical context. I have suggested that empathetic inquiry in history should direct itself towards a specific kind of context – the context in which it was possible for past agents to hold their beliefs as true and to act upon them accordingly. Perhaps this use of 'empathetic inquiry' is still deceptive, and it will need to be stated that historical understanding involves attending to a certain kind of historical context. If this sounds overly intellectual or detached, the person who sets about this study of past forms of life will soon discover that it generates a full range of emotions, feelings and curiosities that themselves fuel further inquiry.

Bibliography

Aldrich, Richard. *The Institute of Education 1902–2002: A Centenary History*. London: Institute of Education University of London, 2002.
——. 'The Training of Teachers and Educational Studies: The London Day Training College, 1902–1932'. *Paedagogica Historica* 45, 5/6 (2004), 617–31.
Anchor, Robert. 'Review Essay *Lebendige Geschichte: Grundzüge einer Historik III*'. *History and Theory* 30, 3 (1991), 347–56.
Ankersmit, Frank. 'Review Essay *Rekonstruktion der Vergangenheit: Grundzüge einer Historik II*'. *History and Theory* 27, 1 (1988), 81–94.
——. 'The Necessity of Historicism'. *Journal of the Philosophy of History* 4, 2 (2010), 226–40.
Appleby, Joyce. 'One Good Turn Deserves Another: Moving beyond the Linguistic; A Response to David Harlan'. *American Historical Review* 94, 5 (1989), 1326–32.
Armitage, David. 'Horizons of History: Space, Time, and the Future of the Past'. *History Australia* 12, 1 (2015), 207–25.
Ashby, Rosalyn, and Peter Lee. 'Children's Concepts of Empathy and Understanding in History', in Christopher Portal (ed.), *The History Curriculum for Teachers* (London: Falmer Press, 1987), 62–88.
Bambach, Charles R. *Heidegger, Dilthey, and the Crisis of Historicism*. Ithaca: Cornell University Press, 1995.
Bann, Stephen. *Romanticism and the Rise of History*. New York: Twayne Publishers, 1995.
Barton, Keith C., and Linda S. Levstik. *Teaching History for the Common Good*. Mahwah: Lawrence Erlbaum, 2004.
Beiser, Frederick. 'Historicism', in Brian Leiter and Michael Rosen (eds), *The Oxford Handbook of Continental Philosophy* (Oxford: Oxford University Press, 2007), 155–79.
——. *The German Historicist Tradition*. Oxford: Oxford University Press, 2011.
Berger, Stefan. 'The Invention of European National Traditions in European Romanticism', in Stuart Macintyre, Juan Maiguashca and Attila Pók (eds), *The Oxford History of Historical Writing, Volume 4: 1800–1945* (Oxford: Oxford University Press, 2011), 19–40.
Berlin, Isaiah. 'History and Theory: The Concept of Scientific History'. *History and Theory* 1, 1 (1960), 1–31.
——. 'A Note on Vico's Concept of Knowledge', in Giorgio Tagliacozzo, Hayden V. White, Isaiah Berlin, Max H. Fisch and Elio Gianturco (eds), *Giambattista Vico: An International Symposium* (Baltimore: Johns Hopkins University Press, 1969), 371–77.
——. *Vico and Herder: Two Studies in the History of Ideas*. London: Hogarth Press, 1976.

Bevir, Mark. *The Logic of the History of Ideas*. Cambridge: Cambridge University Press, 1999.
———. 'How to Be an Intentionalist'. *History and Theory* 41, 2 (2002), 209–17.
———. 'Introduction: Historical Understanding and the Human Sciences'. *Journal of the Philosophy of History* 1, 3 (2007), 259–70.
———. 'In Defence of Historicism'. *Journal of the Philosophy of History* 6, 1 (2012), 111–14.
Bevir, Mark, and Karsten Stueber. 'Empathy, Rationality, and Explanation'. *Journal of the Philosophy of History* 5, 2 (2011), 147–62.
Blackburn, Simon. 'Against False Divisions'. *Times Literary Supplement,* 6 April 1990, 370.
———. *Mirror, Mirror: The Uses and Abuses of Self-Love*. Princeton: Princeton University Press, 2014.
Blake, Christopher. 'Historical Empathy: A Response to Foster and Yeager'. *International Journal of Social Education* 13, 1 (1998), 25–31.
Bloch, Marc. *The Historian's Craft*, trans. Peter Putnam. New York: Alfred A. Knopf, 1953.
Bloom, Benjamin S. (ed.). *Taxonomy of Educational Objectives: The Classification of Educational Goals,* vols 1–2. London: Longmans, 1956–64.
Bloom, Paul. *Against Empathy: The Case for Rational Compassion*. New York: HarperCollins, 2016.
Boddington, Tony. 'Empathy and the Teaching of History'. *British Journal of Educational Studies* 28, 1 (1980), 13–19.
Booth, Martin B. *History Betrayed?* London: Longmans, 1969.
———. 'Skills, Concepts, and Attitudes: The Development of Adolescent Children's Historical Thinking'. *History and Theory* 22, 4 (1983), 101–17.
Booth, Martin B., Christopher Culpin and Henry Macintosh. *Teaching GCSE History*. London: Hodder & Stoughton, 1987.
Boucher, David. *Texts in Context: Revisionist Methods for Studying the History of Ideas*. Dordrecht: Martinus Nijhoff, 1985.
———. *The Social and Political Thought of R.G. Collingwood*. Cambridge: Cambridge University Press, 1989.
———. 'The Life, Times and Legacy of R.G. Collingwood', in David Boucher, James Connelly and Tariq Modood (eds), *Philosophy, History and Civilisation: Interdisciplinary Perspectives on R.G. Collingwood* (Cardiff: University of Wales Press, 1995), 1–31.
Bracke, Sebastian, Colin Flaving, Manuel Köster and Meik Zülsdorf-Kersting. 'History Education Research in Germany: Empirical Attempts at Mapping Historical Thinking and Learning', in Manuel Köster, Holger Thünemann and Meik Zülsdorf-Kersting (eds), *Researching History Education: International Perspectives and Disciplinary Traditions* (Schwalbach am Taunus: Wochenschau Verlag, 2014), 9–55.
Brecht, Arnold. *Political Theory: The Foundations of Twentieth-Century Political Thought*. Princeton: Princeton University Press, 1959.
Breithaupt, Fritz. 'Empathy for Empathy's Sake: Aesthetics and Everyday Empathic Sadism', in Aleida Assmann and Ines Detmers (eds), *Empathy and its Limits* (New York: Palgrave Macmillan, 2015), 151–65.
Brooks, Sarah. 'Historical Empathy in the Social Studies Classroom: A Review of the Literature'. *Journal of Social Studies Research* 33, 2 (2009), 213–34.
Browning, Christopher R. *Ordinary Men: Reserve Police Battalion 101 and the Final Solution in Poland*. New York: Aaron Usher Books, 1992.
Bruner, Jerome S. *The Process of Education*. Cambridge, MA: Harvard University Press, 1960.
Burston, W.H. 'Explanation in History and the Teaching of History'. *British Journal of Educational Studies* 2, 2 (1954), 112–21.
———. 'The Place of History in Education', in W.H. Burston and C.W. Green (eds), *Handbook for History Teachers* (London: Methuen, 1962), 1–14.
———. *Principles of History Teaching*. London: Methuen, 1963.

Callaghan, James. *Time and Chance*. London: Collins, 1987.
Cannadine, David, Jenny Keating and Nicola Sheldon. *The Right Kind of History: Teaching the Past in Twentieth-Century England*. Basingstoke: Palgrave Macmillan, 2011.
Carr, Edward Hallett. *What is History?* London: Macmillan, 1961.
Clark, Penney. 'History Education Research in Canada: A Late Bloomer', in Manuel Köster, Holger Thünemann and Meik Zülsdorf-Kersting (eds), *Researching History Education: International Perspectives and Disciplinary Traditions* (Schwalbach am Taunus: Wochenschau Verlag, 2014), 81–103.
Code, Lorraine. 'Introduction: Why Feminists Do Not Read Gadamer', in Lorraine Code (ed.), *Feminist Interpretations of Hans-Georg Gadamer* (University Park: Pennsylvania State University Press, 2003), 1–36.
Collingwood, R.G. *Speculum Mentis, or the Map of Knowledge*. Oxford: Clarendon Press, 1924.
——. *An Essay on Philosophical Method*. Oxford: Clarendon Press, 1933.
——. 'Philosophy and History: Essays Presented to Ernst Cassirer by Raymond Klibansky; H.J. Paton'. *English Historical Review* 52, 205 (1937), 141–46.
——. *The Principles of Art*. Oxford: Clarendon Press, 1938.
——. *Ruskin's Philosophy: An Address Delivered at the Ruskin Centenary Conference, Coniston, August 8th, 1919*. Chichester: Quentin Nelson, 1971 [1922].
——. *An Autobiography*. Oxford: Clarendon Press, 1978 [1939].
——. *The New Leviathan, or Man, Society, Civilisation and Barbarism*, rev. edn David Boucher. Oxford: Clarendon Press, 1992 [1942].
——. *The Idea of History*, rev. edn Jan van der Dussen. Oxford: Oxford University Press, 1994 [1946].
——. *An Essay on Metaphysics*, rev. edn Rex Martin. Oxford: Clarendon Press, 1998 [1940].
——. *The Principles of History: and Other Writings in Philosophy of History*, W.H. Dray and W.J. van der Dussen (eds). New York: Oxford University Press, 1999.
Coltham, Jeanette, and John Fines. *Educational Objectives for the Study of History: A Suggested Framework*, pamphlet 35. London: Historical Association, 1971.
Colwill, Ian, and Maureen Burns. *Coursework in GCSE History: Planning and Assessment*. London: Hodder & Stoughton, 1989.
Connelly, James. 'Art Thou the Man: Croce, Gentile or de Ruggiero?', in David Boucher, James Connelly and Tariq Modood (eds), *Philosophy, History and Civilisation: Interdisciplinary Perspectives on R.G. Collingwood* (Cardiff: University of Wales Press, 1995), 92–114.
——. *Metaphysics, Method and Politics: The Political Philosophy of R.G. Collingwood*. Exeter: Imprint Academic, 2003.
Cooper, Bridget. *Empathy in Education: Engagement, Values and Achievement*. London: Continuum, 2011.
Coplan, Amy, and Peter Goldie (eds). *Empathy: Philosophical and Psychological Perspectives*. Oxford: Oxford University Press, 2011.
Croce, Benedetto. *The Philosophy of Giambattista Vico*, trans. R.G. Collingwood. London: Howard Latimer, 1913.
Cunningham, Deborah L. 'Understanding Pedagogical Reasoning in History Teaching through the Case of Cultivating Historical Empathy'. *Theory and Research in Social Education* 35, 4 (2007), 592–630.
D'Amico, Robert. 'Historicism', in Aviezer Tucker (ed.), *A Companion to the Philosophy of History and Historiography* (Chichester: Wiley-Blackwell, 2009), 243–52.
Denham, Andrew, and Mark Garnett. *Keith Joseph*. Chesham: Acumen, 2002.
Department of Education and Science. *Teaching History*. London: HMSO, 1952.
——. *Curriculum 11–16. Working Papers by HM Inspectorate: A Contribution to Current Debate*. London: HMSO, 1977.
——. *GCSE: The National Criteria: History*. London: HMSO, 1985.

———. *History in the Primary and Secondary Years: An HMI View*. London: HMSO, 1985.
———. *History from 5 to 16*. London: HMSO, 1988.
———. *National Curriculum History Working Group: Final Report*. London: HMSO, 1990.
Dexter, Colin. *The Jewel That was Ours*. London: Macmillan, 1991.
Dickinson, Alaric. 'What Should History Be?', in Ashley Kent (ed.), *School Subject Teaching: The History and Future of the Curriculum* (London: Kogan Page, 2000), 86–110.
Dilthey, Wilhelm. *Selected Works*, Rudolf A. Makkreel and Frithjof Rodi (eds). Princeton: Princeton University Press. The following volumes were used in this book: Volume I, *Introduction to the Human Sciences*, 1989; Volume III, *The Formation of the Historical World in the Human Sciences*, 2002; Volume IV, *Hermeneutics and the Study of History*, 1996.
Dobb, Maurice. 'Historical Materialism and the Role of the Economic Factor'. *History* 36, 126–27 (1951), 1–11.
Donaldson, Margaret. *Children's Minds*. London: Fontana, 1978.
Dray, William H. *Laws and Explanation in History*. Oxford: Oxford University Press, 1957.
———. 'The Historical Explanation of Actions Reconsidered', in Sidney Hook (ed.), *Philosophy and History: A Symposium* (New York: New York University Press, 1963), 105–35.
———. *On History and Philosophers of History*. Leiden: E.J. Brill, 1989.
———. *History as Re-enactment: R.G. Collingwood's Idea of History*. Oxford: Clarendon Press, 1995.
Dray, William H., and W.J. van der Dussen. Editors' introduction to R.G. Collingwood, *The Principles of History: and Other Writings in Philosophy of History*. New York: Oxford University Press, 1999.
Droysen, Johann Gustav. *Outline of the Principles of History*, trans. E. Benjamin Andrews. Boston: Ginn and Company, 1893.
Dussen, W.J. van der. *History as a Science: The Philosophy of R.G. Collingwood*. The Hague: Martinus Nijhoff, 1981.
Eisenberg, Nancy, and Janet Strayer (eds). *Empathy and its Development*. Cambridge: Cambridge University Press, 1987.
Eley, Geoff. *A Crooked Line: From Cultural History to the History of Society*. Ann Arbor: University of Michigan Press, 2005.
Elton, G.R. *The Practice of History*. Sydney: Sydney University Press, 1967.
———. 'What Sort of History Should We Teach?', in Martin Ballard (ed.), *New Movements in the Study and Teaching of History* (London: Temple Smith, 1970), 221–30.
———. *Return to Essentials: Some Reflections on the Present State of Historical Study*. Cambridge: Cambridge University Press, 1991.
Endacott, Jason L. 'Reconsidering Affective Engagement in Historical Empathy'. *Theory and Research in Social Education* 38, 1 (2010), 6–49.
Ermarth, Michael. 'The Transformation of Hermeneutics: 19th Century Ancients and 20th Century Moderns'. *Monist* 64, 2 (1981), 175–94.
Evans, Ronald R. 'Educational Ideologies and the Teaching of History', in Gaea Leinhardt, Isabel L. Beck and Catherine Stainton (eds), *Teaching and Learning in History* (Hillsdale: Lawrence Erlbaum, 1994), 171–207.
Faulkner, William. *Requiem for a Nun*. New York: Random House, 1951.
Fear, Christopher. 'The Question-and-Answer Logic of Historical Context'. *History of the Human Sciences* 26, 3 (2013), 68–81.
Febvre, Lucien. *Combats pour l'Histoire*. Paris: Librairie Armand Colin, 1953.
Fleming, Marie. 'Gadamer's Conversation: Does the Other Have a Say?', in Lorraine Code (ed.), *Feminist Interpretations of Hans-Georg Gadamer* (University Park: Pennsylvania State University Press, 2003), 109–32.
Forster, Michael N. Introduction to *Herder: Philosophical Writings*, trans. and ed. Michael N. Forster (Cambridge: Cambridge University Press, 2002), vii–xxxv.

Foster, Stuart. 'Using Historical Empathy to Excite Students about the Study of History: Can You Empathize with Neville Chamberlain?' *Social Studies* 90, 1 (1999), 18–24.

Foster, Stuart, and Elizabeth Anne Yeager. 'The Role of Empathy in the Development of Historical Understanding'. *International Journal of Social Education* 13, 1 (1998), 1–7.

Gadamer, Hans-Georg. *Philosophical Hermeneutics,* trans. and ed. David E. Linge. Berkeley: University of California Press, 1976. The following essays were used in this book: 'The Universality of the Hermeneutical Problem' (1966), 3–17; 'On the Scope and Function of Hermeneutical Reflection' (1967), 18–43.

——. *Reason in the Age of Science,* trans. Frederick D. Lawrence. Cambridge, MA: MIT Press, 1981. The following essay was used in this book: 'The Heritage of Hegel' (1979), 38–68.

——. *Philosophical Apprenticeships,* trans. Robert B. Sullivan. Cambridge, MA: MIT Press, 1985.

——. 'The Problem of Historical Consciousness', in Paul Rabinow and William M. Sullivan (eds), *Interpretive Social Science: A Second Look* (Berkeley: University of California Press, 1987), 82–140.

——. 'Introduction to *Denken.* The German Translation of *An Autobiography*', trans. G. Barden and N. McCormick. *The Collingwood Journal* (Spring 1992), 9–14. Collingwood's *Denken* was published in 1955 by K.F. Hoehler Verlag, Stuttgart.

——. *Truth and Method,* 2nd rev. edn and trans. Joel Weinsheimer and Donald G. Marshall. New York: Continuum, 2004. First published in German in 1960.

Gallagher, Shaun. *Hermeneutics and Education.* Albany: State University of New York Press, 1992.

——. 'Simulation Trouble'. *Social Neuroscience* 2, 3/4 (2007), 353–65.

——. 'Narrative Competence and the Massive Hermeneutical Background', in Paul Fairfield (ed.), *Education, Dialogue and Hermeneutics* (London: Continuum, 2010), 21–38.

——. 'In Defense of Phenomenological Approaches to Social Cognition: Interacting with the Critics'. *Review of Philosophy and Psychology* 3, 2 (2012), 187–212.

——. 'Three Questions for Stueber'. *Emotion Review* 4, 1 (2012), 64–5.

——. 'An Education in Narratives'. *Educational Philosophy and Theory* 46, 6 (2014), 600–9.

Gard, A., and P.J. Lee. '"Educational Objectives for the Study of History" Reconsidered', in A.K. Dickinson and P.J. Lee (eds), *History Teaching and Historical Understanding* (London: Heinemann, 1978), 21–38.

Gardiner, Patrick. 'Interpretation in History: Collingwood and Historical Understanding', in Anthony O'Hear (ed.), *Verstehen and Humane Understanding* (Cambridge: Cambridge University Press, 1996), 109–19.

Gardner, Howard. *The Mind's New Science: A History of the Cognitive Revolution.* New York: Basic Books, 1985.

Gay, Peter. *Style in History.* New York: Basic Books, 1974.

Gipps, Caroline. 'GCSE: Some Background', in Caroline Gipps (ed.), *The GCSE: An Uncommon Examination* (London: Institute of Education, 1986), 11–20.

Goldberg, Amos. 'Empathy, Ethics, and Politics in Holocaust Historiography', in Aleida Assmann and Ines Detmers (eds), *Empathy and its Limits* (New York: Palgrave Macmillan, 2015), 52–76.

Goldie, Peter. 'Anti-empathy', in Amy Coplan and Peter Goldie (eds), *Empathy: Philosophical and Psychological Perspectives* (Oxford: Oxford University Press, 2011), 302–17.

Goldstein, Arnold P., and Gerald Y. Michaels, *Empathy: Development, Training, and Consequences.* Hillsdale: Lawrence Erlbaum Associates, 1985.

Gosden, P.H.J.H., and D.W. Sylvester. *History for the Average Child: Suggestions on Teaching History to Pupils of Average and Below Average Ability.* Oxford: Blackwell, 1968.

Grondin, Jean. *Introduction to Philosophical Hermeneutics,* trans. Joel Weinsheimer. New Haven: Yale University Press, 1994.

———. *Hans-Georg Gadamer: A Biography,* trans. Joel Weinsheimer. New Haven: Yale University Press, 2003.
Gutman, Herbert. 'Historical Consciousness in Contemporary America', in Ira Berlin (ed.), *Power and Culture: Essays on the American Working Class by Herbert G. Gutman* (New York: Pantheon Books, 1987), 395–412.
Guyer, Paul. *A History of Modern Aesthetics: Volume 2: The Nineteenth Century.* Cambridge: Cambridge University Press, 2014.
Guyver, Robert. 'The History Working Group and beyond: A Case Study in the UK's History Quarrels', in Tony Taylor and Robert Guyver (eds), *History Wars and the Classroom: Global Perspectives* (Charlotte: Information Age Publishing, 2012), 159–86.
———. 'Michael Gove's History Wars 2010–2014: The Rise, Fall and Transformation of a Neoconservative Dream'. *Agora* 49, 4 (2014), 4–11.
Haddock, B.A. 'Vico, Collingwood and the Character of Historical Philosophy', in David Boucher, James Connelly and Tariq Modood (eds), *Philosophy, History and Civilisation: Interdisciplinary Perspectives on R.G. Collingwood* (Cardiff: University of Wales Press, 1995), 130–51.
Hallam, R.N. 'Piaget and Thinking in History', in Martin Ballard (ed.), *New Movements in the Study and Teaching of History* (London: Temple Smith, 1970), 162–78.
Happold, F.G. *The Approach to History.* London: Christophers, 1928.
Harlan, David. 'Intellectual History and the Return of Literature'. *American Historical Review* 94, 3 (1989), 581–609.
———. *The Degradation of American History.* Chicago: University of Chicago Press, 1997.
Harré, Rom, and Michael Krausz. *Varieties of Relativism.* Oxford: Blackwell, 1996.
Hartley, L.P. *The Go-Between.* New York: New York Review Books, 1953.
Hausheer, Roger. 'Three Major Originators of the Concept of *Verstehen*: Vico, Herder, Schleiermacher', in Anthony O'Hear (ed.), *Verstehen and Humane Understanding* (Cambridge: Cambridge University Press, 1996), 47–72.
Heidegger, Martin. *Ontology: The Hermeneutics of Facticity,* trans. John van Buren. Bloomington: Indiana University Press, 1999.
Heidegger, Martin. *Being and Time,* trans. John Macquarrie and Edward Robinson. New York: Harper & Row, 1962. First published in German in 1927.
———. *Nietzsche,* vols 1–4, trans. David Farrell Krell. New York: Harper & Row, 1979–87.
Helgeby, Stein. 'Collingwood and Croce', in Aviezer Tucker (ed.), *A Companion to the Philosophy of History and Historiography* (Chichester: Wiley-Blackwell, 2009), 498–507.
Hempel, C.G. 'The Function of General Laws in History'. *Journal of Philosophy* 39, 2 (1942), 35–48. Reprinted in Herbert Feigl and Wilfrid Sellars (eds), *Readings in Philosophical Analysis* (New York: Appleton-Century-Crofts, 1949), 459–71; and Patrick Gardiner (ed.), *Theories of History: Readings from Classical and Contemporary Sources* (Glencoe: Free Press, 1959), 344–56.
Herder, Johann Gottfried von. *Herder: Philosophical Writings,* trans. and ed. Michael N. Forster. Cambridge: Cambridge University Press, 2002. The following essays were used in this book: 'This Too a Philosophy of History for the Formation of Humanity' (1774), 272–358; 'On the Cognition and Sensation of the Human Soul' (1778), 187–243.
Hill, Christopher. 'A Whig Historian'. *Modern Quarterly* 3, 1 (1938), 275–84.
———. 'Marxism and History'. *Modern Quarterly* 3, 2 (1948), 52–65.
Hillgruber, Andreas. *Zweierlei Untergang: Die Zerschlagung des Deutschen Reiches und das Ende des europäischen Judentums.* Berlin: Siedler, 1986.
Hirst, Paul H. 'Liberal Education and the Nature of Knowledge', in Reginald D. Archambault (ed.), *Philosophical Analysis and Education* (London: Routledge & Kegan Paul, 1965), 113–38.
Hobsbawm, Eric J. 'From Social History to the History of Society'. *Daedalus* 100, 1 (1971), 20–45.

———. 'Karl Marx's Contribution to Historiography', in Robin Blackburn (ed.), *Ideology in Social Science: Readings in Critical Social Theory* (New York: Pantheon Books, 1972), 265–83.

———. 'Introduction: Inventing Traditions', in Eric Hobsbawm and Terence Ranger (eds), *The Invention of Tradition* (Cambridge: Cambridge University Press, 1983), 1–14.

Hogan, John P. *Collingwood and Theological Hermeneutics*. Lanham: University Press of America, 1989.

Hughes-Warrington, Marnie. *How Good an Historian Shall I Be? R.G. Collingwood, the Historical Imagination and Education*. Exeter: Imprint Academic, 2003.

Humboldt, Wilhelm von. 'On the Historian's Task', in Georg G. Iggers and Konrad von Moltke (eds), *The Theory and Practice of History* (Indianapolis: Bobbs-Merrill Company, 1973), 5–23.

Husbands, Chris, Alison Kitson and Anna Pendry. *Understanding History Teaching*. Maidenhead: Open University Press, 2003.

Iggers, Georg G. 'The Image of Ranke in American and German Historical Thought'. *History and Theory* 2, 1 (1962), 17–40.

———. *The German Conception of History: The National Tradition of Historical Thought from Herder to the Present*, rev. edn. Middletown: Wesleyan University Press, 1983.

———. 'Historicism: The History and Meaning of the Term'. *Journal of the History of Ideas* 56, 1 (1995), 129–52.

———. 'The Intellectual Foundations of Nineteenth-Century "Scientific" History: The German Model', in Stuart Macintyre, Juan Maiguashca and Attila Pók (eds), *The Oxford History of Historical Writing, Volume 4: 1800–1945* (Oxford: Oxford University Press, 2011), 41–58.

Inglis, Fred. *History Man: The Life of R.G. Collingwood*. Princeton: Princeton University Press, 2009.

Jeffreys, M.V.C. *History in Schools: The Study of Development*. London: Sir Isaac Pitman and Sons, 1939.

Jenkins, Keith. *Re-thinking History*. London: Routledge, 1991.

Jenkins, Keith, and Peter Brickley. 'Reflections on the Empathy Debate'. *Teaching History* 55, 18 (1989), 18–23.

Johnson, Peter. *Collingwood's* The Idea of History: *A Reader's Guide*. London: Bloomsbury, 2013.

Jones, Gareth. 'Traditional and New History Teaching: Towards a Synthesis', in Gareth Jones and Lionel Ward (eds), *New History Old Problems: Studies in History Teaching* (Swansea: University College of Swansea Faculty of Education, 1978), 137–54.

———. 'The Debate over the National Curriculum for History in England and Wales, 1989–90: The Role of the Press'. *Curriculum Journal* 11, 3 (2000), 299–322.

Joseph, Keith. 'Speech by the Rt Hon Sir Keith Joseph, Secretary of State for Education and Science, at the North of England Education Conference, Sheffield, on Friday 6 January 1984'. *Oxford Review of Education* 10, 2 (1984), 137–46.

———. 'Why Teach History in School?' *Historian* 2 (Spring 1984), 10–12.

Kant, Immanuel. *Critique of Pure Reason* [1781/1787], trans. and ed. Paul Guyer and Allen W. Wood. Cambridge: Cambridge University Press, 1998.

Keating, Jenny, and Nicola Sheldon. 'History in Education: Trends and Themes in History Teaching, 1900–2010', in Ian Davies (ed.), *Debates in History Teaching* (London: Routledge, 2011), 5–17.

Kelly, Donald R. 'Mythhistory in the Age of Ranke', in Georg G. Iggers and James M. Powell (eds), *Leopold von Ranke and the Shaping of the History Discipline* (Syracuse: Syracuse University Press, 1990), 3–20.

———. *Fortunes of History: Historical Inquiry from Herder to Huizinga*. New Haven: Yale University Press, 2003.

Kingdon, Michael, and Gordon Stobart. *GCSE Examined*. London: Falmer Press, 1988.

Kissell, Michael A. 'Progressive Traditionalism as the Spirit of Collingwood's Philosophy'. *History and Theory* 29, 4 (1990), 51–56.
Kitson Clark, George. *The Critical Historian*. London: Heinemann, 1967.
Klein, Kerwin Lee. *From History to Theory*. Berkeley: University of California Press, 2011.
Knight, Peter. 'Empathy: Concept, Confusion and Consequences in a National Curriculum'. *Oxford Review of Education* 15, 1 (1989), 41–53.
Kobayashi, Chinatsu, and Mathieu Marion. 'Gadamer and Collingwood on Temporal Distance and Understanding'. *History and Theory* 50, 4 (2011), 81–103.
Köhnke, Klaus Christian. *The Rise of Neo-Kantianism: German Academic Philosophy between Idealism and Positivism*, trans. R.J. Hollingdale. Cambridge: Cambridge University Press, 1991.
Körber, Andreas. 'German History Didactics', in Helle Bjerg, Claudia Lenz and Erik Thorstensen (eds), *Historicizing the Uses of the Past: Scandinavian Perspectives on History, Culture, Historical Consciousness and Didactics of History Related to World War II* (New Brunswick: Transcript, 2011), 145–64.
———. 'Translation and its Discontents II: A German Perspective'. *Journal of Curriculum Studies* 48, 4 (2016), 440–56.
Köster, Manuel, Holger Thünemann and Meik Zülsdorf-Kersting (eds). Introduction to *Researching History Education: International Perspectives and Disciplinary Traditions* (Schwalbach am Taunus: Wochenschau Verlag, 2014), 5–8.
Kuehn, Manfred. *Kant: A Biography*. Cambridge: Cambridge University Press, 2001.
Lee, Peter. 'Explanation and Understanding in History', in A.K. Dickinson and P.J. Lee (eds), *History Teaching and Historical Understanding* (London: Heinemann, 1978), 72–93.
———. 'History Teaching and Philosophy of History'. *History and Theory* 22, 4 (1983), 19–49.
———. 'Historical Imagination', in A.K. Dickinson, P.J. Lee and P.J. Rogers (eds), *Learning History* (London: Heinemann, 1984), 85–116.
———. 'Why Learn History', in A.K. Dickinson, P.J. Lee and P.J. Rogers (eds), *Learning History* (London: Heinemann, 1984), 1–19.
———. 'Historical Knowledge and the National Curriculum', in Richard Aldrich (ed.), *History in the National Curriculum* (London: Kogan Page, 1991), 39–65.
———. 'Understanding History', in Peter Seixas (ed.), *Theorizing Historical Consciousness* (Toronto: University of Toronto Press, 2004), 129–64.
———. 'Reflections on Coltham's and Fines': Educational Objectives for the Study of History – A Suggested Framework and Peter Rogers': The New History, Theory into Practice'. *International Journal of Historical Learning, Teaching and Research* 9, 1 (2010), 13–7.
———. 'Historical Literacy and Transformative History', in Lukas Perikleous and Denis Shemilt (eds), *The Future of the Past: Why History Education Matters* (Nicosia: Association for Historical Dialogue and Research, 2011), 129–68.
Lee, Peter, and Rosalyn Ashby. 'Progression in Historical Understanding among Students Ages 7–14', in Peter N. Stearns, Peter Seixas and Sam Wineburg (eds), *Knowing, Teaching, and Learning History: National and International Perspectives* (New York: New York University Press, 2000), 199–222.
———. 'Empathy, Perspective Taking, and Rational Understanding', in O.L. Davis, Jr., Elizabeth Yeager and Stuart Foster (eds), *Historical Empathy and Perspective Taking in the Social Studies* (Lanham: Rowman & Littlefield, 2001), 21–50.
Lee, Peter, Alaric Dickinson and Rosalyn Ashby. 'Researching Children's Ideas about History', in James F. Voss and Mario Carretero (eds), *International Review of History Education, Volume 2: Learning and Reasoning in History* (London: Woburn Press, 1998), 227–51.
Lee, Peter, and Denis Shemilt. 'The Concept that Dares Not Speak its Name: Should Empathy Come out of the Closet?' *Teaching History* 143 (2011), 39–49.
Letwin, Shirley Robin. *The Anatomy of Thatcherism*. London: Fontana, 1992.

Levisohn, Jon A. 'Historical Thinking – and its Alleged Unnaturalness'. *Educational Philosophy and Theory* 49, 6 (2017), 618–30.
Lipps, Theodor. 'Empathy, Inward Imitation, and Sense Feelings', in E.F. Carritt (ed.), *Philosophies of Beauty: From Socrates to Robert Bridges, Being the Sources of Aesthetic Theory* (Oxford: Clarendon Press, 1931), 252–56.
——. 'A Further Consideration of Empathy', in E.F. Carritt (ed.), *Philosophies of Beauty: From Socrates to Robert Bridges, Being the Sources of Aesthetic Theory* (Oxford: Clarendon Press, 1931), 256–58.
Little, Vivienne. 'A National Curriculum in History: A Very Contentious Issue'. *British Journal of Educational Studies* 38, 4 (1990), 319–34.
Lord, Timothy C. 'R.G. Collingwood: A Continental Philosopher?'. *Clio* 23, 3 (2000), 325–36.
Louch, A.R. *Explanation and Human Action*. Berkeley: University of California Press, 1969.
Löwith, Karl. *From Hegel to Nietzsche: The Revolution in Nineteenth-Century Thought*, trans. David E. Green. New York: Holt, Rinehart and Winston, 1964.
Macintosh, Henry. 'The Sacred Cows of Coursework', in Caroline Gipps (ed.), *The GCSE: An Uncommon Examination* (London: Institute of Education, 1986), 21–29.
MacIntyre, Alasdair. *After Virtue*, 2nd edn. Notre Dame: University of Notre Dame Press, 1983.
——. 'On Not Having the Last Word: Thoughts on Our Debts to Gadamer', in Jeff Malpas, Ulrich Arnswald and Jens Kertscher (eds), *Gadamer's Century: Essays in Honor of Hans-Georg Gadamer* (Cambridge, MA: MIT Press, 2002), 157–72.
Macintyre, Stuart. 'The Challenge for History in the National Curriculum'. Keynote Address, Australian Curriculum Studies Association Conference, Canberra, 2 October 2009. Retrieved 21 February 2018 from http://www.acsa.edu.au/pages/images/Stuart%20Macintyre%20Keynote%20address.pdf.
Maclean, Michael J. 'Johann Gustav Droysen and the Development of Historical Hermeneutics'. *History and Theory* 21, 3 (1982), 347–65.
Makkreel, Rudolf A. 'How is Empathy Related to Understanding?', in Thomas Nenon and Lester Embree (eds), *Issues in Husserl's Ideas II* (Dordrecht: Kluwer Academic Publishers, 1996), 199–212.
——. 'From Simulation to Structural Transposition: A Diltheyan Critique of Empathy and Defense of *Verstehen*', in Hans Herbert Kögler and Karsten R. Stueber (eds), *Empathy and Agency: The Problem of Understanding in the Human Sciences* (Boulder: Westview Press, 2000), 181–93.
Marten, C.H.K. 'The Teaching of History in Schools: Practice', in F.W. Maitland, H.M. Gwatkin, R.L. Poole, W.E. Heitland, W. Cunningham, J.R. Turner, W.H. Woodward, C.H.K. Marten and W.J. Ashley, *Essays on the Teaching of History* (Cambridge: Cambridge University Press, 1901), 79–91.
Martin, Rex. *Historical Explanation: Re-enactment and Practical Inference*. Ithaca: Cornell University Press, 1977.
——. 'Collingwood's Claim that Metaphysics is a Historical Discipline', in David Boucher, James Connelly and Tariq Modood (eds), *Philosophy, History and Civilisation: Interdisciplinary Perspectives on R.G. Collingwood* (Cardiff: University of Wales Press, 1995), 203–45.
McGinn, Colin. 'Homage to Education'. *London Review of Books* 12, 15 (1990), 16–17.
McIntyre, Kenneth B. 'Historicity as Methodology or Hermeneutics: Collingwood's Influence on Skinner and Gadamer'. *Journal of the Philosophy of History* 2, 2 (2008), 138–66.
Megill, Allan. 'Jörn Rüsen's Theory of Historiography between Modernism and Rhetoric of Inquiry'. *History and Theory* 33, 1 (1994), 39–60.
Mendelson, Jack. 'The Habermas-Gadamer Debate'. *New German Critique* 18 (Fall 1979), 44–73.

Ministry of Education. *Half Our Future: A Report of the Central Advisory Council for Education (England)*. London: HMSO, 1963.

Mink, Louis O. *Mind, History, and Dialectic: The Philosophy of R.G. Collingwood*. Bloomington: Indiana University Press, 1969.

Munslow, Alun. *Deconstructing History*, 2nd edn. London: Routledge, 2006.

Murphy, Richard. *Collingwood and the Crisis of Western Civilisation: Art, Metaphysics and Dialectic*. Exeter: Imprint Academic, 2008.

National Curriculum Board. *The Shape of the Australian Curriculum*. Canberra: ACARA, 2009.

——. *Shape of the Australian Curriculum: History*. Canberra: ACARA, 2009.

Nietzsche, Friedrich. *Untimely Meditations*, trans. R.J. Hollingdale. Cambridge: Cambridge University Press, 1983. First published in German between 1873 and 1876.

Nora, Pierre. *Realms of Memory: The Construction of the French Past*, trans. Arthur Goldhammer. New York: Columbia University Press, 1996.

Oakeshott, Michael. *Experience and its Modes*. Cambridge: Cambridge University Press, 1933.

Oldfield, Adrian. 'Metaphysics and History in Collingwood's Thought', in David Boucher, James Connelly and Tariq Modood (eds), *Philosophy, History and Civilisation: Interdisciplinary Perspectives on R.G. Collingwood* (Cardiff: University of Wales Press, 1995), 182–202.

Peck, Carla, and Peter Seixas. 'Benchmarks of Historical Thinking: First Steps'. *Canadian Journal of Education* 31, 4 (2008), 1015–38.

Perry, Leslie R. 'The Covering Law Theory of Historical Explanation', in W.H. Burston and D. Thompson (eds), *Studies in the Nature and Teaching of History* (New York: Humanities Press, 1967), 27–48.

——. 'Objective and Practical History'. *Journal of Philosophy of Education* 1, 1 (1967), 35–48.

Peters, Rik. 'Croce, Gentile and Collingwood on the Relation between History and Philosophy', in David Boucher, James Connelly and Tariq Modood (eds), *Philosophy, History and Civilisation: Interdisciplinary Perspectives on R.G. Collingwood* (Cardiff: University of Wales Press, 1995), 152–67.

Phillips, Robert. *History Teaching, Nationhood and the State: A Study in Educational Politics*. London: Cassell, 1998.

Pippin, Robert B. 'Gadamer's Hegel', in Robert J. Dostal (ed.), *The Cambridge Companion to Gadamer* (Cambridge: Cambridge University Press, 2002), 225–46.

Pompa, Leon. *Vico: A Study of the 'New Science'*, 2nd edn. Cambridge: Cambridge University Press, 1990.

Popper, K.R. *The Poverty of Historicism*. London: Routledge & Kegan Paul, 1957.

——. *Objective Knowledge: An Evolutionary Approach*. Oxford: Clarendon Press, 1972.

Postan, M.M. *Fact and Relevance: Essays on Historical Method*. Cambridge: Cambridge University Press, 1971.

Power, Eileen. 'On Medieval History as a Social Study', in N.B. Harte (ed.), *The Study of Economic History: Collected Inaugural Lectures 1893–1970* (London: Frank Cass, 1971), 109–25.

Price, Mary. 'History in Danger'. *History* 53, 179 (1968), 342–47.

Prinz, Jesse J. 'Against Empathy'. *Southern Journal of Philosophy* 49, 1 (2011), 214–33.

——. 'Is Empathy Necessary for Morality?', in Amy Coplan and Peter Goldie (eds), *Empathy: Philosophical and Psychological Perspectives* (Oxford: Oxford University Press, 2011), 211–29.

Ranke, Leopold von. *The Theory and Practice of History*, Georg G. Iggers and Konrad von Moltke (eds). Indianapolis: Bobbs-Merrill Company, 1973. The following essays were used in this book: 'On the Character of Historical Science' (1830s), 33–47; 'The Pitfalls of a Philosophy of History' (1840s), 47–50; 'On Progress in History' (1854), 51–56.

Retz, Tyson. 'A Moderate Hermeneutical Approach to Empathy in History Education'. *Educational Philosophy and Theory* 47, 3 (2015), 214–26.

———. 'At the Interface: Academic History, School History and the Philosophy of History'. *Journal of Curriculum Studies* 48, 4 (2016), 503–17.
———. 'The Structure of Historical Inquiry'. *Educational Philosophy and Theory* 49, 6 (2017), 606–17.
———. 'Why Re-enactment is Not Empathy, Once and for All'. *Journal of the Philosophy of History* 11, 3 (2017), 306–23.
Rickert, Heinrich. *The Limits of Concept Formation in Natural Science: A Logical Introduction to the Historical Sciences,* trans. and ed. Guy Oakes. Cambridge: Cambridge University Press, 1986. First published in German in 1902.
Ricœur, Paul. 'Ethics and Culture: Habermas and Gadamer in Dialogue'. *Philosophy Today* 17, 2 (1973), 153–65.
———. *Main Trends in Philosophy.* New York: Holmes & Meier, 1979.
———. 'Temporal Distance and Death in History', in Jeff Malpas, Ulrich Arnswald and Jens Kertscher (eds), *Gadamer's Century: Essays in Honor of Hans-Georg Gadamer* (Cambridge, MA: MIT Press, 2002), 239–55.
Roberts, David D. *Benedetto Croce and the Uses of Historicism.* Berkeley: University of California Press, 1987.
Roberts, Martin. 'History in the School Curriculum 1972–1990; A Possible Dialectical Sequence: Thesis, Antithesis, Synthesis?'. *Curriculum Journal* 1, 1 (1990), 65–75.
Rogers, Peter. 'History', in Keith Dixon (ed.), *Philosophy of Education and the Curriculum* (Oxford: Pergamon Press, 1972), 75–134.
———. *The New History: Theory into Practice,* pamphlet no. 44. London: Historical Association, 1978.
———. 'History: The Past as a Frame of Reference', in Christopher Portal (ed.), *The History Curriculum for Teachers* (London: Falmer Press, 1987), 3–21.
Rosen, Michael. 'The History of Philosophy as Philosophy', in Brian Leiter and Michael Rosen (eds), *The Oxford Handbook of Continental Philosophy* (Oxford: Oxford University Press, 2007), 122–54.
Rüsen, Jörn. 'The Didactics of History in West Germany: Towards a New Self-Awareness of Historical Studies'. *History and Theory* 26, 3 (1987), 275–86.
———. 'The Development of Narrative Competence in Historical Learning: An Ontogenetic Hypothesis Concerning Moral Consciousness'. *History and Memory* 1, 2 (1989), 35–59.
———. *Studies in Metahistory.* Pretoria: Human Sciences Research Council, 1993.
——— (ed.). *Western Historical Thinking: An Intercultural Debate.* New York: Berghahn Books, 2002.
———. *History: Narration – Interpretation – Orientation.* New York: Berghahn Books, 2005.
Skagestad, Peter. *Making Sense of History: The Philosophies of Popper and Collingwood.* Oslo: Universitetsforlaget, 1975.
Schmidt, Lawrence. 'Hans-Georg Gadamer: A Biographical Sketch', in Jeff Malpas, Ulrich Arnswald and Jens Kertscher (eds), *Gadamer's Century: Essays in Honor of Hans-Georg Gadamer* (Cambridge, MA: MIT Press, 2002), 1–13.
Schools Council. *Humanities for the Young School Leaver: An Approach through English.* London: HMSO, 1968.
Schools Council History 13–16 Project. *A New Look at History.* Edinburgh: Holmes McDougall, 1976.
Secondary Examinations Council. *History: GCSE, A Guide for Teachers.* Milton Keynes: Open University Press, 1986.
Seixas, Peter. 'Parallel Crises: History and the Social Studies Curriculum in the USA'. *Journal of Curriculum Studies* 25, 3 (1993), 235–50.
———. 'Conceptualizing the Growth of Historical Understanding', in David R. Olson and Nancy Torrance (eds), *The Handbook of Education and Human Development* (Oxford: Blackwell, 1996), 765–83.

———. 'Student Teachers Thinking Historically'. *Theory and Research in Social Education* 26, 3 (1998), 310–41.
——— (ed.). *Theorizing Historical Consciousness*. Toronto: University of Toronto Press, 2004.
———. 'Collective Memory, History Education, and Historical Consciousness'. *Historically Speaking* 7, 2 (2005), 17–19.
———. 'Benchmarks of Historical Thinking: A Framework for Assessment in Canada'. Centre for the Study of Historical Consciousness, University of British Columbia, 18 August 2006, 1–12. Retrieved 21 February 2018 from http://historicalthinking.ca/sites/default/files/files/docs/Framework_EN.pdf.
———. Preface to Tony Taylor and Robert Guyver (eds), *History Wars and the Classroom: Global Perspectives* (Charlotte: Information Age Publishing, 2012), xxi–xxii.
———. 'Translation and its Discontents: Key Concepts in English and German History Education'. *Journal of Curriculum Studies* 48, 4 (2016), 427–39.
———. 'A Model of Historical Thinking'. *Educational Philosophy and Theory* 49, 6 (2017), 593–605.
Seixas, Peter, and Tom Morton. *The Big Six Historical Thinking Concepts*. Toronto: Nelson Education, 2013.
Sellar, W.C., and R.J. Yeatman. *1066 and All That: A Memorable History of England, Comprising All the Parts You Can Remember, Including 103 Good Things, 5 Bad Kings and 2 Genuine Dates*. London: Methuen, 1930.
Sheldon, Nicola. 'Jeanette Coltham's, John Fines' and Peter Rogers' Historical Association Pamphlets: Their Relevance to the Development of Ideas about History Teaching Today'. *International Journal of Historical Learning, Teaching and Research* 9, 1 (2010), 9–12.
Shemilt, Denis. *History 13–16 Evaluation Study: Schools Council History 13–16 Project*. Edinburgh: Holmes McDougall, 1980.
———. 'Beauty and the Philosopher: Empathy in History and Classroom', in A.K. Dickinson, P.J. Lee and P.J. Rogers (eds), *Learning History* (London: Heinemann, 1984), 39–84.
Skinner, Quentin. 'Meaning and Understanding in the History of Ideas'. *History and Theory* 8, 1 (1969), 3–53.
———. 'Hermeneutics and the Role of History'. *New Literary History* 7, 1 (1975), 209–32.
———. 'The Rise of, Challenge to and Prospects for a Collingwoodian Approach to the History of Political Thought', in Dario Castiglione and Iain Hampsher-Monk (eds), *The History of Political Thought in National Context* (Cambridge: Cambridge University Press, 2001), 175–88.
———. *Visions of Politics, Volume 1: Regarding Method*. Cambridge: Cambridge University Press, 2002.
———. 'Belief, Truth and Interpretation', Keynote Address, Intellectual History: Traditions and Perspectives, Ruhr Universität Bochum, 18 November 2014.
Slater, John. *The Politics of History Teaching: A Humanity Dehumanized?* London: Institute of Education, 1989.
———. 'History in the National Curriculum: The Final Report of the History Working Group', in Richard Aldrich (ed.), *History in the National Curriculum* (London: Kogan Page, 1991), 8–38.
Southard, Robert. *Droysen and the Prussian School of History*. Lexington: University Press of Kentucky, 1995.
Southern Regional Examinations Board. *Empathy in History: From Definition to Assessment*. Eastleigh: SREB, 1986.
Stedman Jones, Gareth. 'The Pathology of English History'. *New Left Review* 46 (November–December 1967), 29–43. Reprinted as 'History: The Poverty of Empiricism', in Robin Blackburn (ed.), *Ideology in Social Science: Readings in Critical Social Theory* (New York: Pantheon Books, 1972), 96–115.

Stein, Edith. *On the Problem of Empathy*, trans. Waltraut Stein. The Hague: Martinus Nijhoff, 1964. First published in German in 1917.

Stueber, Karsten R. 'The Psychological Basis of Historical Explanation: Reenactment, Simulation, and the Fusion of Horizons'. *History and Theory* 41, 1 (2002), 25–42.

——. *Rediscovering Empathy: Agency, Folk Psychology, and the Human Sciences*. Cambridge, MA: MIT Press, 2006.

——. 'Reasons, Generalizations, Empathy, and Narratives: The Epistemic Structure of Action Explanation'. *History and Theory* 47, 1 (2008), 31–43.

——. 'Theories Explain, and So Do Historical Narratives: But There are Differences'. *Journal of the Philosophy of History* 2, 2 (2008), 237–43.

——. 'Intentionalism, Intentional Realism, and Empathy'. *Journal of the Philosophy of History* 3, 3 (2009), 290–307.

——. 'Empathy versus Narrative: What Exactly is the Debate about? Response to My Critics'. *Emotion Review* 4, 1 (2012), 68–69.

——. 'Understanding versus Explanation? How to Think about the Distinction between the Human and the Natural Sciences'. *Inquiry* 55, 1 (2012), 17–32.

——. 'Varieties of Empathy, Neuroscience and the Narrativist Challenge to the Contemporary Theory of Mind Debate'. *Emotion Review* 4, 1 (2012), 55–63.

Swinnerton, Bronwen, and Isobel Jenkins. *Secondary School History Teaching in England and Wales: A Review of Empirical Research, 1960–1998*. Leeds: Centre for Studies in Science and Mathematics Education, University of Leeds, in Association with the Historical Association, 1999.

Sylvester, David. *The Story of Medicine*. London: Edward Arnold, 1965.

——. 'Change and Continuity in History Teaching 1900–93', in Hilary Bourdillon (ed.), *Teaching History* (London: Routledge, 1994), 9–23.

Tate, Nicolas. *GCSE Coursework: History, A Teachers' Guide to Organisation and Assessment*. Basingstoke: Macmillan Educational, 1987.

Tawney, R.H. 'The Study of Economic History', in N.B. Harte (ed.), *The Study of Economic History: Collected Inaugural Lectures 1893–1970* (London: Frank Cass, 1971), 87–107.

Taylor, Charles. 'Understanding the Other: A Gadamerian View on Conceptual Schemes', in Jeff Malpas, Ulrich Arnswald and Jens Kertscher (eds), *Gadamer's Century: Essays in Honor of Hans-Georg Gadamer* (Cambridge, MA: MIT Press, 2002), 279–97.

——. *A Secular Age*. Cambridge, MA: Belknap Press, 2007.

Taylor, Tony. 'Trying to Connect: Moving from Bad History to Historical Literacy in Schools'. *Australian Cultural History* 23 (2003), 175–90.

Taylor, Tony, and Carmel Young. *Making History: A Guide for the Teaching and Learning of History in Australian Schools*. Melbourne: Curriculum Corporation, 2003.

Thatcher, Margaret. *The Downing Street Years*. London: HarperCollins, 1993.

Thomas, J.B. 'Psychology of Education in the UK: Development in the 1960s'. *Educational Studies* 33, 1 (2007), 53–63.

Thompson, E.P. *The Making of the English Working Class*, rev. edn. Harmondsworth: Penguin, 1980 [1963].

Tollebeek, Jo. 'Seeing the Past with the Mind's Eye: The Consecration of the Romantic Historian'. *Clio* 29, 2 (2000), 167–91.

Toulmin, Stephen. *Human Understanding, Volume 1*. Oxford: Clarendon Press, 1972.

Vardoulakis, Dimitrios. 'The Vicissitude of Completeness: Gadamer's Criticism of Collingwood'. *International Journal of Philosophical Studies* 12, 1 (2004), 3–19.

Vico, Giambattista. *The First New Science*, trans. and ed. Leon Pompa. Cambridge: Cambridge University Press, 2002. First published in Italian in 1725.

Vischer, Robert. 'On the Optical Sense of Form: A Contribution to Aesthetics', in Robert Vischer, Conrad Fiedler, Heinrich Wölfflin, Adolf Göller, Adolf Hildebrand and August

Schmarsow, *Empathy, Form, and Space: Problems in German Aesthetics, 1873–1893,* trans. Harry Francis Mulgrave and Eleftherios Ikonomou (Santa Monica: Getty Center for the History of Art and the Humanities, 1993), 89–123.

Wake, R. 'History as a Separate Discipline: The Case'. *Teaching History* 1, 3 (1970), 153–57.

Walsh, W.H. *An Introduction to Philosophy of History,* rev edn. London: Hutchinson University Library, 1958 [1951].

Weinsheimer, Joel C. *Gadamer's Hermeneutics: A Reading of* Truth and Method. New Haven: Yale University Press, 1985.

Wilkinson, Max. *Lessons from Europe: A Comparison of British and West European Schooling.* London: Centre for Policy Studies, 1977.

Willey, Thomas E. *Back to Kant: The Revival of Kantianism in German Social and Historical Thought 1860–1914.* Detroit: Wayne State University Press, 1978.

Windelband, Wilhelm. 'Rectorial Address, Strasbourg, 1894'. *History and Theory* 19, 2 (1980), 169–85.

Windelband, Wilhelm, and Guy Oakes, 'History and Natural Science'. *History and Theory* 19, 2 (1980), 165–68.

Wineburg, Samuel S. 'On the Reading of Historical Texts: Notes on the Breach between School and Academy'. *American Educational Research Journal* 28, 3 (1991), 495–519.

——. 'The Psychology of Learning and Teaching History', in David C. Berliner and Robert C. Calfee (eds), *Handbook of Educational Psychology* (New York: Macmillan, 1996), 423–37.

——. *Historical Thinking and Other Unnatural Acts: Charting the Future of Teaching the Past.* Philadelphia: Temple University Press, 2001.

Wolfson, Bob. 'Schools Council History 13–16 Project: An Upper School's Experience'. *Teaching History* 27 (1980), 25–30.

Wright, Georg Henrik von. *Explanation and Understanding.* Ithaca: Cornell University Press, 1971.

Yeager, Elizabeth Anne, and Stuart J. Foster. 'The Role of Empathy in the Development of Historical Understanding', in O.L. Davis Jr., Elizabeth Yeager and Stuart Foster (eds), *Historical Empathy and Perspective Taking in the Social Studies* (Lanham: Rowman & Littlefield, 2001), 13–19.

Zahavi, Dan. 'Empathy, Embodiment and Interpersonal Understanding: From Lipps to Schutz'. *Inquiry: An Interdisciplinary Journal of Philosophy* 53, 3 (2010), 285–306.

Newspapers

The Guardian, 1989–90, 2015
The Independent, 1988, 2004
Sunday Times, 1988
The Times, 1990
Times Educational Supplement, 1989

Interviews

Transcripts of interviews conducted by Nicola Sheldon for the History in Education Project, Institute of Historical Research, University of London.

Available at: http://www.history.ac.uk/history-in-education.

Clare, John D. 7 April 2010.
Culpin, Chris. 22 September 2009.
Dawson, Ian. 9 June 2009.
Harrison, Scott. 6 May 2009.
Hennessey, Roger. 11 November 2009.

Lee, Peter, and Rosalyn Ashby. 3 September 2009.
Shemilt, Denis. 3 July 2009.
Sylvester, David. 7 July 2009.

Miscellaneous

'Obama to Graduates: Cultivate Empathy: "The World Doesn't Just Revolve around You"'. Northwestern University Commencement Speech, 19 June 2006. Retrieved 21 February 2018 from http://www.northwestern.edu/newscenter/stories/2006/06/barack.html.

'Tuning the History Discipline in the United States', *American Historical Association*. Retrieved 21 February 2018 from https://www.historians.org/teaching-and-learning/tuning-the-history-discipline.

Index

actions, 2–4, 7, 9–10, 12, 25–26, 38–41, 44, 46, 48, 50–51, 58–64, 67, 74, 76, 78, 80, 83, 85, 91, 97–98, 103, 121–23, 125, 127–28, 139–40, 143n54, 155, 158–59, 176–77, 192–94, 197–201, 216
actuality, 109, 111, 204
aesthetic experience, 75
Alexander, Samuel, 122
American Historical Association, 6
analogical inference, 76–77, 86
Ankersmit, Frank, 80, 201, 205
Annales, 23, 26
Appleby, Joyce, 160–61
Aquinas, Thomas, 161–62
Aristotle, 129, 133, 161–62, 215
Armitage, David, 160
Ashby, Rosalyn, 39, 65
Ast, Friedrich, 92, 96
Australia, 199–201, 204, 206, 211n26
An Autobiography (Collingwood), 11, 16–17n29, 39, 109, 113, 115, 118n11, 119n15, 134, 141, 156–58

Bacon, Francis, 128, 130, 134
Baker, Kenneth, 184–86
Bambach, Charles, 152
Barton, Keith, 5
Being and Time (Heidegger), 146, 150
beliefs, 2–3, 9–10, 13, 37, 40, 50, 58, 62–63, 67, 134, 137, 139, 159, 161, 178, 182, 193, 197–98, 201, 218
Berger, Stefan, 83, 90n28

Berlin, Isaiah, 47, 84
Bevir, Mark, 9–10, 80, 112
black-box problem, 41–43, 61, 133
Blackburn, Simon, 108, 119n13
Blake, Christopher, 5, 64
Bloch, Marc, 26, 51, 173
Bloom, Benjamin, 31, 174
Bloom, Paul, 7
Böckh, August, 97
Boddington, Tony, 57
Booth, Martin, 22
Boucher, David, 112–13
Braudel, Fernand, 26
Brecht, Arnold, 101
Breithaupt, Fritz, 7
Britain, 3, 6, 21, 24–25, 27, 161, 166, 174–75, 184, 186, 188, 194, 205–6. *See also* England; United Kingdom
Brown, Gordon, 188
Browning, Christopher, 162
Bruner, Jerome, 28, 31, 58, 174, 213
Burke, Edmund, 82
Burston, William Hedley, 35, 43–50, 58, 63, 175–76, 193–94

Callaghan, James, 179
Canada, 3, 6, 15, 166, 188, 195–98, 206
Carr, E.H., 2, 24, 43, 173
Centre for Policy Studies, 179, 184
Centre for the Study of Historical Consciousness, University of British Columbia, 195–96, 206

Certificate of Secondary Education, 180–81
chronology, 63–64, 84, 174, 177, 184, 187, 200
Clark, Penney, 194
colligation, 46–49, 58–60, 95–96, 193–94, 209, 214
Collingwood, R.G., 4, 8–12, 14, 15n11, 16n29, 23, 35–43, 45, 48, 58–61, 63, 67–68, 73–74, 80, 85, 92, 103, 106–18, 118n11, 119n12n15n16n18, 121–41, 141n1, 142n35, 145–49, 151, 153–59, 161, 164–66, 173, 175–77, 183, 185, 197–99, 203, 208–9, 213–17
Coltham, Jeanette, 31, 38, 52
comprehensive schools, 27, 30, 68, 174, 177, 179–80
Comte, Auguste, 100
Connelly, James, 106, 137–38
conservatism, 1, 162–63, 165, 183–85, 188
contextualism, 10, 123–25, 129, 132, 160–61, 169n56, 197. *See also* historical context
Cooper, Bridget, 5
covering-law model (including general laws), 3–4, 38, 45–47, 50–51, 81, 154, 175–76, 193
Croce, Benedetto, 22, 81, 85, 106–8, 111, 113, 118n11, 136, 175
cross-curricular and integrated approaches, 8, 28, 30
Cunningham, Deborah, 5

D'Amico, Robert, 100
Dasein, 146, 150
Descartes, René, 76, 85, 128, 152, 163, 176
democracy, 5–6, 21, 199
Department of Education and Science, 179, 182, 184
detachment, 3, 31, 49, 66, 77, 87, 148, 156, 218
detective-historian, 130–31, 133, 158, 198
determinism, 4, 24, 40, 136, 175, 199
Dexter, Colin, 173
dialectic of question and answer, 14, 114, 147, 217
dialogue, 65, 155–56
Die manuscript (Collingwood), 17n29, 108–9, 112, 119n15, 215

Dilthey, Wilhelm, 73, 77–80, 83, 85, 93, 101–3, 106, 112–13, 116–17, 121, 133, 149–50, 152–54, 164, 175, 207
disciplinary concepts, 6, 15, 32, 189, 192–94, 196, 199–200, 205–6, 211n26, 214
disciplinary distillation, 14, 29, 176, 206, 213–14
disciplinary matrix, 202–3, 206, 209
disembedded thinking. *See* Donaldson, Margaret
distance, 42, 60, 66, 78, 111, 122, 125–26, 147–48, 154, 196, 199. *See also* hindsight
Divination, 88, 131, 153
Dobb, Maurice, 23
Donaldson, Margaret, 65
Dray, William, 3, 11, 36, 45, 50, 52, 73–74, 126, 176, 193, 214
Droysen, Johann Gustav, 97–98, 101, 113, 131, 149, 152, 154, 201, 205, 208
Dunn, John, 123
Dussen, W.J. van der, 11, 126, 131

economic history, 22, 48
educational philosophy, 29, 50, 57, 60, 66, 213
educational psychology, 27–28, 31, 44, 57, 66, 213
Einfühlung, 74–75, 78, 84, 215
Eley, Geoff, 23–25
Elton, G.R., 2, 43–44, 61–62, 132, 173, 185
emic and etic perspectives, 8, 39
emotion, 32, 59, 75, 115–16, 195, 218. *See also* empathy; feeling
empathy
    as achievement, 2, 54, 58, 61–63, 65
    and aesthetics, 1, 5, 74–76, 78, 80, 103, 125, 156
    affective aspects of, 1, 3, 5, 7, 38, 42, 57, 64, 75–77, 183, 195, 211n26, 218
    cognitive aspects of, 1–2, 5, 7, 57, 64–65, 77, 211n26, 218
    and Collingwood, 4, 14, 35, 38, 40–43, 58, 68, 73–74, 113–14, 122, 125, 137, 158–59, 166, 175, 178
    dark side of, 7
    disciplinary conception of, 4–5, 54, 58, 63–65

and imagination, 1, 3, 31–32, 38–39, 41, 63–64, 159, 183, 185, 200–201
and mental states, 10, 76–77, 110, 122, 149, 152, 161, 215
as a process, 2, 63–65
and re-enactment (*see* empathy: and Collingwood)
and sympathy, 31, 41, 64, 121
empathy-dependent hermeneutics, 11, 123, 155, 157, 159, 166, 201, 207, 215
empirical/empiricist distinction, 95, 131–32
empiricism, 3, 23–24, 29, 59, 65, 67, 76, 84, 87–88, 96, 98–99, 131–33, 174, 202–3
Endacott, Jason, 5
England, 2, 4, 15, 21–23, 25–27, 30, 40, 47, 82, 106, 110–12, 160, 174–76, 178–79, 181, 196–97, 199, 201, 206, 209. *See also* Britain; United Kingdom
Enlightenment, 14, 83, 87, 99, 107, 162–64, 168n28, 208, 215
epistemology, 4, 8, 11, 28, 41–42, 84, 94, 97–98, 100–3, 112, 115–17, 122, 131–33, 136–37, 140, 149–53, 155, 157, 164, 175, 196, 213–16
Erlebnis, 117, 149
Ermarth, Michael, 149
An Essay on Metaphysics (Collingwood), 114, 122, 133–34, 138, 140
Experience and its Modes (Oakeshott), 23, 110
experiential context, 127–28. *See also* immediate experience
Evans, Richard, 188
evidence, 2–3, 31–32, 38–40, 42, 51–53, 59–64, 68, 73–74, 86–88, 95, 103, 107, 110, 113, 123, 126–27, 129–32, 138, 140, 160, 177, 182, 184, 192, 194–96, 198–201, 206, 209

Faulkner, William, 67
Febvre, Lucien, 26
feeling, 8, 32, 37–38, 41–42, 64, 75–77, 114–16, 185, 198–99, 218. *See also* empathy; emotion
Ferguson, Niall, 188
Fines, John, 31, 38, 52
First World War, 21, 50, 129
fore-conception, 150, 155
fore-meanings, 166
forms of knowledge, 4, 6, 8, 29–30, 44, 58, 61, 85, 95, 118, 174, 176, 186, 188, 192, 194–95, 213–14
Foster, Stuart, 63–64
France, 14, 23, 26, 82–83, 112, 145
freedom, 23, 68, 82, 175
Freeman, Anthony, 183, 185, 187
Fremdheit, 152
Freud, Sigmund, 3, 137
fusion of horizons, 147–48, 156, 159, 201, 217

Gadamer, H.-G., 8–12, 14, 65, 67, 80, 93, 113–14, 131, 141, 145–66, 167n13, 168n28, 169n66, 201, 207–8, 213, 216–17
Gallagher, Shaun, 66, 159
Gardiner, Patrick, 85
Gay, Peter, 3
Geist, 93–94, 152
Geisteswissenschaften. *See* human sciences
General Certificate of Secondary Education, 180–85, 197
generalization, 22–23, 47–48, 87, 96, 215
Gentile, Giovanni, 111, 118n11
geography, 30, 84, 178, 200, 214
Germany, 3, 8, 10, 14, 21, 74–76, 80–85, 87, 92, 96, 98–99, 106–7, 111–14, 116–17, 122, 131, 146–49, 152, 162–63, 167, 169n66, 175, 183, 185, 189, 194, 201–2, 205, 208, 211n30, 213
Goldberg, Amos, 162
Gove, Michael, 188
Gradgrind approach, 174
great tradition of history teaching, 21
Grondin, Jean, 92, 145–46
Gutman, Herbert, 205
Guyer, Paul, 75

Habermas, Jürgen, 147, 162, 169n66, 202
Hallam, Roy, 28
Happold, F.G., 36
Harlan, David, 160
Hartley, L.P., 67
Hegel, Georg Wilhelm Friedrich, 75, 79–81, 84, 94–95, 97–98, 101–2, 104n9, 104n10, 106–7, 111, 113–14, 121, 131, 141, 152, 164, 175, 213, 216

Heidegger, Martin, 145–47, 149–52, 161, 163, 167n13, 208, 216
Helgeby, Stein, 74
Hempel, Carl G., 3–4, 45, 136, 175–76, 193, 214–15
Hennessey, Roger, 184, 186
Herder, Johann Gottfried von, 75, 78, 84–87, 131, 175, 205
Her Majesty's Inspectorate, 37, 176–79, 184
Her Majesty's Stationery Office, 37
hermeneutic circle, 92, 97–98, 103, 113, 133, 149–50, 160, 203, 208
hermeneutics, 5, 9–11, 14, 65–66, 69, 78–81, 84, 87–88, 92, 94, 97–98, 101–2, 106, 112–14, 118, 121–23, 125, 128, 131–33, 140–41, 145–67, 169n56, 194–97, 200–201, 203, 206–8, 213, 215–17. *See also* empathy-dependent hermeneutics
Hill, Christopher, 23, 25
Hillgruber, Andreas, 162
hindsight, 41, 47, 52, 59, 62. *See also* distance
Hirsch, E.D., 188
Hirst, Paul H., 29, 58, 61, 174, 213
Historical Association, 21, 30–31, 60, 178–79
historical competence, 205
historical consciousness, 13, 15, 79–80, 102, 130, 148, 152–54, 161, 167, 194, 201–2, 204–8, 211n26
historical context, 1–2, 4, 6, 8–9, 13–14, 58, 62–64, 80, 121–22, 124, 132, 137, 146, 166, 187, 196, 201, 208, 213, 218. *See also* contextualism
historical judgement, 107, 196–97
historical method, 2–3, 6–8, 36, 40, 42, 63, 69, 73, 81, 83–84, 91, 96, 109, 112, 131, 138, 141, 154–55, 169n56, 176, 187, 202, 213–14
historical school, 94, 102, 104n10, 107, 113, 131, 153–54, 205
historical thinking. *See* disciplinary concepts
Historical Thinking Project, 196, 200
historically effected consciousness, 147, 153–54, 207
historicism, 8–9, 11, 14, 21, 67, 80–84, 87, 91, 94–95, 97–101, 104n9, 107,
112, 114, 118, 123, 130–31, 136, 141, 148–49, 152, 154, 161, 166, 196, 200, 203, 207–9, 213, 215–16
historicity, 65, 112, 123, 148, 153–54, 157–59, 166, 207
Historikerstreit, 162
historiography, 3–4, 23, 26, 82, 92, 96–97, 100, 162, 201–3, 208
History Curriculum Association, 187
history didactics, 189, 201–2, 204–5, 208
history discipline, 1, 8, 12, 22, 26, 30, 41, 44, 51, 65, 74, 80–81, 84, 98, 100, 173, 177, 192, 199, 202–6, 209, 211n30, 213, 215, 217–18
Hobsbawm, Eric, 24, 160
Hogan, John, 112, 147
Holocaust, 64, 163
Holy Roman Empire, 83
humanism, 4, 10, 49, 66, 80, 136, 148, 153, 163, 175, 214, 216
humanities, 30–31
human nature, 42, 45, 85–86
human sciences, 77–80, 85, 100–102, 121, 129, 148–49, 152–53, 156, 163, 216–17
Humboldt, Wilhelm von, 95–97, 113, 131, 152
Hunt, Joe, 37
Husserl, Edmund, 77–78, 80, 145, 152

The Idea of History (Collingwood), 11, 16–17n29, 42, 59, 85, 107, 116, 126–27, 136, 139, 141, 156, 176, 183, 185
idealism, 3, 6, 45–46, 48–50, 68–69, 94–98, 111–13, 122, 152, 156, 175
Iggers, Georg, 81–82, 90n28
imagination, 30–32, 36–39, 44, 48–49, 53, 59, 61, 77, 84–86, 88, 99, 116, 159, 173, 177, 184, 186. *See also under* empathy
immediate experience, 110, 116–17, 121–22, 126, 158. *See also* experiential context
implicit-explicit relation, 137, 165
incapsulation, 103, 109–12, 115, 118, 126, 147
individuality, 4, 45, 51, 59, 78, 80, 87, 97, 99, 110, 126, 207
inside theory, 4, 48, 59, 74, 85, 100, 129, 155, 188

Institute of Education, University of London, 29, 35–36, 43–44, 49, 63, 178, 190n19
intentionalism, 4, 9–11, 50, 52, 74, 136, 175–76, 193–94, 197, 200, 216
intentions, 2, 4, 9–11, 42, 48, 51–52, 61, 74, 88, 113, 121, 123–24, 129, 141, 147, 155–60, 169n56, 176, 187, 193, 199
interpretation. *See* hermeneutics
intuition, 22, 28, 31, 41–42, 53, 59, 66, 74, 77–78, 83–84, 86, 95, 99–100, 107, 111, 118, 121–22, 128, 131–32, 136
irrationalism, 109, 122
Italy, 3, 14, 81, 85, 92, 106–07, 111–13, 175
I-Thou relation, 79, 92, 148, 154

James, William, 115
Jeffreys, M.V.C., 36, 47
Jeismann, Karl-Ernst, 205
Jenkins, Keith, 68–69
Johnson, Peter, 73
Jones, Gareth, 186
Joseph, Keith, 178–80, 184

Kant, Immanuel, 12, 75, 88, 92, 97–101, 129, 131, 133–34, 143n39, 148, 152, 163–64, 170n74
Keatinge, M.W., 36
Kelly, Donald, 92, 94
Kissell, Michael, 164
Kitson Clark, George, 2, 173
Klein, Kerwin Lee, 175
Knight, Peter, 57
Knox, T.M., 11, 136
Kobayashi, Chinatsu, 147
Körber, Andreas, 205, 210n22
Kuhn, Thomas, 143n39, 202, 211n30

Lebenspraxis, 202, 206, 208
Lee, Peter, 2, 32, 36, 39, 43, 49–53, 60–61, 63, 65–66, 74, 174, 176–77, 189, 192–95, 206
Lee, Vernon, 89n9
Leibniz, G.W., 94
Levstik, Linda, 5
Lewes Priory, 183, 185
liberal education, 6, 29–30, 49

liberalism, 1, 4, 23–24, 68, 82–83, 136, 162–63, 167n13
line of development, 36–37, 47, 49, 193
linguistic turn, 92
Lipps, Theodor, 75
Local Education Authority, 179, 181, 186
logic of explanation, 44–46, 175, 193
logic of question and answer, 9, 11, 14, 43, 114, 124–25, 128–30, 132–33, 135–36, 139, 141, 146–47, 154–57, 164, 166, 197, 213, 215, 217. *See also* dialectic of question and answer
logocentrism, 123
Louch, A.R., 74

MacIntyre, Alasdair, 147, 164
Macintyre, Stuart, 200, 211n26
magistra vitae, 81
Major, John, 188
Makkreel, Rudolf, 78–79
Marion, Mathieu, 147
Marten, C.H.K., 21
Martin, Rex, 73–74
Marxism, 23–24
Marx, Karl, 104n9, 163
materialism, 23, 98, 115
McGinn, Colin, 106
McGovern, Chris, 183, 185, 187–88
McIntyre, Kenneth, 124, 147
Megill, Allan, 202, 211n30
memory, 77, 187, 207
metaphysics, 4, 8, 86, 91, 94, 102, 104n9, 112, 116–17, 132–34, 137–38, 140–41, 151–52, 156, 175, 213–16
Michelet, Jules, 82, 92
Mill, John Stuart, 68, 76–77, 100
Mink, Louis, 73, 143n39
modernity, 147, 161, 207
moral imagination, 201
moral judgement, 196, 201, 204
Munslow, Alun, 73, 113
Murphy, Richard, 112

Napoleon, 83
narrative, 63, 97, 158–60, 162, 188, 203–4, 209
narrative competence, 159, 204
narrative forms, 203–4
National Criteria (DES), 182–83, 197

national curriculum, 15, 174, 179, 184–85, 188, 192, 200
National Curriculum History Working Group, 174–75, 184–87
national identity, 83, 99
nationalism, 21, 50, 83, 197
naturalism, 88, 91–92, 104n9, 110, 112, 117, 156
natural-law philosophy, 94, 163
natural science, 40, 45–46, 48, 76, 81, 91, 100, 129–30, 138, 176, 203, 215
neo-Kantianism, 8, 22, 45, 98–101, 106–7, 112–13, 116, 131–32, 146, 153, 215
New Labour, 188
The New Leviathan (Collingwood), 122, 164
New Right, 184
Newton, Isaac, 88, 109, 138
Niebuhr, Barthold Georg, 84, 99
Nietzsche, Friedrich, 152, 163
nominalism, 2, 22
nomothetic/idiographic distinction, 100
Nora, Pierre, 161
North America, 6, 194–95, 199

Oakeshott, Michael, 23, 36, 45, 48–50, 58, 60, 67, 109–10, 175–76, 206
objective spirit, 79, 102, 106
objectivity, 51, 78–79, 91, 97, 100–101, 111, 149, 152, 160, 203
Oldfield, Adrian, 139
O-Level examination, 180–81, 183
ontology, 10–11, 42, 132, 138, 149–51, 156–57, 216
Organization of American Historians, 195

panlogism, 94
Passmore, John, 123
patch approach, 37. *See also* line of development
pedagogy, 8, 40, 47, 53–54, 58, 173, 175, 202, 214
Perry, Leslie, 50
perspective taking (including perspective), 2, 6, 159, 182–83, 196–201, 218
Peters, Rik, 110
phenomenology, 5, 10, 65, 77, 80, 102, 121, 125
philology, 84, 86–87, 93, 97, 145, 154

philosophical judgement, 107, 111
philosophical school, 94, 104n10, 107, 131
philosophy of history, 1, 3, 11, 14, 15n11, 17n29, 45, 73, 94–98, 108–9, 112, 121, 126, 133, 136, 145, 202, 205, 213–15
  analytical/critical, 44, 49, 63, 136, 175–76, 194, 200, 206, 214
  influence on school history, 4, 6, 28, 32, 35, 37–38, 43–44, 46, 49–50, 57, 60, 63, 173–76, 181, 186, 193–94, 197, 200, 206, 213, 217
  speculative, 3, 44, 131, 175
philosophy of mind, 10, 64, 77, 84, 122
Piaget, Jean, 27, 36, 39, 53, 213
Pippen, Robert, 146
Plato, 93, 146, 148, 154–57
Pocock, John, 123, 160
political philosophy, 109
Popper, Karl, 45, 81, 143n54, 144n54
positivism, 45, 50, 52, 74, 88, 91, 96, 98, 100, 110, 112, 155, 175–76, 193, 214
Postan, M.M., 22, 44, 48
Postgraduate Certificate in Education, 181–82
Power, Eileen, 22
practical inferences, 50–53, 59, 61, 63, 121, 192
prejudice, 10, 148, 160, 163, 166
presentism, 66–67, 132, 196–97, 201
presuppositions, 11, 14, 43, 94–95, 128, 133–40, 155, 158, 161, 164, 166, 197, 203, 208, 213, 215–16
Price, Mary, 30
The Principles of History (Collingwood), 16–17n29, 126
Prinz, Jesse, 7
problem of other minds, 76
procedural concepts. *See* disciplinary concepts
processes theory, 108, 110, 115
progressive education, 179–80
Prussia, 82, 84, 95, 97–98
psychological aesthetics. *See* empathy: and aesthetics
psychologism, 8, 14, 73, 78–79, 102, 116, 148, 150, 152, 156–57, 164, 166, 215–16
psychology, 5, 7–8, 27, 31, 36, 39, 52, 57, 59, 64, 74–77, 79–80, 88, 93, 102–3,

114–18, 121, 125–26, 132, 136–37, 141, 150, 156, 199, 213, 217. *See also* educational psychology

Quellenkritik, 84
questioning, 38, 128–29, 147, 151, 166, 199, 205, 209

Ranke, Leopold von, 81–82, 84, 94–100, 104n9, 104n10, 113, 131, 149, 152, 154, 201, 205
rational compassion, 7
rational explanation, 3, 42, 52, 214
rational fact finding, 31, 38
rational understanding, 2, 14, 39, 53–54, 57, 60, 63, 65, 192
rationalism, 4, 74, 82–83, 86, 88, 92, 99, 101–2, 115, 133, 162–63, 202
rationality, 62, 68, 74, 164, 192
realism, 108, 112, 123–24, 128, 132, 136, 146, 155–56
reason. *See* rationalism
reasons, 10, 51–52, 59, 61–62, 124, 159, 192
reconstruction, 11, 26, 36, 38–42, 48, 50–51, 59–60, 62, 73, 81, 85, 88, 93, 96–97, 99, 111, 121, 123, 133, 141, 144n54, 156, 160, 176, 184, 196–97, 199, 214
re-enactment, 8, 10–11, 58, 61, 73–74, 103, 108–12, 114, 118, 122–23, 125–28, 132–33, 136, 141, 142n4, 147, 149, 155–59, 164, 199, 214–15, 217
relativism, 12, 99, 101, 140, 189, 196
relativity, 12, 102, 139–40, 154, 207
Renaissance, 83, 92
Ricœur, Paul, 10, 113, 147, 149–50
Rickert, Heinrich, 85, 99–102, 107, 112, 152
Rogers, Peter, 58–59, 64
Romanticism, 21, 80, 84, 92, 98, 101, 112–13, 118, 122, 125, 132–33, 163–64, 216
Ruggiero, Guido de, 108, 111, 118n11, 119n12
Rüsen, Jörn, 201–9, 211n30, 212n51
Ruskin, John, 138, 143n50

Saunders-Watson, Michael, 186
scientific explanation, 4, 40, 50, 52, 74, 175, 199. *See also* covering-law model

scientific thinking, 122, 139, 203
Schama, Simon, 188
Schleiermacher, Friedrich Daniel, 93, 97, 101–2, 113, 141, 149, 151, 153, 164, 168n28, 201
school history, 1, 22, 25, 28, 35–37, 41, 43–44, 46, 54n10, 57, 60, 64, 166, 173–76, 178, 182, 186, 194, 214, 217
Schools Council, 30–31, 37, 39, 179
Schools Council History Project, 30, 35–40, 42–43, 47, 49, 53, 57–58, 173–78, 180–82, 185
scissors-and-paste history, 130
Scott, Sir Gilbert, 129
second-order concepts. *See* disciplinary concepts
Second World War, 30, 146, 162–63, 175
Seixas, Peter, 6, 188–89, 194–201, 204–5, 207, 210n22
self-criticism, 115
self-knowledge, 40, 85, 107, 119n13, 125, 177
Sellar, W.C., 21
sensation, 87–88, 110, 115–16, 156
Shemilt, Denis, 39–43, 53, 57, 60–61, 133, 176, 181, 192, 195
Simmel, Georg, 99, 112
simulation theory, 76–77, 159
situational analysis, 139, 143n54
Skidelsky, Robert, 185, 187
skills, 177–78, 180, 182, 184, 187
skills versus content, 13, 166, 182, 186, 200
Skinner, Quentin, 9–10, 122–24, 129, 132, 142n4, 155, 157, 169n56, 197
Slater, John, 177–78, 184, 190n19
social cognition, 158–59
social history, 22, 24, 205
social sciences, 8, 10, 22, 24–26, 81, 99, 101, 195, 211n30
social studies, 5, 30, 64, 184, 194
sociology, 22–23, 25–26, 48, 86, 214
sources, 2, 7, 36, 38–39, 43, 46, 59, 67, 84, 97, 129–30, 160, 162, 198, 203, 209
Southern Regional Examinations Board, 181, 183
Speculum Mentis (Collingwood), 108, 137
speech acts, 123–24, 128, 197
spirit, 77–78, 82, 86, 92, 94–96, 101–2, 116–17, 122. *See also* objective spirit

Stedman Jones, Gareth, 23–24
Stein, Edith, 77–78
Stone, Norman, 185–86
storicismo, 81, 107
structural concepts. *See* disciplinary concepts
Stueber, Karsten, 10, 155, 158–59
Sturm und Drang, 86
subjectivity, 59, 75, 80, 92, 97, 101, 112, 131, 133, 148–49, 152, 156, 203, 216
sui generis, 4, 14, 28, 44, 175, 214
Sylvester, David, 35–40, 43, 47, 53, 173, 176–77, 184–85
sympathy, 44, 49, 59, 64, 74, 78, 84, 116, 121, 177–78. *See also under* empathy

Tawney, R.H., 22
Taylor, Charles, 165
teacher training, 1, 25, 27, 36, 44, 167, 181, 218
teleology, 50, 59–60, 95
textualism, 124
Thatcher, Margaret, 174, 178–79, 184, 186–88
theme method, 47, 193
theoretical surplus, 208
theory of mind. *See* philosophy of mind
Thompson, E.P., 25, 51
thought in its mediation, 127, 133, 157–58
Toulmin, Stephen, 140, 161
Toynbee, Arnold, 110
tradition, 11, 139, 147–48, 153, 160–65, 179, 196, 207, 216–17
transcendentalism, 98–101, 131
transposition, 42, 80, 215–16
truth, 12–13, 44, 59, 61, 84–86, 92, 94, 97–98, 100–101, 107, 113–15, 122, 125, 128, 130, 134–35, 138–39, 148, 152, 154–55, 164, 166, 215
Truth and Method (Gadamer), 141, 148, 153–54, 163

United Kingdom, 13, 28, 40, 166, 185, 194. *See also* Britain; England

United States, 5, 6, 28, 31, 40, 64, 160, 162, 189, 194–95, 202, 205–6
universalism, 2, 14, 22, 42, 44, 68, 79–80, 82–83, 86, 88, 91, 95, 98–100, 104n10, 107, 124, 151–52, 176, 199, 203, 208–9, 215
university history, 3, 6, 22, 24–25, 44, 173, 176, 214
University of Berlin, 84, 94, 97
unstated assumptions, 41, 43, 133. *See also* presuppositions

Vardoulakis, Dimitrios, 147, 158
verbum interius, 93
Verstehen, 10, 74, 78–79, 83–84, 96, 131, 149–50, 215
verum factum theory, 85, 100
Volksgeist, 86, 93
vouloir-dire, 145
Vico, Giambattista, 84–85, 91, 100, 129–30, 164, 175, 205
Vischer, Robert, 75
Voltaire, 83, 86

Wake, Roy, 37–38, 173, 178
Walsh, W.H., 36, 44–48, 58, 176
Weber, Max, 99, 101
Weinsheimer, Joel, 151
Whig-liberal tradition, 23–24, 47–48, 193
White, Hayden, 203
Williams, Shirley, 178–80
Windelband, Wilhelm, 99–102, 106, 112, 152
Wineburg, Sam, 66–68, 195–97, 206
Wittgenstein, Ludwig, 50, 76, 123, 143n39
Wolf, Friedrich August, 84
Wolff, Christian, 94
Wright, Georg Henrik von, 50–53, 61, 74, 176, 192–93

Yeager, Elizabeth, 63–64
Yeatman, R.J., 21

Zahavi, Dan, 77
Zeitgeist, 93

MAKING SENSE OF HISTORY
Studies in Historical Cultures
General Editor: Stefan Berger
Founding Editor: Jörn Rüsen

Bridging the gap between historical theory and the study of historical memory, this series crosses the boundaries between both academic disciplines and cultural, social, political and historical contexts. In an age of rapid globalization, which tends to manifest itself on an economic and political level, locating the cultural practices involved in generating its underlying historical sense is an increasingly urgent task.

Volume 1
Western Historical Thinking: An Intercultural Debate
Edited by Jörn Rüsen

Volume 2
Identities: Time, Difference and Boundaries
Edited by Heidrun Friese

Volume 3
Narration, Identity, and Historical Consciousness
Edited by Jürgen Straub

Volume 4
Thinking Utopia: Steps into Other Worlds
Edited by Jörn Rüsen, Michael Fehr and Thomas W. Rieger

Volume 5
History: Narration, Interpretation, Orientation
Jörn Rüsen

Volume 6
The Dynamics of German Industry: Germany's Path toward the New Economy and the American Challenge
Werner Abelshauser

Volume 7
Meaning and Representation in History
Edited by Jörn Rüsen

Volume 8
Remapping Knowledge: Intercultural Studies for a Global Age
Mihai I. Spariosu

Volume 9
Cultures of Technology and the Quest for Innovation
Edited by Helga Nowotny

Volume 10
Time and History: The Variety of Cultures
Edited by Jörn Rüsen

Volume 11
Narrating the Nation: Representations in History, Media and the Arts
Edited by Stefan Berger, Linas Eriksonas and Andrew Mycock

Volume 12
Historical Memory in Africa: Dealing with the Past, Reaching for the Future in an Intercultural Context
Edited by Mamadou Diawara, Bernard Lategan and Jörn Rüsen

Volume 13
New Dangerous Liaisons: Discourses on Europe and Love in the Twentieth Century
Edited by Luisa Passerini, Liliana Ellena and Alexander C.T. Geppert

Volume 14
Dark Traces of the Past: Psychoanalysis and Historical Thinking
Edited by Jürgen Straub and Jörn Rüsen

Volume 15
A Lover's Quarrel with the Past: Romance, Representation, Reading
Ranjan Ghosh

Volume 16
The Holocaust and Historical Methodology
Edited by Dan Stone

Volume 17
What is History For? Johann Gustav Droysen and the Functions of Historiography
Arthur Alfaix Assis

Volume 18
Vanished History: The Holocaust in Czech and Slovak Historical Culture
Tomas Sniegon

Volume 19
Jewish Histories of the Holocaust: New Transnational Approaches
Edited by Norman J. W. Goda

Volume 20
Helmut Kohl's Quest for Normality: His Representation of the German Nation and Himself
Christian Wicke

Volume 21
Marking Evil: Holocaust Memory in the Global Age
Edited by Amos Goldberg and Haim Hazan

Volume 22
The Rhythm of Eternity: The German Youth Movement and the Experience of the Past, 1900–1933
Robbert-Jan Adriaansen

Volume 23
Viktor Frankl's Search for Meaning: An Emblematic 20th-Century Life
Timothy Pytell

Volume 24
Designing Worlds: National Design Histories in an Age of Globalization
Edited by Kjetil Fallan and Grace Lees-Maffei

Volume 25
Doing Conceptual History in Africa
Edited by Axel Fleisch and Rhiannon Stephens

Volume 26
Divining History: Prophetism, Messianism and the Development of Spirit
Jayne Svenungsson

Volume 27
Sensitive Pasts: Questioning Heritage in Education
Edited by Carla van Boxtel, Maria Grever and Stephan Klein

Volume 28
Evidence and Meaning: A Theory of Historical Studies
Jörn Rüsen

Volume 29
The Mirror of the Medieval: An Anthropology of the Western Historical Imagination
K. Patrick Fazioli

Volume 30
Cultural Borders of Europe: Narratives, Concepts and Practices in the Present and the Past
Edited by Mats Andrén, Thomas Lindkvist, Ingmar Söhrman and Katharina Vajta

Volume 31
Contesting Deregulation: Debates, Practices and Developments in the West since the 1970s
Edited by Knud Andresen and Stefan Müller

Volume 32
Making Nordic Historiography: Connections, Tensions and Methodology, 1850–1970
Edited by Pertti Haapala, Marja Jalava and Simon Larsson

Volume 33
History and Belonging: Representations of the Past in Contemporary European Politics
Edited by Stefan Berger and Caner Tekin

Volume 34
The Ethos of History: Time and Responsibility
Edited by Stefan Helgesson and Jayne Svenungsson

Volume 35
Empathy and History: Historical Understanding in Re-enactment, Hermeneutics and Education
Tyson Retz

www.ingramcontent.com/pod-product-compliance
Lightning Source LLC
Chambersburg PA
CBHW072150100526
44589CB00015B/2161